Southeast Humboldt Hinterlands

The Press at Cal Poly Humboldt
Cal Poly Humboldt Library
1 Harpst Street
Arcata, California 95521-8299
press@humboldt.edu

Cover Photo: Shivley (HCHS, colorized by JR).

Cover design and layout by Maximilian Heirich, Sarah Godlin
Interior layout by Maximilian Heirich, Sarah Godlin

ISBN: 978-1-947112-85-8

Southeast Humboldt Hinterlands

Jerry Rohde

The Press at Cal Poly Humboldt

History of Humboldt County People and Places series

Expressions of Gratitude

This book, like its predecessor, *Southwest Humboldt Hinterlands*, had its start in the early 1990s when my wife Gisela and I wrote our first book, *Humboldt Redwoods State Park: the Complete Guide*. We interviewed over 30 southern Humboldt old-timers for that book, and now, three decades later, I am benefitting from their information once again. So, first of all, let me acknowledge those people from that group who told me about the life and times of southeastern Humboldt County, which is the topic of this book. For a second time, my thanks to: Joann Smith Brekke, Richard Childs, Robert Childs, Velma Childs, Max Crismon, Mel Martin, Alice Mortenson, June Ruggles, and Angus Russell. You all helped the now-distant past come alive so that I could write about it.

More recently, I have received much-needed assistance from scores of people who generously gave me their time and the benefit of their expertise. At the Humboldt County Historical Society, Matina Kilkenny, Deb Meador, Linda DeLong, and Jim Garrison all helped me navigate my way through hundreds of maps, written documents, and photographs. At the Humboldt State University Library (as it was then called), Joan Berman, Edie Butler, Erich Schimps, and Carly Marino expertly aided my search for additional hundreds of documents related to southern Humboldt County. Ann Roberts of the Ferndale Museum and Laura Cooskey of the Mattole Valley Historical Society provided often-obscure information that only they knew about, and Laura also reviewed draft chapters of the book.

Postcard enthusiasts Steve Lazar and Jack Irvine graciously allowed me to use many images from there extensive collections. Martha J. Johnson provided a compelling photo of a July 4th picnic at Blocksburg. Herby, the Secretary of the Blocksburg Town Hall Association, kindly allowed me to use photos from the Association's website.

Numerous individuals provided invaluable information with pin-point accuracy. Once again David Heller shared his vast knowledge of southern Humboldt history. Jessie Wheeler recalled important events in the town her family once owned—Bridgeville. Jim and Francene Rizza provided a very obscure and completely fascinating manuscript about early-day Larabee Valley. Theo Atkinson enthusiastically offered a detailed account of the Stafford area, where her parents once owned the Stafford Inn. James Hunt generously gave us access to the Showers Mountain Ranch and to his memories of 80 years in the area. Michele Olsen shared her probing, fascinating research of the Fruitland area. Rowetta Miller helped me connect with the obscure history of Showers Pass, while Merlynn Schroeder shared her riveting stories of earlier days in the same area. Rachel Walton kindly provided information related to her exemplary research about the Coyote Flat murders. Alayne Hunt and Amanda Hunt Laursen offered important details about the Bridgeville Cemetery. Rex and Albert Hunt described important events related to the Fort Baker-Soldiers Grove area when I toured their ranch.

Special thanks are due several people who worked directly on the book. Kyle Morgan, Scholarly Communications and Digital Scholarship Librarian at Cal Poly Humboldt, expertly shepherded my fourth book through the CPH/HSU publication process. Maximilian Heirich, a layout and design specialist at the Press, similarly provided the highest quality of work on this volume, and he had done with the three books that preceded it. Jan Anderson again corrected my many mistakes in the text and thus vastly improved the final version. Any lingering errors are no one's fault but my own.

Lastly, I offer continuing thanks to my wife Gisela, who has always encouraged my writing and helped me with every phase of every book. I could not have done any of this without her.

Acknowledgements

The places described in this book lie within the ancestral homelands of what are commonly called the Sinkyone, Wailaki, Lassik, and Nongatl tribes. In the 1850s and 1860s numerous whites committed genocide against these peoples, killing many of them, sending some to reservations that were often little more than concentration camps, kidnapping others and forcing them into slavery, and driving a few into hiding. By the late 1860s whites claimed possession of all of southern Humboldt County. No payment was ever made to any Indian for the taking of their land nor was any reparation offered for the murders, rapes, kidnappings, and other atrocities that were committed. This book describes some of these events, and one of the previous volume in this series, *Southern Humboldt Indians*, provides additional accounts.

Telling what happened so far in the past can, of course, never right the wrongs that took place. The perpetrators cannot be held accountable, for they are all dead. The victims cannot be compensated, for they, too, are dead. But the information nonetheless has value. It revises the reputations of the perpetrators, and it honors the lost lives of the victims. And one thing further: by bringing the truth of the past into the present, these accounts provide us with an understanding that may help heal the wounds that were inflicted so carelessly, so needlessly, so many generations ago.

Key to Photo Credits

The photo captions use initials to designate the sources. I colorized numerous black and photos using both the colorization feature at myheritage.com and Photoshop Elements 2021, and I have noted this at the end of the relevant captions.

AHC = Arlene Hartin Collection

BL = UC Berkeley, Bancroft Library

CDV = California Division of Highways

CE = United States Army Corps of Engineers

CEFP = California Ethnographic Field Photographs. UC Berkeley: Phoebe A. Hearst Museum of Anthropology; the photographer is Pliny E. Goddard

CPH = Cal Poly Humboldt University Library

CSP = California State Parks

DPR = Department of Parks and Recreation. State of California: the Resources Agency

DTC = Don Tuttle Collection

EDC = Edward Denny Company

FM = Ferndale Museum

FMC = Fritz-Metcalf Photograph Collection. UC Berkeley: Bioscience & Natural Resources Library; the photographer is Emanuel Fritz

GR = Gisela Rohde

HCHS = Humboldt County Historical Society

HRSP = Humboldt Redwood State Park

IA = Internet Archive

JIC = Jack Irvine Collection

JNL = J. N. Lentell, Map of Humboldt County, 1898

JR = Jerry Rohde

JRC = Jerry Rohde Collection

LC = Library of Congress

LI = Leigh Irvine's *Humboldt County California*

MCNAP = Merriam (C. Hart) Collection of Native American Photographs. UC Berkeley: Bancroft Library; the photographer is C. Hart Merriam

MJJC = Martha J. Johnson Collection

MVHS = Mattole Valley Historical Society

NHC = Nancy Holmes Collection

PD = Public Domain

PG = Project Gutenberg

SLR = Save the Redwoods League

TGC = Tom Georgeson Collection

THPO = thehumboldtproject.org

USGS = United States Geographical Survey

WM = Wikimedia

WP = Wikipedia

Preface

One impulse from a vernal wood
May teach you more of man,
Of moral evil and of good,
Than all the sages can.

—Wordsworth

Here, in pictures and in words, is the story of what happened, over little more than a century, to places drained by the Van Duzen and main Eel rivers. We will look at lands claimed by four Indian tribes that together contained more than four dozen tribal groups. We will witness the coming of hundreds and then thousands of whites, most of them intent upon wresting wealth from the forests and the prairies that blanketed the hillsides and the valleys that were everywhere to be seen. We will, if we so choose, discern both "moral evil" and "good" in the way these peoples have treated the land.

Here is Blocksburg, poised atop its rugged ridge, offering succor to the travelers who have reached it by their day-long climb from the Eel.

Here is Pepperwood, with its wagon road running between a band of redwoods and a band of laurels, both trees so useful that soon many will be cut.

Here is Bridgeville, built where two great travel corridors crossed, bypassed by the modern highway when its usefulness had ended.

And here is No-le-bi, a Nongatl village lying deep in the forest, hidden for decades after all its inhabitants had left.

In these southeastern Humboldt places and in many others, the vernal wood may be no more, but here is a record of its impulses, and what they have to teach.

Introduction

This book is the fourth volume in my "History of Humboldt County Peoples and Places" series. It covers 28 areas in the southeastern part of the county, running from Iaqua on the north to the Mendocino county line on the south and from Mail Ridge on the west to the Trinity County line on the east. It generally reports on the time period from 1850, when whites first began taking over the region, to 1964, when the huge Christmas flood rearranged much of the local landscape.

Each chapter tells the story of a particular place, generally presented in chronological order. Certain significant events and processes that are described in detail are placed within sidebars or appendices that speckle the work. The main illustrations are mostly photographs or postcards. If the original image was in black and white, I have colorized it using MyHeritage and Adobe Photoshop Elements software. Several maps appear at key points in the text. These are mostly based on a 1916 United States Army Corps of Engineers series that I have not seen anywhere in print.

As with the other volumes in this series, I have tried to link every factual statement with one or more sources upon which the statement was based. This results in a lengthy set of endnotes. In evaluating the accuracy of sources, I have followed what I call a "hierarchy of reliability." In this system I generally place the highest value on reports that originated at the time of an event, while being mindful of possible bias by the reporter. I also try to find other sources that corroborate such reports, especially when they are of a controversial nature. I usually have less faith in the veracity of accounts given some time after an event, even if provided by one of the observers or participants, since the corrosive effects of time sometimes affect the accuracy of the recollections.

This book, along with the previous one, *Southwest Humboldt Hinterlands*, in part represents a continuation of the accounts given in volume 2 of the series, *Southern Humboldt Indians*. That volume described the ethnogeography of the southern Humboldt area as it appeared in early 1850, the time of stability for the local tribes, and it also provided certain accounts of Indian history after the arrival of the whites. The two hinterlands books contain further reports on the local Indians, which are now localized to the chapter that covers the area where specific events occurred.

Some streams of activity transcended connection with a single place. The construction of Highway 36 and the rise and fall of sheep ranching are two examples of this. In such cases, the main story appears as either a sidebar or an appendix within one of the chapters whose location is closely related to the subject.

The sources upon which I've based my account were acquired during more than 30 years of research. For some locations this has resulted in the collection of ample information, but for a few places there is less coverage than I had hoped. I offer what I have found, knowing that it is only part of the story, but hopefully the most important part.

Chapter Locations

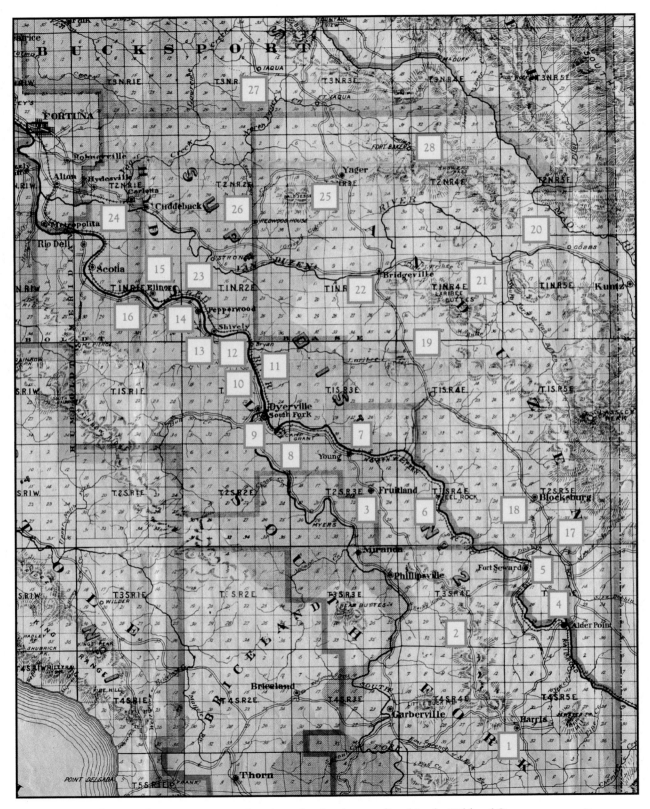

The numbers on the map correspond to those for the chapters listed in the Table of Contents, opposite.

Table of Contents

Chapter 1
Harris

Adieu! adieu! thy plaintive anthem fades
   Past the near meadows, over the still stream,
     Up the hill-side . . .
               —Keats, *Ode to a Nightingale*

Perched on *its* hillside, Harris has endured the decades, an outpost in a far corner of the county, necessary for a few but ignored by many. Whatever anthem of farewell once passed the lips of passing travelers has faded to silence, replaced by the rumble of dusty pickups that may slow but seldom stop. Pause here long enough, however, and other sounds may emanate from the ridgeslope surroundings—the whispering wind passing over the headstones of the half-hidden cemetery, the creak of the rusty barn hinge that has seen no oil for decades—reminders that recollection awaits not only those who look, but also those who listen.

The story of the Harris area begins with words last spoken perhaps a century ago, when Indians from both sides of the Mail Ridge divide told their stories to ethnographers like Pliny E. Goddard and C. Hart Merriam. The ridge separates the South Fork Eel drainage from that of the main Eel. As such, it served as a summer hunting and gathering location for tribal groups that spent their winters close to one of the two rivers. From the west came the To-kub-be ke-ahs,[1] who had winter villages along the South Fork near Benbow and also on the lower East Branch and claimed all of the latter's drainage as part of their territory.[2] A noted location for their summer activity was at Des-an-dun, a summer camp at Spruce Grove, on the ridgeline a mile or so northwest of Harris. A

"little ways north" of Des-an-dun was a second camp, La-cit-el-tci-bi.[3] Over the divide from the head of Tom Long Creek, a major tributary of the East Branch, was Bun-kut-tco-tcin-ne-dun, a large pond where, according to the To-kub-be ke-ah Albert Smith, "that place white man kill all my people. Soldiers."[4]

On the east side of the ridge were three Wailaki tribal groups that came up seasonally from winter villages on the main Eel. The Kai-kichekaiya camped several miles southeast of Harris on Chamise Creek in summer and went there at other times to hunt elk.[5] The Dalsokai-ya likely went onto Walker Ridge, which lies west of Chamise Creek.[6] And the Setaltcitokaiya were located in the Jewett Rock area east of Harris.[7]

Whites came to the locale at least as early as the spring of 1850. It was then that Aristides J. Huestis and a party from Sonoma County rode along "the divide between the main Eel river and the South Fork." Remarkably, Huestis and the group were taking wagons over what was no more than a trail. Most of the vehicles were wrecked along the inappropriate route. Somewhere in the vicinity of what became known as Huestis Rock, they gave up, took the last remaining wagon down to the main Eel, left it there, and continued on wagonless.[8]

In 1851 four prospectors, Thomas Smith, "Redemeyer of Ukiah, Requa of Long Valley," and Enoch Jewett, came through the Harris

Spruce Grove (JR).

area on their way south "through the wilds of Trinity county." They had "found no gold and the Indians were very troublesome, forcing them to take a stand against them where Harris is now situated."[9] The results of the encounter are not described, but the report confirms the existence of an early travel route through the site of the town.

At an undetermined but early date, the ridge became the major travel corridor between Humboldt and Mendocino counties. The 1865 Humboldt County map refers to the route as the "Overland Mail Trail,"[10] but at various times it was also called the Sonoma Trail, the Government Trail, and the Mail Ridge Trail.[11] The last of these became permanent, probably because it referred to the main item carried along the trail. Upon entering Humboldt County from the Bell Springs area, the route went north to the future site of Harris, where it turned northwest and promptly reached what was called "Spruce Grove Station."[12] From there the trail curved around the west side of Pratt Mountain and then more

or less followed the ridgetop until it reached later-day Fruitland, whence it dropped to the west bank of the main Eel to reach Camp Grant.[13]

There was a mail station at Spruce Grove, where trails arrived from the South Fork Eel (at the future site of Garberville) and the East Branch.[14] In September 1861 the station was reportedly attacked "by about seventy-five Indians."[15] It proved to be a lengthy event:

> The station-keeper and one other man were in the house; a few yards distant was the corral, containing about six horses and ten tons of hay. The Indians secured the horses, took them a short distance and killed them. They then returned and set fire to the hay, and attempted to fire the house by throwing burning brands and wisps of hay on the roof. . . .
>
> In the house the occupants fought to save their lives. . . . The two men prevented the house from burning by removing the shingles. There were some fifteen

rifles in the hands of the Indians with which they kept up a desultory fire upon the house; they did not attempt to take possession, as two of their number had been killed in an attempt to approach the door. After destroying the hay and out-buildings the Indians withdrew to where the carcasses of the horses were, when they commenced a feast of roast horse beef. . . .

As the Indians dined in style, three men, on foot, arrived at the besieged station. . . . The Indians returned after a short absence, and renewed their attempt to burn the house and murder the men; but finding that there were more white men than in the morning, and two or three of . . . [the Indians] being dispatched to kingdom come, they concluded it best to be off.[16]

In March 1863 Enoch Phelps Jewett arrived in Little Valley,[17] a flat spot between two ridges about three miles southeast of Spruce Grove. Here he bought a squatter's claim from a Mr. Redd. Jewett married Belle Fenton, "a Wailaki woman," and the couple had four children. Enoch Jewett brought in the first livestock ever seen in the valley.[18] Eventually the Jewett Ranch came to comprise 2,400 acres, upon which grazed some 2,500 sheep, 200 head of cattle, and 100 horses.[19] And Little Valley became Jewett Valley.[20]

Spruce Grove fairly straddled the divide between the main Eel and the South Fork. It still commands a view that raced the pulse of an anonymous resident in 1876:

There are features here for the romantic inclined that cannot be excelled by only a few places in the State. Standing but a few feet from the house one can direct

Jewett Rock looms above Jewett Valley (JR).

the eye over mountains with their for-est-topped peaks and deep solemn look-ing canyon and gaze for miles to either point of the compass. In the west and on a clear day, we cheerfully overlook the fantastic shapped [sic] mountain for a look at the old Pacific, and its many freighted vessels, slowly passing up or down the coast, and wait with no little anxiety for the setting of the sun, a view that is as grand and imposing as was ever witnessed in any clime. . . . The east is not without its attraction or grandeur. Its mountains many of which are higher in altitude than any one on the Coast Range, are generally without the dense forests that cover the latter, and instead are crowned with snow that seems to mock the sun's heat. . . .[21]

By the 1870s there were three focal points near the future site of Harris. To the west was Spruce Grove, to the east was Jewett Valley, and to the south was newly established Dark

Canyon. David M. Stoody and his unnamed wife came to the last location in 1873, claimed 320 acres, and built a hotel, saloon, and feed stable. In 1878 they proved up their homestead, Stoody became postmaster at the newly estab-lished Dark Canyon Post Office, and the place's status as a community was assured.[22]

In 1877 the Overland Road was completed when its two ends, one coming south from Eureka and the other coming north from Mendocino County, met at Dark Canyon.[23] Now wagons and stages could at last travel between Humboldt and San Francisco bays, and the Stoodys' facilities at Dark Canyon served as a stopover on the route.[24]

But the new community faced at least two obstacles to its continued existence, both geo-graphical. First, as one early-day local put it, "Dark Canyon was and still is DARK." The canyon was filled with fir trees, which so en-shadowed the surroundings that one apocry-phal account claimed that "it was necessary to stretch a rope across the road so that the [mail] rider knew he had reached there."[25] Second,

The Overland Road is much lighter south of Dark Canyon (JR).

the new wagon road, after coming south from Alderpoint, passed more than a mile east of Spruce Grove, thereby creating a junction where the new road met the old mail trail that ran up the mountainside and headed north along Mail Ridge. The location of the junction was on an open hillside that offered a hospitable town site.

Thus the town of Harris was a community waiting to happen. All that was required was for someone named Harris to move to the junction and make a few improvements. This occurred in 1881 when William and Amelia Harris gave up their hotel in Blocksburg and purchased 180 acres, a cabin, and a large barn[26] from Jack Robinson. And, faster than you can *say* Jack Robinson, the Harrises turned the property into a town. In short order William Harris built a store, saloon, community hall (that also served as a schoolhouse), and a house that was eventually expanded into a hotel. Harris was aided by the timely arrival of Andrew Haun, who happened to have a portable sawmill with him. Harris took Haun's lumber as fast as it was sawn, hammered a few nails, and soon had his four new buildings.[27]

Meanwhile, David Stoody had sold *his* town, Dark Canyon, to Cornelius Swett in 1881, only to buy it back in 1882 and then sell it that same year to Dick and Perry Drewry.[28] But the property was diminishing in value; on July 25, 1882, the Dark Canyon Post Office moved up the road to Harris.[29]

Despite now having a post office called Harris, there was apparently some hesitation in applying the name to the whole community. The 1886 county map refers to the location, complete with four black squares indicating buildings, as Spruce Grove, while the site of the mail station up the ridge is now shown as "Old Spruce Grove." By then a road went from

Harris/New Spruce Grove on to Old Spruce Grove and then dropped to the East Branch South Fork Eel on its way to Garberville.[30] Never making it onto the maps was another temporary name for Harris: "Dog Town."[31]

Down the road from Dog Town was the Goat Sheds, a location just south of Dark Canyon where school was held. The entire Dark Canyon area was temporarily illuminated when it was burned over by a fire in 1895.[32] By then the local school was safe and sound at Harris, having shed itself of the Goat Sheds in 1891.[33]

While the town of Harris was still wet behind the ears, it was featured at least twice in the Eureka newspapers. First, meandering correspondent "McTavish" stopped there during his 1885 peregrination of southern Humboldt County, sending a lengthy paragraph to the *Daily Humboldt Standard*:

> HARRIS. A public stopping place. Mr. Harris, Sr., owns the hotel, while his son, C. Harris, carries on a general merchandise store; another son, George Harris, has a blacksmith shop and feed stable. They also have a nice farm, orchard and fruit garden. This place was formerly known as Spruce Grove. It seems to be a central point for a large section of country. A stage, conveying the United States mail, leaves on Wednesdays and Saturdays for Garberville, returning the same day. The store of Mr. Harris does a large trade, and is in [the] charge of Mr. Scott, an efficient and accommodating clerk. On the occasion of our visit there were not less than thirty persons stopping at this station—teamsters, sheep-shearers and travelers. The "Troubadours," genuine negroes, gave a minstrel perfor-

Remnant of the old Spruce Grove-East Branch road (JR).

mance, which was well attended. . . . A dance followed the performance, and to say that Harris was a lively place that night but dimly describes the situation. To tell the truth there is always life and stir about this place.[34]

Frank Asbill, who never met a story he couldn't enlarge, elaborated on the liveliness of the town:

At Harris Station I have seen there with my own eyes, fifty people, and many times a great many more, gathered at the little store, stage barn and hill side hotel. . . .

There would be at least fifty or sixty head of saddle horses tied to the long horse rack, and to the large fir post that held the store up, and all along the picket and rail fence on each side of the nar-

row wagon road for a hundred yards or more. . . .

The main part of the store was a room twenty-by-twenty, with a wide board counter on each side and a trap door leading down into what was called the cellar. The whole store set upon large pine poles, for it was built on a sidehill. . . .

On the counter at the east side, the calico, blue jeans, socks, jumpers, shoes and blankets were kept. At the end of the counter, there was a narrow door leading into another part of the building. That room was about fifteen-by-twenty. It was the saloon. The bar was about ten-feet long, and the only other thing of importance in the room was the blanket-covered poker tables, where sometimes a draw poker game would run for as long as a week at a stretch.

Of course these were saddle horse men, but they all had plenty of gold and there never was a game less than a quarter ante, generally half a dollar ante. . . .

All drinks at the bar were two for a quarter or five for a half dollar. Anybody tended bar until he got too drunk, then someone else took his place. The cash register was an old cigar box setting on the shelf with six or seven different shaped bottles with the different kinds of whiskey printed on them in gold letters. Bill Harris tended to the filling of the bottles when they were empty, and it all came out of the same big barrel, in the bottom of which there were nailed two very swelled up plugs of tobacco.

On the counter on the west side of the store was the post office. Bill Harris was

post master, store clerk, and all, but he let anybody tend bar. I heard him say one time he did not think he ever lost a five-cent piece all the time he ran the place.[35]

In 1887 "Rambler" rambled through Harris and reported his (or her) findings to the *Daily Humboldt Times*:

The vicinity of Harris—say within a radius of ten miles—is by far the finest stock-raising region in the county. It is a country of open glade and prairie slope with little timber, and is covered everywhere with a luxurious growth of chess [cheat grass] and foxtail. The entire country is devoted to sheep. Within the regions above described are the magnificent ranges of James Wood, B. Tuttle, J. Smith, Wood

Harris Store, 1905 (DTC, colorized by JR).

and Shroeder [sic], Ben. Arthur, Pierce Asbill, Drewry Bros., J. P. Jewett and John Beaumont. These ranges pasture probably more than sixty thousand sheep and export annually more than a half million pounds of wool.[36]

Then came the "hard winter of 1889." Pierce Asbill, one of the ranchers mentioned by Rambler, lost 3,500 sheep. He had a $12,000 debt at the time, which the sheep loss left him unable to pay off. He was thus "financially ruined." He soon found a new source of income: killing deer out of season. Asbill, with his brother, W. J., and two others, shot "deer by the wholesale," dried the venison, and tanned the hides, sending the latter to a glove factory

in San Francisco. The foursome were caught, found guilty, and sentenced to a $100 fine or 100 days in jail. Only W. J. could pay, so his brother Pierce and the others went to the "Hotel Brown, Eureka," a synonym for the county jail operated by Sheriff Thomas McGinnis Brown.[37]

In 1890 the Harrises sold their namesake town to George J. and Louisa Hart Tooby for $9,000.[38] The Toobys had arrived in the area in 1865, and for years George busied himself "making trips into the mountain fastnesses with his pack trains."[39] Now he took up the more sedentary pursuits of storekeeper, hotelkeeper, and postmaster. In addition, Tooby engaged in stock raising, which allowed him to still spend some time in saddle.[40] The Toobys' hotel came to have a telegraph office, which caused the

Harris clings to its hillside, 1910 (DTC, colorized by JR).

Tooby children to become proficient in Morse Code. At dinnertime they would sometimes insert a knife between the tines of a fork and vibrate coded messages to one another.[41] The telegraph office once proved personally useful to its owner. (See sidebar 1.)

Two of the more interesting ranchers in the area were brothers Graham[42] and John Beaumont,[43] who had property on Island Mountain. In 1871 itinerant bookseller John Morris, carrying a revolver and riding a horse "loaded . . . with books," reached the Beaumont Ranch one evening. There he

. . . found intelligent people. The Beaumont brothers were highly educated Frenchmen who could read the dead languages, and who had a fine library.[44]

In July, 1878, the Beaumonts took 4,500 pounds of wool to Port Kenyon; it was their second delivery of the season."[45] At some point

---

1. Mountain Medical Aid

In January 1906 George Tooby had a toothache. There was "no dentist within a hundred miles," and it was the middle of winter. What was Tooby to do?

He telegraphed Eureka.

There were telephones in Eureka, a device not yet present in Harris, and from the city a phone call was made to Dr. Louis P. Rossier, the physician in Garberville, a town that had telephone but not telegraph service. Rossier was bade come over the ridge to Harris to treat Tooby's ailment. He dutifully rode the ten miles across the mountains and removed the offending molar, adding to his luster as a physician who was reputedly willing to go anywhere for anything.[46]

Another time Rossier rode to the Harris area to treat a more serious case. Stella Lauffer, age 15, had a severe cold that turned into something worse, which the doctor soon diagnosed as diphtheria. By now phone service was locally available and Rossier phoned to Eureka for serum.[47]

The serum was dispatched for Harris, but it took two days to reach the Harris Post Office. Meanwhile, Stella's condition grew ever more critical. Her father, Martin Lauffer, set out on horseback for the post office, nine mountainous miles away. Rossier told him to hurry, for "without the serum his daughter could live but a few hours."[48]

Lauffer did as he was told, riding as fast as possible. As he reached the ranch at the end of his 18-mile round trip, his faithful horse sank to the ground and died. But the serum had arrived in time and Stella's life was spared.[49]

The name of the heroic horse, who gave his life to save another's, was not recorded. Monuments have been raised to humans for far lesser accomplishments.

Lassoing on the Lauffer Ranch, 1905 (DTC, colorized by JR).

John Beaumont joined with Eph Parker to run a 60-mule packtrain.[50]

Frank Asbill, whose father, Pierce, had a nearby ranch, gave an account of John Beaumont that changes his nationality. Asbill, whose "facts" were often fluctuant, described him as

> . . . a Scotchman from the Isle-of-Man. He was a man of letters and owned a fine library. The mountain men called him "the walking encyclopedia," and it was to him they went for most of their advice. Mr. Beaumont was the only educated man in the mountains."[51]

The roads north of Harris made the news twice in 1898. That August, Vic Pedrotti learned the dangers of distracted driving while traveling in his wagon on the Harris to Dyerville road along Mail Ridge. He noticed a deer near the roadside. Good nimrod that he was, Pedrotti reached under the seat for his rifle. While doing so, he knocked the gun in such a way that it discharged, wounding Pedrotti in the neck. The horses, startled by the blast, commenced to run away, tumbling the half-conscious Pedrotti from the wagon onto the road. A wheel from the wagon then passed over his face, "cutting and gashing it in a shocking way."[52] So much for multitasking on Mail Ridge.

Then in October, Assistant Superintendent of Mail Service Rager inspected the local postal routes and found the road from Alderpoint up "Harris Hill" nearly impassable in winter. Rager was fond of the route near Dobbyn Creek, although he noted that it lacked a bridge, and therefore the rather large stream had to be forded.[53]

In a few years the perils of the Dobbyn Creek route would be tested by Eleanor Tracy, who was on her way to teach school at Harris. (See sidebar 2.)

2. High Times at Harris

Eleanor Tracy spent over a year teaching school at Harris, from 1905 to 1906. It was her third teaching position. In 1903 she had taught at nearby Alderpoint but hadn't been asked back; in 1904 she was at Stone Lagoon, and after one of her students died and Tracy had to make the funeral arrangements, she didn't *want* to go back. Instead, in March 1905, she set off for Harris, and it proved to be quite an adventure.[54]

Tracy took the stage up the Van Duzen. There was one other passenger, a Miss Knowles, who carried a geranium in a can. She was the Bridgeville school teacher and got off there. It began raining, and by the time the stage reached Blocksburg Tracy was somewhat damp. The Blocksburg teacher, Emma Swithenbank, loaned Tracy her coat and gloves. Although the road had been very rough all the way from Hydesville, Tracy "did not get sick to my stomach until I reached Dobbyn Creek." Many miles later, she arrived at Harris at 3 A.M.[55]

The Tooby family provided Tracy with "a tiny nest of a room" at their hotel. There was space only for her bed, a "dresser" that consisted of "a box with a glass over it," a wash stand, and her trunk—on which she put two "red cretonne pillows" so she'd have somewhere to sit. Tracy had "good board" but felt somewhat uncomfortable since she was "the only woman at a long table, full of stage drivers and cowboys." Excitement consisted of the arrival and departure of the three daily stages.[56]

The boxlike Harris Hotel was built after Eleanor Tracey stayed in its predecessor across the road (DTC, colorized by JR).

Tracy started with nine pupils, but she expected more to come later. The schoolhouse had "been refitted with a new floor, seats, and stove." It had two porches, but one was partitioned off to provide a place for Mr. Tooby's cattlemen to sleep. As predicted, within a week two more students showed up.[57]

In early April there was snow, and by climbing to "the big rock on the hill," Tracy could see a white-clad panorama from the "Yolla Bollies, to Lassic Peak in Trinity County, and all the ranches from Alder Point to Schroeder's Rock." Despite the cold weather, Tracy found that "the flowers were very early this year." They included "a yellow pansy-like violet" that Tracy had never seen before, "large purple blue-eyed grass,"[58] and even "a few small goldfields."[59]

Vic Pedrotti, having recovered from his earlier Mail Ridge mishap, drove the stage that came from Hydesville. The snow made it hard on all the drivers, but Vic suffered especially because of a landslide between Hydesville and Bridgeville. This slowed him enough that he wouldn't reach Harris until daylight, and he then had to try to sleep while everyone else was having breakfast and bustling around.[60]

School closed near the end of June. Tracy took the stage from Harris to Camp Five (Elinor), where she caught the train to Eureka. After staying there with her family for a month, she returned to Harris and started a new school year in late July. This time she began with 15 pupils, which was just the number of passengers that crowded onto the July 30 stage. The vehicle arrived at Harris already "loaded" and then took on a couple from Garberville, "a man and woman and four squally children," and a Miss Hotorf from the distant Trinity County outpost of Hoagland. Somehow they were all packed into and onto the stage, although for a time it appeared that Miss Hotorf might be left off.[61]

On August 7 there was a crowd at the Harris hotel as "the 3 passengers stayed over—a nice man with a typewriter, a lady who is a fright, and Mr. Tucker." Before he left, the "young and interesting" typewriter man taught Tracy how "to run his machine."[62]

Tracy had just returned from a dance at Alderpoint. She had borrowed a horse, wore a white piqué suit that soon got dirty, and arrived at Alderpoint at 10 P.M. after a four-hour ride. Tracy said that her former Alderpoint students "surprised me by seeming glad to see me." She danced four or five times, stopped at a ranch on the way back for breakfast, and reached Harris a little before 11 A.M.[63]

In mid-August came the dreaded alarm: "fire!" Some travelers had failed to extinguish their campfire before leaving, and it was soon burning the prairie. George Tooby was away in Garberville, but the other residents rallied to keep the flames in check, fighting all afternoon. Tooby was reached by phone and he arrived about 9 P.M. The fire burned into the woods, where it could be better contained. Soon it was "about out," with "only a tree or stump burning."[64]

Tracy wrote her family about all the news in the area. She reported that A. B. Huyck and Joe O'Neil had died.[65] O'Neil's sister and her husband, collectively the Bardins, "were on the verge of a divorce suit that will scandalize even scandalous Blocksburg."[66] A "Mr. Red" from Louisiana had "southern prejudices" and "took a cat fit because he had to eat with our negro hostler." His companion, Mr. Pember, shared Mr. Red's bias.[67] September brought fires on the East Branch and at Whitethorn, sending smoke to Harris at night.[68] In addition, "a large piece of the Prior and Tooby winter range at Blocksburg was burned," but rains in late September ended the fire danger.[69]

In late October Tracy went to the Schroeder-Woods Ranch, about five miles east of Harris. Mrs. Woods played both the violin and banjo and had "a lovely house." The next day Tracy went to the next ranch south, owned by the Lauffers. Getting back to Harris required a 16-mile ride. The distance to

An early, very small "stage" stops at Harris (HCHS, colorized by JR).

the Harris School was so great that the Lauffers maintained a private school on their ranch.[70]

Tracy finished the school term in late fall. Before she left Harris, a snowstorm played havoc with the roads. The stage from the south "tipped over above Bell Springs" and arrived nine hours late. The driver only had time for supper before he turned around and headed back to Laytonville, making two nights and one day of driving in bitter cold without any rest.[71]

In March 1906, Tracy returned to Harris for the next school term. Her good friend Stella Tooby had married a Mr. Hamilton in San Francisco, but they were caught in a snow storm on their way back to Harris and had to stay over at Cummings. During the time that the stages couldn't run, the mail was brought in on pack mules. Tracy got to know Stella's new husband and decided she liked "Mr. Hamilton more than I thought I would." [72]

Tracy's patience with her accommodations at Harris wore thin. She complained that "this 'hotel' is a dreary place to call home. It's all I can do to keep my temper, and sometimes I am pretty mad."[73] And then there was the food: "We have been on a diet of fat salt pork, watery beans, all mushed up, and potatoes, sometimes salted and sometimes sugared to give variety." To make matters worse, Tracy finally ran out of the bananas and oranges she'd brought from Eureka.[74]

In April things improved. The weather warmed up and Tracy and others "visited on the Tooby's porch until after 10 o'clock and never felt cold." Then "Mrs. Fowler invited me over to supper. We had fresh roast pork & spuds, huckleberry dumplings, watercress greens (they are fine) and cake and fruit. Mrs. Fowler was afraid I wasn't being properly fed. . . ."[75]

On April 13 Mr. Davis, the soap salesman from Oakland, arrived. He had traveled the route for 30 years, but this was the first time he found the Harris telegraph operator on duty. So he sent a telegram just for the fun of it. The excitement continued the next day with the appearance of Dr. Waterman the dentist, who "will stay until he mends up the teeth of the community."[76]

In May Tracy and a friend drove a buggy to Garberville. They took the old mail route, which was now a road, up past Spruce Grove and north along Mail Ridge. On the west side of Pratt Mountain they turned west onto the relatively new road to Garberville.[77] The distance of the trip was about 11 miles and required opening and shutting 11 gates along the way. They passed the Robertson Ranch, "a very pretty place," and had four or five views of

Garberville—a little village with white houses right next to the river, which winds in and out of sight in 4 or 5 places. On each side of the river are green grain fields and farms. Then the hills in back are just now golden with poppies and gold fields. There were clouds blowing across a blue sky and resting on the mountains in the background. All together it was one of the prettiest places I have seen, and that scrap of level land looked almost homelike to me.[78]

On June 5, 1906, Tracy boarded the stage for her trip back to Eureka. She was done with her teaching at the Harris School, and for the next four years she taught at Kneeland. Then she was on to the Scotia School and in 1920 finally reached her goal, a teaching position in Eureka. She started at the old Lafayette School and later transferred to Marshall. Tracy retired in 1945, having taught for over 40 years, few of which had the vividness of her time high in the hills at Harris.

George Tooby sold the Harris hotel, post office, and store, which were on the west side of the county road, to George M. Gratto in 1909, at which time Gratto became postmaster. Soon he had built a new hotel and a store with a post office on the *east* side of the road. For a time travelers may have stared in confusion at the twin sets of town buildings, but Gratto solved the problem when he tore down the old hotel, moved the lumber across the street, and used it to enlarge his new hostelry, which for a time was called the Harris House.[79]

In fact, 1909 proved to be a year of hotel fever. In addition to Gratto's new structure in downtown Harris, Lewis Snook began building his own hotel about a mile and a half to the south. Snook finished the East View Hotel the following year but died that October. His widow sold the hotel and associated ranch property to Irvin and Sarah Drewry in December 1913.[80]

The East View Hotel lived up to its name. It was situated on the west side of the Overland Road and faced east, offering a panorama of the Eel River canyon and the mountains beyond. The new owners were siblings who had grown up in Mendocino County. Their family had been associated with the Bell Springs area for three generations, ever since Perry and Elizabeth Drewry took up a homestead there in the 1860s. After they died their oldest son, John, inherited the ranch. He rented out the property and took a job as a sergeant of the guard at Folsom State Prison. This proved to be a bad idea as he was killed there in 1914 by a convict during an escape.[81] John's brother, Dan, continued the family's ranching operation at Bell Springs. In 1889 Dan happened to arrive in Harris after the Forepaugh Circus had stopped there for the night. He came to a dead halt when he saw an elephant unexpectedly emerge from the Harris stable's barn.[82] The barn was used by the stage lines and had a capacity of 30 horses[83] but wasn't rated for its ability to hold elephants.

Sarah Drewry ran the hotel while her brother managed the ranch. On May 4, 1936 Irvin was home alone, playing his violin in the front room

The Harris Barn awaits its next elephant (JR).

of the hotel. He noticed that the building's second story was on fire. Unlike Nero, Irvin stopped his fiddling and went to the phone to call for help. It was a useless undertaking, since the phone was out of order. The hotel burned to the ground, and Drewry sold the ranch to Buck Cann. Two years later, Cann lost the property to Leonard Robertson,[84] who held the mortgage. Eventually the property became part of the Tooby holdings.[85]

Although the Tooby family sold their businesses at Harris in 1909, they remained active in the area. Three of George and Louisa Tooby's sons—Norton, Frank, and Ira—owned ranches, either singly or in partnership, in the Harris and Blocksburg areas.[86] Norton had property southeast of Harris running as far as Chamise Creek. Norton and Frank had a partnership with W. G. Dauphiny, owning land that ran from Harris west to the South Fork Eel.[87] The

partnership later became the Western Livestock Company.[88] Tooby & Prior (Douglas H. Prior) had ranchland southeast and northeast of Blocksburg.[89] In 1949 Ira and Norton Tooby each held various parcels east of Harris.[90] When Norton Tooby died in 1957, "he owned several ranches and thousands of acres in the county." Although Norton was the oldest sibling, his two brothers and two sisters had already passed away.[91]

The Toobys were both successful and fortunate. By 1912 George Tooby had made enough money from the sale of Harris and from his ranches to purchase a 1913 "Little Six" Locomobile,[92] which featured not only a "Sterling Silver Finish" and "Eleven Lights," but also "Woodwork in Solid Mahogany." These amenities were reflected in the Little Six's price, which was $5,350.[93]

Perhaps funds for the auto had come from

George's wife, for the previous year Louisa Tooby had been the beneficiary of a most unusual bequest. When making her will, a childhood friend, Sally B. Stoup, fondly recalled the doll tea parties she, Louisa, and Philip A. Gray had enjoyed together in Fon du Lac, Wisconsin. Stoup left her two friends each $5,000,[94] which would allow for plenty of additional partying.

George Tooby's extravagance in purchasing his Little Six Locomobile may have been justified. The road north of Harris, which the postal inspector had found "nearly impassable" back in the horse-drawn stage day, was apparently little improved by the time the automobile era arrived. A newspaper clipping from early in this period announced that "a man by the name of Willis, who was journeying to Eureka in a White Steamer, is stalled below Harris. He offered to sell his machine for $500."[95]

Also below Harris, but far off the main road was (for a brief time) the most southeasterly post office in Humboldt County. (See sidebar 3.)

Harris owed its start as a community and its continued success to its function as a station on the Overland Road, which served as the main route connecting Humboldt County with Mendocino County and points south. In 1893 the trail that ran from Harris northwest along Mail Ridge was converted to a road,[96] which then became the preferred route to Eureka. This diminished Harris's importance not a whit and perhaps even enhanced its status, since the town now stood at the junction of two major north-south routes. What did diminish Harris was the coming of the Redwood Highway, which was opened for travel between Sausalito and Eureka in 1918.[97] The main travel corridor thus dropped from the ridge to the South Fork Eel, thereby making Garberville, and not Harris, the gateway to Humboldt County.

The highway's effect on Harris was gradual but insistent. Twenty years passed, and then, in March 1940, a sure sign of the town's decline came with the announcement that the Harris

An auto that is not George Tooby's "Little Six" pauses on the road to Harris (HCHS, colorized by JR).

3. Who Was Irma?

On June 15, 1905, a fourth-class post office was established in the extreme southeastern corner of Humboldt County. It was located on the landform known as Island Mountain and was understandably, if misleadingly, called Island. The first postmaster was John J. Morrison, who owned the property upon which the post office stood. The following year, on September 24, Caroline Morrison became postmaster. On August 7, 1907, the post office was moved a half-mile east, into Trinity County, and its name changed to Irma. Caroline Morrison continued as postmaster. Four years passed, and then, On October 26, 1911, the *San Francisco Call* announced, by "Special Dispatch," that there was a "CHANGE AT POSTOFFICE, IRMA, TRINITY COUNTY." The change consisted of Caroline Robertson being appointed the Irma postmaster. She replaced Caroline Morrison, her former self, who had just gotten married.[98]

Time passed, and in June 1915 John C. Buster was listed as the Irma postmaster. Then, on August 16, 1915, the Irma Post Office was discontinued. A new post office, Island Mountain, was established about two miles northeast in the store situated across the tracks from the Island Mountain train station.[99]

The Island Mountain store, long after its post office replaced Irma's (JR).

Ninety years later, the long-abandoned store still clung to the hillside above the station. In its northwestern corner was a small room with perhaps a dozen pigeonhole boxes—the vestige of the Island Mountain, nee Irma, Post Office.[100]

But a question remained: who was Irma?

According to two accounts, she was Irma Morrison, who was allegedly the Irma postmaster and who "rode her horse to Harris three times a week and took the mail and then brought it out,"[101] on a 25-mile-long trip.[102]

But no one named Irma Morrison ever served as the Irma postmaster. Caroline Robertson, nee Morrison, did, however, raising the possibility that she went by the nickname Irma. But no, in the 1914 Humboldt County directory, the listings for the community of Irma includes "Carrie Robertson" as postmaster, indicating that Caroline Robertson went by the name of Carrie.[103]

There was an Irma in the area. She was Irma Asbill, whose parents, Pierce Asbill and Kate Robertson[104] Asbill, had a ranch between Pipe Creek and Jewett Creek on the eastern side of Jewett Rock.[105] The ranch was about five miles from the post office that shared their daughter's name. Irma Asbill Ellery (she had married in 1903[106]) was about 23[107] when the Island Post Office's name was changed to Irma. It is certainly possible that Irma Asbill Ellery made the 25-mile trip with the mail that caused her first name to be given to the post office, but she was not the postmaster at Irma and was not a Morrison.

The nomenclatural confusion continued when the post office moved to Island Mountain, a ridge shaped somewhat like a peninsula but that was certainly not an Island. Another instance of misnomer malaise is found a few miles to the northwest, for there is nary a spruce at Spruce Grove—just lots of Douglas-firs.[108]

Post Office would close on March 7 and its mail would go to Alderpoint. The order was quickly rescinded, however, and George H. Clinkscales was appointed acting postmaster. Anyone with such a last name was no doubt especially adept at weighing letters and packages, and perhaps because of this Clinkscales's appointment was made permanent on June 5, 1940.[109]

By then the heart of Harris was its combination post office-general store, and when a new general store was built three and a half miles to the south in early 1947, the post office (and the town's name) went with it.[110] The new location grew to include other trappings of a town: a Grange hall, "beer parlor," and 15 to 20 houses. It became known informally as New Harris.[111] By 1957 the eight-by-ten-foot post office was housed in the Harris Food Center, whose proprietor, Kenneth W. Popkey, was also the postmaster. Although the "post office did a thriving business, serving about 50 patrons," it was closed in 1974.[112]

The Harris Post Office was gone, but other fixtures remained. In June 1975 Garberville's

More than "three bags full": Harris wool, perhaps from the
Drewrys' ranch, is readied for shipment (CPH, colorized by JR).

newspaper, the *Redwood Record*, confirmed that the Drewrys were still active in the Harris area, maintaining a presence that dated back to the 1860s. Perry and Richard Drewry "had accumulated about 5,000 head of sheep" by the 1880s, but nearly a century later the family's flock had dwindled to about 900.[113] The county as a whole had seen a similar decline; a total of almost 152,000 sheep in 1888[114] had dropped to about 21,000 in 1975. The latest Drewrys to run the ranch were Barbara, whose late husband Dan was the grandson of Perry Drewry, and their son Dick. The diminished size of the Drewrys' flock meant that Dick lived off the property in Redway and worked for the Humboldt County Department of Agriculture as his day job.[115]

So it was that a century after Harris got its start, the words of Keats had become apropos:

Adieu! adieu! thy plaintive anthem
fades. . . .

Chapter 2
Mail Ridge

One of the longer but least-appreciated landforms in northwestern California is the divide between the South Fork and main Eel rivers known as Mail Ridge. It rises, in the north, from redwood-filled Dyerville Flat, just south of the two rivers' confluence, and then runs southeast for about 40 miles to end above the confluence of Rattlesnake and Twin Rocks creeks in Mendocino County. For decades, first by trail and then by road, much of the county's mail was carried along the ridge.

Early-day whites traveled on the route by foot, horse, or mule without notable difficulty, but they soon learned that the roadless ridgeline would not accommodate wagon travel. This became apparent in the spring of 1850, just weeks after the establishment of Eureka and other towns on Humboldt Bay. Two parties set out northward from Sonoma.[116] One was led by the Reverend Aristides Joel Huestis, and another had William Lindsay as a member. The groups soon joined together, driving their wagons north until they reached increasingly rough country between the South Fork and the main Eel. That was it for most of the wagons, the wreckage of which was seen in a deep canyon the following year.[117]

But at least one wagon remained, driven apparently by the redoubtable Reverend Huestis. Along the ridge he went, until a large dome of rock blocked his way. At this point the party turned east and descended to the future site of Fort Seward, where they left their last wagon at the Eel River. Thus unencumbered, the party crossed the Eel, Van Duzen, and Mad rivers before meeting the Union-Trinity trail. Turning west, they eventually reached Humboldt Bay. The ridgetop obstacle that deflected the last wagon was given the name of the driver, becoming Huestis Rock.[118]

John E. Townes encountered the ridge about the same time Huestis did. At first Townes thought he was traveling on a road, but that illusion soon passed:

> I never desire to see a more fatiguing road for both horses and men. . . . In fact it is no road at all, but a constant succession of hills, cañons, and rugged mountain passes. We saw snow in many places twenty feet deep and Eel river we were compelled to cross by swimming. . . .[119]

The exact date that the trail became a postal route is uncertain, but it was used for that purpose at least by the early 1860s. An 1862 military dispatch refers to the "mail trail" that ran north of Camp Grant,[120] while the 1865 county map shows it as the "Overland Mail Trail."[121] The Surveyor General's map, which depicts the area in 1869, labels the northern part of this route as the "Trail from Hydesville to Camp Grant." This trail segment, which ran northward from Camp Grant over the ridge to Strong's Station, was built by the soldiers at Camp Grant for the "transmission of supplies."[122] The southern part was shown, on other survey maps, as the "Mail Trail from Camp Grant to Cahto,"[123] the latter a small community southwest of Laytonville in Mendocino County.[124] At various times the route was also known as the Sonoma Trail, the

The mail trail long after it became a road (JR).

Mail Ridge Trail, the Government Trail, and the Overland Trail.[125]

In late 1893 the county converted the much-used, multi-name trail into a road that connected with the Overland Road at Harris and with the West Side Road at Camp Grant.[126] The new Mail Ridge road shaved many miles off the trip to Humboldt Bay on the Overland Road, which ran through Alderpoint, Blocksburg, and Bridgeville. It thus became the favored route for wagons and stages that departed from or ended at Eureka. Travel from Harris south was unchanged, so that travelers still encountered the "notorious Bell Springs Grade," which lived up to its name with some sections inclined "as high as 30 percent." As the 1916 *California Highway Bulletin* described it,

> . . . after the first rains come which generally occur in October, this road is impassable for motor vehicles and even horse drawn vehicles. When snow storms set in, transportation is limited to saddle and pack animals.[127]

In other words, the road reverted to being a trail.

For many years the main habitation points along the ridge were mail stations and overnight stopping places. Farthest south in Humboldt County was Spruce Grove Station, about two miles northwest of the future site of Harris. Here a secondary trail departed to the west, dividing into branches that led to the South Fork Eel and to the Garberville area.[128] By 1886 the southernmost of these two trails had become a road that connected Harris with Garberville via the South Fork's East Branch.[129] By 1907 the road was gone.[130]

Next, about a mile northwest of the top of Pratt Mountain, was Center Station, where a connecting route ran west to Garberville. Before the establishment of the Garberville Post Office in 1874, mail for the town was left at Center Station. The first homeward-bound Garberville resident to come by would carry the mail back with him.[131] The station also served as an overnight stop of singular repute. In May 1872 Anna Reed and her brother Eddie came along the ridge on her way north. Anna found that

Center Station was a small log hut, where a boy whose name I have forgotten, stayed to look after the horses for the mail carrier. The evening that we arrived the usual week's supplies had not come in, and the sum total of provisions on hand were three withered potatoes, an empty flower sack, an onion and a slice of fat pork. Out of the vegetables and pork I made a stew, shook the flour sack for enough flour to thicken it, and we fared sumptuously. After the collation we retired. The sleeping accommodations were two bunks, one above the other, and several gray blankets, but no mattresses. Eddie and the boy took the upper bunk and I the lower, which was harder than any board on which a Monk had ever done penance, and through a wide chink in the wall of the cabin the wind blew against my head all night. The next morning the supplies arrived, and we had a cup of black coffee before starting.[132]

In addition to the "hut" for human accommodation, there was also a corral and barn for the horses.[133]

A few miles north of Center Station the trail crossed over the top of the ridgeline and began running along the upper eastern slope. It passed through an enchanting prairie area, the profusion of spring wildflowers shaded by stands of Oregon white oaks and punctuated by striking rock outcroppings. The view to the east took in Alderpoint, Zenia, and the distant Yolla Bolly Mountains. The trail then recrossed the ridgeline, offering views of the South Fork Eel drainage. It came to a saddle in the ridge where in later times the road to Fort Seward dropped to the east. West of this was the ranch of Steve

The mountains of Trinity County are seen beyond Oregon white oaks and silverleaf lupine (JR).

Fleming,[134] who had led parties of whites who were hunting Indians. In 1869 Brair Curless and his wife Lovinia[135] stayed with Fleming before they started their own ranch on upper Larabee Creek. Brair claimed that "the trail up from Fleming's house was strewn with skulls still green of the Indians Fleming had killed."[136]

Alexander Porter Guthrie purchased land about two miles west of Huestis Rock in 1877,[137] and "Guthrie's" was a listed location on the 1886 Humboldt County map.[138] In 1890 Orren Williams owned the Guthrie property, where what was previously "only brush and briars is now a vegetable garden, an orchard and a grain field."[139] A mile to the north was the later site of Hubbard Station, where a ramshackle hillside "hotel" offered overnight accommodations.[140] According to one account, the structure was built by a man named Idle, who, despite his name, also constructed a hotel on the Dyerville Flat across the South Fork Eel from the town of Dyerville.[141] The station was named for James C. Hubbard, who had homesteaded 80 acres next to the road in 1898.[142]

Some two miles farther north was another stopping place, variously known as Olsen's or Albee's after whomever was the current owner.[143] In 1896 and 1897 Dwight Felt, Sr., drove the mail wagon from Cummings in northern Mendocino County to what was currently called Olsen's, a distance of 45 miles. He left Cummings at 4 A.M. and reached Bell Springs in time for breakfast. Felt arrived in Harris at lunchtime and then made it to the Olsen place for dinner. Once Felt flipped his wagon north of Harris. Felt and the horses were unhurt but the wagon was upside down and not going anywhere. He freed the team, put the mail sacks on one horse, and leading it while riding the other, made it to Olsen's four hours late.[144]

The road continued north along the ridgetop until it reached Elk Prairie, a large opening where, in the 1890s, the community of Fruitland was established.[145] North of the prairie, the road left the ridge, descending from Fruitland steeply and sinuously to reach the main Eel River at the tiny town of McCann.[146] This section of the route, sometimes called the "Whiplash,"[147] lived up to its name, for near the bottom of the grade were two acutely angled sections of road anatomy known as the Devil's Knee[148] and the Devil's Elbow.[149] The route then followed the Eel downriver to Camp Grant, where it met the southern end of the West Side Road that came up the river from Grizzly Bluff.[150]

In 1908 the ridge that had once defied wagons was so tamed that auto stages began running regularly along it. (See sidebar 1.)

In addition to Smythe's auto stages, other railroad-related traffic raised dust on the Mail Ridge road before the rail line's completion. (See sidebar 2.)

Hubbard Station's "Hotel" (HCHS, colorized by JR).

The completion of the railroad in 1914 dealt the Mail Ridge road a stunning blow, because travelers and goods could now speed along the canyon of the main Eel instead of enduring the rigors of snow, mud, sharp curves, and steep grades found on the overland route. It was left to the Redwood Highway, however, to deliver the coup de grâce, when it was built through the canyon of the South Fork Eel. By 1920 the new highway was considered "passable,"[151] which meant that auto traffic now had an all-weather route that was far less challenging than the Mail Ridge road. The latter then became a mere access route for tiny towns such as McCann, Fruitland, Whitlow, and Eel Rock, eventually gaining the name of Dyerville Loop Road, which nowadays is doubly misleading, because there is neither a loop nor a Dyerville anywhere on it.

Probably the most substantial monument to the ridge's past is hard to see: the enshadowed

---

1. The Seven Summers of the Overland Automobile Stage

In 1908 Fred Smythe and five other entrepreneurs incorporated the "Overland Auto Company." It was designed to carry passengers between the two ends of the Northwestern Pacific Railroad (NWP), which were building towards each other but were still about 100 miles apart.[152] The age of the automobile was just underway, and Smythe's company intended to use the new contraptions to partly replace the horse-drawn stages that were already running along the route.

To this end the Overland Auto Company promptly purchased its predecessor, the Overland Stage Company. The older entity included "about 20 stages, 60 horses, harness, equipment and pasture lands."[153] The new auto stages would run during the dry months, but their horse-drawn counterparts would still operate during the rainy season.[154] For their autos, the new company bought five White steam cars. They featured capacious seating, fold-down fabric tops, and large, gleaming headlamps.[155] The White steamers were already well-known, having gained attention in 1907 when President Theodore Roosevelt allowed his Secret Service guards to ride in one *directly* behind his horse-drawn carriage.[156]

Auto stage service commenced in April 1908.[157] The original route began at the Elinor train station, promptly crossed the Eel[158] to reach the West Side Road downriver from Pepperwood, and followed the road upriver past Dyerville to its terminus at Camp Grant. From there the autos traveled along a newer section of road that ran up the river to Fruitland Grade, by which they ascended Mail Ridge, and then followed the ridge southeast to Harris, where the auto stage connected with the horse stage that then continued south. The following year the auto route was extended south to Cummings, in Mendocino County. The third year the auto stage went all the way to Sherwood, where it connected with the rail line that came north from Sausalito.[159]

As the NWP built south, the northern terminus for the auto stage went with it. By September 1908 the terminus had moved to Holmes,[160] in 1912 South Fork,[161] in 1913 McCann, and by 1914 Fort Seward. At the last location Smythe "built a substantial garage and cottage and there he makes his headquarters in the summer months."[162] The company took the condition of the road seriously. Back in 1908 C. A. Long, traffic manager for the stage line, indicated that "we have taken it upon ourselves to hire a man and with four horses and a scraper he is making trips over the road continuously."[163]

The White steamers may have done well on the streets of Washington, D. C., but despite the scrapings of the scraper, they fared poorly on the Overland Auto Stage route. By July 1909 Smythe had switched to five-passenger Maxwell cars that had had an extra lower gear installed by his master mechanic, Bob Morrison. Next came two seven-passenger Studebaker Garfords, followed in 1910 by specially constructed ten-passenger Pierce-Arrows.[164] Eventual-

Smythe stage at the Fort Seward hotel (THPO, colorized by JR).

ly the company maintained "eight touring cars, mostly of the Pierce-Arrow high-powered type."[165]

In August 1912 Smythe had phone lines built along two sections of the route. He then "equipped [his autos] with telephones, so that in case of trouble it is possible to tap the wire at any place and secure the needed help from town."[166]

When Fred Hadley, a newspaperman from Minnesota, took the auto stage in 1913, he was impressed by the scenery, which differed substantially from that of his relatively flat home state:

> The stage soon climbed high among the mountains to an elevation of about 5,000 feet, passing through dense forest of pine, oak and other timber. From the mountains, we secured a view that was easily worth the trip.
>
> For miles and miles, upon all sides, could be seen a tangled mass of mountain peaks, jutting high into the sky. The forest-clad mountains, the deep canyons and big trees certainly formed an interesting sight. You can talk about the Grand Canyon of Colorado, the garden of the Gods, and other places told of in railroad literature, but for rugged grandeur, we believe this 85 mile auto trip exceeds them all.
>
> The road was more crooked than the letter "S," and it needed a steady hand at the wheel to guide the machine around the tortuous curves. A misslip meant going over the brink of a precipice, and landing on rocks, hundreds of feet below. We negotiated one curve, called the Devil's Elbow, that we rather prefer not going over again. The road dropped about a hundred feet in rounding the curve, and in going around it, the turn is so sharp that it was necessary to point the nose of the machine straight out over a yawning abyss, and then back up, in order to swing the machine around. Straight down below the auto hood, probably three hundred feet beneath, lay the blue-green waters of the Eel river. . . . We fortunately had an exceedingly competent driver on this journey, or we might now be en route home for burial.[167]

Safety was no doubt at the forefront of the minds of many travelers along the Mail Ridge route. Although Smythe claimed that "there has never been an accident"[168] involving his auto stages, he apparently misremembered at least two contrary events. In March 1910 Smythe, accompanied by Frank Nellist, was driving one of the White steamers,

. . . when the steering gear suddenly went wrong and the machine ran into a tree stump, with the result that the steam and gasoline connections were broken. In an instant the car was a mass of flames and the two scarcely had time to get 50 feet away before the gasoline tank exploded. The car, which cost $3000 was totally destroyed.[169]

Then, in early September 1912:

An Overland Stage Company auto collided with a buggy on Fruitland Hill, overturning the lighter horse-drawn vehicle, and breaking its axles. The occupants of the buggy, Mrs. Murphy of the Fruitland House [stage stop] and her grown daughter and two small children, were thrown out of the buggy, but not injured beyond a few bruises.[170]

The Devil's Elbow was a diabolical turn for both autos and wagons (CPH, colorized by JR).

Such incidents might damage or destroy the stage line's vehicles, but the autos could be repaired or replaced. In determining the stage line's future, however, the company was powerless. Each year, with work crews laying tracks in the canyon of the Eel, the two ends of the NWP crept closer to each other, so that the auto stage annually had a shorter route to run. Finally, in the fall of 1914, the cars ran their last. One October day, as a large crowd watched from the nearby hillside, a golden spike was driven at Cain Rock, and the NWP was completed.[171]

Fred Smythe sold his vehicles to fellow stage operator Burr McConnaha, who put them on his Eureka-to-Crescent City route. Smythe took the money from the sale and bought several hundred acres of land at Brock Creek, where "he started a certified dairy and hog raising ranch."[172] The spot was located between Eel Rock and Fort Seward and, appropriately enough, it was right on the route of the NWP.[173]

Fred Smythe's dairy and hog ranch at Brock Creek (CPH, colorized by JR).

2. When Mules Ruled the Ridge

Even more essential than Smythe's stage service was the mule-powered supply delivery system that operated along Mail Ridge between 1911 and 1913. The firm of Klipple and McLean had subcontracted part of the NWP's construction on the Eel, and they needed to have supplies transported to "outpost construction camps" that were upriver from the current end of the tracks. Using Shively as their base, Klipple and McLean sent a squadron of horse- and mule-drawn wagons up the Eel past Camp Grant, onto Mail Ridge, and then down to riverside locations where rail line construction was in progress.[174]

One of the teamsters was Ed Myers, who drove four mules and a wagon. He started at Camp Grant, went downriver and crossed the South Fork, and continued down the main Eel until he reached the Shively Ferry, on which he crossed the river to the Klipple and McLean supply base. After loading up, he recrossed the river and drove south to Holmes Flat, where he and the other drivers "nooned" (had their lunch break). Myers, being the most recent addition to the teamsters, drove last, which meant he breathed the most dust. On his first trip he noticed that "the farther we went, the farther I got behind." One of the other drivers told him that he was driving a "bell team" that was "accustomed to wearing bells," so Myers bought some bells at the Dyerville store and never lagged again.[175]

From Holmes, Myers and his fellow drivers returned upriver to Camp Grant, whence they had started that morning. Here the teamsters stopped for the night and boarded with the Fulwider family. The next day took them to McCann and then up Fruitland Grade past the Devil's Elbow and the Devil's Knee. At the top of the grade, the wagons sometimes dropped back down to the Eel at Sonoma Flat (later known as Sequoia or Whitlow), where the railroad builders had a camp. After unloading and having lunch there the teamsters returned in the afternoon to Camp Grant.[176]

On other occasions the wagoners would bypass the Sonoma Flat turnoff and continue on Mail Ridge through Fruitland and almost to the top of the next grade. Here they would stay overnight at a vacant house and barn. The next day they continued south a mile to the top of the grade, where they sometimes turned off the ridge and descended to Camp 1, at Eel Rock. An even longer trip took them south on Mail Ridge to Hubbard's Station, by then "a former stage stop on the Overland Road, which had a big two-story house and barn." Here they spent the night. The next day they continued south to the Fort Seward turnoff, turned left, and dropped eastward to the railroad camp near the site of the former fort.[177]

In the winter of 1913-1914 Klipple and McLean moved their headquarters to Fort Seward. During the summer of 1914 the railroad was nearing completion. Now only one team and wagon were in use. Come July, the freighting work was finished: "Camp 13, south of Alderpoint, was dismantled and hauled back to Fort Seward and the grade was finished to Cain Rock. . . ."[178] And finished, also, was Mail Ridge as a major cargo route.[179]

remnants of Hubbard Station, reposing in the woods a short distance above the road. It has receded from our awareness just like the origin of the landform's name, for Mail Ridge has been put into the dead-letter file of history, its name providing no more enlightenment than that of Hubbard or Huestis Rock. What has endured, with little change, is what was there long before Huestis, Hubbard, or the mail: the silverleaf lupine and Oregon white oaks that color and soften the contours of the rocky ridgetop, and which beckon travelers who search for beauty rather than a time-saving trip between cities.

No longer do letters travel along Mail Ridge— now the route is suitable only for postcards.

Hubbard Station, 2009; still stationary, it hasn't moved a bit in over 100 years (JR).

Chapter 3
Fruitland

Like Dead Sea fruits, that tempt the eye,
　　But turn to ashes on the lips. . . .
　　　　　　　　　　　　—Thomas Moore

Fruitland, basking upon a sunny ridgetop prairie, was filled with promise for the whites who came there to toil and to abide. But the proclamation of its charms was spoken in a strange tongue that many of the newcomers poorly understood, and the poverty of their understanding meant the dashing of their hopes. Thus many soon departed, far before the ripening of the land's fruits. They left with sorrow in their hearts, as had the Indians who had occupied the place before them. The welcoming prairie did not deceive them, but circumstance did.

The grassland stretched across the ridge that ran between the South Fork and main Eel rivers. It was a hunting and gathering place for Indians from the Sinkyone tribe. Five tribal groups lined the main Eel, two miles north of the prairie,[180] while a sixth group, the Sinkenes, had a winter village called Soldekokbukkidun westward near the confluence of Sol-de-kok (Elk Creek), with the South Fork.[181] George Burtt, a Lolahnkok Sinkyone, called the grassland Hles-yah-kah.[182] Early day whites referred the area Elk Prairie, but it is uncertain when this name was first applied. An early report mentions a detachment of soldiers traveling along the ridgetop in June 1864,[183] a route that was no doubt used often by the military. By the end of the year, the Indians who had once frequented the prairie had either been captured, had fled, or were dead.

An early report on Elk Prairie was provided by Anna M. Reed, who had the "privilege to travel horseback over the old government trail from Cahto, Mendocino County, to Hydesville, in Humboldt" in the spring of 1872 with her brother, Eddie. On May 7 they rode the 20 miles between Center Station, east of Garberville, to

> . . . the trading post and stopping place at Elk Prairie, [which] was kept by Ferris and Carroll. John Ferris, who impressed me as a university man, anyway a scholar and a gentleman, had an Indian wife who cooked venison to perfection. We were very tired and hungry and the meal was delicious. In the large living room were two beds, in opposite corners and in front an immense fireplace, filled with generous logs. The flame lighted the room for ordinary purposes. After supper Eddie and I were assigned one bed, the Indian wife of Ferris and another Indian woman took possession of the other, and presently, when all were still and presumably sleeping, Mr. Ferris and a little Indian boy of about 8 years old came in quietly and laid down before the fire, covered by a blanket, and slept until early morn.[184]

In February 1874 came notice that the stopping place was still assiduously tending to

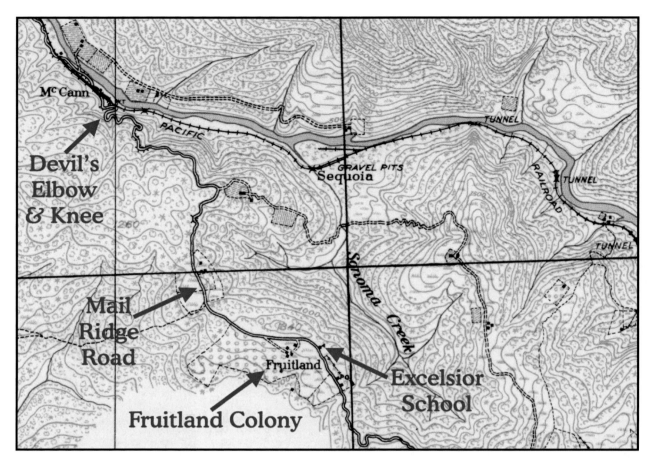

Fruitland – McCann area, 1916 area (CE).

the needs of its guests. A report from Barnett's Ferry, on the lower Eel,[185] indicated that a vessel called the Young Pelican had set forth upriver with, among other items, "a large consignment of whisky for Carroll & Ferris, of Elk Prairie."[186]

By June 1879 there were enough children in the locale that the Excelsior School District was formed.[187] When classes started later in the year, there were ten boys and six girls in attendance. There is no description of the schoolhouse, but ancillary conditions were challenging:

> The furniture was inadequate. There was no water supply. There was no library, and the texts for study had to come from home. There was no outhouse.[188]

These situations changed, slowly, and only sometimes for the better. By the second term two outhouses were under construction. The following year the water supply was "sufficient" and the library contained nine books. Soon, however, "the water in the well was bad and could not be used." It was still bad in 1881, and the furniture remained so sparse that there was "not even a chair for a visitor or teacher to use." By 1889 the furniture was "satisfactory," but "the water supply had not improved at all" and "only one outhouse was usable."[189]

Then in 1896, a new Excelsior School was built.[190] It was about 50 percent larger than the original schoolhouse, with some of the extra space being needed by the library, which now had 149 books. The furniture situation had declined and was again "inadequate." Even in 1947, the school's last year, "many of the desks were homemade." The following year, Fruitland students went to the school in Miranda.[191] There they sat at desks that had not been made at home, but instead had come from the Newburg School near Fortuna when that building was torn down.[192]

John H. Durst published an account in March 1883 of traveling "afoot up Eel River." He found that "from Camp Grant the road is but a trail" that "for seven miles . . . goes up a narrow grade, trodden hard by the trains of pack-mules." The trek brought Durst to Elk Prairie, where there were but two houses. At the second one he asked "for a drink and lodging, and found a Swede living with but one man as his assistant and companion." Durst was given "a pan of milk, cream and all." His host had

owned the property for a year. He had tried raising sheep, but they had not done well, so he had decided to switch to dairying.[193]

The "Swede" was apparently a Dane named Jes N. Gissemann,[194] who in 1880 had bought about a thousand acres of Elk Prairie that was the old Ferris and Carroll place.[195] Four months after Durst's visit, Gissemann was reportedly milking "an average of 50 or 60 cows," and converting the milk "into butter and cheese, both of excellent quality."[196] The property, which included most of the prairie, was evaluated by the Humboldt Standard's traveling correspondent, McTavish, who indicated that the area "was a superior section for fruit culture and in time doubtless every acre of the prairie will be utilized for that purpose."[197] His prediction soon seemed prescient, then problematic. (See sidebar 1.)

Excelsior School, at the time about 50 years old (HCHS, colorized by JR).

1. The Fruitless Hopes of Fruitland

In late September 1890 a commotion occurred at the Eureka waterfront when a group of "60 men, women and children" arrived after a 17-day trip from Amsterdam. The Humboldt Standard reported that

> . . . a large crowd of the curious repaired to the wharf Sunday to witness the landing of the strangers, who aside from their peculiarities of dress looked no different than other human beings.
>
> From the crowd which surged and pressed around them on the wharf as they assorted and picked up their belongings, one would think that it was a band of Fiji islanders or a Wild West show that had just landed.[198]
>
> The arrivals comprised ten families. They wore billowing pants and skirts, woolen or lace caps, and pairs of the distinctive Dutch "klompen"—large wooden clogs. They were dressed like what they were, or intended to become—agriculturalists. They were bound for their new home, which was on Elk Prairie.[199]

Waiting for them was the former Ferris and Carroll property, much of it open grassland with a southern exposure that would stimulate "a general fruit and farming business." The property was now owned by the First Netherland Fruit and Culture Association, an organization formed by Eureka capitalists and Dutch promoters in 1889. The agreement establishing the association was complicated, but essentially it divided the participants into three groups. Four Eureka businessmen—J. P. Monroe, David Cutten, J. A. Livingston, and J. G. Murray—provided the land, most of which had been purchased by them two years earlier for $10,000. It was then sold to the Association, which paid "$15,000 in gold coin for 960 acres."[200] A collection of Dutch investors either bought shares in the association or, in the case of J. P. Koch, recruited colonists from Europe and provided fruit trees. The third group consisted of the ten Dutch families, who paid their own way from Holland and who agreed to labor on the land for "a meager monthly wage." In return each family received one cow, two pigs, and the use of a modest house. After five years of work the families were each to be given a five-acre orchard containing fruit trees that by then would be four years old.[201]

A certain, perhaps intentional, opacity obscures a full understanding of the Association's transactions, but it appears that by the August of 1891 the

The Fruitland colony orchard, getting started (CPH, colorized by JR).

standing of the various participants in the Association was as follows: Three of the four Eureka capitalists—Cutten, Monroe, and Livingston—who had sold the 960 acres to the Association for a $5,000 profit, now held 5,300 shares in the corporation. For his work in providing 10 families of colonists and planting French prune trees, J. P. Koch held 10,000 shares.[202] Five Dutch investors, after paying $1 per share, owned an aggregate 20,000 shares. Ten Dutch families, having endured the considerable expense of transporting themselves from Holland and having worked on the property for nine months, were progressing towards gaining title to part of the property. Lastly, the Bank of Eureka had become an inactive but interested participant in the Association, having loaned the corporation $7,000 on March 21.[203]

It is unclear what the loan was used for; perhaps it was to cover the expenses of feeding and housing the colonists and maintaining the orchard. Crystal clear, however, was the problem soon faced by the Association. On June 22, 1891, a mere three months after providing the loan, the Bank of Eureka filed a complaint against the Association in Humboldt County Superior Court for non-payment.[204] On July 3, 1891, the directors of the Association met and assessed a charge of 30¢ per share on its shareholders. On July 6, the assessment apparently having failed to raise the necessary funds, the court issued a notice of default. The next day the court followed with a decree enabling the foreclosure and sale of the Association's property to satisfy the bank's claim.[205]

The drama moved inexorably towards its conclusion. The Eureka capitalists, having already made a profit when they sold their land to the Association, had nothing they needed to protect. The distant Dutch shareholders, perhaps unaware of the threat to their investment or unable to do anything about it, did not respond. The Dutch colonists, who had spent their money getting to Fruitland, were unable to intervene in a process that, although it threatened their future, took place in a rarified legal and economic arena to which they were not granted access.

When two of the Association's directors, John Livingston and David Cutten, paid a valedictory visit to Fruitland in September, they found the orchard "in good condition." The condition of the colonists was only mentioned as an afterthought; with the foreclosure sale looming, four Dutch families had elected to stay on and "cultivate the land" that would likely never be theirs. The rest had "scattered," although "a number of them . . . [had] found work in the mill and woods at Scotia."[206]

On February 20, 1892, the property was sold by the county sheriff to a group of five Eureka investors headed by I. R. Brown.[207] The following week Brown and his colleagues formed the Fruitland Company, into which they subsequently placed their recently acquired agricultural asset.[208] In August a group including some of the new owners and a Humboldt Times representative visited the property and reported on conditions there: D. L. Miller remained in his previous position as supervisor of the orchard, and Albert Schmidt, once described as "the head of the colony of Hollanders," served as the "budder," or grafter. They were kept busy tending to some 14,000 trees, all of them "French prune." About 20 percent of the orchard was ready to bear fruit for the first time the following year, thus providing the perspicacious owners a quick return on their investment. Concluding with unintentional irony, the article indicated that

> The gentlemen who own the Fruitland property are to be congratulated on the success they have thus far attained. To be sure they have spent considerable money on their venture, but they have the assurance that it will come back to them increased many fold. . . .[209]

Much of the information for the article probably came from David Cutten, who had been the secretary of the Association and was now mingling with the property's new owners. The account included a remarkable revision of the site's history, claiming that

> The Hollanders stayed on the ranch a year or two, but becoming dissatisfied with their condition they left it. Then things went wrong. Money matters were behind, and finally the place was sold at auction.[210]

Thus was the story of the Fruitland Colony rewritten. Three years later the Times issued a sort of unwitting postscript, copying an article from the Ferndale Enterprise that included mention of some of the colonists:

> Supervisor Scott tells us that the family of Hollanders residing on Howe creek . . . are in destitute circumstances and are entitled to assistance from the county. They came to Humboldt a few years ago to work at the Fruitland colony, and later the father was employed at Scotia. He is now ill with consumption and his wife and children dependent upon him.[211]

At this point the Times could have asked—but didn't—how this circumstance might affect the balance sheet of the Fruitland Corporation. Thus the success in growing French prunes would not be measured, as it well could have, against the fate of three score immigrants noted only for their billowing pants, strange caps, and klompen.

Had McTavish returned to Elk Prairie a few years after his first visit, he would have seen the once-open land now speckled with thousands of fruit trees. The First Netherland Fruit and Culture Association, having planted a forest of French prunes, had fallen into the abyss of bankruptcy, taking with it the hopes of ten guiltless but gullible Dutch families, who had come from Holland to tend the trees and eventually receive a piece of the property for their work. Instead the First Netherland Fruit and Culture Association had also become the Last, the Hollanders' promised patrimony became the property of Eureka businessmen, and the landless Netherlanders had taken themselves to the nether lands of Scotia and other lower-elevation communities where they might find work.

Now the prairie was in the hands of the Fruitland Company, and the hands grasped for quick and easy profit. Having taken over the property in February 1892, in 1894 the company added 3,000 trees, mostly French prune, but also included were a few apple, olive, almond, and peach.[212] To some this was taken as evidence of the company's prosperity, but at least four individuals thought otherwise. Almost exactly a

Modest living at Fruitland (HCHS, colorized by JR).

year later, David Cutten and two other former directors of the First Netherland Fruit and Culture Association joined Charles W. Freese in suing the Fruitland Company. The four men had entered into a profit-sharing agreement with the company and, after three years, had found there were no profits to share. Claiming that the business had been improperly managed, they asked "for an accounting and transfer of one-half of the stock of the company."[213]

The suit was proof that the tangled transactions of the various Eureka capitalists had not ended with the formation of the Fruitland Company. The previous year one of the company's co-owners, real estate broker Sam Allard, had offered to sell 16 ten-acre parcels "near Fruitland" for $1,475 each, payable in monthly installments of $10, "without interest or taxes until fully paid for."[214] Maneuverings among the moneyed interests of Eureka

continued. These activities were neither transparent nor accurately reported. When David Cutten's biographical sketch appeared in 1915, it revised reality by claiming that:

> Another important local enterprise of Mr. Cutten was the organization and promotion of the Dutch Colony, owners of one thousand acres at Fruitland, with one hundred sixty acres of the tract planted to prunes, apples, grapes and peaches. A school was built on the land and other improvements made necessary to the permanent well-being of the settlers.[215]

Implied in this account was Cutten's participation in the creation of Fruitland's school. In point of fact, there had been two schools, the first of which was constructed eight years before

Cutten became involved at Fruitland,[216] the second being built four years after the members of the "Dutch Colony" had been dispersed by the bankruptcy and dissolution of the organization that Cutten had helped organize and promote.[217] The alleged "permanent well-being of the settlers" had lasted less than a year.

Also worthy of a closer look was Sam Allard's involvement in the Fruitland property. By 1921 Allard owned the land that had belonged to the "Dutch Colony" and later to the Fruitland Company, of which he had been a principal.[218] In 1900, a barn there that he and I. R. Brown owned there burned with the loss of 13 tons of hay.[219] Twenty-two years later, Allard's property was again scorched, this time resulting in the destruction of a "large dwelling house and fruit dryer and all other outbuildings on the Allard place, seven buildings in all."[220] The loss by fire of two Allard barns at the same location might have merely been coincidence, but those who knew something of the area's true history may have thought there was more to it than that.

Allard's name stretched across a wide area on the 1921 county map and was located just below the word "Fruitland." Nearby, constricted because the acreage involved was far smaller, was the name "Schmidt," a reference to the Fruitland postmaster, Albert Schmidt. When he died in 1925 one headline claimed, with some exaggeration, that the "Founder of Fruitland Succumbs." Unlike the other Dutch colonists, Schmidt not only remained on the ridge; first to graft trees, but then to acquire a small parcel of his own land. On it, he grew peaches, apricots, and plums, for he had arrived from Holland already trained as an "expert nurseryman." Schmidt became the Fruitland postmaster and was serving as such when he died.[221] Ruby Foltz Kelsey, who grew up in Fruitland and picked and packed Schmidt's fruit, recalled that he created an unusual intersection between his work as an orchardist and his job as postmaster:

> Anything in the mail that he did not approve of, such as "funny papers" or religious matter, he threw in the waste basket, no matter to whom it was addressed . . . [he then] used the thrown away papers to line the boxes he shipped plums or peaches in.[222]

So, one way or another, the Fruitland mail did go through.

Schmidt once stated that "I love my orchard, my fruit, and my country."[223] Alone among the Dutch colonists, he had fulfilled at least part of the dream that had brought all of them to Fruitland.

More than fruit was harvested at Fruitland. In 1911 F. H. McKee cut part of the forest that surrounded the prairie, milling timbers on site for the Northwestern Pacific, which was extending its line up the Eel north of Fruitland.[224] More logging was to follow. (See sidebar 2.)

The mail trail that traveled through Fruitland on its way along Mail Ridge was converted into a road in 1893,[225] becoming the principal route to Harris and the Bell Springs Road that led into Mendocino County. The Overland Stage Company and its successor, the Overland Auto Company, carried passengers along the route until 1914, when the completion of the Northwestern Pacific Railroad drained off so many travelers that the auto stage company closed down.[226] A welcome stop along the route was the Fruitland House, which stage driver Frank Nellist recalled as

2. "Henry Loves the Trees"

Fruitland's prairie was surrounded by a mixed conifer forest. To the north stretched a tract belonging to the Hammond Lumber Company,[227] while to the south were lands belonging to a pair of large timberland holders, one a combine that included Miles Standish and Henry Hickey, and the other the Sage Land & Improvement Company.[228] In about 1939 John E. Tsarnas purchased about 600 acres from the latter company. The land was located in the Elk Creek drainage about a half-mile south of the property that had belonged to the Fruitland colony. Tsarnas paid $2 per thousand board feet for an estimated 50,000,000 board of redwood timber on the parcel, resulting in a purchase price of $100,000. Sage threw in all the Douglas-fir timber and the land for free.[229]

At first Tsarnas did split stuff work, using wedges and a broadax to convert redwood bolts into railroad ties, fence posts, grapestakes and similar products that he then trucked to the South Fork train station, about ten miles to the north. Then World War II ended and the demand for redwood lumber escalated. So in 1946 the John E. Tsarnas and Son Company was established, with John's son Henry as a junior partner. They dammed Elk Creek, creating a log pond, and built a small steam-powered mill next to it. They fueled the steam engine with redwood waste but it burned too cool to generate

Tsarnas and Son mill (HCHS, colorized by JR).

maximum power, which limited the mill's production capacity. Then, in 1950 a cutting torch fortuitously ignited the mill building and destroyed the operation. Having done away with the inefficient steam-powered mill, the Tsarnases rebuilt on the same site, this time using a diesel engine, which markedly increased the mill's power. In 1953 the engine was replaced by an electric motor; it required less maintenance than the diesel and thus further increased the mill's efficiency.[230]

The Tsarnases had caught the first wave of the timber boom that swept over Humboldt County in the late 1940s and early 1950s. Other small-scale operators joined in, so that soon there was reportedly "a mill about on every hillside in Elk Creek." The Tsarnas operation was the biggest of the lot and after a time it had cut the 50,000,000 board feet of redwood that had resided on the family's property. Then Tsarnas and Son bought timber on Kerr Peak, across the South Fork from Myers Flat, and trucked it to the mill.[231]

But it was their own trees that supplied the best lumber. According to Henry, the Elk Creek drainage contained "beautiful redwood" that enabled the mill's cut to be about 50 percent "clear" wood, which was the highest grade of lumber and was worth about three times as much as common grade wood. Much of the clear redwood was cut into 20-foot lengths as either 2x10 or 2x12 boards to be used as siding.[232]

At the peak of their production, Tsarnas and Son employed about 40 workers, 25 of which were mill hands, while the rest worked in the woods. Elk Creek, after losing some its water to the millpond, flowed in a westerly direction south of the mill. Across the creek was housing for the married workers.[233]

One day in 1956 Henry Tsarnas noted smoke coming from a pile of bark. Fearing that it would spontaneously combust into a fire, Henry hosed the bark down. A couple of weeks later the bark again heated up, but this time no one noticed it. The bark burst out in flames, starting a fire that engulfed the mill. And that was it for Tsarnas and Son.[234]

Henry Tsarnas left the area in 1965 but returned in 1991. He and his wife Billye lived in the Tsarnas family's house, which had been built with redwood from the mill in about 1950. In 2005 he was interviewed for a cultural survey of the mill area. Henry walked about the rusting ruins of the mill equipment, naming the objects and their purpose. At one point he stood on the top of the millpond's earthen dam, looking across an empty expanse that had not held a log in nearly 50 years. He turned and gazed across the mill site at the stark bulk of the Pawling & Harnischfeger crane, which had moved logs from the pond to the mill. Pointing to the blue and white nameplate at the head of the crane's boom, Henry commented, "P and H—we all said it stood for Poor and Helpless."[235]

The summer sunlight shone on Henry as he said this, his eyes brightened, and it seemed he had been using the Poor and Helpless only yesterday. All day there had been a fondness in his voice as he spoke. It would have been easy to mistake the source of his feelings, but his wife, Billye, had earlier set the record straight. "Henry loves the trees," she said. "His father loved the mill."[236]

Skimpy stage at Fruitland (HCHS, colorized by JR).

. . . a real place to eat, the food was the very best, but there were lots of yellowjackets also looking for lunch and although they never bothered [me] much they made most of the passengers nervous.[237]

An auto stage passenger also noted not only the Fruitland House's cuisine but the advantage of using engines rather than horses to propel vehicles along the route:

Passing Hubbard's at 11:45 we made our way toward Fruitland. Here we stopped to enjoy an elegant chicken dinner prepared for us and to partake of the delicious fruit raised in that section. Here we passed the overland wagon stage which left Sherwood the same time we did and traveled all night.[238]

Fruitland House was run by the Murphy

family. Mrs. Murphy's cooking, praised as it was by the Overland Stage Company's passengers and drivers, was not enough to prevent one of the auto stages from plowing into her buggy on Fruitland Hill in September 1910, "overturning the lighter, horse-drawn vehicle and breaking its axels." Mrs. Murphy and her three passengers "were thrown out of the buggy, but not injured beyond a few bruises."[239]

More than a hundred years later, Fruitland House and its meals were barely remembered, the Excelsior School had been closed for more than half a century, and the villainy that displaced the Dutch colonists was obscured by decades of misinformed or deliberately false reports. Prune trees were no longer prominent on the prairie, but orderly rows of another crop had taken their place. Wine grapes now hung in dark clusters from hundreds of vines, responding to the same benevolent effects of sun and soil that had benefitted the land's earlier fruit. Visitors to the Elk Prairie vineyard could sip its Pinot Noir[240] while ruminating upon the view westward, where above the shadowy confines of the South Fork Eel rose a ridgeslope blanketed with ancient redwoods. The air glowed golden in the afternoon sun. Another glass of wine? Of course. It had taken more than a century, but for a time, at least,[241] the fruits of Fruitland were finally being enjoyed.

Chapter 4
Alderpoint

All the men out here seem nicer than the women.
—Eleanor Ethel Tracy on Alder Point, 1903

The Indians who inhabited the Alderpoint area were the Set-ten-bi-den ke-ah, the southernmost of at least seven groups that comprised the so-called Lassik tribe. They took their name from a rock "near Alder Point" (as the town's name was first rendered), the color of which was variously described (by the same source) as gray or white.[242] The Set-ten-bi-den ke-ahs had a village across the river from today's Alderpoint, but it was terminated in the 1860s, when the villagers were "rounded up by the whites and taken to Fort Seward." Within a few years "the last surviving Lassik adult male had been killed,"[243] and the tribe ceased to exist.

The first white living in the area was probably Thomas Armstrong, who had a 160-acre ranch on the west side of the Eel River. In either 1860 or 1861 mail carrier P. G. Tuttle was at the ranch when it was attacked by Indians. Tuttle indicated that the ranch house was burned and most of the livestock killed.[244] Despite the mishap Armstrong restocked the ranch and still owned it in the late 1860s.[245]

With the Set-ten-bi-den ke-ahs gone from their village and with Armstrong's ranch rebuilt, a gap then appears in the history of the area. Only in the 1870s are new residents reported. George Tooby arrived in 1872.[246] The 1873 land office map shows "Bailiff's House" on the west side of the river where a trail from the Spruce Grove area comes down the ridgeline. Across the river, where the trail resumes, is "Graham & Tooley's

[Tooby's] house." This location put the partners about five miles west of the "Round Valley Trail," which at the time was the main connecting route to northeastern Mendocino County.[247] In 1874 Thomas M. Prior and Emily Tooby Prior arrived at Alder Point.[248] Their marriage had united the Tooby and Prior families, the conjunction of which came to own large areas of rangeland in southern Humboldt County.[249]

Greater change was afoot. The Overland Road, which was the first wagon road from Eureka to Mendocino County, reached Alder Point[250] (whose name was at first spelled as two words) in 1876, where a stage depot was promptly established.[251] The road grading between Blocksburg and Alder Point was done by Chinese workers using picks and shovels.[252] In 1877 Ben Blocksburger, who already operated a store in his namesake town to the north, opened a branch in Alder Point and also set up a ferry.[253] The town's first buildings were located on the east side of the Eel, across the river from where the later community developed.[254] Blocksburger himself came through town on May 11, 1877, "soliciting for wool for a fair in the city." Small wonder then that "sheepshearers . . . [were] riding off in every direction and business in that line has commenced."[255]

The Overland Road was completed in 1877, when the routes from Humboldt and Mendocino counties met at Dark Canyon, south of Harris.[256] Travelers heading north on the Overland had a

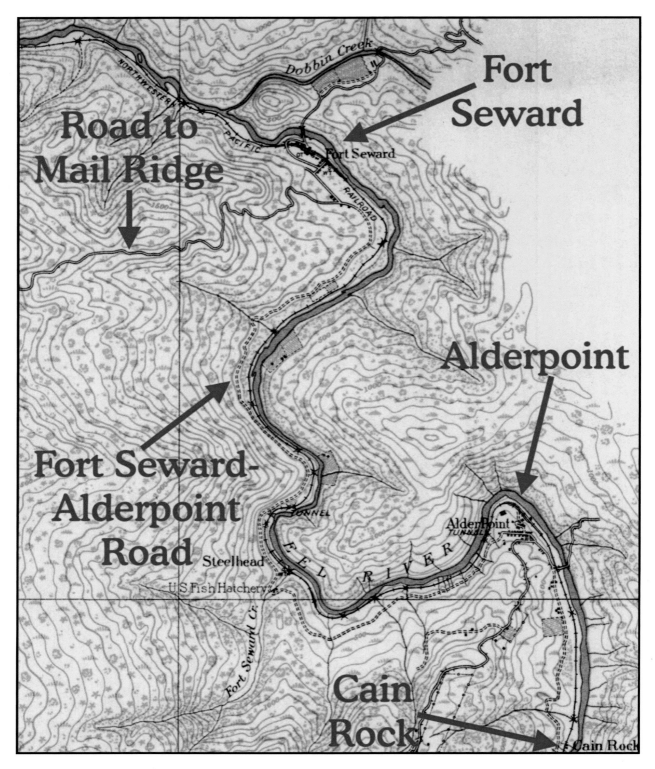

Alderpoint-Fort Seward area, 1916 (CE, colorized by JR).

15-mile trip from Spruce Grove Station, mostly downhill, to Alder Point Station, a stopover accommodation run by Allan Look. Along the way they passed through the "extensive range of

Bailiff and Dyke." Look's station offered "Rest for the Weary and Storage for Trunks."[257]

George Friend had the mail route between Bridgeville and Alder Point. He indicated that lightweight mail was moved across the bridge-less Eel at Alder Point by cable; heavier items were taken by boat. According to Friend it was only after the drowning of George Charles (for whom Charles Mountain, northeast of Blocks-burg, was named) that "the sentiment for the bridge become strong enough to get it built in the [18]80s."[258] Prior to its construction, horses were kept on both sides of the Eel for use by mail carriers who would have to turn around at the river during high water and needed fresh mounts for their return trip.[259]

About 1880 Henry Hyde Ticknor sold his Neafus Peak sheep ranch,[260] which was located about five miles southeast of Alder Point, and moved operations to the budding town. There he "kept a roadside inn and store and owned a ferry." It is likely that Ticknor took over some or all of these businesses from Ben Blocksburg-er. At this time Ticknor also "had charge of the stage at Alderpoint."[261]

By 1885 it was William Perry "who looks out for the stage stock and keeps a public house for the entertainment of travelers." Perry ran the ferry boat during high water in the winter-time; if the water rose too much, passengers and mail were transported across the river in a "car" that ran on a cable. Prominent ranch owners on the northeast side of the Eel were D. T. Woodman and George White,[262] the latter known as the infamous "Cattle King of Round Valley."[263] George White's brother, William Pitt White, co-owned the Kekawaka Ranch, which straddled the Humboldt-Trinity county line and extended to within about two miles of Alder Point.[264] One old-timer provided a 28-word biography of him:

> Pitt White was a large cattleman near
> Alder Point and figured in some early

fracases where a number of men had gun arguments and some got deceased considerable.[265]

Near the end of 1893 the county completed a road that ran along the Mail Ridge divide between the South Fork and main Eel rivers. It connected Harris with Dyerville, and the travel time between those two towns was the same as that between Harris and Blocksburg along the original Overland Road.[266] Since Dyerville was considerably closer to Eureka than Blocksburg, most through traffic switched to the new route. One later account stated that Alder Point was then "abandoned."[267] This was at least a slight exaggeration. Although the town, which had appeared on the 1886 county map,[268] had dis-appeared from the 1898 map,[269] the Alder Point School continued operating during the later 1890s[270] and on into the 1900s.[271] In addition, the allegedly abandoned community acquired a post office, although its name no doubt created a combination of confusion and consterna-tion. Instead of naming the office Alder Point, someone apparently thought to associate the facility with the river that ran nearby. But the process was muddled by poor spelling, and the unfortunate result was a post office named "Eal." Eal existed from August 1889 to December 1890, closed, and then reopened (still with its flawed name) in March 1891, operating until May 1900 when it closed and its mail was sent to Harris.[272]

Edwin Graham homesteaded land in 1893 three miles southwest of Alder Point. His 25-acre orchard included 200 peach and 300 apple trees. He also raised hogs and sold not only the bark from his tanoak trees but also the wood, which was used by furniture makers.[273] Another orchardist was Charles R. Smith, who

The Eel river canyon downstream from Alderpoint (JRC, colorized by JR).

homesteaded about a mile southeast of town. Lavish in his selection of crops, Smith grew peaches, apples, cherries, walnuts, almonds, grapes, and figs.[274]

As the century drew to a close, Bailiff and Dyke still owned a large ranch that stretched south of the Eel to within a mile of Pratt Mountain. North of the river, the Wood-man-White rangeland was now mostly owned by the Petaluma Savings Bank,[275] the result of a forced sale of White's property to meet the demands of a divorce settlement with his third wife, Frankie White.[276]

Southeast of Alder Point Frank L. Cain homesteaded next to the Eel River in 1898. A landform on his property that came to be called Cain Rock was the site of the completion of the Northwestern Pacific Railroad (NWP) in 1914.[277]

During the spring of 1903 Eleanor Ethel Tracy taught at the Alder Point School. In late April she took the stage up to Edwin Dyke's ranch. Tracy was quite taken with the property and its owner:

Mr. Edwin Dyke's house is a little white house (or it was once white) around a turn in the road. It has a wide porch clear around it, and the front yard is full of ros-es and lilacs. . . . The apple trees were all in bloom, too. Inside, the house is paint-ed and papered and carpeted. There is a lovely big fireplace. In fact, it isn't one bit what you would expect of an old bache-lor who has lived there alone for 25 years. Mr. and Mrs. Tompkins live there now and help on the ranch, but Mr. Dyke is the ruling spirit. He is a nice old man with white hair and beard who talked to us about his flowers.[278]

If Tracy considered Mr. Dyke "nice," she found the Alder Point women and children less so. She mentioned a 45-year-old grand-mother who "has a loud voice, which she uses continuously, scolding and aimlessly talking at everything." Her daughter-in-law was "big and fat and soft." This woman had a baby boy who "is redheaded and runs in the mud. He can say a few words—the chief being swear words, and his family think him very cute and don't object—that is the women don't."[279] Tracy was saved from the agonies of prolonged exposure to such persons when the Alder Point School trustees failed to renew her contract.[280] Perhaps her distaste for the women of the district had been too apparent.

A new Alder Point townsite southwest of the Eel was surveyed in 1907. A series of three terraces rise above the river at the location, and the town was to occupy the second, and largest, of these. The first streets were graded in 1910,[281] when the NWP surveyed its route through town.[282] The NWP tracks would run on the southwest side of the river, as they had all the way from the South Fork bridge near Dyerville. About two miles south of Alder Point the rail line would cross to the northeast side of the river at Cain Rock. This alignment left the original Alder Point community on the opposite

(eastern) side of the Eel from the railroad. The "new" Alder Point, which unlike its predecessor was actually on the point itself, was soon embellished with several buildings. The most notable structure was W. H. and John H. Hellard's Alder Point Hotel,[283] which was constructed by Jeptha C. Phillips and his crew in 1911. The men were joined in the mushrooming community by a conglomeration of NWP workers that included "hundreds of laborers, mechanics, engineers and other employees, as well as officials." By June the NWP personnel had made Alder Point "the active center of [rail]road building operations, grading, blasting, tunneling, etc."[284]

In February 1911 the federal government returned to town. It erased the unfortunate earlier memories of "Eal" when it established the "Alderpoint" post office, whose name now conjoined the tree species with the landform by uniting them as a single word.[285] The first postmaster was a Mr. Adin, who had opened a store

Alderpoint's new business district awaits the completion of 4th Street (CPH, colorized by JR).

in town the previous year.[286] Come October 1912, ever-active Jeptha Phillips took over as postmaster. He later acknowledged, in the third person and with minimal modesty, that "he has proved himself admirably fitted for responsibilities, earning the respect and good will of the many with whom he comes in personal contact in the discharge of his duties." Despite Phillips's exertions, the post office was "still in the fourth class,[287] but is doing a steadily increasing business."[288]

Phillips also intimated that he had "driven the first nail at Alderpoint,"[289] presumably in 1911 for the nascent hotel. But vying with him for the distinction was Charles Smith, who that same year built "the first house completed" in Alderpoint along with "a commodious livery barn,"[290] both of which also required the use of nails. In June 1911 Smith married Ellen Mathison. Their wedding trip consisted of riding in a loaded lumber wagon from Hydesville, where Ellen

had formerly resided, to Alderpoint,[291] where Charles got busy on his house and barn. More nails were expended in 1911 by Joe McKnight, who built a store.[292] Then in 1912 McKnight really went to work. He constructed a house and office building[293] and in 1916 sold both, along with his store, to the Helmke Mercantile Co.[294] By then Helmke already had stores in Blocksburg and Fort Seward[295] and was threatening to become the Sears, Roebuck & Co. of southern Humboldt.

By 1911 the Bailiff and Dyke ranch property south of the Eel had changed hands and was now owned by the Monte Vista Land Company, of which John C. Scott of Sonoma County was president. The Monte Vista Rancho, as it was then called, was operated by Scott's son, Joseph. It consisted of 4,700 acres, upon which about 3,000 head of Merino sheep were run,[296] an arrangement that allowed each woolly ruminant about 1.57 acres upon which to ruminate.

The Alderpoint Hotel lends substance to the new town (DTC, colorized by JR).

The Alderpoint School moved to the west side of the river in 1913. At first it lacked a permanent building, so that September classes were "being held in an unfinished butcher shop."[297] The schoolhouse was completed the following year, allowing the students to be replaced by sides of beef in the former classroom. The new building was also used for town meetings, and several years later a dance there welcomed back "the local boys" who had served in World War I.[298] Students from outlying areas rode horses or mules to school and kept them in a stable on the northeast corner of the schoolyard.[299]

Alderpoint was ready for the railroad when it was completed in October 1914. The town had grown to have three hotels, a big store and two smaller ones, a dance hall, and a restaurant. One store also held the post office, a dentist's office, and J. J. Murphy's law office and living quarters.[300] The two small stores sold only groceries. The big store, the Helmke Mercantile Co., "sold just about anything."[301]

If Frank Asbill, a noted storyteller, is to be believed, the coming of the railroad changed the complexion of the town:

> Alderpoint was now wide open, with boot-legging joints, gambling and honky tonks. Few nights passed by that men didn't get killed, a head caved in or a throat cut or maybe just beaten to death.[302]

But another account indicates that Alderpoint was a lively, rather than a deathly, place. In 1915 Leigh Irvine's just-published Humboldt County history claimed that "Alderpoint is one of the newest towns in the county, located on the overland road and the Northwestern Pacific Railway [sic], . . ." In addition to the preexisting sheep and cattle ranges, Irvine noted that "many orchards are now being planted," and that "there are school and hotel facilities and a number of small stores." Despite the recent development there was "only a small population" living at Alderpoint.[303]

But a larger population briefly inhabited Alderpoint each day: persons traveling through on the NWP. In 1915 the still-new railroad ran four passenger trains daily, two in each direction.[304] The schedule allowed people from Alderpoint to catch the 5 A.M. train to Eureka, arrive there about 9 A.M. to shop or attend to business for most of the day, then catch the 5 P.M. train south, and arrive back at Alderpoint around 11 P.M. The same trip in pre-NWP days took most of a week. But with the railroad, every two weeks people from the north could take the southbound evening train, reach Alderpoint about 11 P.M. that evening, dance all night, and return home on the morning train.[305]

The trains unloaded a substantial amount of mail, not just for Alderpoint but for surrounding areas that were not on the rail line, including Harris, Bell Springs, Zenia, Hoaglen Valley, and Lake Mountain. Edmond Wilson owned the first motorized mail stage in the area. It was put on the Alderpoint-Zenia-Lake Mountain-Hoaglen Valley route in 1924.[306]

Freight came to the Alderpoint station six days a week; trains would run between Eureka and Willits one day and then reverse direction the next. The NWP had a section gang housed at Alderpoint; these crews of 10 to 12 men worked an eight-to-ten mile stretch of track year round. A track walker patrolled each section of the railway in a speeder, which was "a hand and foot operated small car." When he discovered a rockslide or other problem on the tracks, he would place a warning device called a torpedo on the track. The next train that came through

J. J. Murphy's multipurpose business building, c. 1915 (CPH, colorized by JR).

would run over the torpedo, causing a small but loud explosion that alerted the train crew to a problem ahead. One torpedo meant "slow down," three torpedoes meant "stop." The track walker contacted the section boss who sent out a crew to repair the track.[307]

Near the end of 1916 the Humboldt Standard reviewed the town and found it to be a "charming village and summer camp." The newspaper noted that the fortunes of Alderpoint had dipped distressingly when the Mail Ridge wagon road usurped most of the town's road traffic. It also lamented the social climate that existed during recent railroad-building days, which brought forth "turbulent characters who to a certain extent are always found engaged on railroad construction work." But now the continuing members of the community were "hard at work developing the country and the town."[308] By 1917 the Alderpoint Hotel confidently advertised that it was

"located amidst the finest hunting and fishing," with not only "cool mountain water" but also "horseback and vehicle trips." The hotel was a bare "209 miles from San Francisco" and only a "ten minutes walk from the depot."[309] The announcement failed to mention that the walk was all uphill.

A prospering Alderpoint activity was the cutting and storing of tanbark for use in leather tanneries. Highly visible were "the immense tanbark sheds which contain 4,000 cords of the tanbark left over from last year's cutting which is worth at least $60,000." The San Francisco owners of the bark found it cheaper to store the material in Alderpoint rather than in the Bay Area, and thanks to the railroad, a supply could quickly be shipped south when needed. The Standard believed that "the bark industry is the principal source of income to the community," and it promised to continue as such "since the

Trains from the south made their first Humboldt County stop at Alderpoint's station (THPO, colorized by JR).

hills are heavily covered with tan oak."[310] Cut tanbark that had partially dried in the woods was hauled to town after the 4th of July. A scale near the bark sheds weighed each cord of tanbark, since payment was made by weight.[311] In 1919 two White trucks were deployed to haul the bark to the rail line, replacing the six-horse teams and wagons.[312] The biggest tanbark hauler in the area was Henry Muir. After the trucks had fully taken over, Muir parked some 15 of his tanbark wagons on a flat above Carter Creek and built a shed over them. There they stayed for about 30 years, awaiting the call that never came, and then someone burned them.[313]

About two miles downriver from Alderpoint, the NWP put in a siding at Steelhead Creek. Tanoaks from the surrounding area were cut, starting in 1915, and their bark taken to the siding. The cutting near Steelhead lasted about five years before all the tanoak was used up.[314]

At Alderpoint livestock corrals next to the rail line held cattle, sheep, and hogs that ranchers had driven "many miles" on the first leg of their trip to the slaughterhouses of South San Francisco and other locations.[315] The local ranchers shipped their fruit by overnight express train so that it arrived still fresh.[316]

Only one cloud enshadowed the dazzling spectacle of Alderpoint that the Standard described. This was the indifference shown by the county supervisors when offered a ready made road connection between Alderpoint and its downstream neighbor, Fort Seward. When the rail line was being built southeastward from Fort Seward, the NWP had constructed a wagon road on a parallel course along the river to bring supplies to the work crew. The road came to extend some 10 miles between Fort Seward and Cain Rock.[317] At the height of activity, in 1913, the route was used by seven "motor trucks" and

37 teams and wagons,[318] but when the railway was completed the NWP abandoned it. The county could have stepped in and maintained the road, which had been costly to build, was scenic, and was by far the shortest route between Fort Seward and Alderpoint. This the county supervisors chose not to do, with the result that the abandoned road had quickly deteriorated. To show their displeasure, Alderpointans made their town the only one in Humboldt County to vote against the state Highway Bond Act.[319] By 1922 the county atlas showed only a one-mile-long remnant of the NWP road running south from Fort Seward before ending at that all-too-common destination, the Oblivion of Unrealized Hopes.[320]

If an old road was lost, a new bridge was won. In 1917[321] Humboldt County replaced its circa 1890 bridge across the Eel with a new, higher one. The increased elevation allowed the NWP trains to pass under its southwestern end.[322]

Another change occurred in 1919 when a fire burned Helmke's store and apartment building and Crete Brasket's blacksmith shop. The owners started rebuilding "as soon as the fire was out." Helmke's new store was more than double the size of its predecessor.[323]

More improvements came in 1921, when the Knapp family moved to Alderpoint. Mrs. Knapp established a branch of the Humboldt County Library in her home. Better yet, the Knapps operated a restaurant and an ice cream parlor.[324]

The 1917 Alderpoint Bridge lasted until 1972[325] (DTC, colorized by JR).

A fire in 1922 burned west from Alderpoint Road towards Steelhead Creek. A backfire was started at Steelhead in an attempt to stop the fire. George Mathison's property lay between the two fires, so he and his eldest son, Horace, created their own backfire in a circle around the family's buildings. The structures were saved but the two Mathisons were trapped on the 10 acres that surrounded their place for four days until the main fire burned itself out. Much of the charred area had been covered with huckleberry bushes, which after the fire regrew with a profusion of berries. H. F. Hall, George Mathison's father-in-law, saw an opportunity and began picking the berries and then taking them to the Alderpoint train station for shipment to market. Others followed his lead and soon "Alderpoint had another industry."[326]

In one instance the industry produced not only huckleberry husbandry but a husband. A Mrs. Richmond, who lived in Berkeley, also had property in Alderpoint, on which grew some of the huckleberries. One year she invited a friend of hers, named Ann, to come up with her for the annual berry picking. Meeting them at the Alderpoint train depot was Mrs. Richmond's brother, John Williamson. For two weeks the women picked berries and then returned to Berkeley. Meanwhile, John Williamson had been doing some picking of his own. Before Ann left, Williamson informed her that he would like to become better acquainted. There followed many trips by Williamson to Berkeley, culminating in his marriage to Ann in December 1926. The couple made their home in Alderpoint. Ann remained there after John's death in 1954. In 1967, at age 89, she was profiled in the Times-Standard. Ann Williamson crusaded against the NWP whenever it suggested terminating passenger service through Alderpoint. To help her cause, according to the article, "she conscientiously rides the train as much as possible to increase passenger service."[327]

Two of the largest local ranching enterprises, Tooby Brothers and Tooby and Prior, hired Basque herders to care for their sheep on the summer range. The two ranches "owned all of the dogs the Basque herders used." The herders gave their commands in the Basque language. Come wintertime, the dogs returned to the main ranches, where the local hands instructed the animals in English. The bilingual dogs obeyed well in either language.[328]

In the early 1920s Henry and Agnes Pulver moved to Alderpoint and built the Riverside Inn. The business took in boarders and served meals. Henry used his pickup to take train crews to and from the station so they could eat at the inn. He dug a well and built a pump house to supply water to the Inn. He was also a barber, and his "shop" was a tiny shack built in a large oak tree. It was reached by a stairway built into the side of the pump house. There was only enough room for Henry and his current customer in the tree house, so anyone waiting for a haircut had to sit on the steps of the stairway.[329]

Eddie Murphy opened the first garage in Alderpoint in the mid-1920s. He also sold gas, as did Helmke's mercantile.[330] The Age of the Automobile was upon Alderpoint. One unforeseen consequence was the "gate problem" that plagued motorists driving to Garberville. There were 11 ranch gates along the route that had to be opened and closed. Several of them were on steep hills, and these locations often provided excitement when a car with primitive early-day brakes was stopped by its driver, who then left the vehicle to open and close the gates, all the while hoping that the brakes would hold.[331]

Another fire hit Alderpoint in 1925. Five buildings burned: a hotel, restaurant, dance hall, livery barn, and house. Only the house and dance hall were rebuilt.[332] The Redwood Highway had siphoned off much of the traffic that once went through Alderpoint, and business declined accordingly. The town was down to one hotel when it once had three.[333]

August 12, 1935, found more than 200 guests witnessing the dedication of Alderpoint Grange #516's new hall. The building "was beautifully decorated with greens and flowers from the wooded hillsides," and "dancing was engaged in until a late hour."[334]

In 1937 Fred Helmke sold his Alderpoint store and then died later that year. After 25 years the Helmke Mercantile Company sign was taken down, only to go back up two years later when Fred's son, Rae, bought the business back. Soon the store was better than ever, with the installation of an ice plant and the addition of a hay-and-grain department.[335]

Road traffic might diminish, but Alderpoint still had the railroad. And if the NWP proved to be the town's lifeblood, one of its engineers

became a lifesaver. It happened on a night just before Christmas in 1938, when engineer Raleigh Christopher noticed flashes of light near the tracks and stopped his train to investigate. He and the rest of the train crew found local rancher Arthur Anthony, who had been mauled by a mountain lion, lighting pieces of paper and throwing them at his attacker in an attempt to fend off the animal. The trainmen chased off the mountain lion and then took Anthony to Alderpoint, where he received medical aid. The train had come just in time; Anthony was down to his last piece of paper when he was rescued.[336]

Alderpoint's slump in activity continued into the 1940s. The NWP still ran four passenger trains through town daily, but there were fewer people on board. The Redwood Highway was periodically improved and became an increasingly appealing travel option as busses ran between Eureka and San Francisco. Lots of livestock was still shipped from Alderpoint, but now only one or two boxcars of tanbark went out. Huckleberries continued as a major export.[337]

As the decades passed, the Cain Rock bridge saw less and less traffic on the NWP's tracks (HCHS, colorized by JR).

During World War II the Stapleton Lumber Co. of San Francisco shipped lots of piling from Alderpoint. The piling was stored on the flat previously occupied by the tanbark sheds. Nearby forested areas were thinned of timber less than 40 years old, which made good piling material.[338]

More changes came to Alderpoint. Rae Helmke, after a brief span of ownership, traded the family store for a cattle ranch in Laytonville. The Pulvers sold the Riverview Inn, and Ray Pulver no longer provided his tree-house haircuts. The Pacific Gas & Electric Company brought in power lines in 1947, and Alderpoint was finally electrified.[339]

As happened elsewhere in rural Humboldt County following World War II, the lumber industry set up shop in Alderpoint. In all, there were four mills that operated at various times. The L & W Lumber Co. first built a planing mill and then a sawmill. Along with several other mills in the vicinity, they shipped their lumber out on the NWP. In 1953 the five Munson brothers built a large sawmill on the site of the Mathisons' peach farm in Alderpoint. They also put in a planing mill and a gang mill, along with a railroad spur that gave them direct access to the NWP. The Munsons added a cookhouse, bunkhouse, several regular houses, and a trailer park for their workers and even ran a daily bus from Garberville to transport employees who lived there.[340] Munson Brothers were serious operators; they bought timber from the U. S. Forest Service and to get it to Alderpoint, they widened Zenia Bluff road so it could accommodate their logging trucks. The Munson mill continued operating until 1982. Over time it had three other owners—Frank Crawford, Georgia-Pacific, and Louisiana-Pacific. After the mill closed, it and the remaining worker housing were torn down.[341]

In the 1950s train traffic diminished. The NWP stopped running regular passenger trains and replaced them with self-propelled, single-unit Budd cars. Local freights were also discontinued, with the hauling taken over by trucks that ran from Garberville. Livestock was shipped out by truck as the NWP focused on shipping lumber and logs, although wool was still sent out by rail and hay was still brought in. Mail came by motor stage rather than train.[342]

The 1955 flood sped Alderpoint's diminishment. The Reverend E. L. Holsinger was on the scene, some distance up the mountainside, to describe an event of biblical proportions:

> The flood came down the several canyons converging right at Alderpoint. The river rose to its greatest height ever known to anyone around here, even the old timers.
>
> The wall of water was seventy five feet high, 75 feet, as it rushed down the canyon carrying everything with it, the railroad, ranchhouses, and barns as well as all the stock and people on the tops of house[s] crying out for help. There was lumber, logs, ready for the mill, uprooted trees, bridge timbers, furniture, butane tanks, etc. Everything one could mention. . . .
>
> Many people were left hanging in the trees and brush all night and many families we knew were separated for days not knowing where each other was.[343]

Reverend Holsinger did note one gleam of light in the storm-wrought darkness: "Fortunately we held our Christmas activities on Dec. 18. So that was out of the way."[344]

Not by flood, but by fire the next time. The Reverend had only to look to Second Peter, verse 3,[345] to find the prophecy for Alderpoint. It took less than nine years for it to be fulfilled.

As more decades passed, the Cain Rock bridge continued to see less and less traffic on the NWP's tracks (HCHS, colorized by JR).

On February 21, 1964, Lawrence Renner was refilling the tanks at Jack's Gas Station in downtown Alderpoint. As he walked away from the locked distributor valve, a "tremendous explosion" rent the area in back of him. Renner turned to see a wall of flames between the gas station and an adjacent warehouse. He jumped into his truck and sped away, tearing loose a gas hose as he did so. Renner's quick action saved his truck, but there was no hope for the station or the warehouse, nor for three nearby houses that were completely destroyed. An entire block of Alderpoint was left in ashes.[346]

And of course, 10 months later came the 1964 flood. There is no known report from Reverend Holsinger about that one.

Amid the traumas of 1964 a more pleasant event occurred. In September the Alderpoint School had its name further particularized by becoming the Alice Jewett School. The honor was richly deserved, for Jewett had taught for 26 years, starting in 1928 at the Long Ridge School in Trinity County, when she had a grand total of two boys as pupils. She moved on to also teach at Island Mountain, Old Harris, and Fort Seward before finally finishing at Alderpoint. When Jewett retired in 1962, "two of her pupils were grandchildren of the owner of the building where she first taught school at Long Ridge."[347]

Gradually the business district shrunk. By the 1990s there was only one store and a "part time" bar and restaurant. The last of the hotels had closed. Enough residents were still present to occupy some 40 to 50 houses and trailers.[348]

As the shadows closed in around Alderpoint, a meteor streaked across the local firmament, illuminating the place in all its past glory. In 1998 local resident Ray Mathison published The History of Alderpoint, an extremely well-written account of the town that filled in many of the gaps in the existing literature.[349] It was a tribute to one of Humboldt County's many remote communities—something they all deserve but far too seldom receive.

Chapter 5

Fort Seward

The flood tide of history has twice washed over the flat at Fort Seward. And twice—once quickly and once very slowly—that tide has ebbed away, each time leaving a set of abiding memories, one of darkness and one of a lingering twilight. The two have crowded together in a very small place.

Before the coming of the whites, the land here was probably within the domain of the Ta kai-ya, a branch of the so-called Lassik tribe.[350] They had two villages, Kuc-to-dun and Di-yic-kuk, across the Eel southeast of the Fort Seward flat.[351] They may have had others on the flat itself, but if so, their names and locations are lost.

Then came the long, somber years when the newly arrived whites imposed themselves on the Indians with a violence that stretched over two decades of conflict. It struck with especial intensity at the area around Fort Seward. Tragedy, however, was preceded by farce. (See Appendix A.)

The United States Army established the fort in the fall of 1861, but in April 1862 the half-built facility was abandoned. During the fort's few months of operation, its soldiers failed to affect the local conflict between Indians and whites, but others of greater determination were about to try their hand at it. Captain Thomas Ketcham wrote from Fort Baker, on the Van Duzen, that

The Lassik Indians traveled far and wide to obtain their food. A few decades later,
the Helmke store would bring food to your door (HCHS, colorized by JR).

. . . a party of whites (citizens) have been out hunting Indians in the vicinity of Eel River, and they say that seventeen bucks were killed by the party and the women and children were turned loose. I have also been informed that there are quite a number of citizens who intend, as soon as the snow goes off, to make a business of killing the bucks wherever they can find them and selling the women and children into slavery. It is supposed that they will make their headquarters somewhere in the neighborhood of Fort Seward, taking their captives into Long Valley,[352] there selling them to certain parties at $37.50 per head, who put them in a covered wagon, take them down to the settlements, and there dispose of them at a very handsome profit. One person is said to have made $15,000 last season in the business. It looks like an exaggerated statement; but say that one ranch is taken with ten women and twenty children; it amounts to the sum of $1,125, which is more money than men of that class can make in any other line of business.[353]

That summer Ketcham was with the 3rd California Volunteer Infantry at Fort Baker, on the Van Duzen River. In late July some 14 Indians were brought to the fort as prisoners. Two women from the group "were liberated and sent to induce the Indians to come in. The result was the appearance and surrender of 112 Indians."[354] Perhaps they were fearful of the killer-slavers that Ketcham had earlier described. Then, on July 31, the leader called Lassik, with 32 other Indians, surrendered.[355] His band was part of a collection of 834 Indians that was subsequently taken to the Smith River Reservation in Del Norte County. In late September about 400 Indians escaped from the reservation, including Lassik "and all the more turbulent among them."[356]

According to one account, Lassik and his followers returned to their home territory, where they became "the most feared of the marauding hostile Indians . . . driving out the settlers in the northern Yolla Bolly Country."[357] But then, at the beginning of 1863, came reports threat had ended. (See sidebar 1.)

The execution of Lassik and his warriors did not end the Indian killings at Fort Seward. Less than three months later, a party of whites

---

1. "Must we die, shoot us."

The January 3, 1863, edition of the *Humboldt Times* carried a short article under the heading "ALL RIGHT." Word had come from Long Valley "that the noted Indian, Lassux [*sic*], was in the hands of the whites at Fort Seward. He is probably [now] in the spirit land. . . ."[358] Three weeks later the *Times* copied an article about the capture from the *Mendocino Herald* that was more euphemistically emphatic about the presumed fate of Lassik and his band:

Revenge—It is pretty well known that an inveterate hatred exists between that of the Wylackie [*sic*] tribe[359] of Indians known as the "Gun Indians" and the whites living in the valleys and canyons north of here. A few days ago a number of them, including Lasseck [*sic*], their chief, were captured by the whites and taken to Fort Seward. From there they attempted to take them to the reservation—to Round Valley we presume—but "on the way they took cold and died." This, at least, is the way we get the word. But knowing as we do, the animosity existing between these Indians and whites inhabiting the region of the Humboldt mail route, and the numerous depredations supposed to have been committed by them, we suppose the "cold" they died of was actually cold lead.[360]

Only decades later was a more complete account of the incident recorded. It came from an elderly woman from the Lassik tribe, Lucy Young, who recalled in 1939 what she had witnessed at Fort Seward 76 years earlier:

At last I come home [Fort Seward, where Lucy's mother was]. Before I get there, I see big fire in lotsa down timber and tree-top. Same time awfully funny smell. I think, somebody get lotsa wood.

I go on to house. Everybody crying. Mother tell me: "All our men killed now." She say white men there, others come from Round Valley, Humboldt County too, kill our old Uncle, Chief Lassik, and all our men.

Stood up about forty Inyan in a row with rope around neck. "What this for?" Chief Lassik askum. "To hang you, dirty dogs," white men tell it. "Hanging, that's dog's death," Chief Lassik say. "We done nothing, be hung for. Must we die, shoot us."

So they shoot. All our men. Then build fire with wood and brush Inyan men been cut for days, never know for their own funeral fire they fix. Build big fire, burn all them bodies. That's funny smell I smell before I get to house. Make hair rise on back of my neck. Make sick stomach, too.[361]

And so Fort Seward, its military buildings never completed, became a charnel house.

murdered three Indians, whom the *Times*, with a coarse attempt at humor, said "forgot to come back to camp." Fresh from these killings, about 15 whites located the Indians' campsite, found 20 more warriors, and left them in a condition where "they will tell no tales."[362]

Following the various vigilante attacks on the Indians, the Fort Seward area receded from the headlines. A property known as the Fort Seward Ranch grew to include some 4,000 acres. It was purchased by J. H. White in 1877 for $12,000.[363] By 1886 the ranch was owned

Humboldt's "second city" promised a "first"
in fruits—"plumbs" (colorized by JR).

by H. T. Fairbank,[364] the president of the Bank of Petaluma.[365] In 1902 Fairbank sold what was now a 10,000-acre stock ranch, along with 700 head of stock, to Thomas Cloney and Henry M. Devoy for about $60,000.[366]

Eventually Devoy acquired all the ranch land around Fort Seward, including property across the Eel in the Dobbyn Creek drainage.[367] In May 1910 he sold the parcel, which then totaled some 22,000 acres, for about $250,000. The purchaser was the Frank K. Mott Company,[368] whose eponymous president[369] was also the mayor of Oakland, California. It was a busy time for Mott, who was currently serving his third term as mayor. The following year he was elected to a fourth term, and then, in 1912, he survived the

city's first recall election, which the Industrial Workers of the World had initiated.[370]

Near the end of 1910, Mott's company ran a full-page ad in *The Californian*; it was modestly headed "FORT SEWARD Destined to Become the Second Largest City in Humboldt County." The Devoy Ranch was to be divided into business and residential lots; townsite acres; orchard, timber, and grazing lands; and riverfront resort frontage.[371] The developers, "taking time by the forelock" in anticipating the completion of the Northwestern Pacific's (NWP's) rail line, paid $250,000 for the land and expected to spend about twice that much improving the parcels.[372] If all the lots and acreage sold, Mott's company would clear about $1,467,000, nearly doubling its money.[373] Motivating the entire enterprise was the ongoing development of the NWP, which was building southward up the Eel River on its way to connecting with the rail line constructing its way north from San Francisco Bay. The tracks would cross the large riverside flat upon which the "city" of Fort Seward, an otherwise isolated municipality in the remote canyon of the Eel, would then come to fruition by the manifold benefits brought by the railroad.

Surveyors were on the scene in December 1911, laying out the townsite. All of Fort Seward's streets would be a generous 75 feet wide, as befit the future second-largest city in the county.[374] By the following month surveyor F. H. Green had platted out 600 acres, including 400 that "were divided up into tracts and were expected to be taken up as summer home sites." In addition, "lumber for a new Fort Seward Hotel was already on the ground."[375] Mott's company had a Pope-Hartford truck that it kept at the tiny town of Young's (later called McCann). Material for building the hotel could be taken by train to

Young's, loaded onto the Pope-Hartford, taken south along the Mail Ridge route to Pepperwood Springs, and then driven down off the ridge to Fort Seward.[376]

Work progressed quickly on the new hotel. A *Humboldt Times* article in August 1912 announced that the building was expected to open in early October. The headline for the story stressed that it would be a "modern hotel . . . lighted with gas and electricity" and would offer "hot and cold water." The three-story structure was to contain 25 guest rooms, four of which were to have private baths. The article revealed that its headline was not entirely accurate—negotiations were under way for securing electric power, but it was possible that "the building will be lighted with ascetylene [sic] gas for the time being." The story concluded by noting optimistically that:

> During the past month the townsite has been visited by many influential people from the central and southern part of the state, all of whom have expressed themselves as delighted with the climate and confident that Fort Seward would become one of the wonder places of the western coast.[377]

However, for the time being,

> Beyond the building of the hotel but little else is moving at Fort Seward, nor will there be until the railroad is completed and trains operated into town.[378]

And, gradually, the railroad moved towards completion. At one time optimists had expected that the rail line would be finished sometime before 1910, but that year had come and gone, and three more besides. The Island Mountain tunnel, just east of Humboldt County, alone took months to complete. Meanwhile,

The Hotel Fort was perhaps the most beautiful hostelry ever built in Humboldt County. It offered the perfect possibility for travelers to rusticate in a high-end example of rustic architecture (JIC, colorized by JR).

. . . the people watched the slow progress that was made. It seemed an interminable time since the work was begun. But finally in October of 1914 the last rail was laid and the date was set for the driving of the golden spike.[379]

But where to drive the spike? The Historical Railroad Celebration Committee debated on the merits of several sites before deciding on Cain Rock, a location where the tracks crossed the Eel southeast of Alderpoint. Committee chairman H. L. Ricks was apparently accused of promoting a different location, for he defensively told the press that "I have not favored Fort Seward."[380]

If Fort Seward lost out on the chance for fleeting fame as the spike-driving site, it certainly won the approval of Leigh Irvine, whose *History of Humboldt County, California* was published a few months later. Within its 1,290 pages were several laudatory references to the predicted "second city" of Humboldt County.

Irvine believed that Fort Seward might become the Switzerland of the Western Hemisphere, despite the difference in elevation, type of scenery, and difference in language, for the opportunities to attract visitors were similar. Look what the clever Swiss have done with their country, Irvine suggested, "where millions of tourists make it possible for hundreds of thousands of Swiss people to reap fortunes from hotels and resorts." Irvine quoted the Reverend William Rader, who had recently traveled from San Francisco to Eureka and recorded his impressions in in a fever of fulsomeness:

> The air is like wine, the sky like that which bends over Venice and Florence. The people one meets on the way are of a class which stands for the best of the Far West. Men of brawn and brain have found their way into these mountain fastnesses, the last of the pioneers, for beyond them rolls the Pacific.[381]

NWP passengers await the arrival of the Fort Seward station's nonexistent porter (colorized by JR).

But Irvine envisioned more than tourism in Fort Seward's future. He saw Frank K. Mott and his Humboldt Land and Development Company (another iteration of Mott's multifaceted business) promoting agricultural activity, noting that

> . . . preparations are being made for cold storage plants, canneries, creameries, and such other modern plants as may be needed in the campaign seeking to command the market. In this connection there will be a concerted effort to raise apples of high quality on a co-operative plan that shall seek to make the output large enough to attract attention in such markets as those of London and New York City.[382]

If the town's brand-new Hotel Fort would serve Swiss-scenery-seeking tourists, nearby the railroad created a facility that suggested such scenery was close at hand. The NWP hired the Mercer-Fraser Company, which had already constructed several of its railroad bridges, to build a train station out of brick,[383] but then camouflage this construction with a faux finish. The façade featured half-timbering in the Tudor Revival style.[384] Upon seeing the station for the first time, train passengers may indeed have wondered if they had been rerouted to a romanticized rendition of rural Europe.

Before the railroad was completed, the locale had received some of its supplies by water. A flat-bottomed river boat ran between Scotia and Fort Seward. It carried a horse on board to pull the boat over the riffles.[385] According to one account, "this horse was trained to load and unload himself. When they came to a riffle, he would jump off and pull the boat up the riffle, and then jump back on the boat." The "boat

had a sail on it that they used to go through the holes. On a good day, when the breeze was brisk, it could come all the way from Scotia to Fort Seward in an afternoon. They used long poles to move the boat upriver when the breeze wasn't blowing."[386]

Once the rail line was operating, river travel became merely a recreational activity. In July 1915,

> Nat Libby and H. J. Kramer shipped a canoe to Fort Seward, followed on the train, launched it on the turbulent Eel River with a supply of food, sleeping bags and camping outfit, and then took passage for a three-day outing on the return journey. At many points the trip was hazardous, heavy swells with short, choppy rapids, immense boulders and treacherous currents, particularly at McCann [where] they encountered a strong wind that for a time caused them much uneasiness. After reaching the mouth of Eel River, they canoed up Seven Mile Slough, then made a portage to Humboldt Bay.[387]

There was no mention of plans for a return trip.

Author Delmar Thornbury first visited Fort Seward before the coming of the railroad, driving a buggy down from the heights of Blocksburg. It was a very hot day. Thornbury acquired a terrific headache, and his horse grew tired. Delmar and his party had to get out and hold the buggy back to help the horse slow the buggy on the downgrade. Having noted that "Fort Seward was a pleasant ranch," Thornbury proceeded to then take the road up to Mail Ridge—a "five mile grade" that climbed 2,500 feet. Now he and his

Along with the Hotel Fort, Fred Smythe's Craftsman cottage gave Fort Seward two masterpieces of rustic architecture (HCHS, colorized by Jerry Rohde).

party again had to leave the buggy, this time to push it uphill to help the horse. His headache became worse.[388]

A few years later Thornbury was able to reach Fort Seward by train, riding up from San Francisco Bay. Now feeling no head pain, he noted that

> Fort Seward was promoted just before the railroad was built, and the promotion has not yet resulted in anything. It [Fort Seward] has merit and eventually will become the most important inland city.[389]

Thornbury proved better at assessing the present than predicting the future. The 1922 Humboldt County atlas showed "Ft. Seward" as a small dot on the NPW rail line, with the dot connected to the county road that ran through the flat by a short, narrow line that represented the Mott company's only city street. Whether it was the requisite 75 feet in width could not be determined by the map. Surrounding "Ft. Seward"—a place so small that the mapmaker

abbreviated its name—were section upon section of vacant land, all bearing the name of Mott's Humboldt County Land & Development Company.[390]

In 1913 the *Eureka Herald* joined the chorus of praise singers with an article entitled "Fort Seward—The Embyro [*sic*] Metropolis," the effect of its laudations being compromised by the misspelling in its headline. While describing a future full of development, the story also noted what was already on the ground. The list was short: "a hotel, a store, a number of tents and temporary buildings, [and] 22 acres of A1 fruit land. . . ."[391] Not mentioned was the Fort Seward "school" that operated in one of stage owner Fred Smythe's garages down near the railroad depot in 1912 and 1913. Rae and Guy Helmke were students there, and their parents, along with other locals, "chipped in to pay for a teacher who came there before the public school was organized in 1914." Then the school moved to improved accommodations: the dining room just north of the Hotel Fort. When the last Fort Seward school was built in 1930, its predecessor "was cut down and became the woodshed for the 'new' school."[392]

Students were sparse in 1934 when Peggy Woodman attended the school. There were just three: teacher Gloria Ritchie's son, Bob; Marie Hammond, whose father had to row her to school across the river; and Peggy, who was allowed to come in an hour late in order to catch a ride from Dobbyn Creek with the mailman.[393] The school hadn't grown much when Goldia Rager started teaching there in 1946. She had five students, but they all came from across the Eel in the Dobbyn Creek drainage. The following year the Trinity National Lumber Company built a mill at Fort Seward, and the town's population explosively expanded. There were 27 pupils in the 1947-1948 school year.[394]

By the early 1950s small sawmills had sprung up throughout much of the Humboldt County back country. In 1952 four were listed in the vicinity of Fort Seward.[395] Although the boom that Frank Mott, Leigh Irvine, and others had predicted for the town had fallen like a thud, now the whine of mill saws finally announced Fort Seward's belated heyday, and even the venerable Hotel Fort ceased functioning as a tourist destination and instead became a bunkhouse for workers at the Trinity National Lumber Company. The transition from resort to mill town was abruptly completed in April 1956, when the former Hotel Fort "crumbled into ashes" as a fire raced through the building shortly after 35 loggers and ranchers had left after lunch. The fire threatened several homes and the Fort Seward School as some 60 firefighters fought the blaze. They were hindered by the absence of equipment, relying on only a single fire engine that was brought over from the nearby Trinity National mill.[396]

By the time of the hotel's demise, another substantial change had occurred. In 1945 Peggy

The Fort Seward School awaits a resumption of classes (JR).

Helmke's Fort Seward store (CPH, colorized by JR).

and Guy Satterlee and a partner, John N. Stuart, purchased the Fort Seward Ranch,[397] which included much of the property that Frank Mott and his Humboldt Land and Development Company had acquired in 1910.[398] The burning of the former Hotel Fort also immolated the last connection between Fort Seward and Frank Mott.

The NWP still maintained a presence in Fort Seward, although by 1966 it had closed the Tudor Revival train station, which was then used as a residence.[399] There had been a bit of excitement in October 1960 when Harold Hardie, in a rush to make a delivery, attempted to drive his truck across the NWP's tracks just as the "Redwood," a self-propelled passenger car, came roaring down the line. The resulting impact "demolished the front portion of the train and twisted the rear section of the truck from the cab back into unrecognizable rubble." Remarkably, no one was killed. The newspaper article failed to report on the condition of the

truck's contents, which happened to be a load of railroad ties.[400]

Although the station had closed, NWP workers could still get a meal at Fort Seward, where the J. V. Moan Commissary Company maintained a cook car. By 1966 the facility was one of only four left on the NWP line.[401] In July of that year another local purveyor of food shut its doors when the Fort Seward store closed. The business had started as the Helmke Mercantile Company. Joseph and Lois Elvidge purchased the store in 1946, when "the mills in the area were just commencing construction and operation." A 1951 fire destroyed the original building and several other structures. Years later, "the mills closed when the good timber was cut in the area [and] the Elvidges reduced the amount of stock in the store to correspond with the dwindling population." By the middle of 1966 the couple "decided that the economy of the area did not warrant the expense of keeping the store open."[402]

Marie Melanson Bair provided a sort of elegy for Fort Seward after she arrived there on the North Coast Daylight in 1989. She had initially visited the area in 1917 when her family made the first of many vacation trips to Boehne's Camp, a summer resort located above the Eel near the north end of the Fort Seward flat. Seventy-two years had passed since Bair's last visit, and she knew that the camp and the early day bridge had been destroyed by the intervening floods, but she

> . . . was unprepared for the total change. The windows of the brick train station were boarded shut. Helmke's store, a block away, was completely gone. The tables for lunch were placed where the railroad workers' cottages once stood. Only Boehne's Butte, a cone shaped hill nearby, was visible and more heavily wooded than I remember.[403]

There were a few other remnants of the earlier town, but not many. Across Railroad Avenue (was it indeed 75 feet wide?) from the train station was much of the striking stonework that remained after the Hotel Fort had burned. Westward up the road was the last Fort Seward schoolhouse, looking more like a house than a school, its front steps sagging but the year of its construction—1930—still displayed in dark numerals beneath the gable above the front porch. And, at the west end of the avenue—the only city street Mott's company ever built—was a long-closed Shell gasoline station, walled and roofed with sheet metal, as if to indicate its expected impermanence, but with its yellow and red shell-shaped sign still unblemished atop its pole. What better emblem for this place of the vanished fort, the burnt hotel, and the fleeting hopes of cityhood than this sign that announces to all that Fort Seward is but a shell of its former self?

The last remnant of the Fort Seward business district (JR).

Appendix A: The Folly of Fort Seward

In the annals of Humboldt County military history, Fort Seward deserves a special place of negative distinction. Not only was it built in the wrong location and at the wrong time, but it also had one of the most wrong-headed officers commanding part of its troops. It took less than four months for this farcical fort to convince nearly everyone that it should never have been constructed.

The trouble started on September 26, 1861, when Captain Charles S. Lovell of the 6th Infantry wrote to headquarters from his "Camp on Eel River," announcing that he had "selected this point as the site for the new military post to be called Fort Seward." Lovell noted that it was "a better location than any that could be found after a diligent and careful examination on Larrabee's [sic] Creek or Van Dusen [sic], besides being in the heart of Indian country." He admitted, however, that in winter it "will be very difficult to pack supplies" to the new fort because "some of the mountains . . . will have from two to five feet of snow on them." To deal with the problem, Lovell recommended that the Army build "a large skiff boat" that could bring the supplies up the Eel, a trip that would take "probably ten or twelve days."[404] He would soon find that there were times when no boat, of any description, could come up the Eel or any other Humboldt County river.

The fort was initially garrisoned by regular army troops, but by the fall of 1861 all such available soldiers were being sent east to fight in the Civil War. They were replaced by militia units composed of California citizens.[405] At the end of October a company from the 2nd Cavalry, California Volunteers, was sent to take over Fort Seward.[406] In mid-November orders went out for the garrison to be supplemented by a company from the 3rd California Volunteer Infantry.[407] For a time little was heard about the infantry unit, but the cavalry company at the fort was about to make the news.

The cavalry commander was Captain David B. Akey, who, as subsequent events bore out, lacked leadership skills. The fall weather marked the beginning of Akey's problems.

November saw the start of what became the epochal 1861-1862 storm season and concomitant flood. It struck everywhere in the West from Washington Territory to northwestern Mexico. In central California it created a temporary lake 300 miles long and 20 miles wide.[408] The rainfall total recorded for November, December, and January at Fort Gaston, in northeastern Humboldt County, was 98.84 inches.[409] At Fort Seward the amount of precipitation was probably similar.

As the rain pounded down and the Eel rose, Akey decided that his orderly and quartermaster sergeants were guilty of being insolent. He arrested them and had them reduced in rank as an example to the other troops. This failed to have a sufficiently intimidating effect. Instead, the soldiers responded by refusing to build both a much-needed supply road and the permanent quarters that might protect them from the incessant storms.[410] The original construction orders had grandly specified that "the buildings erected at Fort Seward will consist of quarters for one company, one medical officer, the company officers actually present, laundresses' quarters, hospital, guardhouse, and stable,"[411] but the recalcitrant troops never achieved this lofty goal. A report from February 1862, found that "no buildings except two log huts, not completed, had been erected there, the troops having refused to build anything but a bake oven."[412] This lack of construction activity was part of a larger problem, which became known as the Fort Seward Mutiny.

It happened thus: with the massive winter flood in full force and without a proper road for supplies, much-needed food and clothing failed to reach the garrison at Fort Seward. At this point Akey "ordered the men to be fed salt pork that had been condemned and left to rot" by the regular army troops who had long ago departed for the war in the east. In response, most of the noncommissioned officers sent a petition to Akey indicating that they refused to serve under him. Akey considered this an act of mutiny. By late December, Akey, the alleged mutineers, and almost all other members of the Fort Seward garrison had returned to Fort Humboldt; only a 20-man mixed infantry and cavalry force, commanded by a Lieutenant Davis, remained.[413] The region-wide flood was now in full swing, and making the trip proved difficult:

> . . . the only means of crossing some of the streams was by felling some lofty tree near the bank [that was] long enough to reach across, on which the men and the entire baggage were passed over, while the animals were made to swim.[414]

The commander of the Humboldt Military District, Col. Francis J. Lippitt, noted the condition of the horses that had just arrived from Fort Seward:

> The horses of the cavalry company are at present entirely unfit for service, being exhausted by continued short forage at Fort Seward and the great fatigue of reaching here [Fort Humboldt] over a route almost impassable from the recent freshets.[415]

Once back at Fort Humboldt, Akey had five noncommissioned officers arrested and placed in the fort's guard house. They remained there for months. By late April Akey had charged 41 soldiers with "a variety of offences ranging from desertion to mutiny." Finally, between April and July of 1862, a court-martial hearing was held at Fort Humboldt.

In July the court eventually found 1st Lieutenant Robert Daly guilty of part of one charge: he had halted his troops three miles short of their destination. He was sentenced to be reprimanded and then returned to duty, but even this minor penalty was cancelled by the commanding general. Two sergeants and a private, charged by Akey with mutiny, "were found *Guilty* of some of the specifications, and *Not Guilty* upon others." They were sentenced to be discharged from the Army.[416]

Subsequently, however, Akey again became involved in court proceedings, although they were of a somewhat different nature. In August, civil authorities in Eureka charged him with assaulting a local citizen. He was released on bail and sent with his company to Red Bluff. There he once more engendered such dissatisfaction that he again charged his command with mutiny. The soldiers were convicted, but their sentences were later revoked. Akey resigned his commission in November 1862, rejoined the cavalry in early 1863, and resigned for good that June.[417]

By early 1862 it was clear to nearly everyone that Fort Seward was a failure. The fort's ambitious construction plans had come to almost nothing. The garrison had suffered from lack of supplies. The commander had lost control of his troops. Added to these three strikes was a fourth: the presence of the fort had so far had little, if any, impact on the Indian-white conflict that had prompted its creation. Even in dry weather, of which there was almost none, the fort's effectiveness was compromised by its location. Although a trail crossed the river near the fort, the main travel routes were high on the mountain slopes above the river canyon. Mail Ridge, the main postal corridor into the county, lay 2,200 feet higher than the fort and three miles to the west. If the soldiers at the fort received word of a mail carrier in distress, it would be a long while before they could reach the scene of the problem. When storms hit, the difficulties were compounded. The fort's contra-strategic location was noted by one of the resident soldiers in February 1862, who, when asked if Fort Seward "was a judicious site for a military post," responded, "Yes. It is a safe place for the troops, for when the streams are up no Indian can get within a thousand yards of the garrison."[418]

In late February Lieutenant William L. Ustick[419] was sent to Fort Seward "with a small pack-train of provisions (the post being out of everything)." Ustick also had a more important assignment: "withdrawing the garrison and the public property."[420] About the time Ustick reached the fort, a member of the garrison, styling himself "Volunteer," wrote to the *Humboldt Times* about the pending closure. He indicated that there were two groups of civilians in the vicinity. The first were southern sympathizers who were "too closely allied to 'Dixie' to suit the times." This group would miss the troops because they had been overcharging them for venison or whenever else the soldiers were "unfortunate enough to need their aid in any way." The other group were "exemplary ex-

Although soldiers disliked the Fort Seward flat, vacationers nearly
a century later found it appealing (CPH, colorized by JR).

ceptions," presumably Unionists, who would be leaving the area when the troops did.[421]

"Volunteer" regretted that soon the soldiers would no longer be available to carry the mail across the Eel, which seemed to be the only duty they were able to discharge effectively. He then declaimed elegiacally about the beauty of the fort's location:

> We all regret to leave this lovely spot just as spring is putting on his[422] mantle of green, which after the severe winter we have experienced is sweet to look upon; the huge old trees covered with ivy, with here and there a vine of velvet green, creeping amidst still darker the hues of the tall firs that line the hillsides and the river banks, which in the warm summer time we had expected would throw their pleasant shade over our now clear and smooth grass decked parade; and we regret to leave the dark woods and quiet valleys around us, with their herds of game and the streams and beautiful little lakes, which so add to the exceeding loveliness of this locality and makes it without an equal in the county. . . .[423]

Volunteer also regretted that "the Indians, too, we must *leave alone*, as we have done all winter—of necessity. . . ." He left it to others, however, to note the biggest regret of all—that Fort Seward had ever been established in the first place.

Chapter 6
Eel Rock

Within the surface of time's fleeting river
　　Its wrinkled image lies . . .
　　　　　　　　　—Shelley

Few places in Humboldt County show better the fleetingness of time than the area around Eel Rock. What today is a small collection of homes and agricultural enterprises was once an arresting stop on the Northwestern Pacific's (NWP's) rail line and, a century before that, a virtual Indian metropolis, with a string of villages lining the east side of the river. But the flood tide of human activity that once washed through the canyon has long ago ebbed, and the floods of the river itself have scoured and scored the landscape, indeed leaving no more than a wrinkled image of what had been here before.

The Indians were the Sununkas, the southernmost branch of the Nongatl tribe. They were separated from their nearest kin, who lived on upper Larabee Creek, by the forbidding hump of Great Butte and its south-running ridge. They were separated from their Sinkyone downriver neighbors by the steep canyonsides of the Eel that threaten to compress the riverway into a gorge. They were separated from their Lassik upriver neighbors by the bulk of Yellow Jacket Butte and the narrow river canyon south of it. So the Sununkas lived, in near-isolation, in six villages near the mouth of Coleman Creek and at two more locations just downriver from Mill Creek.

The 1873 government map for the area displays no trace of the villages. Instead, "Stewart's House" is shown on the east side of the Eel about a mile south of Coleman Creek. It sits next to a trail that runs downstream near the river until it climbs northeastward just north of Coleman Creek.[424]

In 1879 Chester B. Denmark and his family took up land a few miles south of Eel Rock. Denmark became one of the leading sheep raisers in the area but ran afoul of his neighbor, James A. Campbell. In 1919 Campbell, convinced that Denmark was scattering wild mustard seed on his land in hopes of making it unproductive, decided to take direct action. This consisted of shooting and killing Denmark, for which act Campbell was found guilty of second-degree murder.[425]

By 1886 land on both sides of the Eel near Coleman Creek was co-owned by George Edward White,[426] who blazed a trail of infamy through much of the upper Eel River country. (See sidebar 1.)

In 1895 George W. Filkins moved onto the hillside across the Eel from Coleman Creek and developed an apple orchard. He patented land there in 1903.[427] In 1910 his wife announced that the family ranch was "to be cut up into small pieces" and a town called Eel Rock Springs established. A "dozen Eureka business men" were reportedly interested in the project.[428]

This interest ripened, but slowly. The need for a town along a remote stretch of the Eel would manifest itself only with the completion of the NWP, so it was not until the summer of 1914 that "Eel Rock Springs" finally ma-

Everybody needs a hobby: Fred Lippurner operates Eel Rock's mobile water wheel, 1934 (HCHS, colorized by JR).

1. The White Plague of Round Valley

For three decades a remote section of northwestern California was virtually separated from the rest of the state. The rule of law did not apply there, and no level of government could claim effective control. But control there was, exerted by a solitary rancher and his gang of gun-toting cowboys.

The rancher was George Edward White, the notorious "Czar of Round Valley,"[429] who had "gradually acquired over thirty-five thousand acres of the best range in Mendocino, Trinity, and southern Humboldt counties."[430] White used a contingent of "outlaw buckeroos" to keep others from settling within this vast area.[431] He ruled his domain with the proverbial iron fist, but then he opened his hand to caress his young second cousin, Frankie White, who became his third wife in 1881.[432] Less than three years later, George White was making love to Frankie's older sister and plotting to have the inconvenient Frankie murdered.[433] Shakespeare would have loved it. Frankie sought refuge at the Russ House in San Francisco, and George decided on a less drastic method of removing her from his life—he sued for divorce.[434]

It proved to be the biggest mistake White ever made. Frankie responded to the suit by successfully requesting a change in venue. The trial was moved to San Francisco, where George would presumably be less likely to force witnesses to perjure themselves with false testimony in his favor.[435] However, George's chief henchman, Wylackie John Wathan, whose problematic resume included being "a robber, a poisoner, an arsonist, a perjurer, and a murderer,"[436] worked tirelessly on George White's behalf: "early and late he applied himself to getting false evidence against Frankie."[437]

But Frankie White was not without allies, chief of which were her brother, Clarence, and her father, confusingly called "Uncle" Johnny White. They both hated Wylackie John, and he returned the favor, threatening to kill Clarence.[438]

On January 2, 1888, Clarence White and Wylackie John met in a narrow hallway in the Gibson House, a large building in Covelo. Because of the cold winter weather, both men were wearing long coats. The men exchanged "heated words." Then "there was an explosion like a stick of dynamite," and Wylackie John fell down the stairs. He had tried to draw his revolver, but it apparently caught in the lining of his coat pocket. Clarence White's revolver was stuck loosely in his belt, and it was easy for him to draw it and drill Wylackie John, who was still fumbling with his coat.[439] It was the first nail in the coffin that would restrict the power of George White.

Five months later, Clarence White was tried for Wylackie John's murder. After deliberating 55 minutes, the jury returned a verdict of not guilty. A second nail was driven into the coffin: "everyone in Ukiah was so pleased with the verdict that even Judge McGarvey got drunk and became so noisy that the sheriff attempted to arrest him."[440]

Later that year Frankie was granted a divorce from George, who was ordered to give all their community property to her. George had previously deeded all his land to his nephew, John Rohrborough, in an attempt to protect it from an adverse court decision. He resisted complying with the divorce order for several years, but finally, in 1895, Frankie gained control of part of George's land. Although Frankie "was able to obtain only a fraction" of what she was due,[441] it was her name that stretched across the Coleman Creek area when the new Humboldt County map was issued in 1898.[442]

terialized. Ernest Mueller, a Eureka jeweler, arranged for the purchase of the Filkinses' land, and by August the town was "in the process of building." As *The Californian* described it:

There is a considerable flat at this point, prettily surrounded by the high hills of that section, and the river and railroad passing in front.

The best of fishing and hunting are found in the immediate vicinity of Eel Rock Springs, and without doubt this place will soon become a popular summer resort. . . .

Improvements in the town-site are now under way. Streets are being cleared and water systems being put in, and settlers are clearing land for the purpose of planting orchards. It is expected that a girls [sic] boarding school and a sanatorium will be the first public institutions to locate at Eel Rock Springs.[443]

In the event, the new community failed to fulfill *The Californian's* grandiose predictions.

The first public buildings at Eel Rock Springs proved to be a modest public school[444] and a post office.[445] More than a century later, the boarding school and the sanatorium had yet to arrive.

W. L. Douglas prepared for the completion of the railroad by building a store at Eel Rock in 1914, wherein the post office was established the following year. Small as it was, the town managed to merit a stopover by the NWP's most famous passenger. (See sidebar 2).

2. Eel Rock's Hobo Hero

In July 1918 the *Humboldt Times* carried an exciting news dispatch from southern Humboldt. It stated that:

> "Hobo Jack" has just concluded a brief visit to Eel Rock, and, contrary to the usual sensations caused by the visits of hoboes, the populace universally regretted his departure, but considered his call an omen of certain good luck.

Mourners at Boomer Jack's grave in Willits, 1926[446] (CPH, colorized by JR).

This particular hobo is the well known and much loved mascot of the trainmen, a small black bobtailed terrier and is welcome whenever and wherever he chooses to visit. He has a free pass on every freight train on the road. He left the train at Eel Rock Monday evening, enjoyed a refreshing bath in the river, inspected the track and station, visited the school children and talked impartially to each and every one, and accepted several dinner invitations. He is a great favorite with all the little folks and fares well at their hands.

Finding everything to his satisfaction, he entrained on the next freight. Any place on the road where Jack chooses he may flag a train by simply waiting in the middle of the track. He boards the engine via the cowcatcher and fender and finds a certain welcome awaiting him in the caboose. He chooses his own domicile at all times and it is a lucky crew that has the honor of carrying him.[447]

During the 1930s the NWP played a big role in the social life of Eel Rock. The little community had a dance "almost every Saturday night" that was held in the schoolhouse. Dancers coming from the north could drive to the station at South Fork, hop aboard the NWP's evening train to San Francisco Bay, and then get off at Eel Rock at about 9 P.M. They could dance all night, and then catch the morning train to Eureka at about 5 A.M. Easter Sunday was a special event, when "the Greek gandy dancers" from the railroad joined in. A rancher from across the river provided a lamb that was barbecued while the dancers—both gandy and otherwise—worked up an appetite.[448]

Bill Nunnemaker and his wife bought the Eel Rock store in 1923 and maintained it until the 1950s, at which time they built a new store and converted the old one into a home. The post office closed in 1960, and mail was sent instead to Myers Flat. The 1964 flood reached to nearly the second story of the original store building, and shortly thereafter the remains of the 50-year-

old landmark were removed by the Army Corps of Engineers.[449]

The original store had appeared in the March 1951 issue of *Sunset* magazine. The building featured a gravity-flow gas pump, a veranda-like porch, and the false front seen on many early buildings in the West. The caption indicated that Eel Rock was "served only by railroad and, sometimes, a poor dirt road."[450]

Eel Rock's road, which dropped down from the thoroughfare atop Mail Ridge, proved doubly troublesome. It was built about 1949,[451] replacing an even poorer road that dated back to 1913.[452] The alignment of the new road caused it to cut through the Eel Rock School's property, eliminating the playground.[453] This defect perhaps contributed to the school's subsequent condemnation. A new school, "of adequate size, safely constructed . . . [with] a large, level school ground, in a location free from traffic and dust," was expected to be built in time for the start of the fall 1955 term, but construction was delayed.[454] Instead, the students returned to their

Pieces of Eel Rock may line the edge of the river (JR).

. . . crowded, one room school house, which was built 42 years ago, of poor materials, on a steep hillside, where the children have only a small triangle of ground to play in. The school house sits directly below the county road, with only a narrow walk between it and the embankment. There is a large volume of truck traffic along this road, as loaded lumber trucks shuttle from mill to the railroad landing dock, all day long. This school was built to accommodate up to 12 students, while enrollment this September may exceed 25.[455]

The surge of students was due to the postwar logging boom that swept through rural Humboldt County, bringing mills, workers, and their families. Even the remote Eel Rock area felt the effects, with the Rouse Brothers Mill operating there in the 1950s.[456]

A new school was finally built "in the late fifties," but then Eel Rock's population, susceptible to the instability of the timber industry, "dwindled so much that there were not enough children to afford a teacher." The school was closed, and Eel Rock scholars then had to receive their education on the far side of Mail Ridge at Miranda.[457]

By early 1965 Eel Rock had suffered two major diminishments: the removal of its first store building and the closure of its school. Diminishment number three was close at hand. Following the 1964 flood, the town's namesake rock was blown up to create ballast for repairing the flood-ravaged railroad line.[458] Worse yet, plans changed, and the rock fragments were never used for their intended purpose.[459] Instead, they awaited the motive effects of the fleeting, wrinkled river.

Chapter 7
McCann

About three miles southeast of Camp Grant, the Overland Mail Trail (and later the road) gave up following the south side of the Eel River and climbed, with seeming reluctance, to the heights of Mail Ridge, not to return to low ground until reaching northern Mendocino County. The uphill section of the route was sometimes called Fruitland Grade or Fruitland Hill[460] after the community that was established at the top of the climb. The narrow strip of riverside flat at the bottom of the grade came to contain its own community; it was first known as Young's and then as McCann.

The area made the news in March 1869. Eliza Bowman, a widow, lived on the northeast side of the Eel[461] with her six children. Even though the Indian-white conflict was considered finished, on March 26 the Bowman family learned otherwise. As she left her front door, Eliza was struck in the side by a bullet fired by an Indian. Wounded but still mobile, she shepherded her children towards the house of her nephew, David Ward, which lay some 500 yards away. The family departed in plain view of the Indians, who were less than 100 feet distant. The attackers "immediately fired upon . . . [the Bowmans], the bullets whistling around their heads, but without effect." Eliza carried a shotgun with her and, as the Indians gained in their pursuit, she turned and fired at the foremost one, knocking him over. The chase continued until the Indians came within range of Ward's gun. He fired two shots and apparently hit one Indian. The attackers then shot at Ward's house for two or three hours and finally

rushed in, trying to force the door. Ward and Bowman thereupon "fired through the door simultaneously," hitting one or more Indians. This was enough to end the attack. The Indians left the area, taking with them all of the Bowmans' clothing, beds, and bedding, along with $280 in gold. Bowman's wound was serious, but she survived. She was attended by Dr. Theodore Dwight Felt, who also supplied the *Humboldt Times* with his report of the attack.[462]

On hearing about the incident, Wells Fargo & Company presented Bowman with a "fancifully silver mounted" Henry rifle.[463] A grainy photo shows Bowman in front of her rude cabin with what appears to be her new Henry. But rifle or not, she had endured enough Eel River excitement, and she and her children moved to a quieter clime near Laytonville, in Mendocino County.[464]

The Bowmans had occupied part of an inviting river bar where several families established themselves. William Wheat arrived there in 1861, had second thoughts and left, and then had third thoughts and returned in 1864.[465]

By 1872 Thompson's Field was a landmark on the northeast side of the river.[466] Charles L. "Frying Pan"[467] Thompson took over David Ward's place, apparently not long after the 1869 Indian attack on Eliza Bowman's cabin. In 1885 Thompson owned property on both sides of the river: 1,200 acres of grazing land for his sheep, hogs, and horses on his eponymous field and 240 acres of cultivated land and redwood timber on the southwest side of the Eel. Thompson's stallion, Hamlet, had recently "taken the

Eliza Bowman with her old dog and new Henry rifle (DTC, colorized by JR).

premium at the District Fair." Thompson raised alfalfa and corn,[468] presumably leaving grain growing to the Wheat family.

Ed McCann gave the community its name and also a business enterprise when he operated a sawmill there between 1880 and about 1888.[469] Taking advantage of two free but potent resources—gravity and the buoyancy of water—McCann rafted his sawn lumber down the Eel to Port Kenyon.[470]

In 1893 the trail past McCann was converted into a road,[471] and for over two decades it served as the main route connecting locations to the south with Humboldt County. Following the maxim that "one bad turn deserves another," the new road featured both the Devil's Elbow[472] and the Devil's Knee,[473] a pair of hellish hairpin curves just south of McCann a short distance up Fruitland Hill. An early traveler of the road was especially well qualified to assess its infernal qualities; he was an anonymous minister who related, with some repetition, that

> . . . we descended upon a crooked road
> with breathless interest, if not fear—pos-
> sibly the most thrilling and crooked road
> in the world.[474]

The McCann School reportedly opened in 1898, but records for it do not start until 1920, when Marion Smith was the teacher.[475] The school represented the first component of an enlarged community, but it took a while for it to have any company.

In 1908 George Young, who had successfully operated a general merchandise store in Pepperwood for five years, began contemplating expansion. His contemplations followed the tracks of the Northwestern Pacific Railroad (NWP), which were being laid southward up the Eel. By 1911 the work crews had reached McCann, and it was here that Young decided to open his second store. By now, however, Young no longer lived up to his name. He was 67 years old, wanted to become "a man of leisure," and accordingly entrusted the new store's management to a younger Young, George. The new "store" began as a canvas tent, but it was still significant enough that the location, having languished 20 years without McCann's mill, became known as Young's.[476]

The opening of the new store coincided with another inaugural event, the maiden voyage of the *Pepperwood Klipper*. The small steamer carried supplies for—what else?—Young's new store at Young's.[477]

A year and a week after the first trip of the *Klipper*, a post office opened at Young's. At some point it resided within a frame building rather than a tent, for an undated post card shows "Young's Cash Store" as a board-and-batten structure with a sign indicating it is also the post office. Another sign claims that among the items offered for sale are not only cigars, tobacco, and "lunch goods," but also gasoline, a sure indication that automobiles were now testing the grade at Fruitland Hill.

The post office sign came down in January 1914 when the facility was merged with (and moved to) distant Dyerville.[478] By then the railroad builders had made their way south and the few ranches in the area apparently generated little postal activity. But come July 1919, some of the ranchers must have increased their writing, for the McCann Post Office then opened,[479] an event that restored the sawmill owner's name to the maps.

Less than two months after the inauguration of the new post office, tragedy struck McCann when a truck attempted to cross the NWP tracks just north of town and was hit by an oncoming train. The truck was demolished and

Wash day at Young's store (colorized by JR).

its three occupants critically injured. Physicians and nurses were rushed to the scene by a special train and the injured men taken north. William Frye's condition was deemed so grave that he was left at Scotia, where he died soon thereafter. Frank Johnson and Gilbert Cruickshanks were brought to a Eureka hospital, where Johnson promptly passed away.[480]

Nineteen years after the truck-train accident, McCann again made the headlines with another transportation-related incident. In January 1938 two local truck drivers quarreled over a set of "skid chains." George Johnson accused a fellow driver, Joe Whitlow, of stealing his chains. The argument escalated, and Johnson reportedly attacked Whitlow with a knife, stabbing him in the chest. Whitlow responded by drawing a pistol and putting a bullet in Johnson's spine. Neither man's wound was considered serious,[481] but both must have contemplated a possible prison sentence, which, of course, carried with it the ironic opportunity to serve on a "chain" gang.

By 1949 McCann was participating in the post–World War II logging boom. Nearby mills belonging to Fairhurst and Skoog loaded their lumber at the McCann railroad station. Skoog's mill was "owner owned and owner operated," as only Elmer Skoog and his unnamed wife cut the lumber. This activity recalled the days when Ed Ogle logged on the far side of the Eel in 1916 and sent his timber across the river by double cable for shipment by the NWP. Ogle's son, Grover, built many of McCann's houses.[482]

The logging operations probably contributed to the McCann School's enrollment, which soared to 10 pupils. The school, built in 1916, occupied "a sylvan-secluded dell"[483] on the northeast side of the river.[484] It closed in 1962, and McCann's students then took a bus to Weott.[485]

The 1964 flood "swept the west bank [of the Eel] clean," removing the store, post office, and train station. Houses on high ground northeast of the river remained, however, and

The NWP's tracks ran just above the Eel at McCann (HCHS, colorized by JR).

Drivers needed courage to drive downhill around the Devil's Knee (colorized by JR).

additional dwellings were built. A low-water bridge across the Eel washed out in the flood, but it was rebuilt by the Army Corps of Engineers. This structure could be used about 90 percent of the time, but high water rendered it impassable, isolating the McCann residential district. Access to the outer world was then provided by the county's last ferry, an outboard motorboat.[486]

Does riding across the raging Eel in this frail vessel cause McCannites to have transportation trepidation? Probably not. After all, these are people used to driving not only around the Devil's Elbow but also the Devil's Knee.

Chapter 8
Camp Grant

Grant was an uncommon fellow—the most modest, the most disinterested, and the most honest man I ever knew. . . .

—Charles A. Dana[487]

When the Confederate commander at Vicksburg, Mississippi, surrendered to Ulysses S. Grant[488] on July 4, 1863, it ended what some historians have called one of "the twenty clashes that changed the world." A century and a half later, analysts have claimed that "Grant's campaign against Vicksburg . . . [is] the foremost example of operational art during the Civil War."[489] So it is not surprising that three months after the battle, the United States Army, perhaps mindful that the victor of Vicksburg had earlier served at Fort Humboldt, decided to name its new military installation on the Eel River in his honor by calling it Camp Grant.[490] Overlooked was the fact that it was in Humboldt County nine years earlier that then-Captain Grant, despondent in the absence of his wife Julia and possibly facing court-martial for drunkenness, had resigned his commission.[491]

But there it was, an outpost on the north side of the Eel a couple of miles above one of the river's forks, garrisoned by Company E, First Battalion Mountaineers, California Volunteers.[492] The troops were anxious to play their part in the subjugation, and sometimes annihilation, of the native population. Ironically, the volunteers had arrived to replace the soldiers of the regular army, who had gone east to fight in a war against another group of subjugators—the whites of the Confederacy—a war that was to make Grant a hero.

Long before the locale served as a camp for soldiers, members of the so-called Sinkyone tribe had occupied the area along the Eel. A string of at least five small tribal groups held territory beginning just downriver from Eel Rock and ending a short distance below Camp Grant. Little is known about them except their names and approximate location; no member of any of the five groups was ever interviewed.[493]

When Camp Grant was established in October 1863, the only feature noted in the area was the "U. S. mail route" that crossed the river there.[494] It is not known when this route was established,[495] but, under the name of "old Sonoma trail," it was mentioned in a newspaper report from February 1861 regarding the killing of 39 Indians near the trail's crossing of the Eel.[496]

The county map of 1865 shows the "Overland Mail Trail." It ran north along what came to be called Mail Ridge, which separates the South Fork Eel from the main Eel. The route crossed the Main Eel at Camp Grant. It then went over the divide between the main Eel and the Van Duzen River, crossed the latter in the vicinity of Strong's Station, and then ran down the north side of the Van Duzen until it met the county wagon road at Hydesville.[497]

The 1871 Surveyor General's map shows the site of Camp Grant on the north side of the main Eel. Also present is "Dobbin's [sic] Ferry, which connects the former military installation with

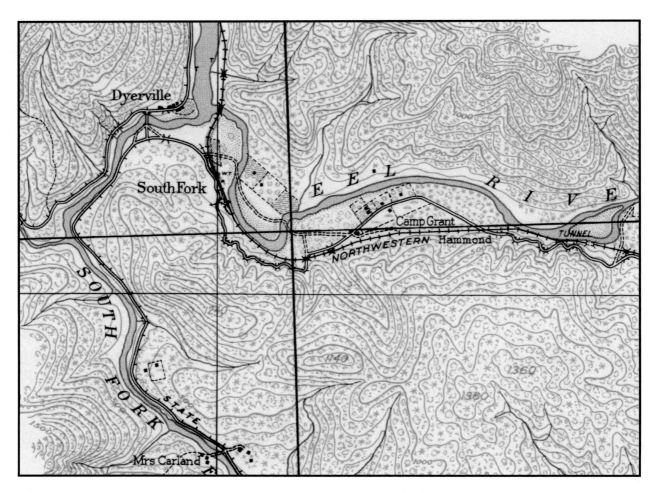

Camp Grant – South Fork area (CE)

the south side of the river, where lies William B. Dobbyn's house and garden.[498] For a time Dobbyn had been the "keeper of the Laribee [sic] mail station," but when Camp Grant was established, he reportedly moved both himself and the station there. Dobbyn subsequently "took up land" across the river from the camp. There he "kept a stopping place,"[499] and "engaged in general farming and stock raising."[500] Dobbyn raised produce on his property, but in the days before a proper road was completed, had difficulty taking his crops to market. The pre-road route went from river bar to river bar, zigzagging across the Eel 23 times in the 25 miles between Camp Grant and Grizzly Bluff.[501] Despite the nearby presence of soldiers, Dobbyn claimed to have been "greatly troubled by the Indians, losing at

one time about $3,000 worth of stock." He temporarily moved his family into town for safety.[502]

Over the years most of Camp Grant's military structures disappeared: "the commissary, officers' quarters, bakery, stables, etc. were gradually dismantled and destroyed." The former camp was reduced to a single building, the guard house, which Dobbyn used as a storage barn for hay. When the Army abandoned the camp, Dobbyn purchased "a considerable amount of stores of various kinds, ferry boat and cable, and other appurtenances which could not well be removed."[503]

In 1869 Dobbyn made use of some of the appurtenances when he was granted a ferry license, which for a while was operated by William Patmore.[504] In 1875 all of the Dobbyns moved to Rohnerville. B. G. Hurlburt took charge of the ferry, but Dobbyn still owned it.[505]

While living at Camp Grant, Dobbyn had an interesting experience involving an unusual combination of animals—a mule and a grouse. He had ridden north on the mail trail with Berkeley Henley to the Van Duzen divide, where Dobbyn dismounted to shoot a grouse. The mule he was riding apparently sympathized with the grouse and kicked Dobbyn in the leg before he could get off a shot. The blow broke Dobbyn's leg. Henley set off for help, leaving Dobbyn on the mountain overnight. It is uncertain if the mule stayed with him. The next day Henley

returned with a rescue party that took Dobbyn by stretcher to Hydesville. Nothing further was heard of the grouse.[506]

For many years Dobbyn was a "staunch Democrat" who, despite living in a "strongly Republican district," managed to serve for eight years as a Humboldt County supervisor. Then, at the start of the new century, Dobbyn stopped swimming against the tide and voted for William McKinley for president.[507]

Sharing the spotlight with Dobbyn at early-day Camp Grant was Amos Hansell Jr., who arrived there in 1872 with his brother, Harry, to join Amos Sr. on his recently established homestead. The

Various Hansells gather for the display of a prime pumpkin (CPH, colorized by JR).

three Hansells (there were no Gretels) "cleared up thirty acres and planted it to apples, pears, prunes, and peaches, and also established a nursery."[508]

When Azel A. Fuller visited Dobbyn's and Hansell's ranches in 1873, he was impressed with the "earlier and more rapid growth of vegetation than is found between them and the ocean." Fuller noted that "peach trees sixteen months old from the graft, bear good fruit; at three years, 15 inches in circumference. Apples at seven years, 26 inches."[509] By 1878 Hansell had achieved noteworthy horticultural diversity; he was growing twenty kinds of apples, sixteen varieties of peaches, six types of cherries, eight different grapes, American and Japanese persimmons, and English and black walnuts.[510]

Camp Grant received a boost in 1877 when the Grizzly Bluff and Camp Grant Road was completed, linking those two locations by a 27.5-mile thoroughfare that was usually called the West Side Road because that was the side of the Eel River it stayed on.[511] Despite this improvement in land transportation, some people preferred traveling *on* the Eel rather than beside it. When Mrs. John O. Mowry ventured from Eureka to Camp Grant in 1883, she used a combination of both methods to reach her destination. She travelled lightly, apparently having left her first name in Eureka. On day one she took the stage from Eureka to McDonald's (later East's) Ferry, a short distance downriver from Alton. Day two was by boat, which transported her only as far as Eagle Prairie (Rio Dell). The third day, again spent on the Eel, brought her to a ranch house, perhaps in the Pepperwood-Shively area. The fourth and last day found her debarking from her boat at Camp Grant at four in the afternoon. Her husband subsequently traveled to Eureka at the same pace, making the round trip in eight days.[512]

The West Side Road, west of Camp Grant, before the right-of-way was taken over by the Northwestern Pacific (HCHS, colorized by JR).

Unlike Mrs. Mowry, another traveler, author John H. Durst, came "afoot up Eel River," as he chronicled in the *Overland Monthly* in March 1883. Durst summarized the history of Camp Grant in a single, insensitive, incongruent paragraph that juxtaposed a biased summary of the Indian-white conflict with a weather report:

> Camp Grant, when reached, proves to be at another "pepperwood bottom," partially cleared, with a couple of orchards occupying almost all of the cleared land, and two houses only. The name alone gives character to the place, and its situation as the terminus of the wagon road gives significance. It was once, as the name indicates, a military station. In the early days, fifteen years or so ago, when the Indians were plentiful and "ugly," the United States soldiers stopped here to awe them by the military arm of the Government. They did good service in impressing the Indians, but the solid fighting, or at least the killing, was done by the settlers. The climate here is delightful. There are no extremes, and there are no harsh ocean winds. Fogs may overcast the sky in the morning, but they never descend, and are soon dissipated; while a balmy breeze blows all day through the orchard trees and corn.[513]

Perhaps it was the same "balmy breeze" that blew through Durst's sensibility, leaving him without comprehension of the tragedy that he disparagingly described.

In the summer of 1881 John Myers was busy in the Camp Grant area cutting, grinding, and shipping tanbark. From every cord of bark, Myers managed to glean more than a ton of ground product, all of which was hauled to Port Kenyon for shipment to San Francisco.[514] That same year Amos Hansell conducted an impressively intense agricultural experiment. He first set out 900 tomato plants; 24 hours later, insects had eaten all 900. Hansell replanted on the same ground, but this time he shaded all the plants. Henceforth he observed "nary a bug."[515]

Other products also left the area. In April 1883 a Captain Bostetter brought down a boat from "above Camp Grant" that carried "over 1,000 pounds of deer skins, mostly collected at Blocksburg; two tons of the finest kind of potatoes, lumber, etc." The etc. included "150 white oak maul heads."[516] There was still room on board for "five passengers, among whom were two ladies."[517]

"McTavish," the roving correspondent for the *Daily Humboldt Standard*, visited Camp Grant in July 1885. He found August Cusa now holding the former Dobbyn property, on which grew both fruit trees and alfalfa. Still on hand was Amos Hansell, who now had "1,200 trees, embracing almost every variety of fruit." He preferred apple trees above all others, so that "whenever a tree dies in his orchard he replaces it with a good variety of apple." The Hansell family lived in a handsome modern house they had built themselves, hand cutting all the timber for it. Also on the premises was the Hansell Nursery and a large stand of redwoods. A mile or so upriver was C. L. Thompson's place, with cultivated land south of the Eel and 1,200 acres for grazing on the north side. Thompson was raising sheep, hogs, and horses.[518]

The county business directory for 1890-1891 noted that Camp Grant was home to 4,000 fruit trees, indicating that the area "is bound to be recognized as the great fruit belt of Northern California." The only drawback to its full devel-

NEAR CAMP GRANT, HUMBOLDT CO., CAL.
BOWMAN FORTUNA, CAL. N°122

The revised road to Camp Grant climbed the hillside south of its
original route that ran next to the Eel (JIC, colorized by JR).

opment was, despite the West Side Road, "the lack of transportation." Northward, across the river, the site of the original camp was now an 80-acre prairie that served as a sheep ranch.[519]

Imprinting himself (or at least his name) on the landscape was J. J. Newman, whose success with fruit and vegetable growing rivaled that of Amos Hansell. In 1890 Newman won awards for the following: best six stalks[520] corn, best display of muskmelons, best display of watermelons, second best display of tomatoes, best apples (five varieties), best display of peaches, and second-best display of fruits of all kinds.[521] In addition to such awards, two further distinctions were bestowed upon him: the ridge face just southwest of Camp Grant was named Newman Bluff, while a stream flowing into the Eel opposite Camp Grant was called Newman Creek.[522]

Newspaperman David E. Gordon arrived at Camp Grant in 1899. He found that Amos Hansell, Sr., had given over operation of his ranch to his sons, Amos, Jr., and Harry. They maintained an orchard of "about 2000 trees" (up from their father's 1,200), which were expected to yield 1,500 to 2,000 boxes of apples. The previous year the brothers had built a "fruit boat" that transported 400 boxes of apples at a time to the "picnic ground four miles above Scotia," whence they were shipped northward in the rail cars of the Pacific Lumber Company.[523]

Gordon noted that the fluvial fluctuations of the Eel had earlier eaten into the river's south bank to the extent that Dobbyn's former orchard there had "almost entirely disappeared." Now the Eel was directing its attention to the north bank, where it was taking away portions of the original Camp Grant site. This property was currently owned by J. J. Newman, and Gordon predicted that "yet many years may elapse before vital injury occurs to the farm which now occupies the site of old Camp Grant."[524]

In 1904 Amos Hansel, Jr., bought out his brother and in 1906 did the same with his father. In the latter year Amos Junior married a widow named Frances Randle. By 1915 the Hansells were specializing in apples, most notably Spitzenbergs, Jonathans, Kings, Rhode Island Greenings, Bellflowers, and Pippins. Cherries and tomatoes were also present, as was an elderly black walnut tree on the property that by then had expanded to a spread of 90 feet.[525]

The river was kind enough to "old Camp Grant" that in the 1910s Joel Sevier Burnell, a Eureka attorney, was developing an apple orchard

at the site.[526] The Patmore family, which had a ranch in the hills northeast of Camp Grant,[527] eventually acquired land on both sides of the river, including Burnell's parcel.[528] George and Elizabeth Patmore came to Camp Grant in 1872, when George "assumed active charge of the ferry." They left the area and then Elizabeth died in 1876. George returned to Camp Grant and took up a timber claim and a homestead. Later George "purchased the old Dobbyn range adjacent his timber claim," ranching cattle and sheep until 1900, when he opened a store in Rohnerville. His son, George William, took over the Camp Grant operation when he was 19. In the 1910s George William gathered stray logs floating down the Eel and converted them into 10,000 railroad ties for the Pacific Lumber Company.[529]

Pumpkins pose in a row at modern-day Camp Grant (JR).

In about 1900 Victor Pedrotti rented the Cusa Ranch and moved his blacksmith shop upriver from Dyerville to Camp Grant.[530] Other changes followed. M. L. Gillogly bought 141 acres, complete with a "fine Jonathan apple orchard" in 1903. At an unknown date, F. L. Read bought Amos Hansell's Camp Grant Ranch from Hansell's widow. Read had been the hired hand on the property and had planted orchards of both Gravenstein and Jonathan apples there in 1910.[531] The decades passed, and in the 1960s Audron and Louise Read Paine bought the Camp Grant Ranch from Louise's parents. They raised "apples, cherries, peaches, pears . . . and many vegetables" until the 1980s when they sold the home ranch and moved to Fortuna. While at Camp Grant they saw one of the floods cover their property "with silt ranging from a depth of nine feet at the upper end to four feet further down the valley."[532]

The original Camp Grant School was an exercise in minimalism. When it started in 1879 it had 12 students, but the building was deemed too small for all the children who wished to attend. There were not enough desks or seats for those who did come. No space was wasted on books, because there weren't any except those that students brought from home. There was no outhouse. By the second term that year only 10 students were present. Furniture was still inadequate, but there were now nine books, so almost all the students could have one. In 1880 enrollment had mushroomed to 20 students. The building size had stayed the same, but now the school had 24 books. Ventilation was reported as being "excellent." It was provided "by holes in the roof." Still no outhouse.

And so it went. By the 1910s some changes had occurred. Attendance fluctuated from about 15 to 35 students. Class now met in what was apparently a larger building, since it had "eight or ten windows on each side." There was neither an anteroom nor a belfry, but there were now two separate outhouses. One of the students, Sid Myers, later recalled a series of events involving both structures:

One time Nell Patmore was locked into the girls' outhouse by three boys. She was a big, strong 8th grader, and she proceeded to kick her way out. Three days later the three boys were seen going into the boys' outhouse for a conference. Nell slipped over and locked them in the boys' outhouse. She then tipped it over, and REVENGE WAS COMPLETE.[533]

Chapter 9
South Fork

When the Northwestern Pacific Railroad (NWP) chose the main Eel River for its route through southern Humboldt County, it left ranchers and other residents on the South Fork Eel to dwell in continued isolation, with only wagon roads to connect them with the outside world. The closest point the NWP would come to the South Fork was just upstream from that river's mouth, where the rail line's tracks would cross from one side of the main Eel to the other. Accordingly, the NWP did the best it could and built a station they eventually named South Fork on the flat just south of the bridge, next to the West Side Road.

In addition to the station, the NWP also constructed several sidings, for the rail line anticipated lots of business from the locals. Now ranchers from the southern Humboldt hills could use the rails to send their produce and livestock on its way to market, while a string of stores along the river could receive their supplies from the south. Most important of all, the vast groves of riverside redwoods could be converted into shingles and split products and sent on their way to carpenters, winery owners, and a host of other distant customers.

Continuing the tracks that the Pacific Lumber Company had laid south of Scotia, the NWP had built upstream along the northeast bank of the main Eel River. Opposite the mouth of the South Fork, the NWP bridged the main Eel, taking the tracks to the southwest

Mercer Fraser constructing the NWP bridge at South Fork (HCHS, colorized by JR).

bank of the river. Staying on low ground near the edge of the river, the railroad usurped the right-of-way for the West Side Road, which had run there since its completion in 1877.[534] This meant that a steep, winding replacement road had to be built south of Newman's Bluff to connect the new community of South Fork with Camp Grant.[535]

At first the NWP called the station Dyerville. This was misleading because the town of that name was located a half-mile to the northwest across the mouth of the South Fork Eel. In 1913 the station was renamed South Fork.[536] This was still misleading but to a lesser degree, as the namesake river was a few hundred feet closer to the station than the town.

For a time the station area became a temporary home for workers building the railroad. Leslie M. Scott, who was a blacksmith and master mechanic, moved his family to South Fork in 1911 while he did construction work on the railroad. His son Bud recalled that his father built a "cabin under the big redwood trees and close to the railroad tracks where the comings and goings of the steam engines and other equipment could be seen firsthand." The family got their supplies at Dyerville. Bud found that

> . . . there were many nationalities among the workers and their families. Each gang had an interpreter as few spoke English. The Russian families in the camp spoke no English but the ladies in our camp got along well with them, and the children became fast friends. The Russian women wore those colorful scarves or kerchiefs called babushkas on their heads.[537]

W. R. Boyce was the first station agent.[538] He aspired to a more exciting occupation, however, and soon ran for county sheriff. Voters, however, decided he should continue living the simple life, and 1915 still found him at South Fork.[539]

Seeking his own kind of simplicity was John W. Alverson, who spent 10 years living in a hollow redwood near the South Fork station. Alverson dealt in split-stuff products, such as grape stakes, that could be easily fashioned in the nearby woods and then brought to the station for shipment. By 1926 Alverson had given up his redwood domicile and moved to a cabin about a hundred yards west of train station. This proved to be a mistake, for one February night, while inebriated, he apparently set fire to his dwelling and perished in the flames.[540]

South Fork was home base for an NWP section crew of about 10 men who maintained the track in both directions from the station. The next section crew to the south was at Fort Seward, while the next one to the north was at Scotia.[541] Railroad cars were used as bunkhouses for the crewmen where as many as 30 might sleep at a time. The NWP also maintained a cookhouse at South Fork to feed the section crews and train crews. At one point there were about 50 families living at South Fork in addition to the railroad employees.[542]

During the 1940s four passenger trains, two from the north and two from the south, passed through South Fork each day, in addition to various freights. Groceries for the NWP's cookhouse came from Eureka by boxcar. Fresh meat was brought by butcher Julio Rovai from Wildwood, fruit was delivered from Fresno several times a month, and smoked meat and Big Loaf bread came in separate shipments. Ivy Patmore worked as the NWP's South Fork cook for a time. Keeping the workers fed required her to bake batches of six loaves of bread in a large coal-burning stove.[543]

By 1949 Melvin Dunn was the station agent at South Fork, and a busy one indeed. The post-World War II lumber boom was in full swing, and things were hopping at the station. Among the businesses loading and receiving at South Fork were the Tacoma Lumber Company, Redwood Garden Materials Company, Morrison and Jackson Lumber Company, J. E. Tsarnas, Stegman Lumber Company, West Coast Lumber Company, Briceland Lumber Company, L. S. Whaley Lumber Company, Bear River Lumber Company, Taylor Lumber Company, Halstead Lumber Company, and "others that come and go." Up to 300 carloads of lumber left South Fork each month.[544]

Three oil companies added to the action. Texaco, Standard Oil, and Tidewater Associated Oil all had distributing depots there, while the state division of highways operated an asphalt heating and storage plant. Not only through trains stopped at the station; many local freights made South Fork either their northern or southern terminus.[545] If the original station master, W. R. Boyce, had only stuck it out, he would have found excitement aplenty at South Fork.

Excitement of a different kind came with the 1964 flood. The South Fork railroad bridge held out for three days, but then the two northern spans gave way.[546] The flood also demolished the railroad facilities on the nearby flat. A newspaper photo showed the station yard littered with debris, reaching a climax where an overturned passenger car and a stack of logs lay atop the main track and several sidings.[547]

South Fork more or less recovered from the flood, but it couldn't fully cope with the diminishment of rail traffic on the NWP. The last passenger train stopped in South Fork in September 1991, when the NWP's successor,

Split stuff at the South Fork Station, 1920: shingles, railroad ties, grape stakes, fenceposts (FMC, colorized by JR).

Most travelers arrived at South Fork on the train, but some chose to come by auto[549] (CPH, colorized by JR).

the Eureka Southern,[548] ran a special excursion trip from Eureka to Fort Seward and back. The tracks by then were in such poor condition that the train was confined to a 20-mile-per-hour speed limit, and as the special slowly moved up the Eel the passengers quickly ate up all the food on board. An emergency stop was made at South Fork so that workers from the Eureka Inn could bring several boxes of coffee cakes on board. As the food was being loaded, pas-

sengers surveyed the remains of South Fork: there was no station house, only a pile of rotting railroad ties and a lone boxcar rusting away on a siding.[550] It had been 80 years since Bud Scott saw a vastly different sight here—the wives of the Russian railroad workers arrayed in their colorful babushkas, no doubt proud that their husbands were creating a part of the future, no doubt unaware of the brevity of the creation.

Tempus edax rerum.[551]

Chapter 10
Redcrest

What pleasure lives in height?
                              —Tennyson

Between Rohnerville and Garberville, there were only two towns that were proof against floods. One was Miranda, more than a hundred feet higher than the South Fork. The other was Redcrest, perched upon a flat some 400 feet above the Eel.

Redcrest was positioned just west of a high bluff that dropped nearly straight down to the Eel, leaving no space for buildings, or even a trail, near the water's edge. When the West Side Road was built up the Eel in 1877[552] it generally ran close to the river. But when it reached the western end of Holmes Flat, it turned into the hills and came up the canyon of Chadd Creek to reach the future site of Redcrest.[553]

There may have been an Indian community in the vicinity, but there is no record of it. George Burtt, a Lolahnkok from Bull Creek, stated that the area was called Kah-li-cho-be but did not indicate if there was a village anywhere nearby.[554] However, members of the Childs family, who first occupied the flat in 1912, over time found "50 or more" arrowheads on their ranch.[555]

According to one report, the first white to take up land in the area was Jesse W. Whitlow, who homesteaded 160 acres in 1865.[556] Ten years later Whitlow received a patent to the western part of the prairie that lies southeast of modern-day Redcrest.[557] The 1869 government survey of the area shows "Wilder's cabin and field," which may include the surveyor's approximation of Whitlow's name.[558]

Then, in the 1870s, two brothers from England, John and Henry Davis, arrived and gave the location not one, but two names. They could easily have called the place Davisville, but love of their homeland overcame any desire for self-glorification, and so they named the prairie Englevale. The area on the flat surrounding the prairie was forested, and so this became Englewood.[559] The latter location received a post office in October 1880.[560] Henry Davis patented the eastern portion of the prairie in 1884.[561]

In July 1885 the *Daily Humboldt Standard's* roving reporter, McTavish, reported on the "Englewood Postoffice" and its surroundings:

H. D. Davis is Postmaster at Englewood and owns 160 acres of land, 40 of which is tillable and 120 timber. There is now in cultivation 20 acres, comprising orchard and grain. Mr. Davis has a comfortable home, good barn and out buildings, and his orchard contains choice varieties of fruit. The locality is as picturesque as its name would indicate, Mr. Davis having an eye to the beautiful in its selection. The Davis Bros. originally owned 320 acres here, which included all the open land. They sold 160 acres to B. F. Spears, who has just completed a good house, which will be open to travel as a stopping place. Mr. Spears has 60 acres of land suitable for cul-

Henry Davis cabin, 1887 (CPH, colorized by JR).

tivation and the remainder is timber. Adjoining Mr. Spears on the west are the places of Paul and A. Romeo, formerly from Tehama county, who each own 160 acres. The land of the former is covered with timber, while that of A. Romeo has 60 acres of open prairie, 20 of which is fenced and under cultivation, a portion being an orchard. The Romeos' [sic] have resided here 8 years and now have comfortable improvements. All the residences about Englewood seem to have a taste for flowers, each home being ornamented with beautiful shrubs and plants, which add greatly to the pleasant surroundings. Stumpage is sold to persons who get out cants and raft them down the river. In this way . . . revenue is realized from the timber.[562]

Despite the manifest charms of the locale, the Englewood Post Office lasted only until September 1891, when it was merged with the Dyerville office. Then the Englevale post office opened in June 1893. No sooner had the paint on its sign dried than it, too, shut down and merged with Dyerville in December 1894.[563]

Meanwhile, other elements of a town developed. By 1890, Henry Davis's son, Henry Jr., and Johnny Garrett were known to "maintain first-class stopping places for the weary traveler" at Englewood.[564] By the following year the latter became "genial Johnny Garrett," who had added a "gentlemanly partner, Mr. George." In addition to possessing "a fine farm, a prolific orchard, and a most comfortable dwelling," the pair had "recently constructed a new barn, and are now better prepared than ever to accommodate the traveling public." Garrett's "most estimable wife" was praised for her cooking but not to the extent that the paper would reveal her first name.[565]

In 1907 "the 160-acre ranch known as Englewood" belonging to "Mr. and Mrs. Cal George, for the past 18 years," was sold to M. P. Endicott of Pepperwood.[566] Mrs. George was formerly Miss Mary Garrett, who had taught at the Englewood School.[567]

The Endicotts kept the ranch only until 1912.[568] The new owners were Fred and Ada Childs, who had two little Childses, Robert and Richard. The family, minus Richard, had arrived at Englewood the previous year. Ada made the trip in the Childs's small wagon, seated atop a stove. She later claimed that, like a cowboy, she "rode the range."[569] They stayed temporarily on the property east of the prairie. While there, Richard was born. The surrounding forest must have impressed his parents, for they gave him the middle name of "Redwood."[570]

The West Side Road, after coming up the Chadd Creek canyon, went through the middle of the Childs Ranch. The barn was in fact right next to the road, a convenience for travelers who could put their horses up there for 50 cents a night and then walk a short distance to the ranch's "inn" where they could get a room and breakfast for a quarter.[571]

After leaving the Childs Ranch, the wagon road curved along the north side of the Englevale prairie before turning south to run near a fringe of forest. At the southeast end of the prairie, positioned so that it would greet travelers arriving from upriver, was a modest cabin designated the "Englewood Inn," which offered "meals."[572] A couple of hundred yards to the north, set in the woods east of the prairie, was a commodious two-story house that served as Henry Davis, Jr.'s stopping place for overnight travelers.[573] Brothers Cornelius and John Daly, who owned a department store in Eureka, took their families

Englewood stopping place, 1911, later the Daly ranch house (CSP, colorized by JR).

The Englewood Inn (JIC, colorized by JR).

there for a summer vacation in 1919. They liked it so much that in 1921 the Dalys bought the entire 160-acre parcel from A. M. Price and turned it into a family retreat.[574] The stopping place was remodeled—several times— and "a colony of summer homes" built around it in the woods. Most notable of the new structures was a Quonset-hut-styled house that was covered with an arch of corrugated sheet metal.[575]

Westward across the vale, the Childs family raised chickens, pigs, and horses on their ranch. They also maintained a small dairy that allowed them to sell milk to the locals. Another popular drink was produced in the area during the 1920s—bootleg liquor. The operators would set up in a "chimney tree" redwood that had previously had its center burned out by a fire. The bootleggers would boil up sour mash at the bottom of the tree, and the smoke and vapor

would rise through the hollow trunk to dissipate undetected in the overstory high above the ground. Much of the whiskey went to dance halls in Eureka, but some made its way south to San Francisco. Competition came from Wildwood (lower Rio Dell), which was described as being "a big winery."[576]

Drawn perhaps by the selection of beverages, people from Eureka and nearby areas began coming to Englewood to camp for a week or so. Travelers still stayed at the Englewood Inn. In the early 1920s a dance hall near the inn attracted "big name bands" and big crowds of people. Twice a week Fred Daggett ran his motor stage, an oversized Pierce-Arrow touring car, down from Eureka and back. By now the Redwood Highway had connected Eureka with San Francisco Bay, its construction aided by Fred Childs, who had used his horse team to pull a Fresno scraper that helped cut the bed of the new road. Soon Englewood became a highway tourist stop.[577]

By the 1910s some of the forest west of Englewood was being cut. L. L. Chapman ran a tie camp west of the Childs Ranch during World War I and on until about 1925. It produced both railroad ties and grapestakes. Clark "Pop" Whetstone operated a shingle mill on nearby Chadd Creek in the mid-1920s. By then, at least one other tie camp and two sawtimber outfits were also busy in the area.[578]

At the top of the hill coming up from Chadd Creek, a small business district developed. L. L. Chapman put in a general merchandise store that was run by Clark Whetstone, while Lee Cathey operated a blacksmith shop.[579] For a

time the location was called Chapman's Camp, while an area of substandard housing down the hill to the north became a sort of suburb derisively referred to as Skiff Town.[580] Up the hill, three families had large land holdings: the Dalys on the east side of the prairie; the Childses on the west side; and farther west, across the highway, the Turners. Bill Turner rented several small cabins to the families of mill and woods workers.[581]

Arland and Ruby Rodenberger took over Chapman's store in the mid-1920s. According to some accounts, it was Ruby who suggested the name "Redcrest" when the town hoped to reinstate its post office; by then Englewood was no longer an option because it was too similar to the town of Inglewood that had sprung up

The Checkerboard Cabin, 1939 (FMC, colorized by JR).

in Southern California.[582] Another account gives the naming honor to Mabel McHenry, who, with her husband, Arthur, established an auto court in about 1931. In this case the name derived from Mabel's shock of red hair.[583] Whatever the actual inspiration, it was slow to inspire the postal service, which waited until 1965 to establish the Redcrest post office.[584]

Marian and Guy Andrews opened Andrews Redwood Novelties in 1929 near the Redcrest store. The biggest novelty was the barber shop that Guy for a time operated in the same building. Later the structure, which "was a traditional log cabin chinked with real mud," served as Shorty's Bar before reprising its role as a gift shop. The building was torn down in 2002. Across the highway, the Redcrest Auto Camp started up in the "early-to-mid 1930s." Accommodations were $1 per night and up, but dishes and cooking utensils were extra. At the entrance

was a small gas station and sandwich shop. By 1949 it had become the Red Crest Motor Inn, which featured, among other attractions, a shuffleboard court. By the 1950s the business district included the Eternal Tree House and the Redcrest Café.[585]

About 1930 Collin's [sic] Englewood Park, featuring a coffee shop, cottages, and "hotel accommodations," was established on the south side of the Redwood Highway opposite the prairie once known as Englevale. It served tourists until it was obliterated by the 101 Freeway in 1958.[586]

In 1951 Bill Herndon and Don Martin built a mill at the southern edge of the prairie. It went into production the following year as the Englewood Lumber Company. Siskiyou Plywood put in an adjacent mill in 1955, which was taken over by the Pacific Lumber Company in 1960. This operation was moved to Scotia in

The Redcrest nasturtium delivery truck will be a little late . . . (GR).

1967. The Englewood Lumber Company was eventually purchased by Mel McLean to become part of his Eel River Sawmills.[587] The mill at one time employed over 100 people. It closed in 2000.[588]

In back of the mill site, at the edge of the Englevale prairie, what is probably the oldest building in Redcrest peeps out from a fringe of forest. It is the reconstructed Englewood School, a log cabin with shake roof that served from 1886 to 1907. When it was nearly a hundred years old, abandoned, and in bad shape, Robert and Richard Childs, who weren't much younger, rescued the dilapidated building from impending oblivion. They numbered all the logs, moved them to where they had built a new foundation, replaced the logs in their proper order, put in a new hardwood floor and put on a new shake roof, and the school was good as new. Vintage desks, a slate blackboard, map rack, and other period features were added. Robert's wife, Velma, a retired schoolteacher, would then conduct "class" for various visitors, including groups of tourists.[589]

So it was that the Childs Ranch preserved a place for children.

Chapter 11
Larabee Area

The community of Larabee and its environs have never had a large population, but it is possible that more people lived there before the arrival of whites than at any time thereafter. The lower two miles of Larabee Creek apparently belonged to the Lolahnkok tribal group, which was part of the Sinkyone tribe. They called the creek Slahn-ko.[590] Upstream from the Lolahnkoks was the territory of the Ne-tcin-dun-kut kai-ya, a Nongatl tribal group. Their name for the creek was Slun-kuk.[591] There were at least two villages along the Ne-tcin-dun-kut kai-ya section of the creek, with one or more summer camps on the side of Chalk Mountain to the north. One of the villages, No-le-bi, was reported by Goddard in 1907 to have 56 house pits.[592] A hundred years later archaeologists visited the site and found many of the pits still present. Some investigators thought that this was evidence of an extremely large village, but they were disabused of this fallacy when reminded that the Nongatls were among the tribes that frequently moved the location of their winter houses, thereby creating multiple pits per family dwelling.[593] As with most of the Indian groups in the area, the Ne-tcin-dun-kut kai-ya failed to survive the Indian-white conflict of the 1850s and 1860s.

The Ne-tcin-dun-kut kai-ya probably faced the first white intrusion on their homeland in 1851, when it appears that the Sonoma Trail was first used. This route came north along the divide between the South Fork and main Eel rivers, descending the ridge to reach a spot about two miles above the rivers' confluence. Here the trail crossed the main Eel to a flat upon which the later military installation known as Camp Grant was built. It proceeded downstream along the eastern side of the river until it crossed Larabee Creek near its mouth. It then left the river valley to run northward over the mountains to the Van Duzen River, crossing the river above Strong's Station on its way to Goose Lake Prairie (Hydesville).[594] This trail became the official government weekly mail route in 1860[595]; it was the "mail trail" that Captain Ketcham and his troops came upon when chasing Indians in 1862.[596] (See sidebar 1.)

This trail served as the main connecting route between Humboldt Bay and areas to the south until the mid-1870s, when its importance was diminished by completion of the West Side Road that ran up the Eel River as far as Camp Grant.[597]

When Van Duzen Pete and Pliny Goddard visited the lower Larabee Creek area in 1907, they found not just remnants of Ne-tcin-dun-kut kai-ya villages but evidence of later white habitation. At one location near the village of No-le-bi, where there were several springs, they came upon "a prairie in the redwoods [with a] deserted house and outbuildings with orchard." Pete remarked that he had "nearly bought it once."[598] On the hillside below Oak Ridge, they found "a prosperous looking farm with buildings."[599] They were seeing an area in transition. In the aftermath of the removal of the Ne-tcin-dun-kut kai-ya, whites had come to ranch the open spaces, with, as Pete and Goddard discovered, mixed results. But as the pair encountered evidence of the past and present,

Camp Balcom was located in Ne-tcin-dun-kut kai-ya territory (CPH, colorized by JR).

1. The Fate of the Ne-tcin-dun-kut kai-ya

In April 1862, Captain Thomas A. Ketcham and 25 soldiers from Company A, Third Infantry, California Volunteers, pursued "a band of Indians who had been killing cattle in the neighborhood of McEntee Crossing, on the Van Duzen River."[600] The soldiers were stationed at Fort Baker. McEntee, or McAtee Crossing, was located near the future site of Bridgeville.[601] On April 25 the detachment

> . . . followed the trace [of the Indians] over the mountain, [and] across the mail trail toward the mouth of Larrabee [sic] Creek. About 3 p. m. [they] discovered a large [Indian] ranch which had been fortified by felling trees around it, but the Indians had deserted the ranch two or three days previously.[602]

The following day the soldiers came

. . . upon the Indians about 9 a. m. encamped in a deep ravine near Eel River. There were 3 Indians and 1 squaw killed, 2 boys, 11 squaws, and 11 children prisoners, two bucks and one squaw escaping.[603]

From the dispatch it appears that the Indians were discovered in or near Ne-tcin-dun-kut kai-ya territory above the mouth of Larabee Creek.[604] With only five adult males out of a group of 31 Indians, it is unlikely the soldiers had encountered a war party; instead, the group was probably what remained of a village population after the warriors had left. Ketcham's report does not indicate that there was a battle against what was likely a peaceful group. Rather, he goes directly to the casualty list: four Indians killed, no soldiers wounded or killed, no weapons taken from the Indians. It appears he was describing a massacre.

Ketcham indicated that the Indian prisoners were taken to Fort Baker, arriving there a day and a half after the attack.[605]

When the ethnographer Pliny Goddard was examining the lower Larabee Creek area with Van Duzen Pete 45 years later, they found another village site, this one with 23 house pits, on a flat called Kac-tco-a-dun. In a nearby creek there had been "lots of salmon." Goddard indicated that "Pete never saw houses there but lots [of Indians from the village] were taken [to the] reservation Crescent City died there."[606]

It may be that Pete failed to see houses because they had been destroyed by the soldiers. It is also possible that the villagers were those captured by Ketcham and his troops and taken to Fort Baker. From there they would likely have been sent to the Smith River Reservation, near Crescent City. According to one Indian witness, the reservation was essentially a concentration camp. The children were given no clothes. Food was minimal and provided only to those who worked for it. Men, women, and children were whipped or jailed "just for trying to get some thing to eat." When Indians got sick, Dr. Wright, the reservation physician, would poison them.[607] No wonder that Pete could report that an entire village population died there.

The Ne-tcin-dun-kut kai-ya inhabited the small, tightly enclosed world that encompassed the drainage of lower Larabee Creek. They had probably lived there, in relative peace and safety, for centuries. But part of their land was good for ranching, and much of it would later be good for logging. As with other desirable places, the whites wanted the Indians gone, and whether it was with a militiaman's bullet or a doctor's poison, they obtained what they wanted.

they also beheld the future, observing, near one village site a "creek bed . . . with big timber on the west side,"[608] and, near No-le-bi, "big timber all about."[609] They were not the first to note the extensive redwood forest.

Before the West Side Road was built, travelers could travel up the bed of the Eel at low water, availing themselves of the river bars whenever possible. One such itinerant, A. A. Fuller, passed the mouth of Larabee Creek in September 1873, noting only the presence of "a few acres of cultivated land and a house."[610]

The Northwestern Pacific Railroad (NWP), building up the Eel River from Shively, reached Bryan's Bluff, a mile northwest of Larabee, in 1910. The bluff presents a sheer rock face to the Eel River—spectacular, but also daunting. The tracks could not go across the face of the bluff, so a tunnel was required. It ran for a quarter mile, and while "drillers and rockmen" worked

their way through the bluff, another crew placed concrete piers for the bridge at Larabee Creek.[611] The NWP had contracted with Mercer Fraser Company to build a 300-foot-long, three-span steel truss bridge over the creek.[612] In 1911 a "huge slide" covered the tracks just west of the tunnel, tipping a locomotive on its side and carrying a string of flatcars nearly to the nearby Eel.[613]

Bryan's Bluff took its name from John and Maggie Bryan, who operated a resort a short distance eastward. In the 1880s they had opened the Bryan House in Rohnerville and subsequently "they conducted the principal hotel in Fortuna." With this experience under their belts, the couple in 1890 purchased 55 acres of land on the flat just north of the mouth of Larabee Creek. Here they opened Bryan's Rest, which included a two-story "attractive and comfortable" hotel building and bottomland "under

Bryan's Rest (THPO, colorized by JR).

Mercer Fraser builds the Larabee Creek Bridge, 1911 (DTC, colorized by JR).

a high state of cultivation." The produce thus produced was "easily marketed" via "shipping facilities."[614] The main such facility eventually became the NWP, which by establishing Bryan station,[615] also assured that vacationers had easy access to the resort.

South of the mouth of Larabee Creek a small community developed. In 1915, Frederick Georgeson, a former mayor of Eureka who also held property at nearby Pepperwood, subdivided a 220-acre tract of land adjacent the Eel just upriver from the creek. He sold lots in five-, ten-, and twenty-acre denominations, the land being "rich in soil and well adapted to horticulture and agriculture, especially the raising of alfalfa and potatoes."[616] In 1917, when a schoolhouse was built at the north end of Georgeson's new subdivision, it was named for him.[617]

On one of Georgeson's 22 lots, Dennis McKinley built a store. Noting that it was the only such business in the area, locals jokingly called it "the Emporium."[618] With his property bounded on the west by the Eel River and on the east by the NWP, McKinley had two shipping options close at hand. When McKinley applied for a post office, he probably realized that the name McKinleyville was already taken; in any event, he produced a perhaps-unique stratagem for selecting an alternative: he took the initial and last name of the surveyor who had platted the Georgeson tract, S. Kelly, combined them, and launched the Skelly post office.[619] With the local school being named Georgeson in honor of the community's developer, it was possible to live in Larabee, send your children to the Georgeson School, and mail a letter at the Skelly post office—all without leaving town.

When the Pacific Lumber Company (PL) opened their mill at Scotia in 1887, they already owned timberland along the Eel up as far as its confluence with the South Fork. They also held the lower two miles of Larabee Creek.[620]

Logging train near Larabee (CPH, colorized by JR).

As the railroad made its way up the Eel, PL cut its nearby timberlands, at last having a way to get their logs to their mill. In 1906, with tracks having reached the area upstream from Shively, PL sent logs from Camp 3, on Chadd Creek, across a summer trestle that connected Holmes Flat with the main line.[621] Ten years later, with the NWP's line completed, PL was cutting in the Larabee area. They had camps at Chris Creek, which flowed into Larabee Creek a half mile east of the Eel, and at Balcom Camp, two miles up Larabee Creek from its mouth. Both camps had their own store.[622]

By the early 1920s PL had five logging camps in the lower Larabee Creek drainage. In addition to camps Chris and Balcom, it added camps Dauphiny, Scott, and Carson, each at or near the mouth of its namesake creek. PL's logging railroad ran three-and-a-half miles up the valley, ending at Arnold Creek. A half mile farther east, just past Smith Creek, the gradually narrowing canyon pinched off into a gorge, Mindful of the obstacle posed by the rugged terrain to the east, PL had extended its land ownership only up to the gorge's mouth.[623]

In addition to their work in the Larabee Creek drainage, PL also logged nearby Bridge (formerly Bryan) Creek. The exact dates of this operation are unknown, but in 1923 there was a "fire in logging slash" some distance up the drainage.[624] PL had run a spur rail line off of the NWP's main line just east of the Bryan's Bluff tunnel that ran up the canyon of Bridge Creek. The space was so confined that the tracks were put on trestles built over the creek bed. Bridge Creek Camp was just a short distance up the canyon. Farther east, an inclined rail line ran up the hillslope from the creek bed to Coolen Camp.[625]

South of Larabee Creek PL logged other locations on the east side of the Eel. They had camps at Georgeson Camp, a mile south of the Larabee train switch, and at Allen Creek, another mile farther south.[626] Farther south yet, PL sent railroad spurs into the drainages of Weber Creek, Perrott Creek, and Newman Creek. The latter two lines each featured an incline that allowed logs to be brought down from the nearby ridges.[627] A series of photographs document the logging operation at Perrott Creek, showing a set of PL's railcars used for worker housing, a busy headquarters area, the inclined rail system, and the devasted drainage.

Reaching the Larabee area by train was easy; the NWP had stops at both Bryan and Larabee.[628] Getting there by other methods, however, was often difficult and sometimes dangerous. In the 1920s a low-water route ran from the northeastern edge of Holmes Flat, angling southeast on the riverbar, and then crossing the river south of Bryan's Rest[629] on what locals called the "Eel River Bridge." After graduating from Georgeson School, Gerald Evans needed to take this route to get to the high school bus in Holmes. At first he tried using a bicycle, but this attempt was defeated by the large rocks on the river bar. George's parents then purchased a 1925 Chevrolet for him to drive to the bus stop. This was a great improvement, but the low-water bridge was usable only "until the first heavy rains in the fall." During the wet months, Evans had to walk two miles north along the railbed to the Paine Ranch, where he met a fellow high school student who had a rowboat. This process was time-consuming; it meant that George left home at six in the morning and didn't get back until six at night. The trip became exciting during stormy weather when the river was rising

Fire in the Bridge Creek drainage, 1923 (FMC, colorized by JR).

Railcar housing at Perrott Creek (colorized by JR).

"as," according to Evans, "floating driftwood in the angry current were [sic] large enough to upset a rowboat if it smashed into it." This never happened, but the boys once contrived to get a floating railroad tie temporarily lodged under the boat. They managed to shove it free and continued on their tumultuous way to school.[630]

Not so fortunate was Arch Crismon, who attempted to reach Larabee in May 1938 on a makeshift "bridge" that was no more than a series of foot-wide planks perched some six feet above the river. It was a temporary means of crossing the Eel while a permanent bridge was being built.[631] Crismon was accompanied by Everett Cyril Ingram, who went first. Crismon placed his hands on Ingram's shoulders, and they proceeded "in almost lockstep formation." When part way across, Crismon missed a step, began to slip, and grabbed tighter hold of

Ingram, so that "together the men toppled into the stream eight feet deep." Ingram managed to make it to shore, but Crismon was lost to the Eel. His body was found two days later a half mile down the river.[632]

When Crismon drowned, Humboldt County lost its most unlikely poet. (See sidebar 2.)

To this day Larabee has never had a high-water bridge. The current structure is a strip of concrete barely elevated above the riverbed. When June Ruggles taught at the Georgeson School, she lived across the Eel in the small town of Bull Creek. Come high water, Ruggles had to be rowed across the river to do her teaching,[633] harkening back to the days when Gerald Evans also went to school by rowboat.

PL made double use of its land holdings on lower Larabee Creek. After the property was logged, much of it was converted into a 20,000-

2. "The Poet of the Redwoods"

Archibald Sterling Crismon led a double life. As Arch Crismon, he was a "chopping boss" for PL, making sure the redwoods were efficiently removed from Larabee Creek.[634] But as Sterling Crismon, he was the "Poet of the Redwoods," writing paeans to the very trees he helped to cut.

The *Humboldt Times* published a short profile of Crismon shortly after his death. It stated that

> Sterling Crismon devoted his life to the study of the flora and bird life of Humboldt county. He lived in a little tree sheltered cabin near his beloved Eel river and there wrote many lyrics depicting the unspoiled wonders of this charmed area. "Some day I'll print them" he said of his poems as he hid them away and allowed only his nearest friends to read them.[635]

The *Times* lamented that Crismon's untimely death likely meant that a wider audience would never see his poems, but the paper did publish one of them, entitled "These Giants Will Stand Again." It read in part:

> We have stood here for countless ages, our proud tops up in the sky,
> But thoughtless man with his wicked hand has us all to fall and wither
>   and die.
> We are a proud race of giants found nowhere else on earth;
> We have the right to live here for this is the land of our birth. . . .[636]

Crismon transmitted his love of nature to his son Max, who also worked in the woods. Late in life Max would name and locate the various species of wildflowers found in the Bull Creek area, where he had grown up. When asked, in 1991, what his dad would have done during the then-current controversy over preserving parts of the redwood forest, Max blurted out, "I don't know—probably join Earth First! I guess."[637]

It would have been a good fit for the Poet of the Redwoods.

acre ranch where, by 1949, about 1,000 head of cattle and 35 quarter horses grazed on the cutover land. The cattle were converted into beefsteak that supplied the company's commissary at Scotia, while the horses were "becoming the nucleus of one of the country's best stables." PL's president, Stanwood Murphey, had a lodge on the ranch to which he could retreat in summer. A full-time resident there was Buck Clayton, registry number 271, a purebred quarter-horse stallion. Buck, in addition to his main duties, allowed himself to be ridden—but only by Dr. Barclay "Doc" Ricks, the manager of the ranch.[638]

Vastly outnumbered by the PL ranch's 35 quarter horses were the nine pupils at the "quaint-appearing little Georgeson School."[639] The number of students varied greatly over the years, depending on local work activity. When PL had been busy logging in the vicinity, several married men with families moved to Larabee to work in the woods. The influx of children prompted the one-room school to double in size, adding both a second room and another teacher. About 1931 the original schoolhouse, which was located just south of the PL railroad line up Larabee Creek, was replaced by a new building next to the NWP tracks just north of the creek. Attendance was in decline by then, so "children were imported" to maintain the minimum requirement.[640]

As the loggers moved on, more than the community's population dropped. The thousand head of cattle and 35 horses on the PL ranch counted for little when it came to providing community services. Accordingly, in August 1943, the Skelly post office closed,[641] requiring residents, when the river permitted, to go to Holmes to get their mail. Georgeson School staged a brief comeback in the early 1950s, when it had 14 students, but then the 1964 flood washed the schoolhouse down the Eel, and it was never rebuilt.[642] As the school headed downriver, one of its former students, Raymond Evans, left Larabee going in the opposite direction. (See sidebar 3.)

Larabee School students, 1919 (CPH, colorized by JR).

3. Making Tracks from Larabee

When Gerald Evans made his perilous passages across the rain-swollen Eel to catch the school bus, he probably thought he was creating the best Evans family river story of all time.

He was wrong. Decades later, his little brother Raymond managed to top him, although Raymond wasn't especially happy he'd done it.

Raymond's story started in late December of 1964. The Eel was already up, and Evans conceived the idea that "some logs suitable for fence posts might be snagged out of the rain-swollen river." Raymond had a 19-foot boat with a new 15-horsepower engine that he thought could do the job. The only problem was getting to the boat at Larabee, which because of the flood couldn't be reached by road. Accordingly, Raymond, accompanied by his brother Art, drove to the tiny town of South Fork, parked his pickup near the NWP tracks, locked the doors, and started down the tracks.[643]

Log landing above Perrott Creek (colorized by JR).

Soon the brothers crossed the NWP bridge over the Eel, where the turbulent river swirled by some 25 feet below them. They reached Larabee in less than an hour and launched the boat. They managed to collect a few logs and tie them to trees along the riverbank. The current proved too strong for them to continue work, so about 2 P.M. the brothers brought the boat ashore and took shelter in the then-unoccupied Evans family house. The river was now rising about four feet per hour.[644]

By 9 P.M. the Evans brothers knew they had to get out. They used the family's 1941 John Deere tractor to haul a smaller tractor to high ground. In back of them, the river "was beginning to make a low roar as it was steadily rising, uprooting cottonwoods and other trees along its bank." They drove off the family's last three head of cattle, stacked tools on the upper deck of the main barn, and tied the boat "to the highest thing in sight." It was now sometime between 3 and 4 A.M.[645]

The fun was just beginning. Raymond and Art now set off towards South Fork, stumbling across the railroad ties at a half-run. They had no flashlight, rain was pelting down in a fury, and the roar of the river had risen in pitch.[646]

They came to the South Fork bridge. The river was now only four or five feet below them. As Raymond and Art made their way across, large logs rammed the bridge. The darkness was pierced by a series of bright flashes; ahead of them power lines were falling and shorting out in a stunning visual display.[647]

Finally they reached land—the elevated berm that the tracks ran on to reach the bridge. The brothers came to the spot where they'd left the pickup. Looking down on the location, they realized the river had flooded the area to a depth of about 10 feet. On the other side of them were the giant trees of the Founders Grove at Humboldt Redwoods State Park, with the floodwaters now far up their trunks. Somewhere beneath the water was the county road that connected to the Redwood Highway.[648]

As daylight approached, Raymond and Art continued along the tracks to the town of South Fork, which sat next to the NWP tracks. All the buildings were flooded, and the brothers left the railbed and climbed the hillside, where several families had their houses. Other buildings on the flat below were now being picked up by the river and carried downstream. Soon the railbed had about four feet of water over it.[649]

It was then that Raymond saw a startling but altogether satisfying sight—his pickup. One of the locals, seeing the truck in danger, had smashed one of the windows and released the brake, allowing the vulnerable vehicle to be towed up the hillside to safety.[650]

Raymond didn't know it at the time, but the pickup was to remain there for a month and a half. Raymond and Art, anxious to avoid being stuck in South Fork, set off along the ridge slope above the flooded Founders Grove and managed to reach the freeway near the Dyerville bridge. The brothers hurried across the South Fork Eel minutes before the river closed over the bridge.[651]

Raymond and Art were able to get a ride from Dyerville to Redcrest, where they stayed overnight in a long-closed restaurant with some refugees from Holmes and Pepperwood. Highway 101 was flooded downriver, so the next morning Raymond, Art, and a young truck driver set out on foot for Rio Dell. Their route from Redcrest took them high above the flooded canyon. They scrambled across wet hillsides and through thick underbrush until, some 20 miles later, they reached the county road below Monument Peak. A microwave technician on his way down the mountain gave the men a jeep ride to Rio Dell. Here Raymond and Art found themselves again temporarily stranded, as the bridge that crossed to Metropolitan had gone out. The next day their luck changed, and they caught a ride to Rohnerville on a cargo plane that had earlier landed on the highway in Rio Dell to deliver emergency supplies. They each paid the pilot $5 for the trip. Both men lived near Rohnerville and were then able to easily make it home.[652]

Two months later Raymond got back to Larabee. Not only had his boat and the logs he'd gathered gone down the river, but also missing were the Evans's house and 34 of the 40 acres that had been the family ranch. Upriver, the South Fork railroad bridge had partly washed away and much of the track he'd stumbled along was a twisted wreck. Yet despite all the losses, Raymond still had his pickup (minus the broken window), his tools, and the memory of a night he'd never forget.

Chapter 12
Holmes

Between the mouth of the Van Duzen and the of mouth Larabee Creek, the topography of the Eel River canyon is defined by a series of point bars, the alluvial deposits that have formed on the inner side of bends in the river. The point bars alternate from one side of the river to the other along the Eel. Each of these bars became the site of a small riverside community: Metropolitan, Rio Dell, Scotia, Stafford, Elinor Junction, Pepperwood, Shively, and Holmes. All of these towns sat astride either the Redwood Highway or the Northwestern Pacific Railroad (NWP) or sometimes both, except one: Holmes.

It appears that before white arrival this section of the main Eel belonged to a branch of the Sinkyone tribe known as the Lolahnkoks, whose territory probably ranged on the main Eel from Scotia to Dyerville and then up the South Fork to include the drainage of Bull Creek.[653] The Lolahnkoks called Holmes Flat Kahs-tes-be,[654] while the Wiyots, who claimed land downriver on the Eel,[655] referred to the flat as Mat-teh-teh-com-ma-me. According to the Wiyot elder Amos Riley, this was as far upriver as the Wiyot language was spoken.[656] As late as the 1940s, residents of Holmes would still find Indian implements in the Eel "when the water was low."[657]

According to one report, Frank Osterlund was the first homesteader on the flat.[658] It is not known when Osterlund came nor when he went, but by 1898 the flat was owned by M. G. Shaw,[659] who subsequently sold the property to the Holmes Eureka lumber company in January 1905.[660] Holmes Eureka had incorporated in

1903 and the following year built a sawmill on the Humboldt Bay waterfront at the north end of Bucksport. At first the company logged two tracts in the Elk River drainage, but in 1905 they moved operations to what subsequently became known as Holmes Flat.[661] In 1908 the name "Holmes" appeared in a news article about activity on the flat,[662] and in 1910 it achieved formal recognition when the Holmes Post Office opened.[663]

Holmes Eureka could cut all the timber they wanted on the flat, but it would do them no good unless they were able to transport it to their mill at Bucksport. Accordingly, in June 1906 they made an agreement with the San Francisco and Northwestern Railway (SF&N), whose tracks had reached Shively across the river, to haul their logs. To connect with the SF&N, Holmes Eureka constructed a timber trestle across the Eel from "Holmes Camp," at the western end of the flat, to a point about a mile south of Shively. Upon completion of the trestle, the SF&N began running both passenger and freight trains to a brand-new station at Holmes. Later that year the SF&N was transformed into the North-western Pacific Railway (NWP).[664] The arrangement between Holmes Eureka and the NWP was uncommon; seldom did a logging railroad also serve as a common carrier.[665] In addition, the Pacific Lumber Company (PL) shared use of the Holmes Eureka spur line, using it to transport logs cut at Camp 3 on Chadd Creek, southwest of Holmes.[666] Between 1908 and 1912, travelers from Humboldt Bay could take the NWP to Holmes and there transfer to Fred

A steam donkey powers a pile driver as Holmes Eureka builds its
annual trestle across the Eel (HCHS, colorized by JR).

Smythe's auto stage, which would carry them south to Sherwood, in Mendocino County, where they could connect with the southern end of the uncompleted railroad.[667] Each winter the frolicsome Eel washed away that year's trestle, so Holmes Eureka had to rebuild it four times before their logging on Holmes Flat was completed.[668]

There were no railings on the trestle, but there were 13[669] saloons in nearby Shively, and members of the Holmes Eureka logging crew "weren't hesitant about taking advantage of the trestle to take in the nightly activities if they missed the work train that came and went each day."[670] In October 1910, the trestle traipsing came to an end. Holmes Eureka had finished logging the flat and closed their camp;

they would not rebuild the trestle following the annual winter washout, and the NWP ceased using it on October 15.[671]

Holmes Eureka may have taken most of the redwood from the Holmes area but they didn't take it all. In 1912 George Young, who owned a store in Pepperwood, formed a partnership with Eureka under-sheriff John Helms and opened the Happy Camp Shingle Mill Company at Holmes. Both men owned timberland in the area; Helms held a parcel high on the hill south of Holmes. The mill could produce 100,000 shingles per day.[672]

Redwood logs, shingle bolts, and . . . farming. Holmes Flat proved usable, and valuable, thrice over. Having finished cutting the flat, Holmes Eureka formed an investment company, had the flat surveyed, and subdivided it into 43 lots that ranged from three to eleven acres in size.[673] Most of these were arranged on either side of what became Holmes Flat Road, which ran predominantly on an east-west axis through the flat.[674] It probably followed the spur line of the former railroad, which had been gradually extended east from Holmes Station to keep up with the timber cutting.[675]

The lots contained land that was exceptionally fertile. The redwood forest on the flat was described as having been

> . . . very dense, with many acres bearing more than a million feet board measure of timber, Humboldt Scale, which is truly exceptional. Old timers familiar with this logging operation and with the resultant stumps, say there were many giant trees on Holmes Flat, some probably taller than the identified and highly publicized trees in today's [1988] parks.[676]

The magnitude of the Holmes Flat redwoods is illustrated by a photo from 1932, which shows a 21-foot-diameter stump on Victor Reback's poultry ranch. The relic is apparently the remnant of a legendary redwood that was over 1,300 years old when cut in the spring of 1909. It required 15 or 16 forty-foot railcars to transport the top 300 feet of the tree, which scaled at 130,000 board feet.[677] Left behind was enough wood "to make 19 cords of shingle bolt material."[678]

This certainly was legendary land for growing redwoods, but the process was slow, and to replenish the flat with full-sized trees would take centuries. Thus the plan to subdivide. Holmes Eureka sold off its stump fields to provide the company with quick cash while it went off to other parts of its old-growth timber holdings to cut. Thus,

> Holmes Flat . . . [became] one of the few instances in the redwood region where

The Holmes Eureka lumber camp (FMC, colorized by JR).

In 1932, squatters have taken over Victor Reback's redwood stump (FMC, colorized by JR).

the stumps were removed and the land converted to general farming, and later to truck gardening.[679]

In 1908 the Holmes school was built on what became Lot A of the post-logging subdivision, replacing a temporary building erected a year earlier.[680] The schoolhouse was located a short distance from the Eel, and "on hot summer-like days school was sometimes held under the trees on the bank of the river."[681] Atop the schoolhouse was a deeply discounted bell. It had originally been one of two sent to the Port Kenyon school, which of course needed only one of them. Although the bells cost $90 apiece, the Port Kenyon trustees offered the second one for $45, whereupon the Holmes trustees purchased it.[682]

Holmes Eureka had operated a company store on the flat while it was logging there. It was located in a swampy area, so the store had been elevated by building it on top of old stumps.[683] By 1912 the Holmes store, perhaps by now a different structure, was run by Obadiah Cyrus Hooper, who was also the postmaster. Hooper lived with his aged mother, Mary, who had the distinction of being "the first white child born on Illinois [Oregon] river." For his part, Obadiah gained limited distinction by becoming a Socialist and a member of the Woodmen of the World.[684]

John Hoffman was "the first rancher to improve property at . . . [Holmes] and make a home there." Taking advantage of the rich riverside soil that had formerly produced mammoth redwoods, Hoffman annually harvested five crops of alfalfa—without having to irrigate. He also took advantage of the redwood remnants on his 40-acre tract, hollowing out one "great redwood stump" and converting it to a cellar and storehouse. Another stump, some 20 feet high, was "mounted with a windmill and reservoir and makes a splendid tower." In such ways Hoffman "utilized the natural resources of the place . . . as to combine beauty and utility in a striking manner."[685]

Ed Ogle established a second shingle mill on the flat at an unknown date, and a man named McIntyre put in a third. Robert Lee Cathey operated a blacksmith shop next to one of the mills. Near the school lived "an old man with white hair and flowing white beard," who made violins for the school children, who in turn would "coax him to play for them."[686]

By 1922 Holmes had between one and three connections with the outside world, depending on the season. Just past the school, Holmes Flat Road bent south, crossed Chadd Creek, and promptly met the Redwood Highway. A

half-mile west of the school, a summer crossing of the Eel led to the southern end of Shively and the NWP. East of Holmes Flat, another summer crossing led to the tiny community of Larabee, the NWP, and Bryan's Rest, a popular resort next to the railroad.[687]

Charles Gragg formed a partnership with Bryant Sappingfield, an expert at truck gardening, and the pair produced notable produce. Gragg's Gravenstein apples grew to have a reputation as "some of the county's finest," and for a time Gragg was known as "the community's tomato king."[688] Then Sam and Rose Stockton arrived in 1937, purchasing the Bradbury ranch with its 20 apple trees. Sam soon offered both fresh apples and cider. Stockton also engaged in truck farming, as he and his family withstood both the 1955 and 1964 floods. By the time of his death in 1983, Stockton had increased his orchard to 270 apple trees. His son Dave continued to maintain the orchard after Sam's death.[689]

A sure sign of agricultural success was the establishment of the Holmes Grange in 1933. It

This may have once been Cathey's blacksmith shop, but at the time of the photo G. W. Hughes owned it (CPH, colorized by JR).

first met in the old Holmes Eureka cookhouse but in the late 1940s moved into a freshly built building. By then, improved auto travel had caused the Holmes stores to close, as locals went to Redcrest, Pepperwood, or Scotia to shop. The post office remained, however. Apples, pears, and cherries were major fruit crops, and both vegetable growing and dairy ranching added to the area's agricultural output. Less practical, but extremely pleasing, were the many flower gardens that abounded in the area. In 1949 *Humboldt Times* reporter Chet Schwarzkopf noted all this in one of his weekly accounts, likening the area to "one big park," claiming that "fortunate are the people who can make their home here, for at their beck and call is nature in her most benevolent mood."[690]

Schwarzkopf may have been correct about the present, but he was no predictor of the future. The 1955 flood brought one and a half feet of water into Sam and Rose Stockton's house, an annoyance that did little other damage. The 1964 flood, however, covered the property with 12 feet of the Eel and lifted the house, which Rose had designed, off its foundation, rendering it uninhabitable.[691] It was perhaps no coincidence that seven months after the flood, the postal service closed its office at Holmes, merging it with the office at higher-elevation Redcrest,[692] where the mail was much less likely to get wet.

Nowadays the community is without any businesses or public buildings. The flat, its redwoods long gone, is dotted with numerous dwellings that are often surrounded by small pieces of pastureland. Now what one mainly sees are the homes of Holmes.

Chapter 13

Shively

Shively is a secluded community. . . .

Chet Schwarzkopf[693]

Bill Shively and his brother, James, settled in Humboldt County in 1853 on the hillside west of Eagle Prairie.[694] In 1860, following a massacre of Indians "above" the prairie (probably at the site of Scotia), Bill Shively participated in a "round-up" of some of the survivors, who were taken to an unspecified reservation.[695] Several years later Bill and his family were "burned out" by Indians, but according to his daughter Abbie, "father made his peace with them and raised two Indian boys, Budds and Ben. . . ."[696] A few years passed, and then in 1869, Bill, accompanied by Budds (whose first name was Charley[697]) and Ben (whose last name is unknown), went up the Eel to hunt and fish. Several miles upriver they came to a large flat on the northeastern side of the Eel that caught Shively's attention. According to Verna Holmes, his granddaughter, Shively

> . . . was greatly impressed, as anyone is today who looks at the location. . . . It was swarming with all kinds of wild game—deer, elk, bear and birds. He was the first white man to see the place. When he came home he told . . . [his wife Carrie] "I have found paradise. We will move there."

Not so fast, Bill, said Carrie, in effect. Negotiations ensued, and Carrie agreed to the family's migration only upon the condition that Bill return her to Rio Dell once they had "proved up"[698] the place at Shively. Five years passed, the property became theirs, and Carrie exercised her prerogative to change her mind: "We won't go home," she stated. "This place is home now."[699]

By then the family's homestead already basked in a glowing reputation. In 1873 a visitor had reported that Bill Shively's

> . . . productive farm enables him to supply the delicate appetites of Eureka with splendid peaches, melons, tomatoes, sweet potatoes and many other edibles.[700]

The area where the Shivelys provided for Eurekans' "delicate appetites" had earlier been the site of an Indian village called Lah-sa-se-ta,[701] but now the locale was being called Bluff Prairie,[702] after a pair of notable features: the open flat that Bill Shively called "paradise" and, just to the northwest, a dramatic bluff that dropped several hundred feet to the Eel River. The same year the Shivelys moved to the prairie, the government surveyor noted its most paradisiacal feature—"land soil 1st rate."[703] The point bar that had developed southeast of the bluff was, as usual with such features, filled with nutrient-rich alluvium.

Other families joined the Shivelys on the fertile flat. Enough of them had arrived by 1874 that the first Bluff Prairie School opened. Over the next hundred years, the school would be housed in four different buildings.[704]

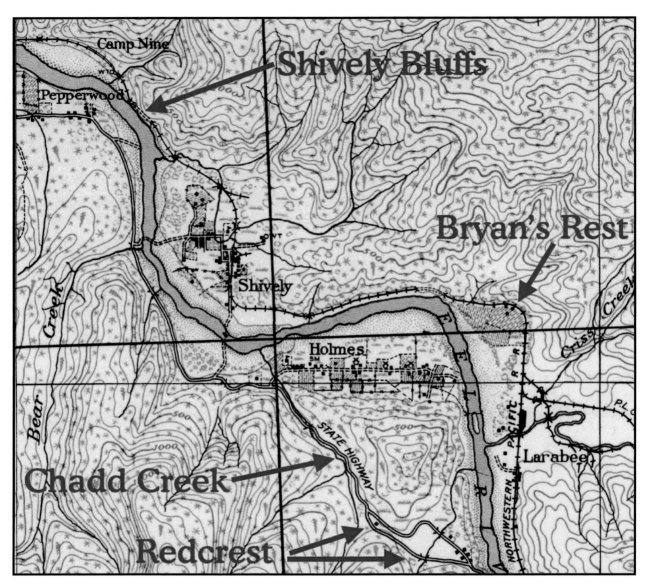

Shively – Holmes area, 1916 (CE)

There may have been an increasing quantity of people and produce on the flat, but growth was hampered by its location. It lay on the east side of the Eel, which by 1877 put the river between it and the area's only thoroughfare, the West Side Road.[705] This route passed through nearby Pepperwood, but the connection from there to Bluff Prairie required either fording the Eel or using the Pepperwood-Shively ferry. (See sidebar 1.)

Bill Shively and an associate named White-horse had built the section of the West Side

Road opposite Bluff Prairie. County surveyor Rufus Herrick inspected their work in August 1877 and found they had created "a splendid road, and that instead of confining themselves to specifications [they] have tried to see how good a road they could build."[706] Herrick's wife, Martha, echoed Rufus's evaluation, indicating that the road was "wider and far better done than the contract calls for, and a road that will stand." Martha, doyenne of the lower Eel, also examined Shively's ranch. She was again impressed:

1. The 50¢ Nighttime Ferry

Of the many ferries that once spanned the rivers of Humboldt County, few were as essential as the one that connected Pepperwood with Shively. The latter location, on the flat called Bluff Prairie, was, in fact, hemmed in by two stretches of nearly vertical cliffs that were high, wide, and frustrating: the Shively Bluff just downriver and Bryan's Bluff a short distance upriver. These massive rock outcroppings prevented riverside travel to and from the prairie, so that crossing the Eel was the only practical way to gain access.

At low water people could walk across the river on a summer footbridge, or they could ride or drive on the sandy river bottom and splash across the wet spots. But when the water was up, they needed the Shively Ferry. Its first operators were all connected with the namesake family. There was William B. Shively himself, his stepson Charley Winemiller, and Charley Budds, one of the two Indians that Shively had brought with him from Rio Dell. Budds even exceeded his responsibilities as ferry keeper, for he would take children to school by boat or canoe when necessary and at other times would walk with them over the summer bridge.[707] Once when high water floated his boat away from shore, Budds swam to the wayward vessel and brought it back.[708]

In 1915 Humboldt County took over operation of the ferry, buying it from Bud Coleman for $400. About then the ferry was moved upriver from its site near the south end of Pepperwood to a spot just north of the mouth of Bear Creek.[709] A century later, traces of the approach road to the latter location could still be found next to the Avenue of the Giants.[710]

The ferry operated from 6 A.M. to 6 P.M. The other half of the day its use was up to the ferryman: if he chose to make a trip then, it cost 50 cents.[711] A full load was a group of passengers and a four-horse team and wagon or, in later years, three autos or a heavy truck and one car. The latter allotment was in place on February 13, 1932,[712] when the ferry broke loose from its cable and sank. The passengers all reached shore safely, but a Standard Oil Company truck and Bud Coleman's auto went into the Eel when the runaway ferry hit some bridge pilings a short distance downriver.[713]

On another occasion, the ferry took a longer impromptu trip, floating all the way to Fortuna. It was brought back upriver by an arduous process: several men in a small boat attached a rope to the ferry, rowed upstream with the other end of the rope, tied it around a tree or some brush, and then pulled on the rope until they had hauled the ferry up to their location. Then

A sign by the Bear Creek bridge states: "One
Mile to Shively Depot" (HCHS, colorized by JR)

the process was repeated, time and again, until the men, boat, rope, and ferry
all reached Shively, more or less simultaneously. It was a three-week job.[714]

The county eventually replaced the winter ferry with a 24-foot rowboat
and later replaced the oars with a 35-horsepower motor.[715] The boat carried
no life jackets. It transported workers, students, hound dogs, and up to "25
cans full of milk." The motor sometimes stopped running, which created
a bit of excitement, but the most dramatic event occurred back in the
rowboat days when an exceptionally strong current took Gilbert "Dooley"[716]
Robinson and his load of milk up against the partially submerged summer
bridge. Dooley nimbly hopped onto the bridge, but the current sucked the
boat under the structure,[717] which may have curdled the milk.

A "low-level" bridge was built across the Eel in 1939; it was supposed to
connect Shively with Pepperwood "year around."[718] This hope, however, proved
overly optimistic, for the bridge "usually was submerged from roughly the first
of November to the middle of May."[719] Even this limited use was eliminated in
January 1948 when a flood swept away 135 feet of the 800-foot structure, along
with the Holmes-Larabee bridge a few miles upriver. The county responded by
providing a 14-foot motorboat that temporarily took over transport, carrying
an average of 50 people per day between Shively and Pepperwood.[720]

By February 1949 the summer bridge had been repaired, but it was still subject to the caprices of the river. Late that month Jack Desmond, a welder for the Northwestern Pacific Railroad, attempted to walk from Shively to Pepperwood across the bridge. It was a bad idea; water was rushing over the top of the bridge, and when Desmond was about halfway across, he was swept into the Eel.[721]

The bridge had proved costlier than the 50 cent ferry.

It is located in a beautiful little valley. Strawberries were abundant, and plums were dropping from the trees. . . . Here I looked at the largest tomato patch I ever saw, and the fruit getting ripe. There will be a bountiful supply of watermelons in their season. . . ."[722]

By 1885 the Shivelys had been on their farm for 16 years. The *Humboldt Standard* reported on the result:

Mr. Shively . . . owns over 182 acres, 120 being redwood timber, the balance open and tillable. At present there are under cultivation 45 acres, principally in corn and small grain. Mr. Shively has paid special attention to cultivating fruit, and his orchard of six acres brings him more clear money than all the balance of the farm. Apples, he claims, are the most profitable to raise. As to varieties, he prefers the King of Tompkins County, Yellow Bell Flower, Rhode Island Greening, Baldwin, Newton pippin and Ben Davis. In the orchard are a great variety of plums, cherries, peaches and nuts, but for profit apples surpass all. They bring a sure crop and have a ready sale.[723]

The Pacific Lumber Company (PL) owned much of the land along the Eel immediately upriver from its headquarters at Scotia. By 1892 its rail line had reached Camp Five, later to be known as Elinor, about four miles downriver from Shively.[724] For several years PL busied itself logging its nearby forests; the company was not eager to extend its rail line upriver, since just beyond Camp Five the right-of-way was disrupted by the Shively Bluff and tunneling through it would be expensive. Then, in 1903, the San Francisco and Northwestern Railway (SF&N), precursor to the Northwestern Pacific, purchased PL's railroad.[725] The following year the SF&N built the necessary tunnel through the Shively Bluff.[726] It was 1,019.4 feet long[727] and opened the way to Bluff Prairie.

Change ensued. According to one report:

Bill Shively sold his extensive timber holdings to The Pacific Lumber Company . . . and the railroad was built into town. Then began the community's heyday. Several hotels were built, . . . a race track was built, and the town staged rodeos, fairs, races, and dances. Logging lasted for over a decade, and it brought money and people into Shively. . . .[728]

In the midst of all this activity, a post office bearing the name of Shively was established in March 1906.[729] But greater excitement was to come. (See sidebar 2.)

Shively Tunnel under construction, 1910 (HCHS, colorized by JR)

2. Sumner Bump's Satirical Summary: Stud Poker, Prostitutes, and the *Poison Oak*

As the railroad built up the Eel, Shively for a time became the center of construction activity. Contractors Klippel and McLean were slated to create 16 miles of railbed, but the going wasn't easy. Klippel soon left for a tuberculosis sanitarium, never to return, and McLean seemed hard pressed to carry on without him. The struggling operation hired an engineer, engagingly named Sumner Bump, who fortunately decided to chronicle the company's flirtation with chaos.[730] Decades later, folklorist-newspaperman Andy Genzoli retold Bump's tale, perhaps adding some of his characteristic embellishments.

Bump found the work camp to be "a helter-skelter set of cabins," the most tumultuous of which was the cook shack. No one ever knew what to expect for meals, for "it was all according to the whim and sobriety of the head cook." If he'd gotten hold of a bottle of whiskey, the result was a plate of "hard, uncooked" beans, and then "all hell broke loose." It was no wonder the workers sought succor at nearby Shively, which Bump described in some detail:

Shively was a town of a few houses, a two-story hotel with 12 bedrooms and thin walls, a dining room to seat 40, a small lobby and a large saloon. Gambling was wide open with solo the favorite four-handed. Draw and stud poker were for the laborers and the suckers.[731]

Railbed-making equipment was basic: "a team and horses, a scraper, or a heavy shovel wielded by a strong-backed worker. . . ." The work gangs were a mixture of Swedes, Spaniards, Italians, and Poles—few of whom spoke much English. They were paid for each 200 feet of work completed, "or on a performance basis." Payday brought a two- or three-day halt to all work, since it was then that

. . . a box car of prostitutes arrived from Eureka to cash in on the lonely workers. A pimp stood by taking care of the cash, and when the work was over, the box car quietly left the scene. In the days after pay day it was a time for a roaring drunk.[732]

Shively, 1911; the church was not the most frequented
building in town (CHP, colorized by JR)

The workers were not McLean's only problem. The company had purchased 60 mules from the Bartlett Springs Water Company to carry supplies, but "the mules fell by the way, when their legs and bellies became infected by [contact with] poison oak." Another system of transport was needed, and this was found, McLean hoped, in a custom-built paddle-wheel boat. Appropriately, McLean dubbed her the *Poison Oak*.[733]

She was the size of a large house, 30 by 84 feet, and was built by Ed Pettengill in Eureka, with A. D. Nash serving as supervising engineer. She was powered by a 75-horsepower gasoline engine that weighed half as much as the boat. A skipper from Sacramento, Captain Joshua Elder, was hired as master of the *Poison Oak*.[734]

Elder's crew came on board straight from a four-day drinking binge in Eureka. Still bleary eyed, they proceeded to tune up the *Poison Oak's* "ear-splitting engine, putting the steering ropes on the steering wheel" in the pilot house, and "adjusting the paddle wheel for balance and weight."[735] Each of these tasks required a certain amount of attentiveness to be successfully completed. The crew, moving from job to job, staggered along the deck.

Work was interrupted while the workers disputed with Captain Elder about the fate of a case of whiskey. Bump reported that "the captain won the argument, but only for a short time." In addition to the contested crate of alcohol, the *Poison Oak* was loaded with gasoline, blasting powder, hay, and food. The supplies were scattered about the deck; nothing was tied down since the boat's maiden voyage was expected to be a placid trip.[736]

It was time for the *Poison Oak* to leave port. A. D. Nash cracked a bottle of Eel River water over the boat's prow, the mooring lines were loosened and brought aboard, the huge engine roared to life, and Captain Elder shouted a barrage of orders that couldn't be heard by the bleary-eyed crew.[737]

The *Poison Oak* moved away from shore. Elder swung the wheel, first to starboard, then to port. Neither maneuver affected the course of the boat. The hungover crew had attached the steering ropes incorrectly, leaving the *Poison Oak's* rudder with no connection to the helm.[738]

Now the Eel's current became apparent, as it caught the *Poison Oak* and began to carry her downriver at a leisurely but steady pace. Elder swore at the crew, but his imprecations were swallowed up by the pounding howl of the useless engine. He watched helplessly as the boat floated past Pepperwood, past Elinor, and onward down the river. Somewhere in the vicinity of Scotia, the hull of the *Poison Oak* scraped across a sand bar and then lodged upon it. As she settled, her deck tilted at a noticeable angle. Elder watched, dumbfounded, while the *Poison Oak's* cargo gently slid into the Eel.[739]

The *Poison Oak* rests after its first voyage (CPH, colorized by JR)

As McLean's supplies bobbed their way down the river, Elder and his mate, accompanied by Bump, went ashore and began the long walk back to Shively. Bump at this point lost track of the crew, but he kept an eye on Elder and the mate, who had each managed to salvage a bottle of whiskey from the case that was on board the *Poison Oak*. The pair were both angry, and they failed to offer Bump a drink, which he found to be both "unkind and cutting."[740]

The party reached Shively, where McLean, who was out thousands of dollars, was angrier than anybody. Elder and the mate quit, and for good measure McLean fired them. He also fired Elder's half-empty whiskey bottle into the bushes. Elder and the mate got their bags and departed Shively on foot. That evening, when Bump went to the company's cookhouse for dinner, he noticed that the cook was drunk. The intermittent inebriate had found Elder's whiskey and finished it.[741]

There is a fine line between persistence and stupidity, and McLean now proceeded to walk it. He acquired a flat-topped barge about a third the size of the *Poison Oak*, installed a Dolbeer steam donkey on deck, and began the second phase of his effort to successfully navigate the Eel.

McLean, sensing a progenitorial relationship between his two vessels, named the new boat the *Poison Ivy*. It became the motive power for the hapless, and heretofore helpless, *Poison Oak*. Once removed from her welcoming sand bar, the *Poison Oak* was reloaded with supplies and a cable connected between her and the *Poison Ivy*. On board the *Ivy*, the Dolbeer donkey's boiler was fired up, and the resulting steam power turned one of the two capstan spools on the donkey. Attached to this capstan was the cable connected to the *Oak*. As the capstan wound the cable up, the *Oak* was pulled upriver a thousand feet to the *Ivy*. A cable was also attached to the second capstan; this cable was taken upriver on a small boat and attached to "a stump or other solid object." Then this second cable was wound round the capstan, which activity pulled the *Ivy* up to the anchor point. Meanwhile, the cable attached to the *Oak* had been allowed to run out, which allowed the *Ivy* to begin repeating the process. Over and over this procedure was repeated, a thousand feet at a time, a little less than a mile for every five trips, mile after mile up the Eel. If the *Ivy* had been given a more powerful donkey engine, the bargelike boat could have pulled both vessels at once, but this was a McLean-run operation, and it was doomed to skirt the edge of failure with continued inefficiency.[742]

The *Oak* and *Ivy*, joined by a steel umbilical cord, ponderously crept up the Eel nine times. They only returned on eight of those occasions, for the vessels were abandoned once they, and the railroad, reached Fort Seward. But the *Poison Oak* was not done traveling. Her engine was removed and taken farther upriver to Alderpoint, where it was used to power an air compressor used in building a nearby Northwestern Pacific tunnel.[743]

By then, Sumner Bump had finished reporting on the two vessels. But earlier he had recalled one further incident involving the *Poison Oak*—and the McLean operation's cook. This person was a new entity—not the impulsive imbiber who'd found the whiskey bottle in the bushes—and she was female, wherein lies the story.[744]

It seems that McLean had persuaded the wife of one of his workers to take over the cooking duties on board the *Poison Oak*. She was apparently a good cook—and good looking. Crewmen on the *Oak* were entitled to dry out at the kitchen stove if they fell overboard, and suddenly one man was regularly splashing into the Eel, and then just as regularly going to the galley, where he stayed a long time. The cook's husband noticed the pattern and finally followed the wet worker into the galley. As Bump put it, "There was a big fight. I lost a good cook and a good oarsman."[745]

Once again, the *Poison Oak* had lived up to its irritating name.

The Pacific Lumber Company redoes the landscape
near Shively, 1908 (CHP, colorized by JR)

The Joseph and Catherine Stockel family moved onto the flat in 1901.[746] They had lived up the South Fork Eel at Phillipsville, but the Stockels sought a better educational opportunity for their children and believed they would find it at the Bluff Prairie School. Joe Stockel bought Bill Shively's house and part of his property.[747] Joe then proceeded to enlarge the town: he built several cottages that he rented "to workmen and their families," and "several store buildings." And, in either 1905[748] or 1906,[749] he erected "Stockel's Resort," a two-story hotel with its name painted in three-foot-high letters between the windows of the first and second floors.[750]

Catherine Stockel ran the resort. According to her grandson, Joe Stockel III,

She prepared and delivered a hot lunch to the woodsmen and the train crew every day. Rooms were available at the resort. For room and board, which included the delivered lunch, family style breakfast and dinner, [the cost was] fifty cents per day. The adjacent casino had a beautiful 'J'-shaped bar and several slot machines. Playing cards were stuck in the ceiling by shooters [who threw] a card toward the ceiling and [shot] it the instant it made contact with the ceiling.[751]

Dr. Eugene Falk had his first office in the Stockel Resort from 1909 to 1910. In December 1910 "he crossed the Eel River to Pepperwood when it was bank full of water to sit with

Stockel's Resort was the centerpiece of Shively (CPH, colorized by Jerry Rohde)

Beatrice Keesey's mother as one of her infant twin sons lay dying. Falk sat all night—it was all he could do—and didn't charge a cent for risking his life.[752]

By 1915 Shively was described as having

> . . . a population of about 300 inhabitants. Logged-off lands surround the town and these are being cleared and planted to orchards and garden truck. There are a number of small Italian hotels and two others. There are a general merchandise store and several smaller stores.[753]

Besides the Stockels, other families were gaining notice. Frank and Fannie Essig ranched at the south end of town, "producing some exceptionally fine apples and making a specialty of raising tomatoes." Two of Frank's sons by a previous marriage were also involved in agriculture: Samuel was a horticultural inspector in Ventura County and Edward was a professor of entomology at University of California at Berkeley who had written *Injurious and Beneficial Insects of California*.[754]

Hitie and Rosie[755] Robinson moved to Shively in 1913, when Hitie went into partnership with the Gribble brothers, who had butchering and retail meat stores in both Fortuna and Shively. Hitie took over managing the Shively portion of the business, which also included a slaughterhouse. His son, Dooley, had started working at the slaughterhouse the previous year, even though he was only 12 at the time. Hitie had left his mark on Shively much earlier, when in 1900 he and Dan Shively had "logged off a straight west-to-east road from the river crossing to the bluffs" behind Shively.[756] Hitie was very particular about his work horses, and every six weeks he would have Martin Jackson, a blacksmith, take the ferry to Shively so that he could give the team new horseshoes.[757] Hitie would have done well to stick with his horses; while ranching in 1948, he was killed in a tractor accident.[758]

Without a family of his own, the Indian Charley Budds was reportedly treated "as a son" by Bill Shively, who provided Charley with 10 acres of land and a cabin. In addition to his jobs as ferry and canoe operator, Budds worked on the Shively ranch, befriended the local children, and did favors for the adults. On occasion, Budds would travel by trail or canoe "to get a doctor when life or death depended on it."[759] He died in March 1916 and was buried in the Shively family plot at the Bull Creek Cemetery. The *Humboldt Beacon* eulogized Budds as "one of the best Indians that ever lived in Humboldt County."[760]

Once the railroad builders moved upriver, Shively had a chance to catch its breath and calm down. For a while. Residents spent several years watching their tomatoes ripen and their corn grow tall before there was another outburst of excitement. It finally came in September 1921 when sparks from the chimney of the Cosmopolitan Hotel ignited that building and quickly spread to nearby structures. A hundred firefighters rallied to finally stop the blaze, but only after it had also destroyed the New Shively Hotel, a rooming house, and two dwellings.[761] For a time it was hard to find a place to sleep in Shively.

Nine years passed, the decade—on schedule—ended, and suddenly there were more diminishments in Shively. On March 1, 1930, the ferry's cable snapped, sending ferryman Clifford Cook

Engine 182 on its side near the Shively Tunnel, 1937 (CHP, colorized by JR)

on a half-mile midnight ride down the Eel that ended only when the gallivanting vessel crashed into the pilings of the old summer bridge. Cook was marooned until friends rescued him with a rowboat. A new cable (ferry) was immediately requested by cable (telegraph) to San Francisco.[762] Later that month, more bad news. The NWP closed its Shively train station, as an increasing number of travelers chose using the Redwood Highway instead of the railroad.[763]

The 1930s found Shively in the news because of its produce. In 1931 the *Humboldt Times* reported that "the first straight carload of Humboldt county tomatoes . . . left Shively last night on the Northwestern Pacific bound for Reno, Nevada." A full 15 tons of the "luscious" salad ingredient were on the tracks, while some 4,000 boxes had already gone to Oakland, San Francisco, Los Angeles, and other locations.[764]

On the morning of August 6, 1937, the railroad and Shively again made the news. Engineer Ed Weatherbee, at the controls of engine 182, rounded a curve north of Shively and threw on the air brakes. Ahead of him was a burning trestle at the approach to the Shively Bluff tunnel. His action came too late—the train slowed but was still rolling when the engine ran onto the trestle, which gave way under the locomotive's weight, plunging the train 50 feet downward into a ravine. Three trainmen were in the engine when it crumpled under the impact. Engineer Weatherbee and fireman Carl Bartlett were killed "as the roof of their cab was crushed like a paper bag." Brakeman C. G. Still was found severely burned but still alive and was taken to the hospital in a Scotia, where he died a short time later.[765]

By 1949 Shively's residents had settled

Shively's long-closed store in 1992 (JR)

into a sort of uneasy rustication, tending their crops and cattle or working in the woods, but also keeping an eye on the Eel, knowing that a rising river could temporarily isolate them. They agitated for an all-year bridge or hoped for a roadway that would run up the east side of the river. Their 38 elementary-age students could safely reach the big Bluff Prairie School, but high schoolers faced the problematic twice-daily passage across the river.

Officials deemed a bridge too costly. But in 1953 the county constructed what is now called Shively Road,[766] which connected with Highway 101 just north of the Stafford bridge.[767]

Shively Road, however, was slow going, and local residents formed the Shively Bridge Committee, which acted to ensure that the Shively Community Bridge, a "low-flow railcar crossing," was in place between Shively and the Avenue of the Giants for approximately four months each summer and fall.[768]

By 1949, the rip-roaring railroad town of the 1910s had seen its business district reduced to a combined store, post office, and telephone exchange.[769] Further losses were soon to come.

The 1955 flood rose to the top of the door at Rosie Robinson's house and covered much of Shively's flat in silt. The 1964 flood removed both houses and four barns on the Robinsons' farm.[770] All the other homes west of the railroad tracks were also washed out.[771]

Today a single monument commemorates the earlier days of Shively. It eloquently conveys a period of time fading into the dimmest recesses of memory, for it is the gas pump that stands in front of the long-closed store, bearing the message: "49.9¢ per gallon."

Rusticate in peace, Shively.

Chapter 14
Pepperwood

There was a place on the Eel River that the local Indians called Ahn-sing ken-tel-te, named for the tree that grew there in abundance.[772] When the whites came, they noted the groves of the same species and at first referred to the area as the Laurel Bottoms.[773] By 1887 the location had become enough of a town to warrant a post office, and—sure enough—it was given another name for the tree—Pepperwood.[774]

For a time it was a difficult-to-reach location. In 1873 a low-water travel route ran up the Eel, frequently crossing the bed of the river as it went from flat to flat. A graveled road led across the Laurel Bottoms on one such flat, passing "prairies and farms, the most noted belonging to Mr. Hazeltine,"[775] who was not himself noted enough to have his name spelled correctly: Hazelton.[776]

When the Eel rose during the rainy season, it covered the sections of the route that crossed the riverbed, isolating the residents who lived on the flats along the river. That changed in 1877, when the county completed what was formally called the "Grizzly Bluff and Camp Grant Road" but was more commonly known as the West Side Road.[777] That September, J. C. Greenlow placed an ad trumpeting "An Inviting Summer Resort!" only "40 miles from Eureka!" that was located at "Pepperwood Bottom,"[778] yet another name variation based on the presence of what botanists called *Umbellularia californica*, or California bay.[779]

Travelers on the West Side Road provided glimpses of the Laurel-Pepperwood Bottom as they passed through. In 1883 John Durst, who was going "afoot up Eel River," noted that

A forest of Pepperwoods shades the West Side Road (HCHS, colorized by JR)

Half-way up to Camp Grant we come to an extended prairie from one-half a mile to a mile in width, mostly covered with laurels—or pepper-woods, as they are called—maple and ash. A number of settlers have claimed here, and have made small clearings, on which they raise corn, peas, and potatoes, and produce vegetables, bacon, butter, and eggs—the dainties backwoodsmen may be most lavish in enjoying. There is little inducement to clear the land and cultivate, as there is no market. It is true, a light boat, or rather a large skiff, plies up and down the river at moderate stages of the water, driven by the breeze that blows up the valley in the summer, and propelled over the rapids and riffles by the aid of poles. This brings supplies and carries down butter and eggs or berries, that will not stand the rough wagon trip down. But there is and can be no extensive navigation. So far as the people here and at Camp Grant sell anything, it is fruit. Wagon-load after wagon-load of apples, pears, and peaches, of superior size and quality go down in the autumn to Eureka and Ferndale. Quite a business is done in cutting down laurel, hewing the sound trunks into square timbers a foot in diameter, and then rafting them at a moderate stage of water down the river to the coast. The lumber is susceptible of a high polish, and when landed in San Francisco brings $50 a thousand for use in making furniture.[780]

The "backwoodsmen"—and women—continued to lavishly enjoy their "dainties," but change was coming. In January 1887 there occurred that most frequent of place-name fixatives, the establishment of a post office. The name chosen was Pepperwood,[781] but earlier appellations die hard, and in announcing the event the *Ferndale Enterprise* steadfastly called the location "Pepperwood Bottom."[782]

In addition to Greenlow's "resort," which was at the west end of Pepperwood,[783] Lemuel Hazelton[784] had a stopping place as early as 1885 on his property east of Greenlow's, with a house that was "large, comfortable, and convenient."[785] And Joseph Barkdull operated the Travelers' Inn on his ranch from about 1882 until 1907[786] that was located in a clearing among the redwoods south of town.[787] Barkdull's ranch facilities "offered barns and feed for passing teams and stock on their journey from Garberville and way points to Humboldt bay."[788] In summer he had an additional "stopping place"—this one for his cattle—at Barkdull Prairie, a ridgeslope opening in the redwoods about three miles southwest of his ranch.[789] During the 1890s another Pepperwood rancher, B. A. Burley, also took in travelers,[790] but he could not offer one of the attractions his competitor did: the telephone toll station for the area was at "Barkdull."[791]

In 1904 William Lucas built a 17-room hotel in downtown Pepperwood, and for the next four years he "served acceptably" as the town's postmaster.[792] At Lucas's hotel weary travelers could recover from such thrilling but tense trips as those recalled by Marjorie Landergen:

I am not sure that "White Gravy" Snider was ever very drunk (if at all), when he pulled into Pepperwood whooping and hollering, horses at a full gallop, stage swaying and careening. It was a special thrill one of the cleverest of the old-time "knights of the ribbons" gave his passengers. They were mostly scared out of a year's growth but wouldn't have missed it for the world.[793]

Making hay on a cloudy day at Pepperwood (HCHS, colorized by JR)

Soon enough things calmed down. By 1914 White Gravy's stagecoach shenanigans were coming to an end as the Redwood Highway replaced the West Side Road as the thoroughfare through Pepperwood. The southern end of the business district started with the Lucas Hotel, located near the current trailhead for the Drury-Chaney Loop. A few hundred feet to the north was Young's Store, which by then also contained the post office and telephone station. A bit farther north, where the new highway bent to the west, was a dance hall; here the old West Side Road branched north from the highway, going past a church, and then, turning west to run next to the Eel, passed the church's antithesis, a saloon. As the new highway completed its westward bend, it passed the Pepperwood School. The highway ran beside orchards, pastures, and cultivated fields before leaving town; then it passed between lands belonging to the Metropolitan Redwood Lumber Company to the south and the Laurel Lumber Company to the north.[794] Notable among the town's buildings was Young's Store, which by then was ten years old and had recently become part of an early-day grocery chain. (See sidebar 1.)

South of town was a side road that dropped southeastward to the Eel. It led to the Shively Ferry, which provided Pepperwood with its closest link to the Northwestern Pacific (NWP) rail line. A second nearby ferry crossing was at Elinor, about two miles west of Pepperwood.[795]

When the rambling writer Delmar L. Thornbury came down the Eel on one of his early-day auto tours, he noticed the contrast between the two sides of the river near Pepperwood:

On the opposite or east bank of Eel River all of the timber has been logged for ten miles down to Scotia, but on the western side, the primeval forest stands serene. The pepperwood or California laurel is the only other forest tree, and several groves sometimes a half mile long are passed through.[796]

The Hotel Lucas, temporarily decorated with colorful bunting (HCHS, colorized by JR)

1. The Old Owner of Young's Stores

George Young was anything but that when he arrived at Pepperwood in the spring of 1903. Born in Illinois in 1844, he'd driven wagons and stages, been attacked by Indians seven times, mined in Nevada and California, and served as a theatrical agent for 12 years. He was 59 years old, had a wife and 10 children, and was now driving a wagon filled with dry goods. It was time to start yet another career—general store owner—and Young chose Pepperwood as the place to do it.[797]

On October 1 Young's Store opened on the west side of the West Side Road near the center of town. The stock of goods Young had brought with him was supplemented by fruits, vegetables, and other foods purchased from the local ranchers. A sign painted by Charley Simmons, a local resident, adorned the store's façade. The store soon "became the official location for Pepperwood's post office," and postmaster William Lucas appointed Young his deputy. Soon Young was writing A. H. Powers, a San Francisco wholesaler, ordering $600 worth of goods with which to restock. The store was a success.[798]

For the people of Pepperwood, the nearby river was both helper and harasser. When it periodically flooded its banks, the lower-lying parts of the community were inundated but Young's Store stood on an elevated spot of ground, and residents would gather there, high and relatively dry, until the surrounding waters receded. When flowing at more normal levels, the Eel was navigable by shallow-draft boats, some of which transported goods to the store. As the railroad built its way up the opposite side of the river, supplies were sometimes sent to construction crews by boat. In February 1911 the ill-fated *Poison Oak* attempted this, but ran aground on her maiden voyage.[799] The following month, little Ina Young, all of 9 years

Young and old alike gather at Young's Store (JIC, colorized by JR)

old, christened the *Pepperwood Klipper*, a small steamer that plied a section of the Eel.[800]

The *Klipper* had a further connection with the family. When it left Pepperwood on its first voyage, it carried as its cargo a load of supplies for Young's brand-new branch store, located up the main Eel at the base of the Fruitland Grade. This location, which was the site of a work camp for the Northwestern Pacific Railroad, was for a time called Young's in honor of its only business. After the railroad was pushed farther up the river, the camp closed, and so did the store.[801]

By then Young had another enterprise. He joined with Undersheriff John Helms to start the Happy Camp Shingle Mill at Holmes, which occupied the next southside flat upriver from Pepperwood. The mill manufactured shooks (panels) for fruit boxes, cutting 100,000 per day.[802]

Come 1917 and Young was short-handed. Most of the younger men were in the service, so George and his wife Camelia were left to run the Pepperwood store. They were assisted by daughter Ina, now 15, who hitched their horse Lucy to the family's wagon and made grocery deliveries. But that fall Ina moved to Fortuna to make school attendance easier. Her parents then listed the store for sale and moved to Weott, where another daughter, Nettie, and her husband, Frank Souza, had a business. It was located in a tent, and—sure enough—it was another store.[803]

But this was about to change, for the laurels that gave Pepperwood its name also gave the town an industry. In 1910 Frederick W. Georgeson, soon to become mayor of Eureka, purchased the Hazelton Ranch at the north end of Pepperwood. In addition to building "a fine two-story country residence," Georgeson also established the Laurel Lumber Company. It had both a sawmill for the laurels, "which grew in considerable abundance on the ranch," and a redwood shingle mill. John French served as the mills' operator.[804] His son Percy French[805] recalled that the mill cut one laurel "that had to about five feet [in diameter], with 80 or 90 feet of barrel (trunk) on it."[806] Navy tests conducted at Mare Island, California, in 1912 found that "Humboldt County laurel was better adapted to the needs of the Navy for blocking and the like,"[807] a reference to the wood's use for

the keel blocks upon which a ship rested while in drydock.[808] In addition, during the latter part of World War I, laurel lumber was used for the interior finish in naval vessels, with straight laurel spars serving as ships' masts.[809] Another report indicated that the versatile wood was also used in airplane construction.[810] The demand was high. By 1918 Pepperwood's namesake trees had been "logged off."[811]

Near the Laurel Lumber Company was the Georgeson Hotel, a "huge" building on the West Side Road. Desirous of protecting his property from the ravages of the Eel, Georgeson "built a system of jetties" at a cost of about $10,000.[812] Despite this prudent effort, the hotel was "taken out by the river,"[813] perhaps during the memorable 1915 flood.

The floods that frequented the community

The Georgeson Hotel seems to float upon a sea of Pepperwood grass (TGC)

did more than wash buildings downriver; they replaced the structures with deposits of nutrient-rich silt. As Pepperwoodians cleared the nearby forest, they created openings where truck farmers could plant crops in the agriculturally beneficial alluvium. The farms prospered. In September 1931 the *Humboldt Times* announced that "the first carload of Humboldt county tomatoes . . . left Shively on the Northwestern Pacific bound for Reno, Nevada." Some 15 tons of "luscious Humboldt tomatoes" from Shively and Pepperwood took to the tracks, while 4,000 boxes had recently been sent to Oakland, San Francisco, Los Angeles, and other locations.[814] In 1949 local resident Frank Johnson allowed

that "we call our crops fair to middlin' here, . . . but the rest of the world calls 'em excellent."[815]

One notable truck farmer was Albert Porter, known "for his fine sweet corn, raised without irrigation." Porter also raised a less-common crop—rocks. An "avid collector of rare minerals," some of which may have washed down the Eel," Porter supplied them to universities and museums.[816]

As the decades moved on, Pepperwood, its namesake trees long gone, continued its tradition of serving travelers. The Lucas, Barkdull, Hazelton, and Georgeson accommodations were no longer available, but during the 1920s, and on into the 1960s, motorists on the

Redwood Highway found a selection of businesses providing gas, food, lodging, and other services. Charlie Leonard sold redwood burls and various souvenirs at Leonard's Curio Shop, the Pepperwood Auto Camp provided groceries and gas, and the Wildwood Café offered "Paul Bunyan Hamburgers."[817] Carl and Aletha Van Noy operated the Tower Lodge Motel and cafe, Fred Schmidt and Charles Mills ran the Pepperwood Cottage Court,[818] and a mile west of town motorists maneuvered their cars through the "Drive-Way Stump."[819] Modern Pepperwood's past was recalled by its "trim little" schoolhouse, built in 1882.[820]

When Chet Schwarzkopf wrote of Pepperwood in 1949 for the *Humboldt Times*, his story was accompanied by several Dick Ryan photographs that depicted a place where the bustle of the Redwood Highway was tempered by surroundings of pastoral peace. Yet Frank Johnson apprised Chet of the town's more turbulent history, recalling the 1937 flood that "hit Pepperwood hard" and "was the worst since April, 1915." With good reason, Johnson concluded that "I hope never to see that again."[821]

And for six more years, no one in Pepperwood did. Although a 1951 freshet crested at 23.5 feet at Fernbridge, this was well below the 1937 mark of 25.54 feet. But then came the Christmas season of 1955, when the Eel reached 27.6 feet at Fernbridge, prompting the *Ferndale Enterprise* to run a special headline proclaiming "**WORST FLOOD!**"[822]

However, this status proved short lived. Exactly nine years later to the day, the *Humboldt Standard*, in an extra edition, proclaimed "**PEPPERWOOD WIPED OUT, OTHER TOWNS CRUSHED!!**" The "hundred-year flood" of

The rich fields of Pepperwood had a Richfield station nearby (HRSP, colorized by JR)

The 1955 flood parked houses along the Redwood Highway (CPH, colorized by JR)

1955 had been topped by the "thousand-year flood" of 1964, and no spot was harder hit than Pepperwood. Photographer Neil Hulbert observed the devastation from the air and reported,

> Pepperwood is completely gone. It's just a huge pile of debris. Houses are stacked on top of houses. The entire area is floating. Nothing is standing . . . nothing but debris."[823]

Two weeks later, Pepperwood resident Fern St. John surveyed the damage:

> Wreckage of cars, washing machines, furniture and farm equipment is everywhere visible. Houses are piled one upon another with sheds, house trailers and barns mixed in the jumble. . . . One of the finest homes at Pepperwood, . . . which was strongly built and bolted to a strong cement foundation failed to withstand the onslaught of the river. The flood of '55 only muddied it. . . . Some of the buildings remain at the Elder's Motel, but they are covered with flotsam and mud. Boehm's Cafe, and the Earl Woolley houses are gone and the large white home of the Angus Russell family somehow missed the row of redwood bordering the St. John place and drifted down to sit topsy-turvy on the Elder's motel buildings.[824]

Pepperwood lost more than buildings. Five people, trapped in the Tower Auto Court, were killed. (See sidebar 2.)

2. One Flood Too Many

For Albert Porter, corn grower and rock collector, the 1964 flood struck with especially tragic force. Porter described what happened to the *Humboldt Times*:

I waited until they cleared off the road. A bulldozer finally did the job. Then I rode up to Pepperwood on a road grader.

The driver and another fella and I were the first back into town. But I wouldn't call it that anymore. Everything was gone.

The only thing left was my home. It had a frame that was bolted down to the concrete foundation. There wasn't any life excepting a chicken and a couple of ducks. We also picked up a couple of rabbits that were somehow still alive.

I stayed below when the two other fellas went up on the top floor of the Tower Auto Court, which stands where Highway 101 used to be.

That was where my wife, Florence, stayed with the four others, Mrs. Aletha Van Noy, Les and Regina Brueck and the Brueck's invalid son, Kelly. She would have been all right if she had stayed with me in the boat, while I rescued those others.

There were two men I took out in the early morning Wednesday. They were staying at the auto court. . . .

But my wife was just horror-stricken. I told her to stay with me in the boat but she just wouldn't do it.

When I finally got the two men, the water had come up too much and I couldn't row against the current. I told the sheriff's office at two o'clock in the afternoon that there were only about two or three hours to save them.

But there was no way. The helicopter was someplace else. They had to be left to perish.

Well, the water went over the top of that two-story building. The building was about 30 to 40 feet high. My wife and the four others were drowned. . . .

I couldn't go up there and I waited below while the others went up and found their bodies. I would have been able to save my wife but it wasn't possible to keep her in the boat.

This flood was worse than the one in '55 and as for me I'm through. First a flood in '37, then one in '55 and now this. That's enough.

> I came here in the 30's and helped to put Pepperwood on the map, but I'm not going to do it again.
>
> I think now I'll get a house trailer and the hell with it.
>
> I probably would have gone overboard if it hadn't been for one thing. That is my rock collection that I've collected through the years.
>
> By the looks of my home, from the outside, I'll be able to save it. Just the roof gone and I think the rocks are still there.[825]

The Millsap family, like others in Pepperwood, lost their home. But they were able to save a few possessions—in spectacular fashion. (See sidebar 3.)

Marjorie and Angus Russells' property lay in northeastern Pepperwood, between the highway and the river. In 1955 the family was trapped in their house as the floodwaters rose to a depth of 18 feet. Afterward there was a foot of mud to clean out. In 1964 the Eel rose to 30 feet, and the Russell house suddenly became photogenic.[826] It held out longer than most buildings in Pepperwood but then took off downriver, coming to rest atop a set of the Elders' motel units. The fractured house looked as if it were a new second floor of the motel, placed there by a powerful but sloppy contractor.[827]

While most of Pepperwood's population relocated after the 1964 flood, the Russells decided to stay. Angus Russell was a logger, and he knew how to operate heavy equipment. He bought a gravel truck, obtained a backhoe, and

3. "Follow That House!"

Rancher Henry Millsap was 82 when the 1964 flood hit Pepperwood. He'd lived there for 75 years and remembered the big freshet of 1915, when his mother had to be taken to safety from the upstairs window of their home. Come December 21, 1964, Henry's wife Florence left early for high ground, but Henry stayed behind, moving valuable items to the second floor and the attic. When water began coming into the house, Henry, grandson John Hower, and others took the Millsaps' livestock to higher ground on the Barkdull Ranch, south of town.

Coming back from the Barkdull place, Henry and John encountered Albert Porter, who told them about his wife and the others who were stranded in the Tower Auto Court. Millsap and Hower tried to reach the motel, but the current was too strong for their light motor boat. They turned back, found a phone still working, and called for help, but it was to no avail.

Let's wait to do the dishes . . . (HCHS, colorized by JR)

But Millsap and Hower could still reach the Millsap house. About three o'clock the next morning, they went there with some others in a convoy that included the motor boat and four rowboats. They found that the water had risen to the fifth step from the top of the stairway. After changing into some dry clothing, they left, going through the same window Henry's mother had 49 years earlier.

After daybreak, Millsap and Hower decided to return to the house yet again. As they approached, Hower told Millsap that the house appeared to be in motion. Millsap strained his 82-year-old eyes to see what Hower meant. After a moment he shouted, "By golly John, it is moving and I've got some stuff in that house I don't want to lose."

The race was on. Millsap gunned the boat's engine as he began to chase his runaway house. As soon as they caught up, Hower launched himself through the upstairs window. Soon he was pitching out items into the boat: Henry's guns, riding boots, spurs, even a mattress and some bedding. Hower again exited through the upstairs window and, back in the boat, watched as the Millsap's house was caught by the current and washed out of sight.[828]

It was the first and only race between a house and boat in Humboldt County history. And, even though the house eventually took the lead, it never reached the winner's circle.

proceeded to recontour his property, creating a small but sufficient hill on his previously flat land. Upon this he put his new house.[829]

The plan worked. When the Eel flooded in 1986, the water came only to the base of the hill.[830] Angus Russell had found permanence in the flooded fluctuations of Pepperwood.

But not many others did. The Pepperwood business district was never rebuilt beyond a scattering of seasonal produce stands that dotted the former highway, which had attained scenic

bypass status as the Avenue of the Giants when U. S. 101 was converted to freeway. Now Pepperwood's big attraction was not produce but prodigious redwoods, a long section of which lay south of town and became part of Humboldt Redwoods State Park. Tourists and local tree lovers could hike the Drury-Chaney Grove, named for two luminaries in the Save the Redwoods League. They would pass under 300-foot-tall *Sequoia sempervirens* and sun-starved California laurels that languished in

The "Drive Way Stump" showed that more than pepperwoods were once cut in Pepperwood (JRC)

the understory, their thin trunks arching delicately over the trail. Or hikers could explore the French Grove, a half mile to the south, where the trunks of redwoods at the trailhead bear the gray staining of Eel River mud, a decoration from the 1964 flood that rises some 20 feet above ground level.

In scenes such as these, it is apparent that nature, batting last, has staged a late-inning rally against the transitory trappings of civilization, erasing the man-made markings that once constituted a town. Now the forest, and the ferns, and the flowers predominate, for the power of the river has said "no" to progress, and reverted the landscape to an earlier, less-populated, but lovelier time.

Chapter 15
Elinor

Elinor, too, was deeply afflicted.

- Jane Austen, *Sense and Sensibility*

There were two Elinors. To get from one to the other sometimes required traveling only a few hundred feet, but at other times making the trip was nigh impossible. This was because the northern part of Elinor was separated from the southern part by the Eel River, whose water flow sometimes prevented travel between the two. When a bridge finally spanned the Eel near Elinor, it still failed to solve the problem, since it was merely a temporary railroad trestle used by the logging trains of the Pacific Lumber Company (PL). "South" Elinor, often the victim of a fluviatile fate, was finally finished off by the 1955 flood.

"North" Elinor nestled in the transitory PL forest (JIC, colorized by JR).

"North" Elinor started as PL's Camp Five, located on an accommodating river bar on the north side of the Eel.[831] In 1885 PL built a rail line northward from its mill site at Scotia; it went to Alton, where it connected with the Eel River & Eureka Railroad.[832] PL's timberlands lay in the opposite direction, however, lining both sides of the Eel upriver from Scotia. To reach their forest, PL began laying track up the Eel, reaching a flat northwest and across the river from Pepperwood in 1892.[833] This became the site for Camp Five.[834]

From Camp Five a short road led down to the Eel, where in wintertime a ferry, first operated by Jerry Meakin, transported travelers across the river.[835] In summertime horses and horse-drawn vehicles could splash across. If at any time of the year the river became too rambunctious, crossing halted. This short but un-

reliable route connected the railroad at Camp Five with the West Side Road, which ran from Grizzly Bluff to Camp Grant. Residents from southern Humboldt would come north by stage or wagon, often bringing produce or other goods to sell. After crossing the river they would arrive at Camp Five. There they would catch the train,[836] which took them to Humboldt Bay or the lower Eel valley.

But the train was not always caught. In February 1914 Grace Johnson Baxter was returning from Bull Creek to her home in Scotia. The weather was stormy. She reached Pepperwood and got a ride across the river in Johnnie Baggett's motorboat. Baxter was wearing a hobble skirt, which slowed her walk from the riverside to the Elinor train station. Once at the station, she learned that a landslide had blocked the tracks and there was no train to

Splashing across the summertime Eel (CPH, colorized by JR).

Scotia. Undaunted, Baxter set off for home on foot. It was an eight-mile hike in the rain, made seemingly longer because her hobble skirt forced her to mince along the ties with the smallest of steps.[837]

In 1903 PL's rail line was purchased by the San Francisco & Northwestern Railroad, a precursor to the Northwestern Pacific (NWP).[838] The train stop at Camp Five was no longer directly linked to PL, and in time the name of the station was changed to Elinor. There are at least three stories as to how this occurred, but the most plausible one indicates that uxorious station agent Tom Flemming named the place for his wife.[839]

Joseph E. Hodgson had received a bachelor's degree from Pacific Methodist College and then taught school for 22 years. Ending his pedagogic pursuits, Hodgson took over the Elinor train station. In 1910 he campaigned for the office of Humboldt County Treasurer and was elected. He was reelected without opposition in 1914.[840] Elinor had proved to be but a brief stop on Hodgson's track to success.

Camp Five/Elinor had few trappings of a community. Besides the train station, there were four houses and a hotel. The latter was a sort of glorified bunkhouse that also served meals.[841] Most of the patrons were PL workers who were logging in the nearby woods.

Angelina Di Basilio ran the hotel. She also did the cooking and in her spare time laundered the men's clothes. While at Camp 5 a daughter, Julia, was born. Julia apparently observed her mother closely, for in 1933 the daughter went to work at—where else?—Bertain's Scotia laundry. There she remained for nine years until one day, on her lunch break, she went to PL's em-

ployment office and hired on as a worker at the mill. She walked to the Scotia store, bought some jeans and a pair of gloves, and went to her new job, missing only two hours of work.[842]

In either 1941 or 1942 PL built a spur line south from the NWP tracks near the Elinor station, put a trestle across the Eel, and ran a route up Jordan Creek to a point just south of today's 101 freeway. From there the tracks turned east, first to Greenlow Creek and then on to a terminus near the mouth of Bear Creek. The spot where the spur line branched off from the NWP's main line was called Elinor Junction.[843]

On the south side of the Eel, a short distance east of Jordan Creek, was "South" Elinor. It was located on a dead-end road that branched off the West Side Road and ran northeastward towards the Eel. The tiny community consisted of five ranches and the Elinor School, which was built in 1912.[844]

Elinor was bucolically depicted by *Humboldt Times* reporter Chet Schwarzkopf in 1949:

> Several comfortable ranch homes, togeth-
> er with rolling fields, give this section an
> appearance of peace and plenty. And right
> in the middle of it, you find the Elinor
> school. Twenty-two fortunate youngsters
> attend there, under the kindly supervi-
> sion of Mrs. Rita Hopper, while across
> the road, Eel river beckons the budding
> nimrod[845] to try his luck after studies are
> done.[846]

The "peace and plenty" seen by Schwarzkopf lasted a little more than six years. Then the "peace" vanished, although there was still "plenty"—of water. (See sidebar 1.)

Bringing out the cut from Jordan creek, 1959 (CSP. Colorized by JR).

1. Nevermore Elinor

Among the 22 students attending the Elinor School in 1949 was 8-year-old Joann Smith, whose family had taken over a 24-acre dairy farm near the school two years earlier. Within the year, Joann would be attending school in Scotia, because its district had consolidated with the Elinor and Stafford districts. And within six years, Joann would be a temporary resident of Scotia because her family's home at Elinor had floated down the Eel.[847]

For a youngster, Elinor was an exciting, if somewhat primitive, place. Joann and her siblings could play in the loose hay in the barn; they could weed the beet field and receive 75 cents for each row they weeded; when the corn was high, the kids could hide among the stalks. At canning time they helped put up a hundred quarts each of cherries, apples, and walnuts. Home-raised chickens and rabbits provided protein. Food that the Smiths didn't grow themselves had to be purchased in Scotia, six miles away. It was also where they went to make phone calls until service finally reached Elinor in the mid-1950s.[848]

It was the radio, not the phone, that Joann's parents, Ivan and Clara Smith, listened to on the night of December 21, 1955. There had been a week of heavy rain, followed by a letup earlier that day. Then the wind rose, and with it came a new storm. The Smiths wanted to keep track of the downpour, since the river might rise enough to force them to take their dairy cows to higher ground.[849]

But about midnight the power went out. The Smiths had no way of knowing that upriver at Alderpoint, some three-and-a-half inches of rain had fallen that day, while farther up the drainage, at Dos Rios, the total was six inches. Soon all of that water would be coming down the Eel past—and through—Elinor.[850]

With the radio out, Ivan and Clara Smith decided to go to bed. Just then, their neighbor, John Smith (no relation), drove into their yard. This prompted Ivan Smith to go out and check the height of the river. He found that it had come up over Elinor Road, which meant that none of them could

Perhaps anticipating the 1955 flood, the Greenlow family finds "high ground" on a convenient stump (HCHS, colorized by JR).

get out of Elinor by car. John Smith went back and brought his family to Ivan and Clara's, where he thought they would be safer than at their own place. Meanwhile, Ivan let his cows and hogs loose, hoping they would head to high ground. The hogs had other ideas. First they rooted around in some sacks of potatoes, and then they tore up the Smith's front lawn. It would prove to be the hogs' last supper.[851]

Jim and Dorothy Luzzi had a large two-story house just to the west of Ivan and Clara's place. Some of the children from both Smith families were taken there, since it was thought to afford more protection from the escalating flood. Ivan and Clara's daughter Darlene stayed with her parents, however, and when dark water began gurgling into their house about dawn, she climbed onto a chair and cried, "Mommy, don't let the water come in!"[852]

But Clara Smith could not comply with her daughter's request. The Smiths had a small boat tied to the back of the back door. They boarded it, grabbing their dog, while Darlene clutched her white Bible, and they headed for high ground. As they left, a house from upriver floated past them.[853]

The Smiths reached an elevated area, where the Luzzi family and the rest of the Smiths had found temporary refuge. As most members of the families headed downriver by pickup truck, Ivan Smith and Jim Luzzi went back towards Elinor in Ivan's boat. They wanted to check on the Joe Mello family, who lived on the upriver side of the Elinor School. The Mellos' house had floated off earlier, and Jim and Ivan were afraid that the family was trapped in it.[854]

Instead, they found the Mellos gathered in their barn. Mrs. Mello had not left their house unprepared. She had brought a cake and an electric percolator with her, but with the power out, only the former was of any use. Smith and Luzzi now plucked the coffeeless Mellos from their barn roof.[855]

That left one Elinor family unaccounted for. Alice and Jim Mortenson lived just west of the Elinor School with Alice's elderly mother, Lucy Barlow. Alice had moved to Elinor in 1909, when she was 3 years old. During the 46 intervening years, she had witnessed only one startling event: the flight of a zeppelin over Elinor that Alice had photographed in July 1932. Now, in a single night, she was having a lifetime of excitement.[856]

Earlier her husband Jim had gone to the barn and brought in his carpentry tools. He could later recall no reason for doing so, but it was good that he did. Jim had also tied a small boat to the back door as a precaution, but when he went to ready it, he found that the rising floodwater was pressing against the door and he could not open it. Instead, the Mortensons decided to seek refuge in their attic.[857]

To their dismay, Jim and Alice discovered that Lucy Barlow could not negotiate the steep stairs. It was then that Jim realized the wisdom of having retrieved his toolbox. Taking out his saw, he cut a hole in the bedroom ceiling. Jim and Alice then managed to lift Lucy up onto the bedroom dresser, and they then were able to reach through the hole in the ceiling and pull her into the attic. Moments later, the floodwater carried the dresser away.[858]

Now Jim again brought his tools into action, cutting a hole in the attic ceiling that gave them access to the roof. There they sat until John Smith came by in his boat and plucked them from their impromptu perch.[859]

Meanwhile, Dorothy Luzzi and Clara Smith left for Rio Dell, where most of their children had been sent. It took a combination of boat and truck rides to get them to town. Once there, they at first couldn't find their children, but the kids were eventually located at the Scotia Inn. Everyone went to Dorothy's sister-in-law's house, which was located just below the PL log pond. The ten children slept crosswise, five to a bed, while the mothers listened to the logs crashing above them and wondering where their husbands were and if the log pond would hold.[860]

The Elinor School waited 43 years for its trip down the Eel (colorized by JR).

The pond held, and the husbands turned up a day later after catching a ride in an army truck. They left little behind them in Elinor. The Mellos' house was gone, the Smiths' house had held out until morning before being swept away, and then the Elinor School departed.[861] Late in the afternoon the big Luzzi house finally gave up. Later, at Rio Dell, Alice Mortenson saw it floating by, and ever ready with her camera, took a picture of it.[862]

Meanwhile, Herb Thompson and Ross Ingram were stacking lumber at Scotia during the height of the flood. Herb reportedly commented that the river was "pretty high all right but not as high as it was in 1914," at which point the Elinor School, with the 1912 date above its door, floated past.[863]

The only house in Elinor left standing was the Dixon place, up near the Redwood Highway. The Mortensons took it over and gradually rebuilt their ranching operation on their old property, growing beans, cucumbers, and hay. They moved to Rohnerville a year and a half later but continued to maintain the ranch at Elinor, camping out there during the summers. In the late 1970s the Mortensons sold the ranch to the Save-the-Redwoods League as part of the continued expansion of Humboldt Redwoods State Park.[864]

In 1992 Alice Mortenson had her story of the flood published in a guidebook to the park. A few years later, after her memory failed her, an attendant at Alice's care home would read her the story, and for a few moments Alice would relive that December night and day when Elinor was washed down the Eel, gone as surely as the zeppelin that had once so briefly flown overhead.[865]

Chapter 16
Stafford

On the south side of the Eel about three miles upriver from Scotia is an inviting flat once covered with redwoods and probably at one time occupied by Athabascan-speaking Indians.[866] It was part of an area called Hah'-tin cho'-be[867] by George Burtt, a Lolahnkok Indian from Bull Creek, but nothing further is known about its ethnogeography.

The 1869 government survey of the area shows a band of pepperwood (California laurel) trees at the eastern end of the flat, near the river, with redwoods to the south. The ridge slope farther south is part of an area labeled "Rolling and Hilly Land densely covered with Valuable Timber."[868] This designation determined a long stretch of the location's future.

A writer for the *Overland Monthly*, walking on the West Side Road in the early 1880s, came upon the flat and remarked on the "Valuable Timber":

> . . . we have reached the forest in its greatest luxuriance. The road is now half the time through the gloom of the woods on the little flats between the river's edge and the mountain. We wind around and among the huge fluted columns of the redwoods, that rise in bare trunks to their tops, which a hundred and fifty feet above form a canopy shutting out the sunlight. . . . The ground is moist, with the fresh, damp, black look of soil in continual shade. The ground is reddish brown with fallen leaves, or covered with tufts of pale green ferns. Scattered about are huge fallen trunks, occasionally hollowed and charred by fire, their sides covered with moss.[869]

By 1885 Cyrus G. Stafford and C. W. Long had each acquired 160 acres on the flat. It was estimated that each parcel would yield 30,000,000 board feet of lumber.[870] Both men appreciated this fact. Long had arrived in Eureka in 1850 and that same year became "engaged . . . in lumbering."[871] Stafford had been a judge, mayor of Eureka, and an organizer of the Elk River Mill and Lumber Company.[872] Despite their interest in timber, neither man retained his property until it was logged. By 1898 Long's parcel had come into the hands of C. A. Rust,[873] while Stafford kept his quarter-section until 1909, when a 30-horsepower Cadillac racing car terminated his ownership. That July, he and his family were watching a road race in Emeryville when Stafford decided he wanted a closer look. He wanted, in fact, to cross the track while the cars were still running their race. Stafford asked a gatekeeper if it was safe to do so, was told no, but he proceeded part way across the track anyway. Just then the three cars came around a blind corner and were on him. Stafford was hit by the lead car, which turned on its side, completed a partial somersault, and ejected its driver, breaking his nose and four ribs. Stafford fared worse; he had nearly every bone in his body broken and was killed, probably instantly, although the *Ferndale Enterprise* prolonged his death by taking three paragraphs to describe it.[874]

A fragment of the Wests Side Road runs eastward from Stafford (JR).

It was left to Stafford's widow, Etta, to dispose of the property, which she did in 1917 when she sold the land to Percy Brown. Over the next few years, Brown added to his holdings by buying the Rust parcel just west of Stafford's and another Rust holding in nearby Pepperwood.[875]

At first Brown intended to use the newly acquired redwoods for "split stuff"—products such as fence posts, railroad ties, and grapestakes that were split by hand from small sections of

each tree. He found, however, that the timber on his property was better for sawing than splitting, which meant he had to build a mill. Wartime demands made it impossible for Brown to buy new equipment, so he located an inactive mill at Occidental, in Sonoma County. This he purchased, had dismantled, and then had shipped by rail to a Pacific Lumber Company spur line that was located just across the Eel from his timber tract. The Northwestern Pacific, in a fit of levity, had named the spur "Perbrow," by conjoining parts of Percy Brown's first and last names.[876] Brown was not amused; he wanted the spur called Stafford after the flat's previous owner.

When the Redwood Highway was completed through the area in 1915, it ran fairly close to the Eel along the course of today's Stafford Road.[877] Brown built his mill in 1918, locating structures on both sides of the highway. To the south was the mill itself, some auxiliary buildings, and the company office. He also constructed "a large two-story cookhouse, ten or twelve good solid houses, and quite a number of spartan four-man cabins." The cookhouse was situated north of the highway, near the river; it is not clear where the dwellings were located. For Brown, the mill was no doubt the most important building in the complex; for the workers it was probably the cookhouse. A near insurrection occurred one day when the cook decided to cut the af-

ter-dinner pies into five pieces instead of the usual four. Order was restored only when Brown commanded the cook to give the workers their full quarter-pie servings.[878]

Prior to the construction of the mill, the area lacked any defining feature. The 1911 official Humboldt County map did not even name the location; in fact, it covered the empty spot with the name of the small community just up the river—Elinor. Then Percy Brown gave the locale a significant enterprise, and soon the spot came to be called Brown's Mill.[879]

The mill began operation in April 1919. Ironically, its main product at first was railroad ties—which were often made by the hand-splitting process that Brown had rejected. But ties were in great demand at the time, so that's what the mill produced. Later Brown switched to cutting dimensional lumber.[880]

Unlike many of the Humboldt County lumber operations of the time, Brown's Mill was

Brown's Mill #1 (HCHS, colorized by JR).

Workers return to Brown's second mill after attending a Chau-
tauqua lecture at lunch, 1923 (FMC, colorized by JR).

adjacent much of its timber supply. This allowed Brown to simplify transportation of his logs. He merely skidded them directly to the mill from where they lay in the nearby woods. A steam donkey at the mill could haul in any logs within a 1,000-yard radius. When Brown's crews began cutting farther away, a second steam donkey was added 1,000 yards out; the logs were then first yarded in by the second donkey, whence they were yarded by the first donkey to the mill. By this method Brown could bring in logs from more than a mile away.[881]

Part of Brown's timber holding was on the opposite side of the highway from mill. According to one account, the state's right-of-way was not exclusive, which gave Brown the right to yard his logs across the highway. When he wished to do so, Brown would notify the state highway office in Eureka, which duly sent down a flagman to stop highway traffic while Brown's steam donkey skidded his logs across the thoroughfare.[882]

The mill Brown had brought from Occidental was of ancient technology and could only cut 30,000 or 40,000 board feet of lumber per shift. Brown subsequently bought a pair of new firetube boilers and then added a ten-foot bandsaw and a seven-foot resaw. This increased the mill's capacity to somewhere between 50,000 and 75,000 board feet per shift.[883] He also added a planing mill, and the expanded operation then employed 125 workers.[884] In August 1923 Brown's neighbor, the Pacific Lumber Company, made a deal to buy almost all of Brown's output.[885]

That same month Brown's Mill experienced a strange and destructive display of unwanted aerodynamics. On August 22 Brown's woods workers began burning slash left from their logging operations. By mid-afternoon

. . . the fire appeared to generate antag-
onistic air currents, for soon a gigantic

funnel shaped cloud of dust, whirling at a tremendous speed, swept down upon the property.

The roof of the boiler shed was torn off, lumber scattered about like straw, and a tree three feet in diameter uprooted. A workman was picked up bodily by the force of the wind and hurled a distance of some fifteen feet, landing in the brush where he escaped any serious injury.

A section of the cook house roof five feet by seven feet was torn away as sharply as if it had been cut away with a large knife. . . .

An automobile standing in the road and containing three people was picked up by the wind and turned around, facing the direction from which it came.[886]

By 1941, motorists on the Redwood Highway found few mature trees in Stafford. The "valuable timber" of sixty years earlier had all been cut (FMC, colorized by JR).

If all this wasn't enough, there was also a rambunctious slash fire to contend with. Brown's workers kept it under control, but the entire episode created about $5,000 in damages.[887]

Calm returned to Brown's Mill. It lasted until 4:10 P.M. on the afternoon of May 20, 1926. At that exact minute the mill's planerman saw a fire under the mill building. He threw a bucket of water on the flames, but it wasn't enough. Nearby was the oil-saturated main belt that brought power to the mill. The fire soon found the belt, and flames "raced along it through the length of the mill." Workers ran for their lives as the building quickly ignited and burned to the ground. It was an exciting but terminating event for mill, as Brown decided not to rebuild.[888]

The now mill-less Brown's Mill was then called Brown's Camp.[889] So things stood until

about 1930, when Tobia Moschini and a Mr. Francesconi bought part of the land, including the former cookhouse. This building was converted into a combination hotel and restaurant. Tobia's daughter, Mary Moschini, was a Fortuna High School student at the time. She knew some local history and suggested that the business honor a former owner of the flat; thus the Stafford Inn was born. It opened in late 1930 or early 1931 and served Italian dinners.[890] In the mid-1930s the original highway, which ran directly in front of the inn, was straightened and moved about a quarter mile to the south. The new route cut through a side of Brown's abandoned log pond.[891] A business district eventually developed along the new alignment, which today is known as North Road. The 101

The stately Stafford Inn (HCHS, colorized by JR).

freeway now parallels North Road to the south and the remnants of the log pond, complete with a covering of yellow pond-lilies, lies just south of the freeway.

The 1930s reroute left the inn in semi-isolation on what became Stafford Road; to reach it, motorists had to detour about a half mile off the new section of highway. The inn had opened during the early stages of the Great Depression; now it languished in side-road obscurity. At an undetermined date, it closed. Then, in the summer of 1950, Ray and Anne Kaspar bought the inn, "which came with a wonderfully dignified and mature spaniel named Magee."[892] The following year the reopened inn reaped the benefit of some government-sponsored publicity when the word "Stafford" appeared on the new United States Geological Survey map of the area.[893]

By then Ray Kaspar had remodeled the

inn's bar, which overlooked three beautiful bits of scenery: a meadow, a pond, and the Eel River. The bar now featured rattan furniture, prompting Ray to name it the Bamboozle Room.[894] One of the local newspapers noted the décor of what it primly called the "Bamboo Room." It featured a

. . . South Sea Isle motif, with striking use made throughout of bamboo, and grass matting. The furniture is of yellow sailcloth with floral print, and the bar stools are done in yellow leatherette. Redwood paneling ties in with the outdoor area around the Stafford Inn.[895]

The rejuvenated inn offered more than the mere melding of bamboo with redwood. Kaspar, a musician who enjoyed enhanced entertainment, arranged for the periodic performance of an unusual duet. When the Northwestern Pacific's late afternoon train came by on the far side of the river, Ray would take his trumpet, play a few licks, and would—remarkably—be answered by a toot of the train's horn. Patrons in the Bamboozle Room were delighted, not realizing that Ray's salute could not be heard by the engineer, who instead looked for a light that Kaspar flashed across the river by flipping a switch under the bar as his cue to respond to the blasts from Ray's trumpet.[896]

If such Stafford Inn serenades were not enough, Kaspar also created unexpected visual displays, the most noted of which were his "hewed [sic] ewes," which were sheep that each spring he dyed the color of Easter eggs.[897] It was simply another way of making features of the inn more ewesful.

Many years later the Kaspars' daughter, Theo, recalled the magic of growing up in Stafford in the 1950s:

> The snapshots in my mind of my childhood at Stafford include: pictures of walking the berry bush lined Stafford Road with my friends to the school bus stop and smelling the fragrance of berries ripening in the sun; sitting in the cherry tree with my brother eating the fruit until we were stuffed; running with my friends down the steep sandy bank of the river with its familiar muddy, musky smell and throwing ourselves full-force into the river, laughing. The abandoned log pond at the former Brown's Mill was a dark and daring place to test our courage as we crept along the water soaked mossy logs as they moved ominously beneath us.[898]

More ominous than the former log pond was the water in the rapidly rising Eel during the December 1955 flood, which battered a corner of the inn. The building held fast, but over the next eight years business slowed at the inn and then came to an abrupt halt in 1963 when Ray Kaspar was killed in a car accident.[899]

Then came December 1964, when the "thousand-year flood" caused the river to wash over Stafford. At the H & H Trailer Park, a jeep-driving Samaritan named Red Nichols pulled three trailers and a Lincoln automobile to high ground. Then, with the water rising above the wheels of his jeep, Nichols switched to a motorboat, also switching his rescue efforts from trailers to people. The next day Red used his boat to bring in a couple named Thompson, who had spent two days above the floodwaters in their water tower.[900]

Even an expert rescuer like Nichols could do nothing for the Stafford Inn, however. The converted cookhouse lay close to the Eel and was among the first of the community's buildings to be hit by the flood. It was also rendered vulnerable by its unusual foundation, which reportedly consisted of "about ten huge redwood stumps."[901] And so the Stafford Inn soon became part of the vast armada of structures propelled by the flood towards the sea.

Later years have found Stafford connected to the outside world by a single freeway interchange. The community has been of interest primarily to its few residents and to knowledgeable neighboring locals who used a remnant of the West Side Road for river access. In the late 1990s the hillside south of Stafford became quite famous, however, for controversies related to the logging conducted there by the Pacific Lumber Company (PL), which by then was owned by

Stafford (in foreground) awash during the 1964 flood (AHC, colorized by JR).

Charles Hurwitz's MAXXAM. On New Year's Eve 1996, a landslide triggered by PL's clear-cutting sent "up to 17 feet of mud and debris" down onto the south side of Stafford, destroying eight homes.[902] Starting in December 1997, environmental activist Julia "Butterfly" Hill occupied an old-growth redwood named Luna on the ridge slope above the slide. Hill stayed on her perch for over two years. Her high-altitude inhabitancy not only prevented PL from cutting Luna down but, with Stafford as the focus, also publicized the controversial forestry practices the company was using on thousands of acres of timberlands.[903]

So it was that Stafford, once a blank space on the map, finally made a name for itself.

Chapter 17
Dobbyn Creek Area

There never was a white community at Dobbyn Creek, but before whites took over the area there were many Indian villages. Three groups usually subsumed within the so-called Lassik tribe lived in the drainage, while a fourth group occupied a nearby stretch of the Eel River.

On South Dobbyn Creek (sometimes called "Big" Dobbyn) were the Tai-tci-kuk kai-ya.[904] They had several villages[905] in the canyon of South Dobbyn, including Sai-to-tci, located not far west of the Zenia Bluffs.[906] North Dobbyn Creek ("Little" Dobbyn) was home to the Se-ta-kuk kai-ya.[907] This group had several villages along the creek, one of which was Sa-tci-ni-tci-dun, "where salmon ran."[908] The Tec-ta-kuk kai-ya were the "Conley Creek people," who occupied the area south and east of Blocksburg and had at least two villages plus Se-kuh-ne, a rock shelter.[909] The Ta kai-ya were the "people on main Eel River."[910] Pliny Goddard, using information from the Lassik Indian Jim Willburn, mapped two villages, kuc-to-dun and di-yic-kuk, that probably belonged to this group, locating them on the east side of the Eel opposite the southern end of the Fort Seward flat.[911] According to Willburn, who was a small boy at the time, the Indian leader called Lassik "used to camp on Little Dobbins [and] sometimes Big Dobbins."[912]

The Lassik tribe was all but wiped out during the Indian genocide of the 1850s and 1860s. The last of the tribe's men, including Lassik himself, were shot and burned by whites at Fort Seward.[913] Some of the remaining women then cohabited (whether willingly or not) with white men; the children were sent south, probably to become slaves.[914]

An accused slaver lived in the area. In 1867 the Hog Ranch, near the mouth of Dobbyn Creek, was put up for sale after the death of its owner, S. D. Ross.[915] Six years earlier Samuel D. Ross had written the *Humboldt Times* to defend himself against charges of "trading in Indians."[916]

Dobbyn Creek was reportedly named for William B. Dobbyn. In the early 1860s he was keeper of what was vaguely called the "overland Laribee [sic] mail station."[917] In 1864 the station and its keeper moved to Camp Grant, where Dobbyn also farmed, maintained a stopping place, and owned a ferry. He is shown in that location on the 1865 county map.[918] In about 1875 Dobbyn and his family moved to Rohnerville; while living there he served two terms as county supervisor.[919] His connection with the Dobbyn Creek area is unclear.[920] However, his probable presence in Lassik country at an early date is indicated by the subsequent existence of "Bill Dobbins," a part Lassik Indian who was born about 1867.[921]

The county map from 1886 shows three large land ownerships in the Dobbyn Creek drainage: A. S. Rogers held property along the Overland Road east of Conley Creek; M. A. Casterlin owned much of the area north of North Dobbyn Creek; and Watts and Huyck had land on South Dobbyn Creek.[922] By the late 1890s several other landowners were present, and the cumulative effect was such that the Dobbyn School opened on Friday, July 2, 1897,[923] just in time for students to enjoy the Fourth of July holiday. (See sidebar 1.)

1. Dobbyn School

Like several other remote areas in Humboldt County, Dobbyn Creek had the absolute minimum (one) of facilities that allowed it to be called a community. In this case it was a school.

Dobbyn School[924] originally met in a house on Mrs. L. M. Wilson's property.[925] The first teacher was Helen Augusta Fawcett, who arrived in 1897 in dramatic fashion. She "rode her high-stepping little mare, Maude," from Eureka all the way to the school, stopping overnight in Bridgeville.[926] She taught two grammar and eight primary students. The school report for the year indicated that there were 12 seats but "not enough furniture." There was one outhouse, and "the water and the grounds around the school were satisfactory."[927]

In 1912 the school moved to "a building near a spring between property of Anderson Lyons and L. E. McCowley." The following year the district issued bonds in the amount of $550 for a new school and had it completed

Dobbyn School (HCHS, Colorized by JR).

by April 1914.[928] It was located about three miles east of the Overland Road and a mile north of North Dobbyn Creek and was reached by what is today known as Casterlin Road.[929]

Some 25 years after Helen Fawcett's memorable arrival at Dobbyn Creek, Doris Kildale came there in 1922 to teach. She was only 18 and had just qualified for her teaching credential under the regulations of the time. Like her predecessors, Kildale taught grades one through eight in the one-room building. She never had more than 22 regular students, but for a time she also taught two ninth-graders. The pair lived too far away to attend the nearest high school, which was in Fortuna. Kildale then went to Stanford University to complete her bachelor and master's degrees. She taught for a time at Humboldt Normal School (which is now Cal Poly Humboldt), studied at Harvard, and then returned to Stanford, where she received her doctoral degree in botany. Kildale married rancher Arthur Dewey Niles in 1938, raised a family, and then went back to teaching. In 1960 she taught for the University of California extension program, visiting numerous locations in northern California. To facilitate her traveling, Niles became a pilot and flew to her assignments in a four-seater Cessna plane. She helped found and then direct the Nature Discovery Volunteers, which trained people to give presentations about Humboldt County's natural history. In the 1980s Niles taught University of California, Davis classes at her Sea Breeze Ranch, which was on the old Kinman property on the north side of Table Bluff.[930]

The Dobbyn School caught fire at an unknown date; the flames were extinguished by "students and a few nearby parents [who] formed a bucket brigade," getting their water from a nearby spring. Between 1926 and 1929 the school closed because of deficient enrollment. It then reopened and lasted until 1948, when it closed for good.[931] It was well it did, for at the time the Dobbyn School was "probably the most inadequate [school] of 19 in southern Humboldt." It was situated on a half-acre hillside lot with no playground, no artificial lighting, no water, and no sanitary facilities. The board-and-batten building was apparently little changed from the time of its construction in 1914. Its closure was one of the first acts of the newly established Southern Humboldt Unified School District.[932]

When its seven students left and teacher Willa Patton closed its door for the last time, the Dobbyn School had operated for nearly 50 years in rural obscurity.[933] It had seen a lot in less than half a century, from Helen Fawcett's Maude, high-stepping mare, to Doris Niles, the high-flying teacher.

Delmar L. Thornbury, Humboldt County educator and expeditionist, came through the Dobbyn Creek area about 1920 and described it thus:

> The main road south of Blocksburg is very crooked, but presents new and novel scenery at every turn. Along Dobbyn Creek, the country sobers down somewhat, and there are thousands of acres of land presented to the view along the road, which will make farms and fruit ranches. It has been the very heart of the great sheep raising country of Humboldt, it will be its greatest agricultural section.[934]

Time has proven Thornbury to be a better historian than prognosticator.

The Trinity County town of Zenia is located high up in the South Dobbyn Creek drainage. For years a connecting road branched off the Overland Road about four miles north of Alderpoint and ran east along the divide between North Dobbyn and South Dobbyn creeks until it reached Zenia. About a mile west of town the road "crossed a big blue slide on Mud Creek" that "could not be kept open in stormy weather." Between 1922 and 1923 a new road was built up South Dobbyn Creek, cutting across the spectacular Zenia Bluffs that rose north of the creek. The road construction was also spectacular: men were lowered by rope from the top of the bluffs to the cliff face; once there they drilled holes for the blasting powder that would create a ledge for the road to run on. The three major creeks along the route were spanned by bridges. It was a big job, given the primitive equipment of the times, but the result was a year-round road.[935]

Just north of the junction where the original Zenia Road met the Overland Road was a flat at the mouth of North Dobbyn Creek. In the late 1940s, Sig (or Sid) Lindroth's Capitol Lumber

One of the bridges on Zenia Road (DTC, Colorized by JR).

Company[936] "bought the Tooby and Prior timber on their Blocksburg Ranch and built a mill and planer" on the flat. The resultant lumber was hauled to the Fort Seward railroad station for shipment. Lindroth also constructed employee housing and a cookhouse.[937] In 1960 he paid $283,197 for 14.4 million board feet of timber in the Six Rivers National Forest. The trees were located on the Mad River about 12 miles northeast of Zenia. Five species were included: Ponderosa pine, sugar pine, white fir, Douglas-fir, and incense cedar.[938] Lindroth reaped the benefits of the road building done 37 years earlier as his log trucks rumbled along the Zenia Bluffs, perhaps putting a pothole or two in an earlier generation's work.

Seven years after the Dobbyn School closed a replacement came on line. The Casterlin School was completed in 1955. It is located only a couple of miles west of the site of the Dobbyn School[939] and, like its predecessor, has been the only public building in the area.

Chapter 18
Blocksburg

As Blocksburg begins to loom up as a town . . .

Evening Star, 1877

And loom, at least for travelers from the south, Blocksburg did. Perched astride the divide between the Larabee Creek and Eel River drainages, the lights from its stores and hotels twinkling in the twilight, Blocksburg beckoned road-weary riders as they ascended the gradual but lengthy grade from Dobbyn Creek, promising that the ridgetop saloons and stables would offer succor to man and beast. It was the perfect location for a travel-route community in the days when a conveyance had from one to six horsepower, but the arrival of the Age of the Auto rendered the town redundant. Today Blocksburg's business district barely meets the minimum requirement—one building, a small and youngish-looking post office. On side streets are found the icons of early-day communities: a cemetery to the west and a church and long-closed school to the east. Year after year the juggernaut of the present has swept over the ridge, carrying away pieces of the past with each turn of the calendar. Stop now, Blocksburg tells the traveler, not for necessity, but to sense the dwindling scenes that recall another century.

Blocksburg's ridge formed the approximate boundary between the so-called Nongatl and Lassik Indian tribes. The Tec-ta-kuk kai-ya were a tribal group, subsumed under the Lassik name,

Distant Blocksburg sits far up the mountainside at the top of the ridge (BTHA, colorized by JR)

that occupied the Conley Creek drainage south and east of Blocksburg.[940] In the upper Larabee Creek area north of Blocksburg was a Nongatl group called the Senunka.[941] When Victor Hope took up property just north of Blocksburg in 1875,[942] he built his house on a site that had previously been an Indian meeting place. Here, Hope stated, with perhaps some magnification,

> . . . they congregated and held their war dances. Often as many as five hundred bucks and squaws were assembled here, but there was never any resultant trouble.[943]

But Hope was talking about the 1870s. The previous decade there had been plenty of trouble, most of it caused by the U. S. Army.

In the spring of 1861 three detachments of soldiers conducted a coordinated campaign against the Indians of southern and eastern Humboldt County. The unit in the middle consisted of Lieutenant Joseph B. Collins and a detachment of 45 men. For a time they camped near the headwaters of Larabee Creek, which would have put them just north of the future site of Blocksburg. Between April and June Collins's unit killed at least 92 Indians, while army casualties were limited to two wounded.[944] The disparity is indicative of army-Indian encounters that were not battles but massacres.

The community that eventually became known as Blocksburg started in the late 1860s. There are many accounts of the town's early days, seldom in agreement with one another. The most plausible story runs as follows.

According to Rosa Curless, when her parents Biar and Lovina Curless homesteaded on upper Larabee Creek in 1869,[945] "there was no town then, only a store run by a squaw-man named 'Beanie' Powell." This single business was amplified into a community by calling the location Powellville or Powellsville. Some 25 years later and long after his name was put to such use, Joseph James "Beanie" Powell was "said to have died of food poisoning, possibly caused by eating sour beans,"[946] which suggests that he received his nickname posthumously.

George Friend indicated that when he was 15 or 16, he came into the area as the bell boy for Henry Dix[947] on "the first pack train of goods ever to come into Blocksburg in 1872 to open [Ben] Blocksburger's store there." There was already a store at the townsite, according to Friend; it belonged to Joe Stemmons: "He had a little shed with a few pairs of overalls and other necessities," Friend recalled, "but his chief commodity was whiskey."[948]

Stemmons's "shed" was otherwise referred to as a "small log house" that was reputedly the first building completed in the town. Stemmons gained the honor by default; Dan Young had come over from Hayfork in the late 1860s, had some logs hauled in, and then put some of them together to start a structure but never finished it.

Ben Blocksburger arrived on the scene in 1871. Depending on which account is preferred, he came either in the spring or the fall of that year, and he was accompanied by either Ben Rickett or Gus Ellis.[949] Blocksburger wanted to open a store right away, but he was unable to get the necessary supplies. Meanwhile John Coates "put up a house and brought in goods for sale."[950] Come the spring of 1872 Blocksburger bought out Coates's stock, supplemented it with the contents of George Friend's pack train, and "opened a store with a full supply of general goods." Ben's store had a notable clerk (See sidebar 1). That same year Robert G. Coates opened a hotel in the suddenly growing community.[951]

By 1961 few travelers stopped at the (former) Blocksburg hotel (BTHA, colorized by JR)

1. "2-B or not 2-B"

According to Frank Asbill, a sort of local historian, Ben Blockburger's store featured an unusual employee:

The clerk Ben hired was George Cooper. He'd been a buckaroo, a saloon keeper, and what have you. George had not been educated; he didn't know what two and two was. When George wanted some merchandise, he simply drew a picture of whatever he wanted. One time he wanted a grindstone. He drew a picture but when it arrived it was a head of cheese. George always carried his pencil behind his ear but when he saw the cheese, he took the pencil, wiggled it behind his ear, and said: "Well, I'll be damned if I didn't forget to put the hole in the damned thing."

There was a man who was packing for John Graham, George J. Toobey [sic] by name. He ran a bill at the store. When Ben Block balanced his books, he kept seeing a figure 2-B, and on the next page it would appear in several places again. Ben called George, and said: "George, what in the hell is this 2-B in the ledger so many times for, you damned fool?"

George replied, "It's Toobey, George Toobey's account."[952]

A couple of other notable families held land on the outskirts of the townsite. George S. Kneeland and Charles W. Kneeland had property about two miles to the south in the Conley Creek drainage, some of which they claimed as early as 1874 and 1875.[953] George S. Kneeland's house was apparently a short distance off the trail that led from Blocksburg southwest to the Eel River.[954] Silas Hoaglen[955] became Kneeland's neighbor when he bought 160 acres directly south of town in 1876.[956] George Friend recalled the saga of the Hoaglen family:

> I was at the Kneeland house one time when Hoagland [sic] lived there. Hoagland and Kneeland were married to two squaws who were sisters. Their names were Sally Kneeland and Sue Hoagland, and they were wonderful cooks. It took

about 35 Indians to run the place and it was quite a sight to see these two squaws cooking and serving the meals to the large crew. Hoaglands were the first settlers in Bridgeville. They didn't care much for civilization, and as other settlers moved in they kept moving further out. They went out to Blocksburg and then moved to New Mexico where Si Hoagland died. Tom Ragland, his old partner, went down there and brought the family back, and they settled over in Hoagland Valley, which is named for this family.[957]

In September 1897 four Hoaglen brothers—Charles, Hank, Brick, and George—were sheering sheep on the Kneeland Ranch and got to drinking. Hank proceeded to hit his brother Charles on the head with a picket. Charles

Built in 1907, Blocksburg's iconic church still perches on its hill slope east of town (CPH, colorized by JR).

"moved off" and no one thought much about it at the time. The next morning, however, Charles was found nearby "in an unconscious condition." He was taken to the Kneeland house, where "he died a few hours afterward."[958] No wonder the Hoaglens kept moving "further out."

In 1875 and 1880 Robert G. Coates patented land immediately north of Blocksburg.[959] Robert and John Coates were likely related, and one or both of them apparently stayed in Blocksburg for some time. Either or both of the men had probably fled Mendocino County, where the Coates and Frost families had recently staged what was considered the deadliest shootout in northwestern California history. The two families were based in the Little Lake area, where the town of Willits later developed. They had engaged in a low-scale feud since the early 1860s, brought on at least in part by the Coateses' support of the Union and the Frosts' allegiance to the Confederacy during the Civil War. Then, on election day in October 1867, several men from each family came together in front of Baechtel's store, which was near the Little Lake polling place. Some intemperate remarks were made, some blows struck, and then suddenly the air was filled with bullets and buckshot. When the smoke cleared and the dust settled, five Coateses and a Frost were either dead or dying, and another Coates and two members of the Frost family were wounded.[960] Years later, some of the Frosts also arrived in Blocksburg, where some Coateses still lived. The result was not murder but marriage, as a young member of each family improved on the doleful example set by Romeo and Juliet.[961]

The original Overland Road reached Blocksburg in 1875, having come from Eureka via Kneeland and Bridgeville, and suddenly supplies began arriving in trains of nine or ten wagons. Pack trains still departed Blocksburg for outlying communities that were not yet reached by road. Nearly all the wagoners sported colorful names—Dirty Face Rader, Easy Thompson, High Weather Perry, Tallow-Faced Davis, Hay Buckus Rodgers—but the most memorable driver, for local juvenile Everett Kay at least, was Lee Short, who made up for his lack of nickname by leaving candy for Everett under the dining room table cloth. Lee later made a dramatic career change and became superintendent of Napa State Hospital.[962]

After a brief spell of being called "Powellville or "Powellsville," the town for a time became "Laribee" or "Larrabee,"[963] probably because it lay at the head of Larabee Creek. In 1876 Ben Blocksburger placed an ad for his dry goods store in the *West Coast Signal* that gave the location as "Larrabee."[964] The following year an ad for the "Larabee Hotel, Blocksburg, Humboldt Co." marked the current phase of the nomenclatural transition.[965]

Meanwhile the ridgetop town expanded. John Stemmons, having given up his store, built a shop with a forge in it, and duly became a blacksmith.[966] By May 1876 the *West Coast Signal* could report that

> Blocksburg is improving very fast. A townsite has been surveyed and lots sell readily at $100. The place has one store, one hotel, one blacksmith shop, . . . one schoolhouse, a dozen dwellings and more going up.[967]

But additional components of a community were needed. Ben Blocksburger made a contribution when, on January 23, 1877, he generously allowed the use of 83 percent of his name for the town's new post office. The effect was diminished somewhat when a postal official in Washington, apparently having Pittsburgh in mind, added a superfluous "h" to the end of the office's name, thereby creating "Blocksburgh." This of course wasn't right, but the wheels of bureaucracy turned so slowly that only some 5,823 days later, on April 29, 1893, did the post office's name officially become Blocksburg.[968] Meanwhile the office served as the hub for outlying areas that could only be reached by trail. Mail for Zenia, Hoaglin, Ruth, and Caution came through Blocksburg(h).[969]

The post office was followed later in 1877 by a second store, this one operated in the Minor house by a Mr. Sweet.[970] Given the proprietor's name, he likely stocked lots of penny candy. Goods for both stores were packed in from Hydesville.[971] It was reported that "just before winter each year a double pack train of 60 mules would make the long trek to bring in the winter supplies." There was a strict division between the two trains: one brought all the regular merchandise, the other brought whiskey.[972]

Adding to the abundance of significant 1877 events was the completion of what came to be called the Overland Road, which linked Humboldt County with Mendocino County and points south.[973] On July 25th the Humboldt and Mendocino Counties Stages announced their "Overland" route, which went from Eureka to Cloverdale, where there was a rail line connection to San Francisco Bay. Included was a stop at "Blockburg"[974] as the struggle to correctly spell the town's name continued. With Blocksburg strategically positioned along the route at the top of a major grade, business in town could not help but increase. A wide-ranging tally in May, provided by a loquacious local styling himself "Larribie," showed that

Blocksburg Post Office (CPH, colorized by JR).

Blocksburg has one store, two hotels, one restaurant, a meat market, two saloons, a blacksmith shop, a boot and shoe shop, two stables connected with the hotels, while another is being built . . . as a regular livery, feed and sale stable. . . . So you see we have plenty of accommodation for both man and beast. . . . Our public school has a regular attendance of 25. . . . Wool buyers are coming around. . . . Sheep shearing is about to begin. . . . Block[s-burger] weighs two hundred and thirty pounds. . . . Got a brick-yard here. . . . Increase in sheep will average over 100 per cent in this locality. . . .[975]

In July came an account on how Blocksburg celebrated the hundred-and-first anniversary of the signing of the Declaration of Independence:

We went so far in the old grove as to fire off a salute of a hundred guns, accompanied with numerous discharges of fire-crackers, baby-wakers, etc., and your correspondent read the immortal declaration. About fifty aborigines, male and female, dressed in gala costume, mounted on horseback, each bearing the stars and stripes, proceeded through all the peripheral streets, and were greeted with enthusiastic cheers by the caucassion [sic] lookers-on.[976]

Many stories were told about Ben Blocksburger, and some of them were probably true. One that was reportedly "well authenticated" claimed that "Blocksburger was the champion snorer in northern California." According to this account Ben took a trip to Eureka, leaving the two Indian women who were living with

him at home. The first night of his absence the women couldn't sleep; they had grown so accustomed to his "stentorian sounds" that the sudden silence kept them awake. They pondered their problem for a while and then hit on a solution. Down from the shelf came Ben's hand-crank coffee grinder, into it went a handful of beans, and then, as one woman cranked away, the other found slumber sweet. After a time the cranker woke the sleeper, they changed positions, and the second woman caught if not 40, at least 20, winks. Come morning, they had plenty of ground coffee beans ready to go into the pot.[977]

With the Overland Road completed and sheep ranching going strong, Blocksburg entered its heyday. In 1878, a little more than a year after Larribie's account of the town, the *Humboldt Times* described an enlarged community that had added a second general merchandise store, a second blacksmith shop, a third saloon, and "two billiard tables." In addition, a school was scheduled to be built. The *Times* noted that

By some Blocksburg is given rather a hard name in some respects, as for instance sporting and whisky drinking. But we believe this to be to a great extent unjust, or if it at any time has deserved this reputation a manifest change for the better is now discoverable.

Perhaps a "manifest change" was temporarily "discoverable," but it had vanished by 1882, when writer and traveler Warren B. Johnson came through town. He found fewer businesses than those reported in 1878, but the activity within some of them harkened back to Blocksburg's "hard name" days:

Local Indians celebrate the Fourth of July near Blocksburg (MJJC, colorized by JR)

Blocksburg is a small town comprised of a hotel, two stores, blacksmith, wheelwright shop, two saloons and a few houses. Saloons are well patronized, I counted twenty-two horses at one. Their riders were inside drinking and gambling. "I asked what business they followed?" I was told that they "were wool growers, but their main business was drinking and gambling." Those that follow this business, and they are many, have nothing but gold. I have seen piles of gold on the tables. They do not appear to be afraid of each other. They do not count out their money; it is laid in piles; they go by the height. Their money consists of five, ten and twenty dollar gold pieces, I have seen heaps four inches high of

twenties. Their money lays [sic] on the table until they get through, with their revolvers beside them.[978]

Fortunately the revolvers usually stayed put, but the saloon frequenters found less-lethal activities to keep them amused. One of the bartenders created a "championship belt," a wide swath of leather to which numerous sheepbells and cowbells were attached. It functioned like this:

Whenever there was a fight, the belt which hung in one of the saloons, was brought forth and hung on the winner. Scarcely had it found its new champion when another fight was started and the belt probably found a new wearer because the former champion met ignominious defeat. . . . The belt changed hands three to five times every day, after the boys from the ranches had taken aboard drinks enough to make some of them belligerent.[979]

Any place with such amusements was bound to prove popular, so it was no surprise that the 1880 census found that Blocksburg was the seventh largest community in Humboldt County, with 121 inhabitants.[980] Two of its businesses had new owners who would operate them for decades. In 1878 Martin Frederick Helmke bought Simon Sweet's general merchandise store. His son, Frederick Martin Helmke, joined his father in running the store in 1898 and then became sole owner in 1905. In 1911 the business became the Helmke Mercantile Company and

Store No. 2 was opened in Fort Seward.[981] The Helmke empire made its final expansion in 1916 by adding a store in Alderpoint.[982] But all too soon the Blocksburg store closed 1921.[983]

Meanwhile, in about 1882, Addison McLean and his wife took over the Harris House, renamed it the Overland Hotel, and ran it until 1906.[984] In 1889 ethnographer Jeremiah Curtin and his wife Alma arrived by "private conveyance" at Blocksburg after a "wearisome ride of 44 miles" above the Van Duzen and through the hills. They took a room at the Overland after their driver advised them about the McLeans, stating that Mrs. McLean "was the better man of the two."[985]

The wool growers who so strongly supported Blocksburg's saloons were riding the crest of a wave of government-induced prosperity. (See sidebar 2.)

The Overland Hotel, with Helmke's store in the background (CPH, colorized by JR)

2. Pulling the Wool over American Commerce

When Congress passed the Tariff Act of 1867, Blocksburg was nothing more than a few logs waiting to become a cabin. Yet, by enacting this act, the federal government had just reached across the continent and assured the future success of this nascent Humboldt County community.

The act increased import duties on both raw wool and various woolen products. Such a protectionist tariff benefitted businessmen, workers, and ranchers associated with the wool industry, many of whom were located in the northern and western states. By approving the act in 1867, Republican legislators bolstered their chances in the upcoming 1868 presidential election.[986] Sure enough, Ulysses S. Grant won the contest, although his popularity as a Civil War hero may have also been a factor in the outcome.

Not long after passage of the 1867 tariff, both the number of sheep and the amount of wool produced in the United States increased dramatically. Congress determined that in 1870 some 28,477,961 sheep provided just over 100 million pounds of wool. By 1874 there were 50,626,626 sheep and they produced about 308 million pounds of wool, a threefold production increase in only four years.[987] According to another report, the years

Sheep shearing at the Kneeland Ranch, Blocksburg (BTHA, colorized by JR)

between 1873 and 1883 saw a "very rapid advance" in wool output. Most of the gain was found in the West, including various territories that were not yet states, along with Texas and California.[988]

By 1879 wool production and wool prices had advanced to the point that the *Weekly Humboldt Times* could report that

> The proceeds received from the shipment of wool from this county places that interest far ahead of any other, *lumber even not being except-ed.* (Italics mine.) The wool shipment from Humboldt ranks among the best in the market and commands the highest price. This year the wool clip was large and the price ranging above the average, our wool men will realize handsome profits.[989]

A new tariff act in 1883 reduced duties on imported wool. This caused a gradual reduction in the number of domestic sheep and in domestic wool production. Then in 1890 the tariff was again raised and sheep and wool production again increased. A new, lower tariff in 1894 caused another decrease.[990]

In the midst of the fluctuations induced by tariff changes, domestic production produced some startling statistics. In 1888 the United States produced about one-sixth of the wool grown worldwide. It was the only country that in recent years had seen an increase in wool production. It ranked as the country's sixth most important agricultural enterprise, "surpassed only by corn, hay, wheat, cotton, and oats." Domestic consump-tion of wool had risen 70 percent between 1870 and 1880. Perhaps most impressively, the sheep themselves had cleverly increased their individual production; while an average fleece weighed only three pounds in 1860, by 1880 the average fleece weighed a whopping six pounds. This far surpassed the sluggardly sheep of Great Britain, whose fleeces averaged a paltry four pounds.[991]

In 1888 some 151,973 sheep produced 1,667,248 pounds of wool in Humboldt County. Between then and 1892 those figures plummeted, with the number of sheep decreasing by more than a third and the amount of wool produced declining by almost half. The two main causes given were "depression in the woolen trade," and "encroachment of the settler and his plow."[992] A third factor was the "hard winter" of 1889-1890, when the heavy snows killed both livestock and crops. During the boom times of the early 1880s, ranchers had "mortgaged their property up to the limit in order to

Wool pack train waiting to leave Blocksburg, 1890 (DTC, colorized by JR).

buy more sheep and cattle." Now their investments lay dead in the snow. The onetime poker players had gambled on livestock and lost, and many of them lost their ranches and moved elsewhere.[993] Ben Blocksburger, who had been a wool buyer[994] in addition to running his store, went bankrupt.[995]

Gambling of course didn't have to occur in a bar room, and Blocksburgians created another venue when they established a race track about three miles north of town. It was "laid out on a flat among the willows" that was later the location of the Lost Flat Ranch and was operating as early as 1881.[996] In 1885 the Blocksburg Jockey Club held two days of races in late October, attracting "a large number of people from all parts of the county."[997] Purses ran as high as $75 per race.[998] With few tracks anywhere in the state, racing devotees came from as far away as Los Angles.[999]

In addition to racehorses such as Saltwater Jim, Peavine, and Black Jack,[1000] another quadruped attracted notice in Blocksburg. She was Empress, an elephant with the Forepaugh Circus, which came through town in 1889.[1001] Some locals, perhaps thinking of Empress's large feet, called the circus the "Four Paws Show."[1002]

As the new century moved forward, Blocksburg fell back, becoming one of those communities whose best days receded into the past. Five fires and the decline of sheep ranching would have been enough to diminish the town's importance, but the loss of traffic on the Overland Road caused by a new route on Mail Ridge[1003] and then the opening of the Redwood Highway had relegated Blocksburg to full backwater status.

Besides the stimulation provided by gold-piece gambling, horse racing, and circuses, Blocksburg found another way to have excitement—watch fires burn down part of the town. The first such incident occurred in 1886, when Frank Hendrickson's saloon, Herman's meat market, and Helmke's store all burned.[1004] Then, in 1899, a conflagration started in the Methodist Church and soon spread to Helmke's barn and warehouse before finishing up with the blacksmith shop and Curless's saloon.[1005] Next,

in 1907, the post office ignited, taking with it Levi Wheat's warehouse; the Blocksburg town hall; and Robinson's hotel, saloon, and barn.[1006] The town then cooled off until 1920, when Helmke's store and Seth Frank's home went alight; only a strenuous effort by the citizenry kept the hotel from also incinerating.[1007] Barely a year later it was the Blocksburg School's turn. Even though the school was reduced to a pile of ashes, classes continued; for a time they were held the old Bosworth home and then moved to a better location—the school's woodshed, which had been renovated to accommodate scholars rather than scrap wood.[1008]

So it was that when Delmar L. Thornbury came by in the early 1920s, he looked at the shrunken town, and, dismissing its earlier heyday, pontifically pronounced that

Blocksburg's 1907 fire (BTHA, colorized by JR)

Blocksburg with its Shell station, center, in the 1930s (BTHA, colorized by JR).

Most of the buildings of Blocksburg were burned some years ago, but the place has never been of much importance, and was [now] made up only of a store, church, postoffice with three or four dwellings.[1009]

But others, with a better sense of history, knew of a different Blocksburg, one that for a time was probably the most important community in southeastern Humboldt County. After the post office opened in 1877, Blocksburg became "the congregating point and trading post for ranchers for three counties: Humboldt, Mendocino, and Trinity."[1010] It was the place where ranchers, warmed by their wool-raising profits and whiskey, were transformed into dev-

il-may-care gamblers, treating $20 gold pieces as if they were pennies. It was a place that kept hold of its people as it kept hold of its past, so that when the Blocksburg School closed in 1955, old Ed Burgess could go to his even older desk and show former stage driver J. S. Madden the spot where he'd carved his initials 70 years earlier.[1011] (See sidebar 3.) It was, and would continue to be, the Blocksburg of bucolic beauty that Thornbury beheld from a distance before he came closer to criticize it:

At the very head of Larribee Creek, on a low pass, in a range of hills, high up on the summit of a ridge, with fresh spring water and purest atmosphere, is the mountain town of Blocksburg.[1012]

3. Kindness Remembered

Ed Burgess was not the only Blocksburg student to carve his initials in his desk. Sometime in the 1880s Tom Murphy did the same thing, and his handiwork was there for his granddaughter to see 40 years later.[1013]

The years passed, and Murphy's granddaughter, June Reger, wanted to share the stories of her early life in Blocksburg. Out of this came a book of reminiscences by June and other students who attended the area's schools. Many people participated, but no one offered more than Reger. She had a lot to say.

Reger recalled "the wonderful steam engines . . . that could be heard up and down the mountainsides . . . all the way to Grizzly Mountain." The sounds were plentiful in those early times of the railroad, since every day four passenger trains and various freights passed through the canyon below, stopping at the Fort Seward station.

Closer to home, Reger viewed with alarm the unused Blocksburg church, which "was leaning sideways and threatening to fall over." Her stepfather, Bill Heinze, and Fred Lang "managed to straighten it up by placing cables in it from side to side. The cables held the church in an upright position until later when extensive repairs were made."

Tom Murphy, with his two best bear dogs, Button and Baldy (PG, colorized by JR)

June told of shopping with her brother and grandfather during the Great Depression at "Bill Campbell's little store." Money was tight, and the children "would never think of asking for treats," but Bill always invited them to pick out a piece of free candy when the shopping was done. It was a small kindness but a big thing for the kids, and June kept it in her memory for more than 70 years.

Her grandfather knew a thing or two about kindness, although he didn't advertise it. He and his wife Etta had a ranch a couple of miles south of Blocksburg, and one day in the early 1900s they were visited by some of the local Indians who lived in the area. Tom Murphy had learned their language, and he understood them when they asked permission to pick bear clover on his property. Murphy said sure, and added that they could also take any apples they found lying on the ground. Soon he saw the Indians up in his apple trees, shaking the limbs so that more apples would become eligible for the taking. Etta saved some of the Murphys' apple crop by persuading the Indians to come up onto the porch and have some bread and milk.

Granddaughter June did not learn about her grandfather's deepest connection with the Indians until near the end of Tom's life. It had to do with the "hardship winter" of 1889-1890, which brought a series of severe snowstorms. Decades later, when Tom was dying of cancer in 1934, June observed

> . . . two lovely Indian ladies [who] came to see if they could help him. They told our family they nearly starved to death in the winter of 1889 because the snow had made it impossible to gather food. At the age of 17, Tom had loaded up a packhorse with all possible types of food available at the ranch and broke a trail up through the snow to their camp. This was the reason they were still alive and they wanted to help him in any way they could.[1014]

Forty-five years had passed since Tom Murphy had rescued the Indians from starvation, and this was the first time anyone in his family had heard about it.

Chapter 19
Burr Creek & Upper Larabee Creek

The largest stream between the Van Duzen and main Eel rivers is Larabee Creek. One of its main tributaries is Burr Creek. Most of the travel corridor between Bridgeville and Blocksburg runs through the drainages of these two creeks, and all of the ranches in this area connect with this corridor.

Before the ranches, the area was within the territory of the Nongatl tribe. Little is known about the Indians who lived there because none of them were ever interviewed, but it appears that at least four Nongatl tribal groups occupied portions of the locale. The Senunkas had a series of at least nine villages along upper Larabee Creek, starting at its confluences with Boulder Flat Creek and Thurman Creek and running downstream to the vicinity of the Curless (Payton) Ranch. One village, Tokintcabi, reportedly had "many Indians."[1015] Directly north of the Senunkas were the Tcin-nun-un ki-yas.[1016] No villages are described for this group, and it is unclear how far north their territory went. A third Nongatl group, the Bus-ta-dun ki-yas, lived in the vicinity of Boulder Flat Creek.[1017] Finally, the Ye-lin-din kai-ya, whose name refers to Larabee Creek, apparently occupied a stretch of the stream canyon near the Curless Ranch.[1018]

In May 1861 Lieutenant Joseph Collins of the Fourth U. S. Infantry wrote from a "camp near the head of Larrabee [sic] Creek" that his troops "had attacked two ranches and killed 15 Indians." He noted that

> . . . the entire country is mountainous, well timbered, watered, and furnishes sufficient grass all the year for large herds of beef cattle and horses; indeed, it is one of the finest mountain grazing countries I have ever seen.[1019]

Collins found that there were a "considerable" number of inhabitants "located over a country of more than fifty miles." It was clear he was counting only the whites who lived there.[1020] The Indians who had dwelt in the area for centuries were even more "considerable" in number, but by Collins's calculations they apparently did not qualify as inhabitants.

One of the soldiers who participated in the attacks, E. E. Turk, sent the *Humboldt Times* a sequel to Collins's dispatch. He indicated that

> May 30th was one of the greatest days in our campaign. . . . We came in sight of the [Indian] ranches just as the Indians were going out hunting. We commenced firing, and after a fight of half an hour we went out to count the dead—found about 25 bucks killed and about ten wounded. We found no guns, just got twelve quivers full of arrows the Indians made use of very fast. Then comes June 2nd and with it another fight, showing evident signs that but few escaped the lead or knife. Men were stationed in all directions. Here we counted twenty-three killed and some wounded; we then burned the ranches and started back to camp very sleepy.[1021]

Turk does not call these engagements battles, nor were they. No soldiers were reported wounded or killed. The Indians were armed only with bows and arrows. Soldiers surrounded the Indians' camp site. No indication is given that the trapped, poorly armed Indians were offered a chance to surrender. Turk is describing what were massacres. In the aftermath the soldiers were "very sleepy" but the Indians were dead.

Many of the ranchers had fled their recently built homes as they came under attack by the Nongatls, who were residents of long standing, apparently struck by the quaint idea that they were defending *their* homeland. Lt. Collins believed a continuing military presence was necessary to assure the whites that they could safely resume ranching. He recommended the

construction of a post "on Eel River, near the head of Larrabee [sic] Creek,"[1022] failing to understand that the latter location was actually three rugged mountainous miles from the former. In the event, his superiors followed half of his advice, soon establishing Fort Seward in the canyon of the Eel River, a location that proved so inaccessible and useless that the fort was abandoned less than a year later.[1023]

Larabee Creek may be divided into three geomorphological sections.[1024] From its headwaters just north of Blocksburg, it runs north-northwest along a nearly level valley floor for about 11 miles before turning west. It subsequently enters a second, more confined section, which gradually narrows to become a deep gorge. Near its confluence with Smith Creek, it leaves the gorge and, in its third section, continues west for

Chalk Mountain separates the Van Duzen from Burr Creek (JR).

about five miles through an expanding canyon until it reaches the Eel at the small community of Larabee. Along the upper portion of the creek, the Round Valley and Hydesville Trail[1025] was established at an early but uncertain date. It was certainly in place by August 1864, when the *Humboldt Times* carried a report on "Larabee's Station," claiming "that the diggers had destroyed it by fire and killed a white man."[1026] Four years later and a few miles to the north, one of the last encounters between Indians and the local whites ended near Little Burr Creek[1027] with the deaths of vigilante Joe Drinkwater and an Indian named Big Foot.[1028]

Once almost all the Nongatls in the area had been killed or taken to reservations, ranching intensified, filling in the 22 miles[1029] between the head of Larabee Creek and the Van Duzen River. One of the ranchers, Alexander Robertson, started acquiring land there in 1874. By 1880 he had accumulated 33 parcels, most of which had previously been owned as quarter sections (160 acres).[1030]

When the government surveyed the area in 1872, a reincarnated "Laribee [sic][1031] Station"

appeared just north of where the Round Valley and Hydesville Trail crossed Mill Creek.[1032] In 1875 the trail was superseded by the Overland Road, which that year was completed between Bridgeport (Bridgeville) and Blocksburg.[1033] The area was further glorified in 1888 when Laribee Station was expanded by the opening of the Laribee Post Office at the same location.[1034] The 1890 county directory went so far as to include "Laribee, via Bridgeville" as a "town" 64 miles distant from Eureka. Three other nearby locations also made the directory's list,[1035] all reached by way of the mountain-encircled metropolis of Bridgeville. "Bur[r] Creek Station" was 50 miles from Eureka and was just north of the Overland Road crossing at Little Burr Creek.[1036] "French," no distance given, was a farm on Little Burr Creek named for its owner, Greenleaf C. French.[1037] "Curless," also no distance given, was the ranch of Biar and Lovina Curless, who homesteaded there in 1869.[1038] All four of the above locations were either stage stations or stopping places, or both. One local knew the road through these spots especially well. (See sidebar 1.)

---

1. "I was mud and blood from head to foot."

Between 1877 and 1894 or 1895, George Friend ran the Alderpoint stage station in summer and carried the mail between that point and Bridgeville in winter. Over 50 years later he recalled both activities but lingered on describing his mail carrying. As Friend put it,

> This was no snap. Heavy snow and rain storms made the trail doubly dangerous, and the worst part of it, in order to make proper connections and get the mail through on time, it was necessary to make the trip at night. I rode a horse and drove a pack horse ahead of me because I could make better time driving the horse instead of leading it.

The pack horse had three bells on his harness so I could locate him in the dark. I have often thought how handy it would have been if flashlights had been invented at the time.

The only lights we had on these long night trips were "coach candles." These candles were about 1½ inches in diameter and 6 inches long. We carried them in a little box strapped to our leg. The box had a glass front, something like old carriage lights, and on a clear night the candles would show as far as the toe of your boot.

But it did help the mail carriers to locate each other in the dark. On some of the runs there would be carriers going each way and they would try to calculate by the length of the candle just how long it would be before they met the other carrier. That is they would burn two lengths of candle this trip, or an actual time of about 4 hours for the 22 miles.[1039]

The mail route from Cloverdale, in Mendocino County, to Eureka was 217 miles long. In summertime the carriers were given 36 hours to complete the run. In winter the men were allocated 80 hours, "and," according to Friend, "we needed every minute of it."[1040] He gave a couple of examples of the delays he'd encountered.

Once Friend came to the Charles Ranch and found that Larabee Creek had washed out the trail. His horse didn't realize the change, however, and kept going. The bank caved in, Friend said,

. . . throwing the horse and myself into the raging current. I left the horse as we hit the water and started to swim to shore. I was wearing heavy oilskins because of the storm and it didn't help my swimming one bit. There was a swift current running and it was nip and tuck with me, but I made it.

In the meantime my horse, who had landed out in the main current, was swept away down stream several hundred yards. There was some drift wood along there with a long ash pole sticking out into the stream and the horn of the saddle hooked up on that pole, and there the horse hung, teetering back and forth, sometimes with his head under and sometimes his tail under.

I ran down and tried to figure out some way to get the poor beast loose before he drowned, but just then the saddle girths gave way and the horse scrambled ashore. I rounded up the pack horse, and rode my saddle horse bareback to Burr Creek, a distance of some 12 miles, where I had another saddle. I tell you, it was the coldest ride I ever had. I nearly froze before I got there—but the mail went through. I never did find the saddle, but it belonged to the stage company anyway.[1041]

That was a tough tale to top, but Friend managed it with this one:

One particularly nasty winter's night, I was riding through a heavy snow storm when the horse missed his footing and fell off of the trail down into Little Dobbins Creek. When he landed I was pinned under him by one leg, and he was down in such a shape he couldn't get himself up. So there we lay, and it seemed a mighty long time to me, though perhaps it might not have been over half an hour.

The horse in his struggles cut my forehead, and it was pretty uncomfortable there wallowing in the snow and mud on the edge of the river with blood streaming down my face. After a while I managed to get my boot off and got my leg out from under the horse and then helped the horse get up.

The mail went through all right, but I was a pretty hard looking specimen when I reached the hotel the next morning, as I was mud and blood from head to foot.[1042]

No community ever developed in the area between Bridgeville and Blocksburg. A Laribee School, nine miles north of Blocksburg, began in 1873. It reportedly operated until 1922; thereafter local students went to the school in Blocksburg.[1043] Joel Whitmore built a sawmill at Larabee Station in 1876,[1044] but nothing more was heard of it. Two years later the station, run by a Mr. Dyer, was deemed "a fine summer resort for invalids,"[1045] apparently languishing in disuse the rest of the year. It, too, faded from the news. In 1885 McTavish, an itinerant reporter, told the *Humboldt Standard* that rancher George Charles had nearly 12,000 acres on which to graze 8,000 to 10,000 sheep, but it was apparent that his "very handsome

two-story residence"[1046] hardly qualified for the start of a town. The most public place along the road, the Laribee post office, came and went—twice. Its first run, from 1888 to 1891, ended when it merged with the Blocksburg office, but it reopened the next year and lasted until 1899. This time it merged with Bridgeville's P. O.[1047] The Burr Creek School was of longer duration but was a hit-and-miss operation. It started in 1887 with Frank Cuddeback teaching six boys and six girls. There was one book in the library and no outhouse. The following year the library had grown to seven books. In 1889 there were now 14 students, still evenly divided, and there was still no outhouse. By 1905 the library had mushroomed to 137 volumes. The presence or

Burr Creek School, 1907, with or without an outhouse (HCHS, colorized by JR).

absence of an outhouse was not mentioned. Ruth Moorehead French taught intermittently at the school between 1916 and 1939, the longest tenure by far of any teacher. In 1942 the Burr Creek School closed, and students then went to Bridgeville.[1048]

But not for long. The timber boom in the late 1940s brought enough families into the area that by 1947 the one-room Bridgeville School was filled to overflowing. To deal with the problem an "emergency school" was set up in the "in the camp at Chalk Mountain Ranch Road." This was not an ideal venue, and so the next year the Burr Creek School was brought

out of retirement. It took some work to refurbish the building for it was just "an empty room with a porch on it." The schoolhouse had no electricity, phone, or running water, but at least there were now two outhouses. After serving for one year, the school was again closed, and the students returned to Bridgeville for their studies.[1049] Fifty years later the weatherbeaten building still stood by what was now Alderpoint Road,[1050] but it failed to long withstand the rigors of the new millennium and is now marked only in the memories of those who studied in it or drove past it.

Sic transit gloria ludus.[1051]

Chapter 20
Dinsmore

Just west of the Trinity County line, the Van Duzen River runs through an open valley for several miles before reaching a constricted canyon that bends around the north-facing bulk of McClellan Mountain. When the valley was mapped in 1872, "Wyckoff's House" was shown on the north side of the river about where the small community of Dinsmore later developed.[1052]

Nothing more is known about Wyckoff. His predecessors in the area were probably a tribal group called the Na-ai-tci ki-yas. It appears they were a division of the so-called Nongatl tribe. Van Duzen Pete, a Nongatl, reported that there were "lots" of Na-ai-tci ki-yas on both the "Big" (main) Van Duzen and the Little Van Duzen. According to Pete the group occupied the area from Hogback Ridge, on the main Van Duzen just above the original Fort Baker, up to the forks of the Van Duzen, and then up the South Fork, or Little Van Duzen.[1053] At the forks of the Van Duzen Goddard mapped a Na-ai-tci ki-ya village called Le-gi-li-me with "lots of Indian houses. On both sides Little V[an] D[uzen]."[1054] Pete also indicated that the Na-ai-tci ki-yas were located "over near Low Gap."[1055] Based on this information, it is probable that the area between the forks of the Van Duzen and Low Gap was also Na-ai-tci ki-ya territory.

By 1876[1056] George and Almeria Eaton had a cattle and sheep ranch north of the forks. The property contained some dramatically barren rock outcroppings that became known as the Eaton Roughs.[1057] John Owen Dinsmore, who had a dairy farm at Grizzly Bluff, purchased the Eatons' ranch "of about three thousand acres" in 1901.[1058] He added to this acreage in 1905 when he bought the Green Bartlett[1059] Ranch on Bartlett's Flat, which lay just east of the former Eaton Ranch.[1060] John Owen Dinsmore sold both his Grizzly Bluff and Van Duzen River ranches to four of his sons in 1906.[1061]

Part of the Green Bartlett property came down to the north side of the Van Duzen River, and by 1911 the road to Trinity County ran through the edge of what was by then the Dinsmore Ranch.[1062] Now that the location was accessible by auto, the Dinsmores built a lodge[1063] and started a resort by the roadside. Each season some 50 to 75 "sports" came to stay at "Dinsmore's" to fish or hunt in the surrounding area.[1064]

On August 19, 1913, a note was delivered to Dinsmore's Resort. It was from Earl P. Burns, who had a neighboring ranch. He informed the brothers that some of their milk cows had strayed over to Burns's place, where they entered and destroyed his garden. Burns was notifying the Dinsmores "to take possession of their stock and settle for the damages they had done to his garden." The four Dinsmore boys and a hired man saddled up and rode over to the Burns place where, according to subsequent court testimony, they "settled up" in dramatic fashion. They found Burns at his ranch with his two young sons, Lee, age 9, and Bobbie, 6. According to Lee's testimony at the trial, the five men attacked his father, while "he stood off a few yards hurling rocks at the man who had his father down until one of the men struck him and knocked him senseless." Bobbie took the

Dinsmore's Resort in early days (THPO, colorized by JR).

stand and testified that he was kicked by one of the riders and then fled into the house and climbed into bed. Earl Burns sued the Dinsmore brothers. The jury, no doubt impressed by the Burns boys' testimony, awarded Earl $2,500.[1065]

The Dinsmore family was not the only owner of a resort in the area. Arthur and Louise Renfroe had a 160-acre ranch about a mile and a half northwest of Dinsmore. They built a six-bedroom house there in 1921. Sometime after that two doctors from the Bay Area drove up to the ranch, looking for good deer-hunting ground. Art Renfroe guided them to such a location, and Lou, who had cooked at the Star Hotel in Fortuna, fixed their meals. The doctors enjoyed their vacation, and once back in San Francisco they spread the word of their happy days in the mountains of eastern Humboldt. The next year they returned, bringing some friends with them. Thus started "Art Renfroe's Resort." Eventually entire families came, including some from Humboldt County. It seemed that "all of Fortuna" visited, according to Charlene Kanahele, the Renfroes' niece. In 1990 she wrote a memoir of the place, noting that

Arthur and Louise Renfroe are gone, as are many of those who enjoyed their hospitality. The old house burned long ago; once well-defined trails are overgrown with brush and trees. Is the old barn still standing? Do the owls still hoot in the woods bordering Charley Cavagnarro's place? Surely the tiny, flavorful wild strawberries still flourish along certain sunny banks, the abundant bed of fawn lilies still bloom down below the gate and the lady slippers and tiger lilies thrive in their secret places—And, after the mad torrents of winter, the quiet, green pools form in Mad River, as "in those old days of the lost sunshine of youth."[1066]

The road to Renfroes' ranch, which eventually diminished to a trail, left the main road about a half-mile east of Dinsmore. Another half-mile east on the main road was a stop important enough to be marked on the maps—Cobb's. Accounts are fragmentary, but it appears that Joseph D. Cobb, his wife Sarah, and their family moved from Bridgeville to the upper Van Duzen in 1907, at which time they opened a roadside store. Joseph Cobb died in 1931.[1067] His son William operated the store from 1932 until his retirement in 1946.[1068]

Three miles east of Cobb's store was another marked location called either Kunz or Kuntz that lay almost exactly on the county line.[1069] It was named for Frank Kuntz, who had property east of the Cobbs that stretched across both counties.[1070] The locale made the news in the late 1880s. (See sidebar 1).

The Dinsmore Lodge served for a time as a stage stop. John Friend drove the mail stage from Bridgeville to Ruth in 1917-1918. It took him six hours to reach Dinsmore, where he had lunch, which "was always good," and changed teams. Then Friend drove five more hours to

---

1. The Death of an "Honest Norwegian"

A mile east of Kuntz was a ranch that in the 1880s belonged to "industrious George Ericson, an honest Norwegian who was brave and a good shot." None of these sterling qualities were of any help, however, when Ericson acquired sufficient land to attract the notice of George Edward White, the notorious "autocrat of Round Valley."[1071] Not content to control the ranch land of northeastern Mendocino County, White extended his realm to include property in both southeastern Humboldt County and southwestern Trinity County. White determined to drive Ericson out of the area:

> Ericson was soon subjected to every kind of abuse known to White's unscrupulous hirelings: his stock was run off; his fences were broken; and false charges of illicit distilling, sheep stealing, and misappropriation of wool were brought against him in the courts, which almost ruined him financially. But still he stayed and defied White and his henchmen. A man named Schappe was sent to shoot him but missed, and Ericson fired many bullets after the man, intentionally coming close to frighten him. Then Ericson was arrested on a charge of assault to murder, but the district attorney failed to "file an information," and the case lapsed. Ericson refused to leave his claim, thinking that he had finally outwitted White's gang.[1072]

But then:

> In early part of September, 1886, Ericson's riderless horse came out of the woods with the saddle covered with blood. Some sheepherders who had heard the shots found his body, which had been shot in the back from ambush.[1073]

Evidence was subsequently discovered indicating that five men had put up money to have Ericson murdered. Two of them, George Orr and Trinity County Deputy Sheriff George Kuntz, were arrested and Kuntz brought to trial for the murder. Orr confessed to involvement in the killing but claimed that Kuntz did the actual shooting. According to Orr, he and Kuntz waited for Ericson on the trail. But Ericson didn't show up, and Orr and Kuntz left to go fix a fence. Kuntz, however, "took his gun and returned to the trail." Orr heard four shots and shortly afterward Kuntz returned. Orr claimed that the following conversation then occurred:

"Well, I got some big game down there," Kuntz said.

"What was it?"

"George Ericson."

"What were the four shots about?"

"To fool anyone who might have heard the shooting. They would lay it to some poor shot and never suspect me. I shot him in the back as he rode by on his mule. He threw up his hands and yelled and rode on. But I fixed him."[1074]

As murdering Ericson was not enough, Kuntz then inflicted further pain on the dead man's relatives, for "at the funeral, Kuntz furnished the boards for Ericson's coffin and charged his family $250."[1075]

Kuntz was tried for murder in Weaverville, found guilty, and sentenced to hang on March 18, 1887. His lawyers appealed the verdict, which was reversed by the state supreme court. A new trial was held in August 1888 that resulted in a verdict of not guilty. At $2,500, it was considered "the most important and costly . . . trial ever held in Trinity County." The *Trinity Journal* venomously attacked the verdict, urging "that if ever a similar case comes before courts" the accused should be lynched.[1076]

Justice, however slight, came only decades later. By 1922 the name Kuntz had vanished from that year's map, but 36 years after the murder, the words "Ericson Ranch" were still present.[1077]

Ruth. The next day he reversed the trip. The stage, which must have been no more than a glorified buckboard, was pulled by two horses and had a yellow umbrella instead of a roof. Friend could carry up to three passengers in addition to the mail. There was sometimes excitement at the Van Duzen River crossing west of Dinsmore, which had no bridge until 1920. If the river was high, "you swum it or didn't get across," according to Friend. By the 1920s mechanization had taken over, and motor stages ran from Eureka to Red Bluff. Arriving from each direction at about the same time, the drivers stopped for lunch at Dinsmore; then the passengers changed vehicles, completing their trips as the drivers returned to their starting points.[1078]

Dinsmore's Resort in later days (THPO, colorized by JR).

More than humans made the trip east to the Central Valley. In December 1930 the "Dinsmore brothers drove a large herd of cattle to Tehama county for winter pasture."[1079] Unlike the auto-stage passengers, the cattle had failed to find adequate food at Dinsmore.

In 1943 brothers Bob and Jay Dinsmore bought the family's Dinsmore property from their uncles. The brothers divided the holdings in 1949. Bob and his wife Gloria took over the former Eaton Ranch while Jay and his wife Leona kept the resort on Highway 36.[1080] A guest at Dinsmore's, Les Pierce of Pierce Flying Services, talked Jay into buying a plane and gave him flying lessons that involved using the hayfield east of the resort. In 1955 Dinsmore gave the field to Humboldt County, and it became the Dinsmore Airport.[1081]

In 1955, George Lennon bought the Dinsmore Lodge, the nearby store, and other buildings from Jay Dinsmore. In the 1960s three

fraternity brothers bought out Lennon. After two of them died in a plane crash, the last of the three, Jim Hartley, sold the property to Corky Korkowski and Bill Hulse in 1972. The pair had driven up from Los Angeles "looking for country property." They found 430 acres that ran along two and a half miles of the Van Duzen, but there was a catch: the buildings that went with the land were almost in ruins. Hulse was so shocked he couldn't talk. He found that "the lodge and the cabins were riddled with bullet holes, 57 windows were broken, the plumbing was sustained by coffee cans. . . ." Nonetheless, after sleeping on it for a night, the pair decided to buy what was left of Dinsmore.[1082]

The purchase was made, and Bill and Corky moved up from Los Angeles. They had been at their new property for only an hour when their first customers—Jim and Donna Hall from Montana—showed up. The lodge, with its bullet holes and broken windows, wasn't ready to receive guests yet, so the Halls "paid three dollars for sleeping outside and for dining on food cooked in an iron skillet over an open fire." The lodge officially reopened that July, "when the major repairs and redecorating were completed." Korkowski had known just how to revamp the premises; he was an interior designer by profession and had just completed plans for basketball star Wilt Chamberlain's 8,300-square foot mansion in Southern California.[1083]

Hulse and Korkowski wound up spending about $40,000 to restore the lodge, but even with nearby airport access, the place "never really lived up to expectations as a tourist destination." By 2006 the lodge still had rooms available for tourists, but the accommodations were politely described as "quaint" or "inexpensive."[1084] It was a far cry from the days when John Friend—and up to three passengers—could hardly wait until they arrived, just in time for lunch, at Dinsmore.

Chapter 21
Larabee Valley

The Larabee Valley is a nearly flat expanse of upland prairie—an island of grassy openness enclosed by a turbulent sea of forested mountains. On lower Butte Creek, near the southern edge of the prairie, two Nongatl villages occupied the valley the Indians called Kosdun. The people from these villages apparently formed the entirety of a tribal group called the Kos-dun ki-ya.[1085]

The valley's elevation is about 2,500 feet, so it saw snow at times when lower-elevation Nongatl villages on the Van Duzen had only rain. Despite this, about 25 Kos-dun ki-ya "used to stay there all winter."[1086]

One of the first reports from the valley came in early June 1861, when Lieutenant Joseph Collins and soldiers from the Fourth Infantry, who were searching for Indians in eastern Humboldt County, moved into the vicinity of Larabee Valley. Collins reported that on

> June 2, attacked a rancheria about five miles from Larrabee's [sic] house; killed 20 Indians. June 8, attacked a rancheria about three miles south of Larrabee's house; killed 4 and wounded 1. June 16, attacked a rancheria near Kettenshaw Valley; killed 4 Indians. Corporal Larrabee, of the volunteers, wounded in the left arm by an arrow. This rancheria was occupied by Las-sic's [sic] band, probably the most desperate and troublesome Indians in the mountains. They have frequently been engaged in murdering whites, burning houses, and killing

horses and cattle. I regret so few of them were killed, but they were constantly on the alert and could only be caught by following them day and night, the troop carrying their provisions and blankets on their backs. The attack was made near noon, and as the Indians were prepared for it, many of them escaped through the almost impassable brush.[1087]

Collins's condemnation of Lassik's Indians, who were defending their homeland, could have more aptly been applied to the lieutenant's wounded corporal, Henry Larabee.[1088] The man who left the valley his name also left a legacy of death and destruction unequaled in Humboldt County history. (See sidebar 1.)

In 1867 Hugh McClellan and an unnamed partner purchased 2,200 sheep and drove them to the mountainous area east of Bridgeville. After five years McClellan bought out his partner and gradually expanded his ranch.[1089] The property came to extend over much of the Larabee Valley, with additional parcels northeastward in the vicinity of "northern" Burr Creek,[1090] while it also covered so much of the mountainous area northwest of Larabee Valley that the landform took the name McClellan Mountain.[1091] The ranch comprised more than 11,000 acres, with an equal amount of government land being used for grazing. This combination provided enough grass to feed 5,000 sheep. Small wonder that McClellan became one of the organizers of the Humboldt Bay Woolen Mills Company in Eureka.[1092] Hugh McClellan died

1. A Name That Lives in Infamy

Henry Larabee was born in Ohio in about 1828. He came to California in 1849, and ten years later "established a ranch east of what is now known as Bridgeville."[1093] The 1859 assessment rolls indicate that Larabee" had livestock valued at $2,080 and was living on public land.[1094] Larabee operated his ranch in partnership with Wallace M. Hagans.[1095] Their ranch house was near the headwaters of the north fork of Little Larabee Creek, about halfway between McClellan Rock and Sweasey Lake.[1096] In 1862 Larabee moved to Montana, where he became sheriff of Missoula County. During his three-year stay in Humboldt County, he committed multiple murders of Indians. Larabee reportedly "boasted of having killed *sixty infants* with his own hatchet at the different slaughter grounds." Angered because an Indian boy who worked for him left to visit his relatives, Larabee went to their place and "slaughtered the whole family." He then put the bodies on a raft of logs and sent it down the Van Duzen to another rancher who was sympathetic to the Indians.[1097] When Lieutenant Daniel Lyons of the Sixth U. S. Infantry visited Larabee Valley in March 1861, he reported on the area's most infamous inhabitant:

> I had no conversation with Mr. Larrabee. . . . I heard no man speak in his favor, or even intimate one redeeming trait in his character. The universal cry was against him. . . . [He was] an accomplice and actor in the massacre at Indian Island and South Beach; the murderer of Yo-keel-la-bah; recently engaged in killing unoffending Indians, his party, according to their own story, having killed eighteen at one time . . . and now at work imbruing his hands in the blood of slaughtered innocence, I do not think Mr. Larrabee can be too emphatically condemned.[1098]

By the time Lyons filed his report, Larabee and Hagans's house was in ashes and their cook, Ann Quinn,[1099] dead. More than 60 years later, "Black Jim" Euret recalled that he was working on the ranch, "in the timber making rails," when he heard a rifle shot. Then another ranch hand, David King, came running to him, shouting, "Injuns, Injuns. They've killed the cook!" Euret looked towards the ranch house and saw "about a dozen Indians and under a large oak tree the young woman lying dead." Euret headed west to get help but had trouble finding any. He came upon a Portuguese man herding cattle and borrowed his horse, riding to the closest community, which was

Yager. Euret found that many residents had fled because of several Indian attacks, and consequently its population consisted of Al Frame. After staying at Frame's overnight, Euret rode west to Redwood House, where there were two soldiers. He continued on to the mouth of Yager Creek, where he found Henry Larabee. Euret and Larabee headed back to the burnt ranch, picking up the soldiers, Frame, the Portuguese cowboy, and King along the way. The six men started after the Indian band, which they found early the next morning. They killed seven of the Indians, "and that," according to Euret, "was the end of that."[1100]

Larabee lived in Humboldt County at a time when whites, who ignored what local Indians called various locations, were busy attaching new names to geographical features. Over the years Larabee's last name was attached to three such features: a valley, a creek, and (somewhat later) a small community. Persons who are offended by seeing his name thus displayed on county maps can at least take heart in knowing that in all three instances, the family's spelling for their name, "Larrabee," has been misspelled as "Larabee," a small diminishment but nonetheless a start.

in 1911. Three years later, following the "devastation of . . . [the] flock by coyotes," his son John sold all of the ranch's sheep. They were replaced with Hereford and Durham cattle.[1101]

In 1901 five ranchers from the Larabee Valley-Buck Mountain area—George Friend, J. A. Albee, H. M. Devoy, William Bankhead, and C. T. Schreiner—began constructing, at their own expense, a private road that connected their properties with the county road at McClellan Rock.[1102] Eleven years later the ranchers' road provided a way for Larabee Valley children to reach the area's brand-new school.

Families were scattered across the Larabee Valley ranchlands, but by 1912 enough children could be centralized that the Buck Mountain School opened. It was located nowhere near Buck Mountain, which lay about 10 miles to the east. It could have more accurately been named for McClellan Mountain, which rose up directly

behind the school.[1103] But the local namers, who may have grown up schoolless, had perhaps never learned their geography.

In 1913 seven children from the Stockhoff, Williams, Heston, and Friend families attended the school.[1104] The Williams and Heston properties were about a mile south of McClellan Rock on upper Little Larabee Creek, and by using the 1901 private road, it was about three miles to the school. The Friend and Stockhoff ranches were farther away, some five or six miles southeast of the school near the confluence of Butte Creek with the South Fork Van Duzen.[1105] It was a long walk for little kids like Helen, Dorothy, and Kenneth Stockhoff, who carried their lunches in repurposed tobacco cans. The school was a frail-looking board-and-batten structure that was approximately 12 feet long and 8 feet wide, about right for seven students and their teacher.[1106]

Buck Mountain School in winter, 1913 (HCHS, colorized by JR).

The school stood next to the county road about a mile west of McClellan Rock. The road had recently been extended from McClellan Rock to the Trinity County line, where it connected with a Trinity County road on a route that reached all the way to Red Bluff.[1107] One of its more exciting sections was at the southeastern end of McClellan Mountain, where it dropped and twisted through a mile or so of hairpin curves to reach a bridge over the South Fork Van Duzen near the mouth of Burr Creek.[1108]

On December 6, 1913, two new residents arrived in Larabee Valley. They had traveled a long way to get there. (See Appendix A.)

The tide of time washed quietly over Larabee Valley. Then, in 1929, the Alton-Red Bluff road was rerouted so that it dropped south from McClellan Rock on the route of the 1901 private ranch road. Starting at Butte Creek, a new section of road was constructed; after crossing the South Fork Van Duzen, it met the existing Alton-Red Bluff road near the mouth of Burr Creek. Although the new route was longer, it eliminated the tortuous curves and steep grades of the earlier route that cut across the side of McClellan Mountain. To complete the new route, contractor Thomas Englehart planned on using two steam shovels and set a tentative completion date of July 1.[1109]

As the 1920s moved into the 1930s, the Larabee Valley road excitement ebbed, and the area returned to the calm of ranchland rusticity. Events merited no more than a sentence or two in the local newspapers. In October 1932 Emmett Atwell returned to Fortuna from Larabee Valley where he had spent "a couple of weeks . . . helping O. Hodges."[1110] What Atwell was helping Hodges do was not reported. In July 1933 John F. Quinn, his wife, and their niece left the damp confines of Eureka and motored out to the Quinns' summer home to experience a bit of southeastern Humboldt heat.[1111] Then, in September 1937, Guy Felt, who had property on Horse Creek next to the Friends, discovered that panthers had killed some of his goats.[1112] So went the events of the valley.

Meanwhile the Buck Mountain School continued to serve a small group of students. There was no electricity at the school (or anywhere else in the area), so all the light came from windows on three sides of the building. According to Shirley Schelling Tommila, a student there in the 1940s, the children walked to school every day, "sometimes in deep snow." One boy rode his horse and stabled it in a small shed. The schoolhouse sat on the hillside above the road, "so there was very little flat land to play ball."[1113]

Attendance increased in the latter part of the decade[1114] as Larabee Valley felt the impact of the post-World War I housing boom. By 1952 the Hinton Lumber Company had a mill on Butte Creek, and Sauer's Mill sat nearby. C. R. Schelling's mill was also located in the Larabee Valley area, eight miles east of Bridgeville.[1115]

The loggers logged and the mills cut until there were no logs left to cut. The workers left Larabee Creek. The Buck Mountain School closed in 1961. Cattle still grazed the grasses of Kosdun but eventually "dope growers" noted the area's remoteness and established proscribed plantations of marijuana. Times changed, "pot" became permissible, and the 2010s saw an influx of "cannabis cultivators," some of whom fulfilled the necessary requirements for legalized growing. Now anyone looking down at night from the Charles Mountain ridge would no longer see the dim glimmer of a solitary kerosene lamp in a window; instead they would witness the ghostly glow of dozens of Humboldt hoop houses, whose interior lights stimulate the growth of the backcountry's cash crop.

Appendix A. The Light in the Window

Henry Schneider was a carpenter. Emil Pfeil was a blacksmith. Their skills had allowed them to become sailors, and for years they traveled far from their home in Marburg, Germany, where

Buck Mountain School students (HCHS, colorized by JR).

they had grown up as best friends. In 1912 they decided to go to the United States. They did some additional sailing and met up in New York in the fall of 1913. Schneider and Pfeil took a train to San Francisco, apparently, with the insouciance of youth, having no ultimate destination in mind. After their arrival they spent time at the Ferry Building, studying a relief map of California. Humboldt County caught their interest, so they read up on the area and, as Henry put it, were attracted by "those big trees, dairy farms, stock ranches, and above all government land to be homesteaded." They took the steamer *Phoenix* to Eureka, thinking they could later go farther north if they didn't like Humboldt.[1116]

But like it they did. They found a "homestead locator" who drove them out to Larabee Valley where they looked at a promising claim. Once back in Eureka, Emil took a blacksmithing job at the jetty, while Henry took the train to Carlotta, where the tracks ended, and walked up the Van Duzen to Bridgeville. There he encountered Sam Stockhoff[1117] and his two sons and accompanied them as they drove cattle and hauled supplies back to their Larabee Valley ranch. Stockhoff showed Schneider the claim and indicated it was worth filing on. Schneider accordingly walked the 50 miles back to Eureka, discussed the claim with Pfeil, made another trip to see the property, and then filed for it.[1118]

The men purchased "a gun and ammunition, saws, axes, shovels, pots and pans, a Dutch oven, provisions and bedding, a big piece of canvas and plenty of matches." It was enough of a load that they traveled by stage to Bridgeville and then took another stage to McClellan Rock. From there Stockhoff took their belongings to an old barn on his property, where he let the men stay as they built their cabin. It was

early December, not a propitious time to begin house building in snow country. Sure enough, "it rained or snowed nearly everyday," but Schneider and Pfeil worked through it, cutting down trees, peeling the bark, and carrying the logs to the cabin site. They split shakes for roofing and hewed boards for flooring, and in late January they moved into their cabin.[1119] The locals watched the pair struggling in the snow to finish the cabin and dubbed them "the two crazy sailors."[1120]

That spring they bought a span of mules, Belle and Judith, along with a wagon and farm tools. Then in April Henry went to the East Coast to join the crew of a yacht for the summer. He had held the job previously, and the wages would come in handy. Emil was busy at the homestead, clearing and fencing a field, putting in a garden, and hewing timbers for a barn. He bought a pony, "little Billy," and made a hay wagon. After Henry returned in November, they built a barn "so," as Henry said, "that the animals were sheltered as we sat in our snug cabin while the storms raged outside." He added that "we spent our evenings reading, writing letters or exchanging stories of our sailing days and the ports we visited." Henry told of a Chilean sailor on the *Oranazia* who had experienced a frightful voyage:

> They left Liverpool for Seattle and broke the fore gallant mast around Cape Horn and lost most of their sails so they were obliged to go to Cape Town, South Africa, for repairs which took about two months. They went through the Indian Ocean to the Pacific heading for Seattle, but the journey had been so long that they were short of provisions, lost two men overboard, the Captain died, and

only a few men were left who were able to work, so they couldn't manage the sails. They sighted a steamer near the California Coast. A tug boat was sent out to bring them into San Diego where the crew was hospitalized and a new crew took the ship to Seattle.[1121]

Emil and Henry had landed far from such perils of the ocean when they homesteaded in Larabee Valley. Instead of the boundless expanse of the blue Pacific, they now had the confined waters of Butte Creek, a tributary of the South Fork Van Duzen that headed at Charles Mountain and the Larabee Buttes. In addition to including two branches of the creek, about a third of their homestead was prairie. The rest of the property was wooded, and its western side tilted upward towards the buttes.[1122]

Emil filed for his own homestead in the spring of 1915, having found a parcel about two miles east of Henry's. In addition to the Stock-hoffs, their only neighbors were George and Addie Friend, who had a ranch directly east of Henry's place.[1123]

Then came the "hard winter of 1915-1916 . . . [when] it snowed or froze nearly every day until the middle of February." At the homesteads "there was usually four feet of snow on the ground." Fortunately Henry and Emil had left their mules at Bridgeville and were able to use their small supply of hay for the cows, which would have starved otherwise.[1124]

Henry and Emil found that even though America had yet to enter World War I, they were victims of an anti-German attitude. Henry indicated that they "felt a coolness from those whom we thought were our friends." For a time Emil wanted to leave the country. Instead, he sold his claim to neighbor George Friend and went to work in the Sacramento Valley. Henry referred to the elderly Friends as "Uncle George" and "Aunt Addie."[1125] During the summer of 1917 Henry met a woman at the Friends' house who definitely did not have an anti-German attitude. She was the Buck Mountain school teacher, Jenny Alfred. Jenny's husband had died of tuberculosis, leaving her a single parent with two children. Now Henry began helping Jenny with her chores, fixing fences and repairing the children's shoes.[1126]

On April 1, 1917, Henry checked with the Humboldt County Clerk regarding his pending citizenship papers. Henry learned that the five-year waiting period for granting his citizenship would expire on April 16. On April 6 the United States entered the World War I,[1127] and Henry, having committed the crime of being ten days short of gaining his citizenship, immediately became an "alien enemy."[1128]

A few months later, Henry learned that ship carpenters were needed in Eureka. Mindful of his alien enemy status, he checked with the district attorney to see if it was all right to apply for the job. The D.A. told him "no," adding that "reports have come in that you and Emil are under investigation." The D.A. advised Henry "to go home and stay away from Eureka." Henry, who had been working for the Holmes Eureka Lumber Company, took a more remote job at a tanbark camp near Blocksburg.

In January 1918 Henry and Jenny were married. That fall they rented a ranch near Blocksburg. Henry found it was "a more pleasant environment" than Larabee Valley, where some of the residents still could not forgive him for being German.[1129]

Emil returned to Humboldt County in March 1919. He and Henry went for their citizenship examination in January 1920. The hearing judge asked them no questions. Instead he said, "their record in the East is excellent. Admitted."[1130]

Emil went to Seattle in the fall of 1920 and the following year continued north to Alaska. Despite now being a United States citizen, Henry still faced hostility. Jenny's mother was part of the Rackliff family, who were long-time ranchers on the Mattole. The mother had opposed her daughter's marriage to a German. The depth of her opposition became apparent when she died in 1921; her will provided that all of Jenny's siblings would inherit the Rackliff home ranch property.[1131] As punishment for marrying Henry, Jenny was willed a parcel of marshy farm land near Oxnard.[1132]

Henry and Jenny reluctantly left Humboldt County and moved to Oxnard. Henry busied himself reclaiming the marsh land, and then Fate, in one of her ironical caprices, determined that the property would become highway frontage, resulting in the Schneiders gaining remarkable wealth.[1133]

The Schneiders kept their Larabee Valley ranch but were in Oxnard in November 1929 when a wildfire burned through the homestead, destroying all the buildings. Henry and Jenny rebuilt, constructing two cabins, a barn, a woodshed, and a garage on the site.[1134]

Emil stayed in Alaska. Henry learned that his friend "became a successful businessman. He married a highschool teacher in Anchorage and built a home there." Emil visited the Schneiders in Oxnard in 1944, and Henry visited Emil and his family in Anchorage in the summer of 1950. Later that year Henry and Emil returned to their "childhood home in Marburg, Germany and

found a few boyhood friends who had survived two worldwars." In 1954 Emil was killed in an airplane crash in Alaska.[1135]

Jenny and Henry continued to spend time at what they still called "the homestead." By 1960 Jenny was suffering so badly from arthritis that she could no longer make the trip from Larabee Valley to Fortuna to get supplies. The Schneiders sold the property to Doug and Elizabeth Clayton. Henry and Jenny spent their last years at a rest home in Berkeley. Their daughter, a nurse, lived nearby.[1136]

Decades earlier, not long after Henry and Jenny were married, Jenny received word that Henry needed to go to Bridgeville to register as an alien. Henry was away over the ridge, working in Blocksburg. Jenny was anxious to get more information, so she tried to borrow a horse from a neighbor. He responded in a neighborly way, for someone who disliked Germans, by offering her a mule instead. She refused the blighted offer and instead walked to Bridgeville. There she learned that there was no rush required to sign the papers, so she borrowed a horse from Henry Cox, the store owner, and rode to Blocksburg to find Henry. When she arrived she learned that Henry had already departed for home. Jenny promptly left Blocksburg and headed north along Larabee Creek. Probably at the Charles Corrals, she took the trail that crossed Charles Mountain. The sun set and there was no moon. Jenny lost the trail and had to follow the fence lines over the mountain. She finally crossed the ridge and looked down upon Larabee Valley. In the distance she made out a faint light—it was the kerosene lantern in their cabin's window. She rode towards the light and her crazy sailor.

Chapter 22
Bridgeville

The location that became Bridgeville was a town site waiting to happen. Here lay a crossing point on the Van Duzen, "the only safe ford . . . for many miles." Here also were two stream canyons, Brown Creek to the north and Hoagland Creek to the south, that offered access routes into the mountainous areas that rose abruptly from the river. Finally, upstream from the crossing, the river corridor narrowed from a canyon to a gorge, rendering travel along it almost impossible, forcing anyone who may have come east beside the Van Duzen to here leave the river.

The demands of the local Nongatl Indians, who were horseless and therefore traveled by foot, did not require much of the spot except for the river crossing. Once whites arrived, however, the location became servant to their several needs. The ford was superseded by a ferry and then a bridge, packers and travelers were accommodated by a hotel, the local ranchers supplied by a store. A community developed, and by a naming process more tortuous than most, eventually came to be called Bridgeville.

First, however, the place belonged to the Indians. A Nongatl tribal group called the Kit-tel ki-ya claimed a stretch of the Van Duzen from Goat Rock, two miles west of the future site of Bridgeville, to Hogback Ridge, which lay

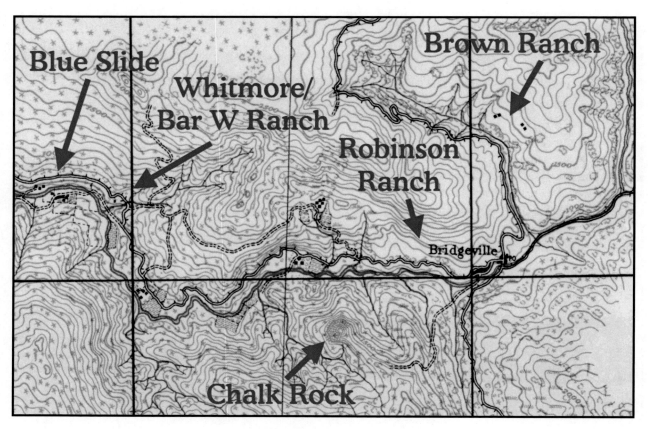

Bridgeville area, 1916 (CE).

about nine river miles upstream from the town site.[1137] The Kit-tel ki-ya had no village at Bridgeville-to-be, but upriver there was a string of communities near the water. The closest village to the town site was west of Goat Rock and belonged to the Kik ki-ya, the next tribal group downstream from the Kit-tel ki-ya.[1138]

What might be the first mention of the river crossing is in an army dispatch. On May 25, 1864, Sergeant R. B. Harris and a detachment from the First Battalion Mountaineers "camped on the Van Duzen, at the McAtee crossing." The following day they reached the south side of the river en route to Camp Grant. Harris and the other soldiers had been chasing Indians since April 13, going as far east as Hayfork, in Trinity County. When they reached Camp Grant on May 30, they claimed, perhaps too lavishly, to have marched "about 600 miles, mostly over very rough and mountainous country." The troops had encountered a large group of Indians

only once, between Pilot and Grouse creeks, when they killed nine and "wounded many others."[1139] No mention is made of any Indians in the McAtee's crossing area. By then, most of the former residents were either dead, confined to a reservation, or in hiding. In 1868, however, there was a final encounter in the vicinity. (See sidebar 1).

In 1865 McAtee's Crossing appeared on the first official Humboldt County map.[1140] James McAtee and his wife Owney had raised stock on the Van Duzen[1141] at least as early as 1860, when James sent an affidavit to the governor regarding cattle that he claimed Indians had killed in the vicinity. His statement was one of dozens submitted by local ranchers the week following the 1860 Indian massacres at Humboldt Bay and in the lower Eel valley.[1142]

The only other name on the map near the crossing was "Whitmore."[1143] This was Joel S. Whitmore, who at some point in the 1860s

---

1. Drinkwater Stays (Forever) in Humboldt County

By 1868 it appeared that the Indian-white conflict that had long convulsed Humboldt County had ended. On March 8, however, Albert DeLassaux learned otherwise when he was plowing a field northeast of Hydesville near the Cooper family's mills. A raiding party of seven Indians shot him dead and then sacked his house.[1144] Several local men attempted to pursue the Indians but failed to find them. Then that fall noted Indian tracker Steve Fleming led several other men "on a scout to the headwaters of Larabee Creek." They had only reached Burr Creek[1145] when that night they found the camp "of a marauding band of Indians," waited until daybreak, and then attacked from ambush. Five Indians were killed, while a sixth "was badly wounded [and] left a bloody trail behind him as he fled." One of the whites, Joe Drinkwater, insisted on hastily pursuing the Indian. Fleming tried to keep Drinkwater with the rest of the party but couldn't.[1146] Drinkwater was apparently bent on revenge, since a member of his family had earlier been killed by Indians near Hayfork.[1147] On the southern side of Chalk Mountain,[1148] the wounded Indian, who was named Big Foot,[1149] hid behind a log. When Drinkwater approached, following the blood, Big Foot propped his gun over the log[1150] and "shot him all to pieces." Fleming and the other whites came up, and Fleming killed Big Foot.[1151]

Two of the whites then scouted around the area and found a young Indian woman and a young boy. One of the men, Bill Crabtree, took the woman back with him, reportedly married her, and together they "raised a large family."[1152] No further mention was made of the boy.

Drinkwater's body was brought north, back across the Van Duzen, and was buried at what became the Bridgeville Cemetery. George Friend was 12 years old at the time. He later stated that "my brother and I happened along at Bridgeville the day they buried Drinkwater, so we attended the funeral."[1153]

It was good that Friend was there. Drinkwater had a ranch east of Peanut in Trinity County. Later some Trinitarians would claim that he was buried on his ranch,[1154] but Friend's eyewitness account has quashed their attempt to anecdotally appropriate Drinkwater's remains. As it is, his grave is the oldest marked burial in the Bridgeville Cemetery.

Drinkwater's remains remain at Bridgeville (JR).

In about 1903 "a hot fire swept through the cemetery and the granite of many stones crumbled in the extreme heat." On another occasion some of the graves were washed away by the creek that bounded the graveyard on its north side. In 1955 the 8th grade class at Bridgeville Elementary School not only "researched the cemetery" but also "built a picket fence around the grave of Josiah Drinkwater to recognize him as a historical figure."[1155] A later student project added further information about the cemetery and refurbished it. Visitors can easily locate Drinkwater's fenced grave and read the marker, which states:

Josiah Drinkwater

d. Nov. 28, 1868

Last whiteman in Humboldt County

who was killed in the Indian wars.

Drinkwater's distinction, however, is unmerited. Nearly two months after his death, Rufus B. Emory was killed by Indians at Redwood House,[1156] thereby becoming the final white fatality in the prolonged conflict. Perhaps the next restoration of the Bridgeville Cemetery will see the erroneous final lines on Drinkwater's wooden marker painted over. At least the mistake will be easy to correct. The statement could have been etched in marble.

---

started a ranch about three miles west of Bridgeville.[1157] In the 1920s the property came to be the setting for a strange and sorrowful story. (See sidebar 2.)

Various members of the Hoaglen[1158] family were reportedly the first whites to locate at Bridgeville. In 1869 Sam Hoagland sold several hundred acres of "squatter's rights" south of the Van Duzen to Thomas M. Burns.[1159] The dubious rights were converted into legal ownership, and Burns developed a large ranch that straddled the Overland Road for several miles and extended up and over Chalk Mountain to the west.[1160] Burns "had trouble with the Indians several times" but survived these encounters and was still "riding the range" until his death in 1933 at age 93. His son, Ed, who was then 65, then took over the ranch after a lengthy apprenticeship.[1161]

As for Sam Hoaglen's brother, Silas, and his family, they

> . . . didn't care much for civilization and as other settlers moved in they kept moving further out. They went out to Blocksburg and then moved to New Mexico where Si Hoagland died. Tom Ragland, his old partner, went down there and brought the family back and they settled in Hoagland Valley, which is named for this family.[1162]

2. Leaving the Bar for the Bar-W

Hans Weisel, a Progressive Republican, was elected to the California Assembly in 1912. He found, however, that "machine politics" were distasteful and therefore set up a law practice in Anaheim, soon becoming city attorney. Unfortunately for him, the Ku Klux Klan gained power within the Anaheim city government. The Klan apparently offered Weisel $100 in gold coins as a bribe. So it was that in 1925 Weisel, again appalled by the pitfalls of public office, abruptly quit his job as city attorney, left a partially built home in Anaheim, and took his wife Eva and their two children to northern California. There, above the Van Duzen river, he purchased Joel Whitmore's old Bar-W Ranch.[1163]

In more recent times the ranch had been known as Rogers Resort. In 1915 Ed Rogers ran what was rated "an excellent hotel" on the property.[1164] By 1922 the land had changed hands,[1165] but the new hands didn't move much, and when the Weisels arrived the ranch was in need of restoration. The entire family pitched in. They grew almost all of their food. Eva canned vegetables from their garden and Hans caught trout in the Van Duzen. Soon the Weisels opened a refurbished resort they called the "Bar-W Ranch," which enjoyed success as city folk from San Francisco, Orange County, Los Angeles, and elsewhere came to rusticate by the Van Duzen River.[1166]

The Whitmore Ranch, west of Bridgeville (CPH, colorized by JR).

Then, in 1930, Eva Weisel died of pneumonia. At the same time, the Great Depression made itself felt on the Van Duzen, as vacationers could no long afford to travel to remote destinations like the Bar-W Ranch. Hans Weisel found himself without income, and soon he was writing letters to old political friends like former governors Hiram Johnson and Friend Richardson, begging them to help him find work. No luck. Weisel had to return to Orange County, where he stood in breadlines with his daughter Anita. He tried to restart his law practice. Again, no luck. Weisel lost all his law books because he couldn't raise $50 to pay off his creditors. He moved to a house at Newport Beach where, in 1934, he committed suicide.[1167]

It had been less than 10 years since Weisel and his family had arrived in the hills of Humboldt County, coming to a magical place where he wrote about "the wonderful roses in the old garden" and of "the wild lilies blooming everywhere." For a brief time the family had lived in a rural paradise, far from the hurly burly of crowded cities and corrupt politics. It was an idyllic existence, but, like most idylls, also fragile. An unexpected death of a loved one, a sudden rent in the economic fabric of the country, and the stars fell from the heavens, dropping to the Van Duzen, their dimming light rushing, without pause, to the sea. Did Hans Weisel still hear the river in those last days before he took his life? What sound did it make, washing over a broken heart?

By 1870, with civilization encroaching, Silas Hoaglen sold 1,520 acres of land north of the Van Duzen to William Slaughter Robinson in 1870,[1168] and McAtee's Crossing became Robinson's Crossing.[1169] The Surveyor General's map of 1872 showed a trail coming up the Van Duzen to meet the "Round Valley Trail" at a spot on the north side of the river labeled "Robinson's."[1170] The Robinson family first "lived in a double cabin where the present [1949] school is . . . and the first school in the district was on the family's ranch."[1171] Much of the Robinsons' property covered the vast swatch of hillside prairie northwest of Bridgeville.[1172] In the early 1870s Robinson upgraded the crossing by putting in a ferry.[1173]

Bordering the Robinson property on the east

was the Salmon and Abbie Brown ranch.[1174] The Brown family took up land there the same year Robinson did. By 1881 their ranch supported 2,000 sheep on its 3,340 acres.[1175] Salmon Brown was the son of abolitionist John Brown Sr. He had not joined his father in the ill-fated attack on the federal arsenal at Harper's Ferry in 1859 (if he had, he would probably have been executed), but three years earlier he and his four brothers had participated with their father in the Pottawatomie Massacre in which five pro-slavery men were murdered in retaliation for the sacking, three days earlier, of the abolitionist town of Lawrence, Kansas. There are conflicting accounts of the massacre, but it appears that Salmon helped kill at least three of the five victims. In the 1880s Brown sold his ranch and

The Pottawatomie Massacre as depicted by the press (PD, colorized JR).

moved to Oregon.[1176] There, "in 1919, at the age of 83, Salmon Brown celebrated his father's birthday one last time alone," and with a violence that had lain dormant for 63 years, "picked up his old Kansas pistol and killed himself."[1177]

The trails that converged at Robinson's ranch typified the transportation infrastructure of Humboldt County in the early 1870s. The larger towns had a few streets; there were several connecting roads near the coast; and for use by buggies, wagons, and stage coaches, that was about it.[1178] Thus almost all rural areas, with their scatterings of large ranches and small communities, could be reached only by mule or horse or on foot. The transporting of people and goods to and from San Francisco was by ship. But then, in the mid-1870s, the county embarked on a road-building frenzy, and soon Robinson's Ferry was in the middle of it. (See sidebar 3.)

3. It's Ho! for Mendocino

The *Humboldt Times* began publication in the fall of 1854. Almost immediately (September 23), it carried a hopeful article regarding "an overland road to San Francisco."[1179] During the next few years money was raised to explore possible routes, but exploration was not forthcoming. Finally, in 1859, the Humboldt and Mendocino county surveyors "examined the route from Long Valley to Hydesville, Humboldt County, and reported favorably on the location of a road along this route." There were insufficient funds to begin work on such a project, however, and soon the escalation of the Indian-white conflict "prevented any improvements of this kind."[1180]

Thus to leave the county by land, travelers still had to go by trail and not by road. In 1861 Haskell & Force, a Hydesville company, attempted to assist the traveling public by providing "good riding animals" that could be used for the long, intercounty trip between "regular stage roads."[1181]

In 1872, the county supervisors, mindful of the increase in both population and general activity in the eastern Humboldt ranching areas, approved a thoroughfare that started at the Eureka-Arcata road near Freshwater Slough and climbed the hills to Kneeland Prairie. The logical continuation of this route would take the road through Yager, Robinson's Crossing, and Blocksburg, but those locations could also be reached by coming up the Van Duzen from Hydesville, and the county chose not to choose between the two routes at this time.[1182] People were already talking of an even more ambitious project: a road that would reach Mendocino County and there connect with some preëxisting road that ran south all the way to San Francisco Bay. There was, however, debate about the route. One faction favored going down the coast (more or less) from Ferndale, while the other preferred a road through the mountains in the eastern part of the county,[1183] a course that could be a continuation of the road to Kneeland. A premonitory analysis of the coast route had been provided by former soldier H. Neibur in 1867, when he stated, based on his travels pursuing Indians in northern Mendocino and southern Humboldt counties,

> . . . that the trail from Shelter Cove in this county to Ten Mile River, in Mendocino county is the roughest trail I ever saw in California anywhere.[1184]

And indeed, the only road ever built along the middle of this route, the infamously difficult Usal Road, has remained dirt to this day and all but impassable at certain times and for certain vehicles.

Finally, in March 1874, not one or two but *three* roads were launched. First came an act to levy and collect taxes for "the construction of a road from Hydesville to what is known as Robinson's crossing of Van Duzen Creek."[1185] Then the state legislature empowered Humboldt County to issue bonds for the construction of two additional roads, one "to run from Kneeland Prairie and Yager Creek south to the county line, the other to follow as nearly as possible the route of the telegraph line along the coast."[1186] The coastal route never

The second Bridgeville bridge replaced the one washed out in 1879 (THPO, colorized by JR).

became a viable thoroughfare; as late as the 1900s, travelers still braved the "Beach Road" for five miles south of Centerville as they rode or drove along the wave-swept sands on their way to Petrolia,[1187] while farther south there were sections of the road that never rose to pavement status.[1188]

The inland route was officially known, at first, as the "Kneeland's Prairie and Round Valley Wagon Road," those being the endpoints of the road to be constructed.[1189] At Robinson's Crossing it would meet the recently approved county road that came up the Van Duzen from Hydesville.

By the end of September 1874, the Hydesville-Robinson's Crossing road was open, and Bullard & Sweasey began semiweekly stage runs between those two locations. The *West Coast Signal* effused that

> The new line will prove a great convenience to the people in the hills, and will give pleasure-seekers of the town an easy and reliable mode of transit to new and romantic scenes from which they have henceforth been shut out.[1190]

Scenic the road might have been. Reliable it was not. What should have been emphasized was the fragility of the route, which at times was etched across the steep, unstable slopes on the north side of the Van Duzen canyon. A notorious stretch at what came to be called Blue Slide sometimes confronted both "people in the hills" and "pleasure-seekers of the town" with a mass of slumping, pale indigo hillside that blocked their way forward.[1191]

Despite these difficulties, the road from Hydesville at least sometimes brought people as far as Robinson's Crossing, apparently in enough quantity that before 1874 was over, H. P. Linton had opened a store there.[1192] That fall, John Colby was supervising work at the crossing on what was termed "the Van Duzen Bridge." It was noted that "the bridge will be 250 feet long and a ton and a half of iron will be used in its construction." In addition, work on the first five miles of road south of the bridge was in progress and was expected to be completed later in the fall.[1193] Near the end of November, a flood surged down the Van Duzen as "that furious stream rose nearly 20 feet in 24 hours." The bridge was unfinished, but "the structure 'saw the raise [sic] nobly.'"[1194] The excitement was not yet over. A week later C. A. Eastman fell 40 feet from the bridge into the river but "was most miraculously got out alive."[1195] By January 1875, the bridge (instead of Eastman) was finished and ready for inspection by the road commissioners. The *Humboldt Weekly Times* did not wait for their report, instead noting that

> On every hand we hear the structure spoken of as a most substantial one, and the belief expressed that it will withstand any assault that . . . will be made upon it by the elements.[1196]

Bold words that while glorifying the event, also invited hubris.

With the structure now manifested, Robinson's Crossing became Bridgeport.[1197] By August "Carr Brothers & Leary" had completed the first 27-plus miles of the Round Valley road, from Kneeland Prairie to Gibson & Hessig's Store on South Yager Creek.[1198] Work on the remaining seven miles to newly named Bridgeport was delayed because of a damage claim by the landowner through which the road was to pass, but south of the Van Duzen a segment of the road had been built all the way to Blocksburg.[1199] This latter section was viewed in 1876 by the editor of the *West Coast Signal*, who commented that "we have the opinion that there is no better road in the State than that from Van Duzen bridge to Blocksburg."[1200] George Friend, who lived in the area at the time, recalled that John Carr "built this road with Chinamen and wheelbarrows,"[1201] always an effective combination. For a time there was even a "Chinatown" on a flat near the Van Duzen just west of Bridgeport.[1202] Using the Van Duzen road to reach Bridgeport and then continuing on to the Round Valley road, Bullard & Sweasey offered a stage line that transport-

Bridgeville's main buildings, 1916 (DTC, colorized by JR).

ed travelers from Eureka to Blocksburg on Sundays and Wednesdays for only $5. Included in the fee was "40 pounds of baggage."[1203] The weight of the passengers apparently had no bearing on the assessment.

By April 1877 the road was completed, having reached the route coming north from Mendocino County at Dark Canyon, about five miles south of Harris.[1204] For the next 16 years, the Overland Road, as it came to be called,[1205] was the major connecting route between Humboldt and San Francisco bays,[1206] and Bridgeport, soon to become Bridgeville, was an essential stop along the way.

In April 1877 Bridgeport received a post office[1207] but during the transaction lost its name, there being a Bridgeport already in place on the eastern side of the Sierra Nevada Mountains. Mail would instead go to Bridge*ville*, a minor change in spelling and a more accurate description of the location, for the Van Duzen was not navigable and was therefore unable to serve as a *port*. The first postmaster was John J. Hale, who was also the proprietor of Bridgeville Station,[1208] an important stop on the now-completed Overland Road. Hale indicated that "the sooner the old name is forgotten, the better." The recipient of this sentiment responded, with studied redundancy, that postmaster Hale "looked hale and hearty."[1209]

Later that year the bridge made the news when it was the scene of a fatal shooting. A man named Gibbs, who kept a saloon between Ryan Slough and Freshwater Corners, shot and killed his wife in July 1877 and was arrested for her murder. While awaiting trial, he was confined in the county jail on the corner of Second and J streets in Eureka. The jail was on the second story of a wooden building that was "a flimsy affair." One night Gibbs and two other prisoners managed to get out of their cells and reach the cupola that sat atop the structure. From there they lowered themselves to the ground by tying together their jail blankets. Gibbs, now an escapee wanted dead or alive, hightailed it for the mountains, where he stayed for a time with a man named Noble. While there Gibbs "procured a horse and saddle intending to make his way out of the county." However, there was a reward offered for his capture, and desirous of obtaining this, Noble notified Sheriff T. M. Brown of Gibbs's intentions and the route he planned to take, which would involve crossing the Van Duzen at Bridgeville. Brown accordingly swore in two deputies, one of whom was Ben Emerson, "who was recognized as a dead shot," and the three men went to Bridgeville, arriving after dark. Brown stationed the deputies at the north end of the bridge, which Gibbs would reach first, while the sheriff himself waited at the far end in case their quarry got past the deputies. Sure enough, at the expected time, a lone rider showed up. He was commanded to halt but instead turned his horse around and attempted to escape. Emerson brought him down with a single shot. The miniposse identified the fallen man in the dark "by feeling one of his hands from which several fingers were known to be missing." Gibbs wasn't dead—yet. He was taken back to Eureka where he expired

from his wound a few days later,[1210] thereby confirming Emerson's reputation with a rifle.

Almost two years of calmness ensued following the shooting of Gibbs. Then on March 5, 1879, postmaster Hale, three additional male Hales, and four other locals went out to the middle of Bridgeville's namesake bridge to check on the rate of rise of the river, which was coming up fast. Having ascertained this, the group turned and was heading back to the riverbank

> . . . when all at once there was a terrible commotion like an earthquake, followed by a terrible crash, which caused a stampede, quick as thought, among the crowd. At this time Mr. Hall and Mr. Coleman thought of the little boy [Johnny Hale], turned and looked back. All behind them was falling plank, bridge timbers, and the river in chaos and away they all went for the bank on the double quick, with the bridge or what was left of it sliding into the mad stream as fast as the surging current could pull it from the bank, and the men fell in every conceivable shape at the end of the bridge as it left the bank, some going with the plank, falling on their heads ten feet on the rocks below, others on timbers and stumps, and one, Mr. Coleman, fell in the river and was pulled out with a rope. Elmer Hale was picked up on the rocks insensible, and remained so for about twelve hours, and is getting better now. But little Johnny Hale has gone back to the infinite. . . .[1211]

The Van Duzen, as it turned out, had reached lethal intensity after receiving 12 inches of rain

Bridgeville before the removal of the 1879 covered bridge (THPO, colorized by JR).

in 48 hours. Achel Look, the mail carrier, subsequently found Johnny Hale's body 12 miles downstream.[1212]

By December the frail and fatal bridge had been replaced by a new span.[1213] This time the structure "was raised many feet higher and set on piers made of metal and filled with cement." The planks and timbers were hand-hewn, as were the roof shakes.[1214] Photos show that the bridge sides were clad with some of the planks. About that time a traveler on the Overland Road noted that "the river bed is deep, and the stream is a canyon river, with a rocky and boulder bed," characteristics that the survivors of the March mishap could readily attest to. At Bridgeville, the station was described (with problematic punctuation) to consist "of a store, hotel, saloon. Postoffice and stable, and is the resort of many hunters, as game is found here in abundance, both deer and bear."[1215]

In 1882 temporary vagabond Warren B. Johnson found Bridgeville to be "a small place,"

perhaps supporting this contention by conflating some of the businesses, so that he noted only "a hotel, store, blacksmith shop, and one other house." Johnson gave his attention to the hotel; he found that "the building is cheap, but still it has many things for the comfort of travelers." A few of these he described: no room was available, but he was allowed to sleep on a lounge in the lobby. The hotel-keeper told Johnson that "we can give you something to eat and all the whisky you want."[1216] The combination persuaded Johnson to overnight in Bridgeville.

The *Daily Humboldt Standard's* roaming reporter, McTavish, traveled through the Van Duzen's redwoods in May 1885, stopped at Bridgeville, and filed a report. He noted Slaughter Robinson's 1,700-acre ranch, which included an orchard and garden. Robinson's 1884 wheat crop had averaged 40 bushels per acre. The Whitmore Ranch was still to the west, the Salmon Brown Ranch still to the east. E. B.[1217] Barnum, who had bought out John J. Hale, was now the business bigwig in downtown Bridgeville, owning the store, hotel, and blacksmith shop. A half-mile west of town was a competitor, Tom Kelly, who had both a store and blacksmith shop.[1218]

By 1888 Barnum had "completed one of the most roomy and convenient hotels on the line of the overland road until Ukiah is reached." Summer sojourners "could wander off to the Larribee [sic] or Burr creek with the fishingrod [sic] and basket, or stalk deer in the hidden retreats of Buck mountain." Beyond these nearby locations were similar attractions that extended "to the head of Yager [Creek], to Fort Baker range, to Showers' Pass, to the big bend of Mad river, or to the South Fork mountain in Trinity."[1219] After a pause, Barnum continued his improvements. In October 1897 came the report that he "will soon commence the erection

of a new store on the site of the old one, which will be moved back and used as a warehouse."[1220]

Barnum may have succeeded in attracting visitors to Bridgeville, but he failed to keep at least one local in town. In April 1903, 10-year-old Elmer Norgard set out

> . . . on foot and alone for Round Valley, a distance of forty miles, which he traveled in two days' time, reaching his destination without getting lost or doing anything of a remarkable nature, or performing an unusual feat in his estimation.[1221]

Henry Cox, Maria Jane Cox, and their family arrived in Bridgeville in 1909 after moving around much of Humboldt County. The couple had met in Eureka[1222] and were married there in 1881. They went to Sproul Creek in 1888,

Downtown Bridgeville, 1925 (HCHS, colorized by JR).

farmed there for a time, moved north and ran the Briceland Hotel for a year, moved farther north to Hydesville to again run a hotel, returned to Eureka in 1904 to take over a boarding house, and five years later went to Bridgeville[1223] as—of course—proprietors of the hotel there.[1224] In 1912 Henry bought Bridgeville from Ed Barnum's estate,[1225] and one of his sons, George, came on board to help run things.[1226]

And things apparently ran pretty well until December 14, 1919, when they ground to a halt. "During a spell of freezing weather,"[1227] "when the mercury stood at 16 degrees,"[1228] a fire warmed up the town by burning down both Bridgeville's hotel and store.[1229] A faulty flue in the office of the hotel started the blaze, which grew hot enough that it caused a tank of gasoline on the porch of the nearby store to explode, so that it "sprayed the store building with its inflammable [sic] contents." No other buildings were damaged, but the town also lost its post office and branch library, which were housed in the store.[1230]

The Coxes, father and son, promptly converted the town's old saloon and the blacksmith shop that stood beside it into a replacement store. They operated it together until Henry Cox died in 1934.[1231] George Cox then ran the store until he retired in 1955.[1232] During the 1940s and 1950s, the store segregated some of its merchandise by age group. There were two large coolers, one for beer and one for soda pop. There were also two magazine racks, one with comic books (for the soda pop crowd) and the other with "detective magazines, True Confessions, Saturday Evening Post, Life, and pulp fiction" (for the beer crowd). Like all good country stores, there was a pot-bellied stove, complete with benches and a spittoon.[1233] Almost every ranch in the area had an account at the store.[1234]

Offsetting the fire-induced reduction of the business district was the construction, in about 1910, of a large barn that served for a time as a livery stable.[1235] Then in 1925, the fifth, and last, of John Buck Leonard's string of Van Duzen bridges replaced the 1879 covered bridge. Like the other four, it was made of reinforced concrete, a Leonard trademark. George Cox's 8-year-old daughter, Laura June, watched the Mercer Fraser construction crew intently as they built the bridge. As a reward, Laura June was allowed to press her footprints into the wet concrete of the bridge deck before the surface was paved,[1236] an architectural enhancement not foreseen by Leonard.

The 1910 barn kept pace with the times. As motor vehicles replaced horses, George Cox converted the building's hay loft into a skating rink and removed the stalls on the first floor. In the 1920s the barn became a commercial garage.[1237]

By the late 1940s another transformation was taking place. Ranching, which had long dominated the local economy, found its supremacy challenged by lumbering. In 1949 there were "no less than a dozen tie mills and camps in the surrounding area."[1238] By 1952 the total was up to 22, with mills at such diverse locations as Swain's Flat, Larabee Valley, and Burr Creek.[1239] As early as 1947 one local lumberman, Jack Fairhurst, steadfastly stated that "our 13 mills in Bridgeville and Carlotta are here for good."[1240]

As wood went out of the Bridgeville area, timber workers and their families came in, swelling the Bridgeville School's 1949 enrollment to 45 students and requiring the hiring of a second teacher.[1241] At Cox's store the soda pop cooler and comic book rack worked overtime.

The wave of timber cutting came and went. Fairhurst's many mills turned out not to be there "for good" but "for a while." When George Cox died in 1966, his daughter, now Laura June Pawlus, became the owner of Bridgeville. In 1973 Pawlus sold the town, starting it on a series of ownership misadventures that did no service to the dignity of the community's earlier history. In 1997 CalTrans added to Bridgeville's distress by constructing a neo-brutalist bridge that bypassed the town and caused the closure of Leonard's 1925 concrete masterpiece.[1242] It is unlikely that Laura June would have deigned to have her footprints adorn the stark bed of the new structure.

Nowadays anyone wanting to gain a sense of earlier Bridgeville can go to two locations. Leonard's bridge, although blocked to vehicular traffic, can still be walked across, its graceful stolidity perhaps more apparent than when it was viewed at 25 miles an hour by car. And at the opposite end of town, the white fence of the Bridgeville Cemetery invites observers to pass through the gate and view the smaller monuments of the town's history—the headstone for little Johnny Hale, swept to his death from the first Bridgeville bridge; the nearby stone for William Friend, who died at 90 instead of Hale's 3; the wooden marker for Josiah Drinkwater, who never returned to Trinity County but whose story returns a bit of Bridgeville to the past.

Chapter 23
Strong's Station

"Before the hotel comes the road." The truth in this little-known maxim of geography[1243] is borne out by the establishment of Strong's Station in 1878,[1244] some four years after the road that ran by it was completed.[1245] A mail trail had come through the area at least as early as 1861,[1246] but a trail meant solitary walkers or riders or at best a small party—not enough to fill a hotel should they want a place to sleep. Instead, trail travelers were accommodated by overnight "stopping places" that were usually either ranch houses or the occasional mail station that was often no more than a rude cabin. Only with the coming of a road would stages and carriages carrying multiple people make hotels worth building.

Samuel Strong no doubt understood this. Starting in 1853 he spent his early years in Humboldt County in the vicinity of Rohnerville. He ranched, owned the Rohnerville town hall, and introduced roller skating to Humboldt County.[1247] Strong's Skating Pavilion opened in 1871[1248] and was an instant success.[1249] And Sam, watching his patrons glide across his rink with the tiny wheels of their skates whirling, may have dreamed of other wheels, far larger, at last rolling up the Van Duzen past Hydesville, past that town's last hotel, to some point where the stages and wagons to which these wheels were attached came to a halt, and the persons who rode in them debarked, travel-worn and in need of a pleasant place to rest.

Every day, as skaters handed over their coins at his Pavilion, Sam gathered the resources

Redwoods (FMC, colorized JR).

needed to provide those travelers with what they would need. So it was that by June 1878 he had, a few miles east of Carlotta, "built a fine, large house for the accommodation of the traveling public.[1250]

In just two short years the place had become "one of most delightful pleasure resorts in Humboldt County" that left departing guests "well pleased." More specifically,

The house is large, roomy and comfortable. Mrs. Strong presides, and having everything, in the way of fruit and vegetables at hand, the table is loaded with all

The fields that fed the famished at Strongs' Station (DTC, colorized by JR).

that is good to eat. There are ample accommodations for horses and the greatest of care is taken of everything. The
house is situated in one of the loveliest
nooks on the Van Duzen River. . . .[1251]

And indeed, the nook was lovely. The hotel
backed up against the hillslope that rose towards
a peak called Bald Jessie, while its front view
looked out across a large vegetable garden to a
wide bend in the Van Duzen River. The porch at
the hotel's front was shaded by a climbing vine
that rose like a leafy filigree before the building's
entrance. No wonder that in the spring of 1881
the hotel "was filled with people from Eureka,
Arcata and elsewhere." In addition to the hotel's
"wholesome" food, there were site-specific attractions:

Game is abundant, deer in the immediate neighborhood, elk, fish, jack-rabbits,
quail, etc. There are swings, croquet
grounds, etc. The Van Duzen, at this
point is deep, and Mr. Strong has placed
upon the river a fine boat that will carry
eight persons comfortably. Every little
detail has been attended to, and for a
week of fun enjoyment in the country,
there is no place like Strong's."[1252]

Soon, however, the founder of the resort was
no longer on hand to supervise it. The Strongs
moved to Napa in the "early eighties,"[1253] and
by May 1883 traveling correspondent McTavish
wrote from the station that "young, active, and
buoyant" D. A. Dunlap now made guests "feel
welcome."[1254] The Strongs' daughter, known on

the printed page as "Mrs. Dunlap," remained at the station.[1255]

"Cherries Are Now Ripe and plentiful at STRONG'S STATION" announced the *Humboldt Times* in June 1911. The "beautiful resort situated eight miles from the railroad" was now "open for the season, under new management," J. E. Wilson by name.[1256] Lured perhaps by this notice, Delmar L. Thornbury and party came through and stopped for dinner, with Thornbury subsequently confirming, in his guidebook to Humboldt County, that "the luscious cherries temp, and tempt, and nowhere in the world are there superior ones in size and flavor."[1257] Wide-ranging traveler that he was, Thornbury nonetheless exceeded himself by

implying that he had sampled cherries across the globe.

On May 12, 1887, Strong's Station came under absentee ownership when the property was purchased by Russell A. Alger.[1258] By 1898 it was co-owned by an associate of Alger's, Aaron T. Bliss.[1259] As was to happen later with the Pacific Lumber Company,[1260] it was a case of Great Lakes capital coming west. (See sidebar 1.)

J. B. Barber leased the hotel at Strong's from 1887 to 1889. He was followed by several other proprietors, including George W. Porter, George Foster, David Nevers, and G. W. Byard. At an unknown date Elmer Wilson purchased the property. He sold out to W. L. Robinson in 1917[1261] but took over the station again

Sunlit Strong's Station (CPH, colorized by JR).

1. The Governors of Strong's Station

The land at and around Strong's Station was far removed from that of Michigan, or Puget Sound, but it bore an important resemblance to both locations: it was heavily covered with first-rate timber. This explains why Russell A. Alger and Aaron T. Bliss took an interest in it.

When Alger purchased the property that contained Strong's Station in 1887, he had just finished a two-year term as governor of Michigan. Having declined renomination,[1262] Alger was temporarily unemployed, but rather than taking on the role of hotel-keeper, he leased the property to J. B. Barber.[1263] This gave Alger time in 1888 to seek the Republican nomination for President; at the party's convention he polled 142 votes before seeing Benjamin Harrison gain the candidacy. Undeterred, in 1889 Alger became the commander-in-chief of the veterans' organization known as the Grand Army of the Republic. Then in 1897 he was selected by William McKinley to be Secretary of War. In April 1898 the United States declared war on Spain, and Alger was subsequently criticized for his handling of the War Department. At McKinley's request he resigned as secretary in August 1899. Not finished with politics, Alger served in the United States Senate from 1902 until his death in 1907.[1264]

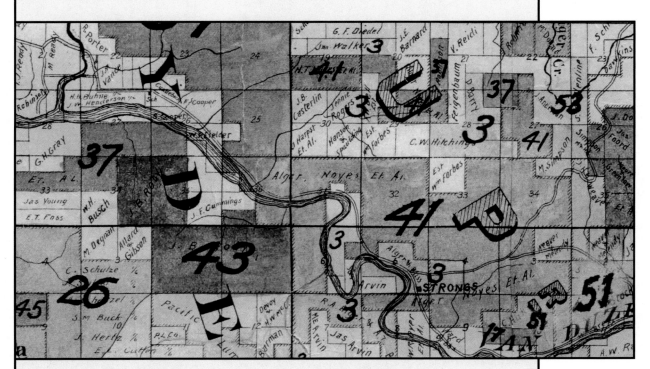

The Alger, Bliss and Noyes brothers' properties; Strong's Station; and, northeast of J. F. Cummings's parcel, Cummings Creek; 1898 (JNL, colorized by JR).

Alger came to the Senate as an appointee to finish out the term of James McMillan. The ex-governor was appointed by Michigan's current governor, Aaron T. Bliss,[1265] who had served as Alger's aide when the latter was governor. They were both officers in the Grand Army of the Republic, and they both took a deep interest in sawtimber.[1266]

Bliss had headed the interestingly named firm of A. T. Bliss & Brother, and he became active in various timber operations in the Saginaw area. In 1890 he organized the Central Lumber Company, which held "large tracts of pine lands in the Georgian Bay region of Canada." One of the company's stockholders was Alger's son, Russell Jr. Bliss also had timber holdings in the "Iron region of Minnesota," yellow pine acreage in Virginia and Arkansas, fir forests in Oregon and Washington, and an estimated 240,000,000 board feet of redwood in Mendocino County, California. By 1898 Bliss was ranked "among the more prominent of the lumbermen in Eastern Michigan."[1267]

Alger, for his part, was involved in various timberland companies that often specialized in "long lengths" of wood, cutting 1,000,000,000 board feet in Michigan's Alcona County that were sent to mills in Michigan, Ohio, and New York. Like Bliss, Alger had additional holdings in Georgian Bay, Puget Sound, and Mendocino County.[1268]

The 1898 Humboldt County map shows the former governor and the governor-to-be co-owning a parcel of 480 acres on the Van Duzen that included Strong's Station. Southwest across the river they owned another 800 acres, and they also held close to 3,000 acres scattered among three parcels a few miles upriver from Strong's.[1269]

But the 1898 map shows more than this. Almost surrounding the Strong's Station property and extending off to the north were three other parcels that Alger co-owned, totaling over 5,000 acres. Here Alger's partners were Henry T. Noyes and John S. Noyes,[1270] the latter being known as the "dean of the Buffalo [New York] lumber and timber trade."[1271]

In 1882 and 1883 some 5,198.44 acres of redwood timberland on the Van Duzen were purchased by the Noyeses and others for $32,550.64. John S. Noyes subsequently sold a quarter interest in the property to Alger. On August 6, 1883, the owners were offered $25 per acre for these lands, for a total price of $129,963.25. The owners, however, refused the offer, which triggered a lawsuit by J. E. Barnard, who by terms of an earlier sale agreement, was due a commission of 7.5 percent when the property was resold.[1272]

Where tourists saw scenery the governors of Michigan saw profits (HCHS, colorized by JR).

If anyone wondered why lumbermen from New York and Michigan would cast their eyes upon timber tracts along the Van Duzen River in far-distant California, and then open their pocketbooks to purchase such tracts, they had only to review the financial figures revealed in the lawsuit. If Alger and the Noyeses had accepted the 1883 purchase offer, they would have received almost exactly *four times* what they had paid for the land no more than 14 months earlier. They would have made a profit of $87,665.37.[1273] In 2018 dollars the profit would be about $2,250,000.[1274]

And yet the offer was refused.

Why?

It was because Alger and the Noyeses and other timbermen were aware of two equations:

1) redwoods alone = 0

2) redwoods + transportation for redwood logs = $$$$$

When the investors completed their timberland purchases on the Van Duzen in 1883, it was just a year before the Eel River & Eureka Railroad (ER&ERR) opened its line from Fields Landing, on Humboldt Bay, to Burnell's, on the lower Van Duzen. For the first time in Humboldt County's history, the products of the lower Eel River (and its tributary, the Van Duzen) could be easily shipped to Humboldt Bay, whence it could then be reshipped to San Francisco and other port cities, and indeed, even across the Seven

Seas. And what was most desired at these ports of call, what of the multitudinous bounty of Humboldt County products was most longed for and greeted with the most eager outlay of money? What, indeed, except lumber milled from the county's redwoods.

And, just as the ER&ERR was soon to extend its northwestern terminus to Eureka, would it not, in the approaching fullness of time, also extend its Van Duzen terminus, laying rails up the river valley until it reached the forests around Carlotta, and then, not that much later, touch the tracts of timber that surrounded Strong's Station? If you were wealthy enough to allow investments to accrue value at their leisure, if you already had money enough to live in not just affluence, but in sumptuous affluence, then why not wait until you were offered not just a fourfold profit but instead a fivefold profit, or even more? And if that eventual plateau of profit was not to be reached in your lifetime, wasn't it enough to know that when it arrived, members of your family would be there to receive its benefits and would perhaps intone a quiet "thank you" to the memory of the forebear who had made this addition to their affluence possible?

If this understanding was not within the calculus of common folk, it was certainly something that the Russell Algers, and the Aaron Blisses, and the

Fulfilled in the fullness of time: the railroad at Cummings Creek, on the Michigan governors' former property (HCHS, colorized by JR).

Did one of these gents put the bullet hole in the bar room door? (CPH, colorized by JR).

John Noyeses were capable of contemplating, and it was such contemplation that no doubt prompted the rejection of the offer to purchase the redwood acreage on the Van Duzen. Subsequent events confirmed the wisdom of this decision.

The California Midland Railroad was incorporated in in April 1902. It purchased a right-of-way up the Van Duzen from Burnell's, where ER&ERR tracks currently ended, to a point about two miles southeast of Carlotta.[1275] The new endpoint was directly adjacent the western end of the Noyes-Alger timber tract.[1276] It therefore came as no surprise when, in February 1903, a five-eighths interest in 5,653.66 acres[1277] of the property was sold to "Samuel H. Stephenson and Isaac Stephenson, wealthy Michigan lumbermen." The price was not announced but was rumored to be "in the neighborhood of $150,000.[1278] Based on that figure, the profit on the sale would have been $129,655.85. In addition, the Noyes-Alger combine retained three-eighths of their original holding, which was worth $56,250.00 based on the per-acre value established by the Stephensons' purchase. That left Noyes-Alger with assets of $177,905.85, representing a profit of $145,355.21. By declining the 1893 offer and waiting a decade until rail access was obtained, Noyes-Alger had accumulated an additional $57,689.84 in profit. In the 20 years since the property was purchased by Noyes, et al., its value had increased 547%.

Redwoods + transportation for redwood logs = $$$$$. QED.

in 1920.[1279] In 1934 Steve Angelini and his unnamed wife began running the hotel. They were still running it 25 years later when genial Andy Genzoli stopped by on December 2, 1959. Andy was prompted to make the trip because three months earlier, Angelini had been given orders to vacate the property by its owner, the Georgia-Pacific Lumber Company (G-P). G-P indicated that it might tear the building down sometime after November 1. Genzoli, apparently unconcerned about the possible demolition date, waited another month before driving out there and learning that the building was still standing.[1280] He toured the old hotel and provided his readers with a brief travelogue:

> I looked at the big dining room where many a couple has skipped across the old wooden floor . . . went into the kitchen with its seven-feet long range . . . big enough to cook an entire beef. The grills and huge ovens could do the trick easily, and yet have room to spare for the pots of mashed potatoes, the gravy and the vegetables.

Upstairs there are twelve bedrooms. . . . Off the south porch the old bar-room still sports a bullet hole through the door from a gun which not only punctured the door, but one of the patrons. . . . This happened long ago. . . .

The automobile had a lot to do with Strong's Station Hotel's decline. . . . Better roads and better cars now get you in and out of the redwoods a lot faster than did horses, years ago. . . . The old hotel was built in 1872 [1878] and is still sound. . . .[1281]

Sound it might have been, but the hotel was indeed nearing its end. By 1969 the stretch of Highway 36 that passed in front of the station had been rerouted to the hillside in back of the building, leaving on the flat below a truncated section of the highway's old pavement and not much else. The topographic map for that year showed no buildings still standing. In their place were the words "Strongs Station (Site)".[1282]

The hotel that had lived by the road had also died by the road.

Chapter 24

Carlotta

You let me kiss you, Carlotta. Remember?

George S. Kaufman and Edna Ferber, *Dinner at Eight*

Downtown Carlotta occupies the floodplain at the mouth of Yager Creek. Adjacent to the east is the suburb of Cuddeback, which extends along the alluvial flat on the north side of the Van Duzen River. A Nongatl tribal group called the Tce-lin-dun ki-ya occupied the lower Yager Creek drainage. West of them, in the Hydesville area, was the northeastern extension of the Bear River (Nekanni) tribe.[1283]

Samuel and Laura Hoover reportedly became the first whites to inhabit the area when they homesteaded 160 acres in November 1858. In May 1861 Samuel died and Laura inherited the property. The following year she married Peter Donnelly, a "friend and neighbor." In 1860 Donnelly had served as a private in the Humboldt Cavalry Company,[1284] a would-be militia unit that had formed in Hydesville. Some members of the company were implicated in the multiple Indian massacres that occurred earlier that year.[1285] In 1861 he indentured a 12-year-old Indian boy he called George Washington Donally [sic] under the state law that legalized this type of slavery.[1286]

When Laura Hoover became Laura Donnelly, she also became victim of the sexist laws of the time, losing her ownership of the Hoover property and her right to administer Samuel's estate, both of which went to her replacement husband, Donnelly. The new marriage lasted only until 1866, when, "for obscure reasons," Donnelly left the area and he and Laura divorced. It was then discovered that more than $700 in funds and property were missing from Samuel Hoover's estate. In February 1868 an order was issued for Donnelly to appear in court. There is no known record that he did so.[1287]

The locale had previously made the news in July 1862. Henry and Martha Cuddeback had a small farm just east of the modern-day intersection of Highway 36 and Wilder Road.[1288] One day, according to their daughter Laura, Henry was with a hired man "plowing a field some distance from the house." Martha was resting upstairs after the noon meal, when she was roused by the barking of their dog. Going downstairs to investigate, Martha opened the front door and "a shot fired from ambush hit her." The bullet, however, "struck the wire of her hoop skirt, split, and the two pieces bounded back, one fragment embedding itself in the door and the other in a table."[1289]

Her adrenaline activated, Martha exited by another door and, keeping the house between her and her attackers, ran down the hill to the road. She looked back to see that her dog, though wounded, was following her. She realized that the dog "had kept the Indians at bay and made possible her escape." Martha then "ran through brush, mud, and timber in her thin slippers until she reached their neighbor's home. . . ."[1290] This was the Simmons family, who lived about two miles to the northwest, near where the pack train trail to Trinity County crossed Yager Creek.[1291]

The rustic Carlotta business district of a bygone time (THPO, colorized by JR).

Henry and his helper had heard both the barking of the dog and Martha's scream when she was shot. They "came rushing to the house in time to see five Indians leaving with their arms full of blankets and clothing." Henry and his hired man fired at the Indians, wounding one of them, and then set off to find Martha. They tracked her to the Simmonses' farm.[1292] By good fortune Laura Cuddeback had gone there earlier and was safe from harm.[1293] Laura indicated that "soon all the men in the surrounding country formed a posse to hunt the Indians,"[1294] but she gave no report about the result. The Cuddebacks' heroic dog died from its wounds, the location of his demise later being marked by a large California laurel tree.[1295] For their part, the Cuddebacks moved to Hydesville, where they remained for five years.[1296]

It was not a propitious time for the local residents. The same week as the attack on the Cuddebacks, their neighbor to the east, Hiram Lyons, was killed by Indians at the "upper Mad river crossing."[1297]

There followed three decades of diminished drama, during which the most notable event was the construction of the road connecting Hydesville with Bridgeville in 1874. (See Appendix A.) Then, in 1893, a power broker from Eureka bought some land a short distance east of Yager Creek, and the tempo of activity gradually increased.

John M. Vance was the nephew of mill owner John Vance, who died in 1892 while serving as mayor of Eureka.[1298] Before he passed away, John Vance turned over control of many of his business interests to John M.[1299] About a year later John M. used some of his recently endowed wealth to buy a parcel of land east of Yager Creek and build a "sumptuous home" at the base of the ridge that rose northward from the Van Duzen floodplain.[1300]

So things stood for nearly a decade. Then, in 1902, John M. Vance did two things to advance his plans for the area. He purchased 40 additional acres west of his existing property, and he began buying up railroad right-of-way easements between the Cuddeback area and Burnell's. The latter location, situated in the Van Duzen valley about two miles east of Alton, was the southeast terminus for the Eel River and Eureka Railroad (ER&ERR).[1301] Vance was the rail line's president.[1302]

Now Vance's vision of the locale's future soon became manifest. On April 26, 1902, the California Midland Railroad was incorporated. The new railway was intended to extend the ER&ERR's line eastward from Burnell's, crossing Yager Creek and ending a short distance east of the Cuddeback area.[1303]

The California Midland was a short line, both in distance and in longevity. Not only was its right-of-way a mere 5.5 miles in length, but the Midland itself existed little more than a year. It was started during the rise of the prolonged railroad frenzy that saw two gigantic rivals, the Southern Pacific and the Santa Fe, gobble up the various existing Humboldt rail lines as they attempted to string together a series of rights-of-way that would offer access to the shores of San Francisco Bay. On July 7, 1903, the California Midland, along with the ER&ERR, was purchased by the San Francisco & Northwestern Railway, which was the instrument the Santa Fe used to acquire various Humboldt rail lines.[1304] After more such machinations, in 1907 the Santa Fe and the Southern Pacific, tired of butting heads in Humboldt County, consolidated their local rail lines, including the San Francisco & Northwestern, and formed the Northwestern Pacific Railroad (NWP).[1305]

The abandoned Vance mansion, 1985 (CPH, colorized by JR).

Meanwhile, Vance was busy east of Yager Creek. In August 1903 the *Humboldt Daily Standard* proclaimed "Carlotta New Railroad Town," enthusing that

> Nowhere in southern Humboldt is there a prettier site for a town than at this point. A broad, level prairie, well protected from the winds by the forest-clad hills surrounding it, and close to the sinuous windings of the Yager and Van Duzen rivers. . . .[1306]

Interviewed for the article was Vance, "owner of the land hereabouts." He indicated that work would commence that week on a three-story, 30-room hotel, to be followed by a store, livery stable, and blacksmith shop, after which building lots would be sold.[1307] This was enough to constitute a town, which was duly named for one of Vance's daughters, Carlotta.[1308]

On the exact day the California Midland was purchased by the San Francisco & Northwestern, the line opened between Carlotta and Burnell's, ensuring that the trains never ran under the original company's name[1309] and thereby reducing the Midland's operating history to nothing.

By extending the rails to Carlotta, Vance preempted the attempt of another railroader, A. W. Foster, to run a line up the Van Duzen. Foster already operated the San Francisco and North Pacific, which had tracks in Mendocino, Sonoma, and Marin counties. Desiring to extend his empire, Foster formed the San Francisco and Eureka Railroad (SF&ERR).[1310] In 1902 the SF&ERR announced its intent to build

> . . . a new line at a cost of one million dollars. The line was to run from Eureka to Alton, thence up the Van Duzen to Root Creek[1311] and across the divide to Dyerville, there to effect a junction with the projected Humboldt Company's line.[1312]

Proposing such a route was either fanciful or fat-headed, for it would entail crossing the steeply sloped ridgeline that divides the Van Duzen from the main Eel, thus requiring a rapid climb of over a thousand feet—far beyond the capabilities of any train engine. Yet, proof that the plan was considered is found on a copy of Lentell's 1901 Humboldt County map, where, drawn in red ink, is a dashed line that runs from Burnell's to Dyerville over that very route, along with branches going to Bridgeville and up Yager Creek.[1313]

By 1904 the brand-new town possessed the striking Carlotta Hotel and a livery stable, both run by James Elliott, and a branch store of the Fortuna Merchandising Company operated by Mark Mitchell. In 1906 E. A. Light and his unnamed wife took over the hotel.[1314] Then, in May 1907, as Carlotta was still getting up steam, John M. Vance died. His son, Harry P. Vance, took over management of the family's estate.[1315]

With its rail connection to Scotia and Humboldt Bay, Carlotta was on its way to becoming a transportation hub. The redwood timber on Yager Creek and on the Van Duzen could, by the extension of spur lines, be taken to the mills. One timberman, Frank L. Smith, found he could do without the spurs; in 1907 he floated 30,000 railroad ties down the river from his camp on Grizzly Creek to the tracks that awaited the wood at Carlotta.[1316]

In March 1911 the *Humboldt Times* announced: "ENTIRE TOWN OF CARLOTTA SOLD," with "TRANSFER IN A FEW DAYS." By then, the community consisted of the eponymous

For decades the Carlotta Hotel was the area's most popular resort (HCHS, colorized by JR).

hotel, six cottages, a store, saloon, blacksmith shop, town hall, and livery barn. The purchaser was something called the Carlotta Townsite and Development Company, "an organization formed by San Francisco capital." Just *whose* capital was not announced,[1317] and perhaps not enough of it was available, for the deal failed to go through.

In 1913 Charles Willis Ward, an expansive New York businessman, came to Humboldt County. He was in ill health but the local climate agreed with him, and he decided to stay. Before Ward left the East Coast, he'd developed a highly successful nursery business on Long Island, and soon he started a similar enterprise in Humboldt County. He established a part of what he called Cottage Garden Nurseries in cool, coastal Myrtletown, added a McKinleyville bulb farm operation, and acquired a 232-acre farm in warmer, fertile Carlotta.[1318] When Ward published a promotional book on Humboldt County in 1915, it featured several

photos of "Cottage Gardens Nurseries' Plant at Yager Creek."[1319] The parcel extended from the county road north along the creek's floodplain. The area had recently been logged of its old-growth redwood, and Ward had the stumps removed and the land leveled. The property was then planted in alfalfa and corn and more than a thousand fruit and nut trees. Ward also used the site for a "model dairy ranch" that was "stocked with a herd of thoroughbred registered Jersey cows." The barn had concrete floors, electric lights, a water system, and other up-to-date features. Ward reportedly had music played for the cows to induce higher milk production.[1320] All of Ward's projects came to an end with his death in 1920.[1321] His model dairy at Carlotta was sold at a mortgage foreclosure auction for $37,000 to Henry Rohner, who subsequently died. The ranch was then taken over by the Mantova brothers.[1322]

When Ward wanted to serenade his cows, he could have utilized a local resource. The

Charles Willis Ward's walnut field at Carlotta (CPH, colorized by JR).

Playtime at American Tank (HCHS, colorized by JR).

five-piece Bryant Orchestra was based at the Carlotta ranch of Charles C. Bryant. It featured his daughter, Ruby, who was deemed "an accomplished pianist and a great credit to her profession."[1323]

East of Cuddeback the American Tank and Equipment Company in 1919 constructed a mill across the road from the future site of the Carlotta fire station.[1324] American Tank

built oil storage tanks for use in Oklahoma and Texas, where the oil lands had "a high content of sulphur and salt." The best tank staves for this type of oil were milled from cypress and redwood. To get a supply of the latter, American Tank had purchased a tract of redwood timber on Yager Creek and then created the mill to produce the staves. Eventually the Hammond Lumber Company made a deal with American Tank whereby the latter sold its mill, lumber inventory, and Yager Creek timberlands to Hammond, while also agreeing to buy all their tank stock from Hammond in the future.[1325] When American Tank had set up its Carlotta operation, company owner J. T. Simmons purchased equipment formerly used by Robinson's Mill on Loop Road, east of Fortuna. Sometime after American Tank sold out to Hammond in 1928, the peripatetic mill equipment made its way to Sandy McPherson's sawmill on South Fork Yager Creek, just over the ridge from Redwood House.[1326]

E. W. Haight, A. C. Edson, and M. F. Mitchell bought the town of Carlotta from the John M. Vance Estate in 1920. The 40-acre property included the hotel, store, and various other buildings.[1327] The new owners refurbished the structures, and by January 1921 the freshly painted hotel was leased to W. J. Riley, while the Whitney brothers, "both expert mechanics," began operating a brand-new garage.[1328]

Meanwhile, the area experienced extreme ornithological excitement in the summer of 1916 when William Leon Dawson, author of the magisterial *Birds of California*, visited Mr. and Mrs. H. D. Wilder at their home in Carlotta. On the morning of July 1, Dawson awoke and "thrusting [his] head out the window . . . distinctly heard two birds as they made their way down the valley." They happened to be marbled murrelets, and "were twenty miles from tide-water"—much farther inland than Dawson, and other murrelet experts, had ever suspected.[1329]

By the time Carlotta was sold, another vestige of the Vance legacy had gone through its own transformation. The rails of the short-lived California Midland now belonged to the NWP, promising speedy transport for the products of both Yager Creek and the Van Duzen. And the product of greatest importance was redwood timber, which filled both drainages for many miles and, by timbermen's standards, was ripe for harvest.

The Holmes Eureka Lumber Company began logging in Yager Creek in 1912. It had formed a partnership with the Dessert Redwood Company, which was based in Mosinee, Wisconsin. Dessert Redwood originally purchased 10,500 acres of its namesake tree north and east of Carlotta for $300,000. Eventually their holdings extended northward into the Lawrence Creek drainage and beyond into Bell Creek, coming to within a mile of Kneeland's Barry Ridge. The tract held more than a billion board feet of timber. Holmes Eureka, which controlled the merged companies, took Dessert's logs to their mill at Bucksport and converted them into lumber.[1330] In 1924 Holmes Eureka was still logging in the Carlotta area, but the company expected to focus on Fortuna-area tracts of timber the following year.[1331]

To facilitate transport of the Yager Creek timber, Holmes Eureka in 1916 constructed a spur line off the NWP's tracks in Carlotta that ran northward along the west side of Yager Creek. Holmes Eureka used its own locomotives to bring their logs down the Yager Creek drainage to a station called Kniss, where their short rail line met the NWP's tracks in the western part of Carlotta.[1332] Holmes Eureka operated a logging camp about a mile north of the town, a short distance west of Cooper Mill Creek.[1333] With the log-loaded railcars rolling down the tracks, the elimination of passenger service between Carlotta and Alton in 1914 was probably soon forgotten.[1334]

The NWP extended its tracks 1,762 feet east of its Carlotta terminus in 1923. This allowed the Bayside Mill and Lumber Company

Fred Holmes, in white shirt, looking over a Carlotta-area Holmes Eureka logging show (NHC, colorized by JR).

(BM&LC) to build a short spur northward and begin cutting the slopes above Cuddeback. In 1928 NWP track was laid an additional 4,300 feet eastward to Cuddeback Creek, where the BM&LC put in a second spur. Both spurs connected to incline tracks that allowed the company to lower their logs down the steep hillside grade.[1335]

In 1930 the Hammond Lumber Company began building five miles of railroad east of the NWP's Cuddeback terminus to reach its 20,000-acre tract of timber in the Strong's Station area. This led to Hammond's first logging operation in the southern part of the county.[1336] Hammond laid track southeast from Cuddeback Creek on the NWP's right-of-way to a location that was unimaginatively named Railhead,[1337] which was located across Highway 36 from the current Carlotta fire station. From

there, Hammond continued the tracks on their own right-of-way,[1338] eventually ending a short distance south of Strong's Station near today's Highway 36 turnoff for Swimmer's Delight. In later years the end portion of the line was converted into a logging truck road.[1339]

Holmes Eureka owned timberlands on the south side of the Van Duzen. The company ran a rail line from Carlotta south and crossed the river near Fisher Road. The line then split into two spurs, one of which ran upriver and the other downriver. In 1933 they ran a three-mile stub line east from the NWP tracks at Baxter, a railroad stop southeast of the mouth of the Van Duzen.[1340] Holmes Eureka also had some scattered holdings farther up the river, and in 1936, having logged off their Yager Creek and lower Van Duzen timber, they began cutting in the Grizzly Creek drainage. The logs were

In 1935, a Hammond Lumber Company truck is dwarfed by its load (FMC, colorized by JR).

brought by truck to Carlotta, where they were transferred to railcars. It was announced that newfangled "caterpillar tractors" would be used for the logging operations in the woods.[1341]

At an unknown date in the 1920s the Carlotta Hotel closed. It was reopened by Joe Matteucci about 1936 and "was known for its fine Italian food." The Matteucci family ran the hotel for "thirty or so years."[1342]

Meanwhile, logging operations moved up the timber-rich canyons. In 1940 PL bought the Holmes Eureka logging railroad that ran up Yager Creek and began extending their line up the drainage.[1343] That same year PL purchased tracts in the Yager and Lawrence creek drainages from the Deseret Redwood Company, the Hicks-Vaughn Redwood Company, the Hammond Redwood Company, and the Holmes Eureka

Redwood Company. The result was "a solid block of timber twelve miles long and seven miles wide and [which] contained twenty-two thousand acres of virgin timber."[1344] PL began running their logging trains on the Yager Creek route in November 1941.[1345] Ultimately the line extended to a junction with Lawrence Creek, whence one set of tracks went about two miles up Lawrence Creek and another set about a mile and a half farther up Yager Creek.[1346] PL installed its logging headquarters at the site of the former Holmes Eureka camp, three miles up Yager Creek from Carlotta. PL announced that, unlike many earlier camps, "living accommodations will be built for only 50 men at the start, since a large part of the crew will be made of residents of the community." The locals would reach the camp by a "private motor road."[1347]

PL's Yager Creek Camp, 1942 (FMC, colorized by JR).

PL indicated that it planned an intensive operation. It would activate three separate "sides," or logging units, simultaneously. Two sides would work in continuous production while the third side would be "rigged ahead for quick changes." One of the two active sides was to use steam-powered equipment while the other featured four tractor units, "two with arches[1348] and two with bulldozers." The northern end of the cutting area abutted PL's holdings in the Freshwater drainage. The company planned to transport logs from its Lawrence Creek cutting area over the ridge to its rail line in Freshwater via tractor haul and inclined railroad. Logs from lower in the Yager Creek drainage would go down the canyon to Carlotta for transport by rail to Scotia.[1349] In 1946 the Carlotta train depot, unused for 22 years,[1350]

"was torn down to make additional room for loading cars of lumber.[1351]

Reporter Chet Schwarzkopf visited Carlotta in 1949, mentioning in the first paragraph of his subsequent *Humboldt Times* article that the beauty of the area included "age-old redwoods [that] look down from the hills." Without missing a beat, Schwarzkopf segued into paragraph two, which noted the three lumber mills and "a railroad terminal for logging operations nearby."[1352] Readers were left to wonder how many of the "age-old" trees would still be looking down on Carlotta were Schwarzkopf to file an updated report a few years later.

The Carlotta that Schwarzkopf observed in 1949 had changed dramatically from the town that John M. Vance had started more than 45 years earlier. In addition to being the rail hub for the logging operations of the Hammond, Holmes Eureka, and Pacific Lumber (PL) companies, Carlotta featured on-site sawing at the Mark Mitchell, Carter Brothers, and Jack Fairhurst mills. The Carlotta store now catered to the loggers and truckers who were removing the nearby forests. Nearby, the Carlotta Hotel no longer served as a vacationer's resort; instead, it now housed "lumbermen entirely."[1353]

Thanks to the intensity of tree removal, mid-century Carlotta was booming. Some 300 persons resided in the area, while about 130 young scholars attended the Cuddeback School. Some students were bussed in from as far away as Bridgeville, 20 miles up the Van Duzen.[1354]

The town reached its apogee in 1952 when the Carlotta Hotel costarred with Kirk Douglas in *The Big Trees*, a remake of the redwood lumbering saga, *The Valley of the Giants*. In it, Douglas romances one of his leading ladies in front of the hotel's gingerbreaded, Technicolored façade.[1355]

Despite its flirtation with Hollywood, the hotel did not thrive. It closed again, except for a bar at its south end. The bar lasted until 1977, when a fire destroyed the kitchen annex.[1356] That same year the building was purchased by Angelo and Sharon Batini and was subsequently restored and reopened.[1357] The hotel's resurrected dining room drew many locals before the building ignited on a June 1995 morning.[1358] The Carlotta Fire Department had one small truck in a garage less than a block away, another several miles up the Van Duzen, and a water tanker at a fireman's house.[1359] They were no match for the fire, which left a vacant lot whose space has never been filled.

Although less than a hundred yards distant, Carlotta's Fire Department
lacked the capacity to quell the flames at the Carlotta Hotel (JR).

Appendix A: Vanquishing the Van Duzen

Like female film stars from the 1930s, the Van Duzen River canyon between Carlotta and Bridgeville is beautiful, tantalizing, and defiant. Here and there tall cliffs line the river, sometimes releasing slides of clay and rock that plunge dramatically to the riverbed. Near Bridgeville the dark bulk of Goat Rock, a huge, moss-covered section of former cliff, rises upward from the water, forcing the river to curve its way around it. A dense redwood forest covers the riverside flats, wrapping the locations in shadowy silence. Stones of varying size, their surfaces smoothed by the Van Duzen's tumbling water, lie in a patchwork of hues by the riverside. For travelers, the temptation is to linger at a dozen places to admire these sights. But somewhere ahead a destination beckons, and so the trip must continue, if it can, for the canyon often challenges those who come to it, as when a hillside slumps across the roadway or a tree falls to block the way. Such events still happen, but less often than a hundred years or so ago, when travelling up the Van Duzen was fraught with peril, or at least with disappointment.

The first road between Carlotta and Bridgeville was completed in 1874.[1360] It stayed on the north side of the river for its entire distance,[1361] which removed the need for bridges, but this also meant having to cut across unstable, nearly vertical cliffs at locations such as Blue Slide, where clay-colored earth flows were indeed commonplace. Lower Blue Slide was divided by Blue Slide Creek, about a mile southeast of Strong's Station. According to one observer, it "contained layers of blue mud, that during the winter rains washed down across

Repairing the Van Duzen River road, 1915 (FMC, colorized by JR).

the road, causing a lot of trouble every year for the people who lived at Bridgeville and other locations past Blue Slide. At times, they could not get through for days."[1362] Nonetheless, in 1877 the Humboldt and Mendocino Stage Company boldly announced that it would offer daily stages between Eureka and Cloverdale over a route that included the Van Duzen road. At Cloverdale passengers could board a train that would take them, via a bay ferry, all the way to San Francisco. The charge: $21.25.[1363]

In July 1883 an incident occurred about two miles west of Strong's Station that hovered on the edge of tragedy. Eureka banker J. W. Henderson, his family, and William Carson's daughter Lottie left the station in a buggy and a carriage. At a point where the road skirted the edge of a deep canyon, one of the horses pulling the carriage, in a display of equine excitability, "commenced kicking, rearing and backing." The carriage was "forced backwards towards the edge of the precipice." A log momentarily slowed its progress, allowing everyone to leap or scramble from the vehicle except 21-month-old Stella Henderson. Although the horses struggled to regain their footing, the force of gravity proved stronger, and the carriage, horses, and little Stella were, as one of the newspapers breathlessly reported it, "compelled to submit to the death-plunge into eternity."[1364]

But not entirely. Edward Henderson, Stella's older brother, made his way down the hillslope and was soon at the scene of the wreck. He found the "carriage literally smashed to pieces, the two horses badly crushed and dead, and little Stella lying beside the horses' legs. She was crying, and "her face and head were bruised and considerably swollen," but that was about it. Somehow the "sweet-faced, flaxen-haired little

girl" had survived the tumble without serious injury. It was, as the unrestrained account put it, "one of the most . . . wonderful escapes from death on record."[1365]

In 1888 a ray of hope shined down upon those seeking the road's improvement. Ed Barnum wrote from Bridgeville[1366] that a new section of the road east of Strong's Station had been built by two men named Francis and Good. Barnum indicated that

> It was anticipated that the road being new would slide badly as the result of the winter storms. But notwithstanding the severe test to which it has been subjugated . . . wagon travel and horsemen are continually passing over it without being delayed. It is because the road was properly built, and the cuttings properly sloped—because the work was not slighted.[1367]

An alternative to the Blue Slide route involved this summer-only crossing of the Van Duzen east of Grizzly Creek (HCHS, colorized by JR).

However, Barnum noted, Francis and Good's good job took so much time that they lost money on the project, and Barnum believed, with unrequited optimism, that they should be reimbursed for their loss by the county supervisors.[1368]

Austin Wiley, editor of the *Humboldt Times*, traveled the route in June 1892 and reported to his readers:

> To anyone who has never been over the road from Hydesville to Bridgeville we would recommend a trip by moonlight. Thus a weird view of the grand scenery may be obtained and the less attractive features of the road escaped. But returning by daylight the traveler will be astonished at his temerity in having gone over such dangerous looking grades at night, and be set wondering how four-horse teams with heavy loads of wool or goods can safely pass over such roads in the daylight.[1369]

By 1898 there was a way to avoid Blue Slide. It involved leaving the river route near Strong's Station, taking Redwood House Road some two miles into the hills, and then branching off to the southeast on a road that reached the main Van Duzen road near the mouth of Grizzly Creek.[1370] In February 1905 Eleanor Tracy took a stage along this route, going over what she called Grizzly Mountain. She described it as "a long climb and rough descent over a corduroy road."[1371] In addition to Blue Slide, another trouble spot was Blackburn Grade, which ran along the cliff across the river from Swain's Flat.[1372] By 1911 it, too, had a bypass route that crossed to the south side of the Van Duzen and ran through the flat before returning to the north side of the river.[1373]

At Bridgeville the road up the Van Duzen met the original Overland Road that came through Kneeland, Iaqua, and Yager on its way south to Blocksburg, Alderpoint, Harris, and Mendocino County. Much of the Van Duzen traffic turned south at Bridgeville and took the Overland towards Blocksburg.[1374]

An eastward continuation of the Van Duzen road ran from Bridgeville to McClellan Rock, at the northwestern edge of Larabee Valley. It appeared in this guise on the 1898 Humboldt County map.[1375] In 1909 the state began work on completing a route from the coast to the Central Valley. It improved the existing county wagon road that ran up the Van Duzen, creating a 12-foot-wide roadway with 18-foot-wide turnouts.[1376] The road was extended eastward from McClellan Rock, bypassing Larabee Valley as it ran across the southeastern flank of McClellan Mountain. It crossed the South Fork Van Duzen near the mouth of Burr Creek, crossed the main Van Duzen just west of Dinsmore, and followed the Van Duzen for another five miles, where it met a preexisting Trinity County road at the county line.[1377] From there the route led eastward through Peanut and the mountains of Trinity County, and crossed the Tehama County woodlands on its way to Red Bluff. Finally, "on October 3, 1912, Department of Highway road engineer Filson drove an automobile from the Mad River over the road . . . to Red Bluff—the first motor vehicle over the new road."[1378]

By 1913 newspapers were mentioning "the new State Highway from Eureka to Red Bluff."[1379] On August 20 some 22 autos from a "Three States Good Roads Rally" stopped at Dinsmore en route to Eureka, arraying themselves on a grassy field through which passed the narrow dirt road that was the highway.[1380]

"Three States Good Roads rally" at Dinsmore, 1913 (CPH, colorized by JR).

The remotely situated rally was firm in- dication that the Automotive Age was upon the country and had even reached remote Humboldt County. However, as is so often the case, enthusiasm had outpaced engineering, with at least one spectacular result. In 1912 the freighting company of Light & Condon began operating out of Carlotta. Light & Condon started off with a brand-new Mack truck. It had hard-rubber tires and wooden sides around its bed. The vehicle's first run was in September. The Mack had a three-man crew and was "loaded to the gunwales for their customers in Blocksburg." The truck came to the first bridge (exact location unknown) on the road. The structure was built in the traditional style

The Yager Creek covered bridge at Carlotta, 1916, (CPH, colorized by JR).

Unstable slopes on the VanDuzen: landslide opposite Swain's Flat, 1938 (FMC, colorized by JR).

then in use for country roads, with a decking of wooden planks nailed lengthwise. The Mack motored onto the bridge, which promptly collapsed. The crew managed to get the truck to the far side of the bridge and then continue on their way. They came to bridge number 2, which also collapsed, as did bridges number 3 and number 4. The juggernauting Mack kept going, trailing wrecked bridges in its wake. It took six days, through mud that sometimes reached the Mack's axles, to reach Blocksburg, but Light & Condon delivered the goods. Only one bridge along the route remained standing. When the wrecked bridges were repaired, the planking was nailed crosswise, which became a common strengthening practice to meet the just-demonstrated threat of heavily loaded trucks.[1381]

The bridges were repaired, at no known cost to the perpetrators of the problem, and along the new but fragile highway "heavy traffic" ensued, with 200 automobiles and 50 teams and wagons using the route in 1914, a staggering statistic that was soon eclipsed by the 670 autos and 150 teams and wagons that traveled the road in 1915.[1382]

But problems persisted. In March 1921 a report stated that

> Blue Slide Road beyond Strong's Station has been impassable for some time past, and the whole mountainside seems to be sliding into the river. It is the general opinion that the only way the road can be kept open through to Bridgeville is by bridging the Van Duzen River twice,

thus cutting out the Blue Slide. At present some traffic is going over the mountain by way of the Redwood House.[1383]

However, help with the Van Duzen road situation was at hand. In the early 1920s engineers from the California Highway Commission designated what was then known as the Fortuna-Red Bluff Highway "as the main route between the north coast and the upper Sacramento Valley." Soon after this, the Humboldt County Board of Supervisors initiated a road improvement program that included the construction of five bridges along the lower Van Duzen. In an unusual move, the Board bypassed the normal bidding process and hired the bridge designer directly—and no wonder, for he was John Buck Leonard, who had developed

the plans for that quintessential monument to reinforced concrete and a Humboldt County showpiece, Fernbridge, a decade earlier.[1384]

First came a pair of bridges that allowed the highway to bypass Blue Slide. In 1922[1385] Napa contractors Boardwell and Zimmerman built the Lower Blue Slide Bridge for $33,000 and the Upper Blue Slide Bridge for $42,000. Then, in 1925, Leonard's Lower Blackburn Grade, Upper Blackburn Grade, and Bridgeville bridges were all completed. The first two allowed bypassing the other Van Duzen trouble spot, Blackburn Grade, while the third replaced a wooden covered bridge built in 1879.[1386]

The most interesting of the five structures, from a motorist's point of view, was the Upper Blackburn Grade Bridge, which was narrower than the others, allowing only one-way traffic.

"Let's wait for the truck": Upper Blackburn Grade Bridge, 1952 (HCHS, colorized by JR).

Many were the eastbound automobilists who suddenly shifted into reverse when confronted by a fully loaded log truck approaching them on the bridge. Downriver from it stands the loveliest of Leonard's laudable Van Duzen structures, the Lower Blackburn Grade Bridge. It is a through-arch bridge, where the deck, which contains the driving surface, runs through the lower part of the arch, unlike a deck-arch bridge where the deck rests upon the top of the arch. An example of the latter is Leonard's Bridgeville bridge, which, along with the Lower Blackburn Grade Bridge, was retained by CalTrans as an architectural monument when all five Leonard bridges were replaced by technologically superior but aesthetically inferior structures in the 1980s and 1990s.[1387]

The route up the Van Duzen remained a county road until August 1933, when the State of California took over control and made it part of State Highway 36.[1388] In December 1940 the highway had been within the state system for over seven years but was not in good shape. That month a special committee of the Eureka Lions Club sent two of its members roaring along the route "to determine freight-carrying capacity . . . and discuss needed improvements." Driver Alling Davis and observer John Langer made their inspection tour in a 1941 Hudson, provided by "Car-A-Day" Hodges and equipped with both an altimeter and a gradometer.[1389] They took with them 10 copies of the Sunday *Humboldt Times* with which to gift "people living on the outer fringe of the Eureka trading district." The round trip from Eureka to Red Bluff, with a swing through Redding and Weaverville, covered 327.5 miles and took 14 hours and 26 minutes, including

Scenery on 36: Carlotta's last conical burner adorns the highway just east of the Yager Creek bridge (JR).

three breaks. Davis and Langer reported, with startling syntax, that

> These roads can be traveled safely only by experienced drivers and only then when the vehicle has unusual safety built into it. The ability of the car to be completely decelerated as it rounds a severe curve down a 20 percent grade [!] of country rock is often the margin of safety over such highways as were traversed on this trip. When brakes grip evenly while none of the four wheels are on the same plane then both the driver and passenger are free to gain some pleasure from the spectacularly rugged country through which they travel.[1390]

While the Hudson was up to the task, the road itself failed the highway committee's test. The testers concluded that:

> Definitely State Route No. 36 between Alton and Red Bluff is not now suited to the transportation of munitions, foodstuff nor other commodities. The low capacity of the bridges,[1391] the lack of [additional] bridges and culverts, the roadbed, the snow problem, the sometimes-more-than-twenty percent grades make this a highway in urgent need of much improvement before it can be useful for the handling of vital supplies.[1392]

The trip was made on December 8, 1940,[1393] a day less than a year before the attack on Pearl Harbor and the United States' entry into World War II. Anyone who scoffed at the safety committee's concern about the "transportation of munitions" then had their comeuppance.

Thirty years after Davis and Langer's evaluation of Highway 36, another examination was made. This time it was done by British race car driver Sterling Moss, who concluded that the highway was "not only beautiful, but also a test in driving techniques, a course in safety."[1394]

Moss made his trip 96 years after the first road twisted its way up the canyon of the Van Duzen. As he zoomed across the Lower Blue Slide Bridge, he may have noticed, off to his right, the scar on the hillside where the original route went. If Moss truly wanted a "test in driving techniques," he had missed his chance.

Chapter 25

Yager

The upper drainage of South Yager Creek is one of the loveliest locations in Humboldt County. The stream heads in an open, grassy valley, with an oaken border that fringes the gently rising hillslopes. Two miles westward the valley, never wide, narrows to a canyon. Here a rocky cliff is colored in late spring with both cañon and poison delphiniums and, amid their deep reds and indigo blues, grows a soft rosy hybrid of the two, and hybrids of the hybrids that display several gradations of the parent colors.

The rest of the setting is similarly picturesque. Cattle graze peacefully on the grasslands near the road that runs through the canyon, while South Yager Creek wends its way past low rock outcroppings that punctuate a softly colored pattern of prairies and woodlands. There are no reminders of the area's earlier, turbulent history, when ranch families, fearful of Indian raids, fled towards the coast while Indians tried to hide from the soldiers and vigilantes who pursued them without mercy. Time has erased the marks that fighting left upon the landscape, but stories of what happened in this now-peaceful place still linger.

The Yager townsite was part of the territory of the Nongatl tribe, but we know not which specific group within the tribe lived there, nor do we know anything about their villages.[1395] Early in the 1850s, the South Yager Creek area became a travel corridor for pack trains, while ranchers soon began placing their cattle on the prairies. For the resident Indians, this was an invasion of their homeland, and the clash of cultures could only end in tragedy.

In October 1858 a "Letter from Yager Creek" appeared in the *Humboldt Times*. "A. L. W." wrote that:

> The number of settlers at present on the North and South Forks of Yager Creek and Van Duzen is about thirty, and they are coming in fast from Shasta and other northern counties. We have between one thousand and fifteen hundred head of cattle. . . .
>
> The Indians in our section have done us no other damage than burning off a considerable portion of our grass, but we have plenty left.
>
> I should be glad if you could pay our section a visit, so you might be able to tell people what a fine grazing and farming country this is. For stock ranches it cannot be beat.[1396]

"Burning off a considerable portion of our grass"—for the Nongatls, this was their age-old method of keeping the prairies open, thus avoiding conifer encroachment that would diminish Indian food sources such as edible flower bulbs, berries, seeds, and acorns.[1397] A. L. W. had managed to chronicle the tipping point where recently arrived whites suddenly saw the prairies as containing "*our* grass," probably without realizing or caring that the Nongatls had seen the grass as part of *their* prairie. The honeymoon year of 1858, where the Yager whites were tolerant of the Nongatls' behavior, was followed by the desperate year of 1859,

The picturesque Palace Rock Ranch lies just over the ridge from the headwaters of South Yager Creek (JR)

when the Indians, losing their traditional food sources, began supplying themselves with meat taken from the whites. (See sidebar 1.)

The locale became busier in 1875 when the Kneeland Prairie and Round Valley Road (KP&RVR) came through, reaching both Gibson and Hessig's store[1398] and "William's Hotel" on Yager Creek.[1399] That September, it was claimed that a driver leaving Humboldt Bay

> . . . in a buggy, behind a good substantial
> team, at 7 o'clock A.M, and without do-

ing injury to the animals can be at Yagerville at 4 P.M. The distance is given as 43 miles, but they will seem to be very long ones on the first trip.[1400]

By 1880 it was time again to try maintaining a post office. Now called merely "Yager," it lasted until 1932, when it was merged with the office at distant Kneeland.[1401]

Despite the new post office's name, the community was shown as "Yagerville" on the 1886 county map, its substantiality suggested by four dark rectangles designating buildings.[1402]

1. The Black Jager

> . . . in arms arise,
>   Spirits of revenge incite us!
>
>   The Black Jager's Song[1403]

It is unclear how the name Yager came to be applied to a creek and a small town in rural Humboldt County. It could have acknowledged someone of that name who was linked to the area, but if so, that person has never been identified. It could have been a reference to a type of rifle, common at the time, that had a "short barrel and large bore." It could have been an anglicization of Jäger, the German word for hunter. It could have, somewhat obscurely, referred to a military unit in the Napoleonic wars, Lutzow's "Black Jäger" army corps.[1404] In any case, by 1860 the town certainly had a connection with the sentiments expressed in the "Black Jager's Song," with its call to the "spirits of revenge," for Yager was linked with one of the most vindictive episodes in Humboldt County history.

In April 1859 the *Humboldt Times* lamented that "every few days we hear of cattle being killed by Indians in the vicinity of the Bald Hills and Yager Creek," urging that some of the roughly "one hundred soldiers lying idle in the garrison at Bucksport" be sent out to protect travelers and to safeguard stock.[1405] By May, the martial drumbeat grew louder as the *Times* reported "More Trouble with Indians":

> For the last five or six weeks the Indians have been killing cattle in the vicinity of Yager Creek, and knowing that the few settlers there were not able to protect the stock, we have been urging the commander of the Post here [Fort Humboldt] to send out troops.[1406]

The *Times* included a letter from a Hydesville resident providing more details. It stated that a group of whites had pursued some 20 to 30 cattle-killing Indians and while on Yager Creek, one of the vigilantes, James C. Ellison, had forged ahead and, "after killing two or three, was fired upon from the brush by as many more." He "was wounded in the groin by an arrow." The Indians had allegedly "killed as many as two hundred head of stock within a short time."[1407]

And, as it turned out, they had also killed Ellison. On May 21 the *Trinity Journal* announced that Ellison had died at "Iroquois ranch,"[1408] probably

The Kneeland Prairie and Round Valley Road zigzags through the distant prairie below Iaqua
Butte. The military installation called Camp Iaqua was situated to the left of the road (JR).

a garbled reference to the ranch at Iaqua on North Fork Yager Creek. The
article concluded by claiming that "nothing short of extirpation will subdue
the ferocious devils."[1409] Thereupon Yager ranchers, seeking protection for
their herds, moved most of their remaining cattle to the Mattole.[1410]

Also moving were Wesley Underwood and his unnamed wife, who in
January 1859 left Yager for the lower Eel. The transition must have pleased
Mrs. Underwood, who, while living at Yager, "did not see a white woman for
six months."[1411]

Before the end of May, a contingent of 25 men was organized in Hydesville "to go in search of the Indians who murdered Ellison."[1412] The company
divided into two squads, one going to Mad River and the other to North
Yager Creek. By the end of June they had driven off many of the Indian bands
in those areas. But in fall the Indians resumed their raids, and the vigilantes
continued pursuing them on into December.[1413] Near the end of the month,
"Y. Z." sent the *Northern Californian* an account of the conflict that cast it in
monumental terms:

Our end of the country is now mixed up in as bad a war as ever were
the "Medes and Persians," and that, too, with a worse foe, for the In-

dians out here have not only waged war against the whites, but have carried their depredations to the horned stock, and are killing cattle every day. Yet the citizens are chastising them every day. . . .

The company that is out on "Yager" has so far effected but little; the limited number of the company prevents them from doing much more than to protect themselves and the families that are out there; in fact they cannot protect the numerous herds of stock that "graze upon a thousand hills,"[1414] for they [the Indians] are killing them every day.[1415]

On February 4, 1860, the *Weekly Humboldt Times* announced that "the Indians have about taken possession of the Bald Hills country."[1416] That very day, citizens meeting in Hydesville formed a "Volunteer Company," 67 men strong, with Seaman [Seman] Wright as commanding officer."[1417] By mid-February "the Company had been provisioned and were in the field, scouting on the Van Duzen."[1418] On February 23 a petition asked Governor John G. Downey to "commission and call into immediate service the company recently organized in this county as the 'Humboldt Cavalry Company' to proceed to the said districts [Yager Creek and the Van Duzen] to chastise the Indians and to protect the settlers thereof in their property."[1419]

The volunteer company did not fulfill their stated purpose of going east to protect the Yager Creek and the Van Duzen areas, but instead went to the South Fork Eel River, where they managed to kill about 40 Indians.[1420] After that, they still did not go east, but instead some of them participated in the series of late February Indian massacres (including the one on Indian Island) designed to compel Downey to commission them. Downey, however, steadfastly refused to commission the company, which soon disbanded, having never acted to directly defend the Yager area.[1421]

According to Owen C. Coy, in his history of early Humboldt County, "the ranges on Yager Creek were those most seriously affected during the earlier years of the war. . . ."[1422] Coy provides no proof for this statement, but more than 30 years after the event came a report that listed the damage claims made by the Yager ranchers. In 1884 one of them, William White,[1423] filed a claim for losses suffered during the height of the conflict in 1862 and 1863. White indicated that he had lost 43 head of dairy cows, 73 head of beef cattle, 287 cows and stock cattle, 128 head of hogs, and 9 head of horses. In addition, his house and improvements on the ranch were all burned.[1424] At the time of the Indian attacks "the only persons living in this vicinity were James R. McAtee, Wm. White, Martha Linley, Amos Frame, Margery Campton, and Levi Linley."[1425] The list was short because by then other Yager residents had fled, including White's wife, Catherine, and their baby daughter, Bertie, who was born at Yager in 1859 and while still in swaddling clothes left for Hydesville by pack mule.[1426] According to the claim application, "eventually all the whites (including William) "were robbed and barely escaped with their lives."[1427]

Many of the Indians did not escape with *their* lives. They were massacred in the mountains or sent to distant reservations where many of them died.[1428] By the late 1860s the valley of South Yager Creek was again available to white ranchers and to the pack trains that trod its trails. Enough repopulation had occurred by 1872 that a post office called "Yagerville" opened that November, but the gesture was premature; the office closed two years later.[1429]

The county directory of 1890-1891 listed hoteliers William Dawkins and T. B. Kelly, Justice of the Peace A. C. Friend, Road Overseer F. Jameson, and W. E. Feenaty (no occupation given).[1430]

In 1887, well before the invention of Monday night football, local ranchers created their own competitive amusement by staging a September sheep shearing contest at Yager. When the fleece had settled, the home team won, defeating Iaqua seven strings to six.[1431]

During the hard winter of 1889-1890, neither Yager hotel did much business as the weather made traveling nearly impossible. One hotel owner, William "Bill" Dawkins, woke up one morning to find that it had snowed so heavily that "the fences were out of sight." Dawkins was also a rancher, and he and his brother Jim headed out to a lower-elevation barn where they kept their sheep during bad storms. They had gotten as far as the Yager schoolhouse when they realized they wouldn't make it on foot. "So," as Bill related it,

We hunted up some six-inch redwood flooring and nailed cleats on the end of it. Well, we had a devil of a time in getting there. The old barn and sheds were down and a lot of the sheep killed.[1432]

Bill and Jim then found some pine flooring that made better skis. They used them for over a month because

. . . riding a horse was out of the question for the snow was so deep all they could do was flounder about. The sheep slept at night in a willow patch next to the creek and one night after a warm rain, the whole patch of willows was flooded and about a third of the sheep were drowned. . . . Ramus Jensen, who lived on the Dinsmore Place on Mad River at the time, had only 24 sheep out of 2000 left.[1433]

Other roads came to form connections with the KP&RVR near Yager. The 1898

The Niles ranch, part of which is shown here in 1958,
included the Thousand Arce Field (CPH, colorized by JR)

county map depicted a route that left the Van Duzen near Strong's Station, rose to the ridge at Redwood House, dropped to South Yager Creek, and then followed the stream canyon east to meet the KP&RVR about a quarter-mile west of Yager.[1434] The next county map, in 1911, showed a road branching northeast from the KP&RVR about a half mile east of Yager to reach the Russ-Porter ranch west of Showers Pass.[1435] Both new roads replaced older trail routes.

Despite these new connections, travel over the KP&RVR lessened with time. Even before the completion of a series of five bridges up the Van Duzen in 1925, the river road, landslides and all, was preferred over the mountain-

ous KP&RVR. In 1923 hardened Humboldt traveler Delmar Thornbury wrote witheringly that the KP&RVR

. . . is the shortest route leading from Eureka to Bridgeville, but travel is very slight on account of the enormous and many repeated grades. Yet Humboldt County went into debt many thousands of dollars to build this road over which perhaps one wagon is driven each week, and which serves not more than ten sheep ranches.[1436]

Thornbury found the approach to Yager especially irksome:

The former Yager School in 1959 (HCHS, colorized by JR)

From Iaqua, the overland road winds its crooked, wearisome length for six or seven miles down to a bridge across North Yager, then winds its eternally crooked way up the tedious hill beyond, makes a long detour around the head of another branch of the same stream, and finally descends to South Yager Creek at Yager post office.[1437]

Would Delmar be so easily daunted today? The road, still almost entirely dirt and following the same route nearly a hundred years later, surely ranks as one of the most scenic in Humboldt County. The spring green prairies, the rustic barns and ranch houses have, if anything, greater distinction than a hundred years ago, and if some (or all) of the "ten sheep ranches" are now instead inhabited by cattle, the effect is to amplify rather than diminish the bucolic beauty that makes every slow-driven mile a welcome event.

In 1908 Dan East, who, with various brothers, had operated East's Ferry east of Grizzly Bluff, "bought the old Humphrey Sevastes place on middle Yager . . . known as Thousand Acre Field." Despite the name, East's ranch contained only 657 acres,[1438] but it included lovely grasslands west of the KP&RVR. East had at least two unusual experiences during his life. First, he was a student at the short-lived St. Joseph's College[1439] southwest of Rohnerville, a Catholic institution that operated in the 1870s and was briefly resurrected as Mount St. Joseph's in the 1880s and 1890s.[1440] Second, at age 76, he attempted to engage in a fistfight with a young worker on the Russ ranch who had disrespectfully ordered him off the property.[1441] East continued operating his ranch until his death in 1941 at age 84.[1442]

Another long-time rancher in the area was Fred G. Hinckley, whose property was directly south of downtown Yager.[1443] Hinckley and his brother Rudolph purchased about 3,000 acres there in the 1900s. Rudolph had his headquarters at another Hinckley ranch that the brothers owned downstream from Low Gap on Mad River, while Fred made the Yager ranch his home starting in 1909.[1444] By 1922 Harry McWhorter had bought the land between East's ranch on the north and Hinckley's ranch on the south.[1445] In 1923 Hinckley and McWhorter donated land for the Yager School.[1446]

Over time Yager lost the various attributes of a community—the post office gone in 1932,[1447] the school closing in 1943,[1448] the store and hotel shutting down at unknown dates. Finally, the townsite came to have only ranch buildings, one of which, if observed carefully, proves to be the old schoolhouse. The road that Delmar Thornbury scorned still sees only the occasional vehicle, while the dust the drivers raise still settles gently upon the nearby foliage as it did a century and more ago. Time's thread, so taut in the times of William White and the Nongatls, has slackened, and the Yager valley is now merely a place to pass through, rather than a location to flee. The edges of adversity, that here once cut as deeply as a knife blade, have been smoothed by the peaceful progression of the decades, and the Black Yager has vanished like a shadow in the ensuing sunlight.

Chapter 26
Redwood House

The early Humboldt County pack trails kept to the ridges whenever possible, avoiding problematic travel along stream and river corridors. So it was that the location known as Redwood House came to be an important stopping place for packers and other travelers. Situated near the top of the divide between the Van Duzen River and South Yager Creek, the ranch and its welcoming house stood about a mile east of the spot where trails from Rohnerville and Hydesville met near the top of the ridgeline, just south of the canyon of South Yager Creek. Redwood House itself was located high on the southern slope of the ridge. To the east a single trail climbed the daunting bulk of a mountain

called Bald Jessie, headed towards the small community of Yager, and continued beyond it to Showers Pass and Trinity County.[1449]

Redwood House was established in the early 1850s:

> One of the oldest houses in Humboldt County was located about 12 miles directly east of Fortuna on the old horse trail from Rohnerville to Iaqua. Another important pack trail led off from the bottom of the Hydesville trail and met the Rohnerville trail about six miles west of Iaqua. . . . The cabin was built . . . before 1855 by Brown and

The barn at modern-day Redwood House Ranch (JR).

Gibson, two squaw men. Brown and Gibson kept a few cows, the squaws churned the butter.[1450]

The location is mentioned in October 1860, when a trail traveler named A. J. Tyrrell crossed over Bald Jessie on his way west, saw the Pacific Ocean from the top, and "reached Reed's Ranch in the Bald Hills." Tyrrell reported that:

> There is a comfortable frame house here and a corral enclosed by a high board fence. The owner of the place, G. W. Reed, informs the public by a notice posted on the door that he has not abandoned the premises but has left on account of the unsettled state of Indian affairs and intends to return when they become settled. There is a fireplace in the house and we have moved in and taken possession for the present.[1451]

Reed apparently made good on his claim to return, for the location is shown as "Reed's R[anc]h" on the 1865 Humboldt county map.[1452] The following year, however, it is listed as belonging to "Dix and Whitmore—Eel River."[1453]

Reed's fear of Indian attack received belated confirmation in January 1869, when Rufus Burman Emory, who lived in the vicinity, was killed by Indians,[1454] probably the last white victim of Humboldt county's prolonged Indian-white conflict.[1455] One of the men who found Emory's body was William Slaughter Robinson, the owner of what by then was called Redwood House.[1456] Robinson owned the place from 1868 to 1870 before migrating east to Bridgeville.[1457]

Other brief reports followed intermittently from Redwood House. David and Mary Gibson operated a store there from 1872 to 1874, subse-

quently moving to Hydesville.[1458] In November 1877 "Mr. Myers of the Redwood House" lost two children to a diphtheria epidemic.[1459] The house burned in July 1879; at the time it was owned by Winfield Scott Lamb and Alexander Lamb, whose Lamb Brothers Company came to include over 9,000 acres of ranch land in eastern Humboldt County and a slaughterhouse in Rohnerville. The brothers' Redwood House Ranch ran east and north from the trailside ranch buildings, eventually including much of Bald Jessie, going nearly to the small community of Yager and all the way to Middle Yager Creek.[1460] The company still owned the ranch in 1949.[1461] At some point the property was leased to the Tooby brothers, who also did extensive ranching in southern Humboldt County.[1462]

In October 1892 a contractor named Wood started, "with a force of men," to build the Redwood House Road.[1463] It began at the Van Duzen River road just north of Strong's Station and when completed had climbed up the mountainside to pass west of Redwood House, cross the divide and drop into the canyon of South Yager Creek, and then follow the creek upstream to meet the Bridgeville-Kneeland road just west of the community of Yager.

In the mid-1920s one-armed Sandy McPherson set up a sawmill about a half mile north of Redwood House where Redwood House Road crossed South Yager Creek. McPherson had bought his mill machinery from the American Tank Company whose mill had been located east of Carlotta. The well-traveled equipment had first been used at Robinson's Mill on Loop Road, east of Fortuna.[1464]

McPherson hired a number of married workers with families, so the employees built what was called the Redwood House School,

The Redwood House School sat at the ridgetop between South Yager Creek and the Van Duzen River (JR).

perching it right atop the ridgeline that was uphill and south of the mill. It had one room and for a time had two teachers and about 50 students. By 1938 there were only four students left: three were from the Crabtree family, which owned property near the mill, and the fourth was a cousin. Minimum enrollment for a Humboldt school at the time was five, and the county wanted to close the school. Mrs. Crabtree, however, reportedly went to Sacramento and obtained "emergency school" status, the reason apparently being that winter snow would prevent her driving her children down Redwood House Road to the Cuddeback School in Carlotta.[1465]

The teacher that year was Virginia Frederickson Miller. She found that "the Crabtree children were good and obedient kids," with one memorable exception. One day Pat Crabtree had an argument with Miller and "stormed out of the classroom." Pat proceeded to climb up onto the schoolhouse roof, where he sat for "a couple of hours," perhaps enjoying the magnificent view of the Van Duzen watershed. Then, having made his point, Pat came down and "strode back in and settled into school life as if nothing had just happened."[1466]

After Redwood House's turbulent early times, the area had lapsed into more than a century of calmness, with Pat Crabtree's roof-climbing experience producing the peak of local excitement. Then, in 1992, an old-growth redwood forest area less than two miles northwest of Redwood House became the site of what is known as the "Owl Creek Massacre."

In June 1992 the Pacific Lumber Company, which had been taken over by Charles Hurwitz's Maxxam corporation, illegally cut the Owl

Creek drainage a month after one of the grove's residents, the marbled murrelet, had been designated a threatened species. The Environmental Protection Information Center sued MAXXAM and in 1995 won its case, but by then "a million dollars worth of old-growth redwood [had been] removed from the grove." In September 1996, after years of protest that included a blockade of Maxxam's access road to Owl Creek, an agreement was reached with Maxxam to establish the Headwaters Forest, creating a federally owned reserve that contained some of the last publicly owned old-growth redwoods, along with nearby cutover areas that included Owl Creek.[1467]

Did anyone see the irony? There, so close to Redwood House, Maxxam had destroyed the marbled murrelets' redwood home.

Chapter 27
Showers Pass

Perhaps, eons ago, some giant being, wielding some giant tool—it could have been a huge hoe—dug into an obscure mountainside and carved a small canyon, pulling the earth and stones northward and upward and depositing them at the top of the ridge. Over time all of this excavated material formed into a single, enormous mass of mineral that is now called Showers Rock. Below it, the gash in the mountainside became known as the canyon of Baker Creek. The creek flows south, into the Van Duzen River.

A German, looking west towards the rock, would have been stymied when trying to describe it, for it appeared to be something between a "Berg" (mountain) and a "Burg" (castle)—a stone formation rising from the surrounding forest like a dark fortification with a tower at each end. But for the local Nongatl Indians or for the white trail travelers that first arrived in the 1850s, it was neither. Instead, it was a gigantic obstacle that blocked easy travel through the high country north of the Van Duzen. A tale was told about an early-day incident when the rock became a flashpoint between the two disparate, already clashing cultures.

According to this story, sometime in the

Mountain? Or castle? Showers Rock (JR).

1850s Jacob Oscar Showers found himself on the ridgeline pursued by a band of Indians. Showers was on horseback or perhaps was riding a mule. The Indians were mounted— an unusual, or, more likely, apocryphal occurrence—and were gaining on Showers. Heading west, he found himself atop a huge outcropping of rock that terminated in a tall, steep cliff. Rather than be caught by the Indians, Showers urged his mount forward. Amazingly, the animal kept its footing during the long, plunging descent down the perilous precipice and brought Showers to safety at the base of the rock. None of the Indians dared to follow, and Showers made his way westward to safety. The rock was of course subsequently named for him, and the route that was eventually discovered around the rock became Showers Pass. The horse or mule, which was the true hero of the story, had nothing named for it.[1468]

By the time Showers did or didn't ride down the eponymous rock, the vast upland area surrounding it had long been home to various branches of the Nongatl Indian tribe. South of Showers Rock the Kit-tel ki-ya occupied the Van Duzen canyon from Hogback Ridge downstream to the Bridgeville area.[1469] North of Showers Rock were the Bus-a-kot kai-ya, who lived in the upper drainage of North Fork Yager Creek.[1470] A third Nongatl tribal group, repetitiously and confusingly called simply the Nongatls, lived east of the rock, on the Mad River from Deer Creek to about Olsen Creek.[1471] Each of these groups probably passed through the Showers Rock area for summertime hunting and gathering.

After the arrival of whites at Humboldt Bay in 1850, the Showers Pass area was soon frequented by pack trains, mail carriers, cattle drives, and

Hogback Ridge culminates in a diagonal of dark, mossy rock that plunges into the Van Duzen River far below (JR).

assorted other travelers. Several trails headed east from the bay and the lower Eel River valley, gradually combining with one or another until only two crossed through or near Showers Pass. East of the pass the trail system expanded again to reach various locations in Trinity County.

To the resident Nongatls, the trails represented incursions into their homeland. Their response was to attack those whites, like Jacob Oscar Showers, who traveled the various routes. If a rancher brought cattle into the Nongatls' traditional hunting and gathering areas, the animals were considered eligible for capture and conversion into food. In November 1858 the *Humboldt Times* chronicled a response by Captain

J. G. Messic and his recently formed volunteer company called the Trinity Rangers.[1472] In the middle of the month Messic

> . . . engaged a band of Indians near Showers Pass in the Yager Creek country, and as near as we can ascertain, killed some of them and took the remainder prisoners. One of Messic' [sic] company, Henry Allen, was wounded in the attack by the accidental discharge of a gun in the hands of one of his comrades.[1473]

The Trinity Rangers were not an elite force. According to one account, they spent much of their time "drinking and hunting,"[1474] but roused themselves long enough to attack three bands of Indians in the fall of 1858. These "engagements" followed a pattern typical during the prolonged Indian-White conflict. The soldiers would take a small group of Indians by surprise, shoot several, and capture any others who failed to escape. Seldom was more than a single soldier killed or wounded, sometimes, as in Henry Allen's case, by another soldier—who quite possibly was drunk.

The editor of the *Times* did not suffer such foolishness gladly, and continued his account by venting his genocidal rage upon the Indians:

> . . . We hope that Capt. Messic will succeed in totally breaking up or exterminating the skulking bands of savages in that section, that have preyed upon the lives and property of our people for the last seven years. These Yager Creek and Van Dusen [sic] Indians are the very worst in the country, and have never manifested any other feeling toward the whites than that of hostility. . . .[1475]

This statement begged the question: when had the whites ever manifested anything but hostility towards the Indians?

The constriction of the trail system caused by the protuberance of Showers Rock made the area a profitable place for Indians to attack. The military was mindful of the situation, and accordingly an outpost called Fort Baker was duly established in March 1862.[1476] Less than two years earlier, a similar facility call Fort Seward had been constructed above the Eel River. Fort Seward had proved to be a monumental failure. It had been located at low elevation in the river valley, and thus was several miles away from the main trail it was meant to protect, which ran high along the ridge to the west. In less than a year, the half-completed fort had been abandoned.[1477] Now the army wanted to police another high-elevation trail route, which was situated about three-and-a-half miles north of the Van Duzen River. Showing that they had learned absolutely nothing from the Fort Seward fiasco, the army located Fort Baker on a flat above the river at an elevation that was exactly 2,500 feet lower than the top of Showers Rock. The climb from the fort to the rock was, if anything, steeper than the incline at Fort Seward.

Although Fort Baker was thus useless for directly protecting the Showers Pass trail system, it did prove useful as a base for sending patrols into the back country. A few weeks after the fort's establishment, Captain Thomas Ketcham reported on a "successful scout," indicating that

> We have killed 3 Indians and 1 squaw (who was mistaken for a buck), and we have 24 prisoners, big and little, among them two boys, respectively sixteen and eighteen years of age, who were found

A junction at Soldiers Grove, about two miles southeast of Showers Pass. Members of the state militia reportedly camped among the oaks, which allowed them direct access to the ridgetop trail system that was frustratingly far from Fort Baker. One of the oaks still bears the marks of a cross carved into its trunk that memorialized the burial place of three soldiers who never left the grove.[1478] (JR).

secreted after the firing ceased, and were without weapons. *If it meet the views of the colonel commanding I would respectfully request that their lives be spared*, as it will be likely to have a tendency to induce others to surrender. (italics mine)

Ketcham was compelled to plead for the boys' lives because earlier that month, General George Wright, the commander of the Department of the Pacific, had issued orders to the commander at Fort Humboldt requiring that: "Every Indian you may capture, and who has been engaged in hostilities present or past, shall be hung [sic] on the spot."[1479]

It is not known whether Ketcham's plea was heeded.

Four months after it was established, Fort Baker's limitations were dramatically illustrated by an event a few miles to the east. On the morning of July 11, 1862, "two citizens residing in the neighborhood of the fort" reported an Indian attack where the Weaverville trail crossed the Mad River. Ketcham and 15 soldiers promptly started for the scene of the incident but didn't arrive there until 2:30 in the afternoon. They found Hiram Lyons dead and William T. Olmstead shot through both the thigh and hip. Olmstead had survived only by making his way to the river and hiding in a pile of drift wood.[1480]

Fort Baker remained in operation until September 1863. That month, Lieutenant Colonel S. G. Whipple reported on the deficiencies of the fort. He indicated that it

. . . is surrounded by high mountains, making it unapproachable a great portion of the winter season. There are no Indians inhabiting the country about Camp Baker within a day's march, while all the white settlements to be protected by the force stationed there are north and west from the camp. At the time Camp Baker was established an influential citizen had large herds upon the ranch on which the camp is located, but during the year past no cattle have been there except those belonging to Government. If ever there was a good cause for the continued presence of troops at that point it is not necessary now.[1481]

Whipple recommended that Fort Baker be abandoned and replaced by a new installation, to be called Fort Iaqua, on North Fork Yager Creek.[1482] And indeed, that same month, the troops left Fort Baker and company A of the Mountaineers Battalion was "ordered to go into quarters at 'Iaqua,' between Kneeland's prairie and the head of [North Fork] Yager [Creek]."[1483]

In the mid-1860s the Indian-white conflict diminished to the point where Camp Iaqua was abandoned in August 1866.[1484] With the Showers Pass area now relatively secure from further fighting, Joseph Russ made his first land purchase there in October 1868—some 320 acres on Indian Creek.[1485] Once started, Russ assiduously acquired a series of other parcels in the area. These were often homesteaded properties of 160 acres that Russ bought from the original owners. It was said that "Russ had a standing offer to buy any homestead in an area in which he was interested, for $400, and in addition he would cancel any indebtedness the seller might have had at a Russ Store."[1486]

Russ was not the only person buying land in the Showers Pass vicinity. In 1866 or 1867 Chris Hansen brought Merino sheep into the area and subsequently obtained lands adjacent Russ's that were "on the slope to the Van Duzen River." Robert Porter, who owned stores in Eureka and Hydesville, formed a partnership with Hansen about 1874. Some four years later, Hansen and Porter "threw in with Russ" to create what came to be called the Fort Baker Ranch.[1487] The name, however, was a misnomer. It was based on the incorrect belief that there had been a second, later army post called Fort Baker, one that was located on upper Indian Creek where Robert Porter built his ranch house about 1878.[1488]

By 1881 the Russ, Porter, and Hansen ranch was "considered the largest in the county." That June, they brought together a crew of over 50 men for the wool clip, including 38 shearers. In 12 days they sheared 14,000 sheep. On one of the days they put up 62 bales of wool, which was "considered the biggest day's work ever done on any ranch in the county."[1489]

The three-way partnership lasted 20 years, until 1898, when Robert Porter bought out Chris Hansen's interest in the ranch for $40,000.[1490] Before Hansen leaves the pages of this book, however, two stories about him must be repeated. The first involves Hansen's 1866 trip to Humboldt County, when he brought his sheep from the Sacramento Valley. Near Blocksburg "Hansen was shot in the chest by an Indian arrow, which he cut out with his razor." This alone is a remarkable demonstration of fortitude, but it may have been even greater than generally thought if it occurred after Hansen had received injuries that left him with only one arm and one finger on the other hand.[1491] Story two involves Hansen's "enormous Newfoundland dog by the name of Nero." Hansen had a brother who lived some 30 miles away in Hydesville, and, according to George Friend:

The Porter Ranch headquarters, built about 1878 on the supposed site of the notional second Fort Baker (JR).

When Hansen needed supplies or wanted to send through some important message, the letter was fastened to Nero's collar and he was started out in the evening. Next morning he would arrive in Hydesville, deliver his message, rest up for the day and make a return trip next night, carrying with him a reply, often in the form of much needed supplies or medicines.[1492]

With Nero on duty, who needed the postal service?

The 1898 county map showed the Russ-Porter ranch stretching from the Van Duzen River to the Mad River, centered on the Indian Creek area about midway between the two rivers. By then additions the ranch had extended it southeast to encompass the site of Fort Baker, so the name "Fort Baker Ranch" had finally become appropriate.[1493]

Joseph Russ died in 1886 and Robert Porter died in 1906. Their heirs continued the partnership until 1918, when the Porters took sole control of the eastern part of ranch, including the headquarters on Indian Creek. The Russes took 10,000 acres to the west and built their own headquarters on Dairy Ridge, about three miles from the Porters' counterpart.[1494] A look at the 1911 county map shows a stripe of small landholdings, running north to south and mostly a half-mile wide, that roughly separated what became the discrete Russ and Porter landholdings. Other small parcels formed a partial ring around the edge of the Russ-Porter ranch. Most of these properties were 160 acres in size— the amount of land that could be filed on for an individual homestead.[1495] These parcels were useful only as ranchland, but 160 acres was generally too little on which to maintain a successful ranch. When the Russ-Porter ranch was split up, the Porters sold some of their land to

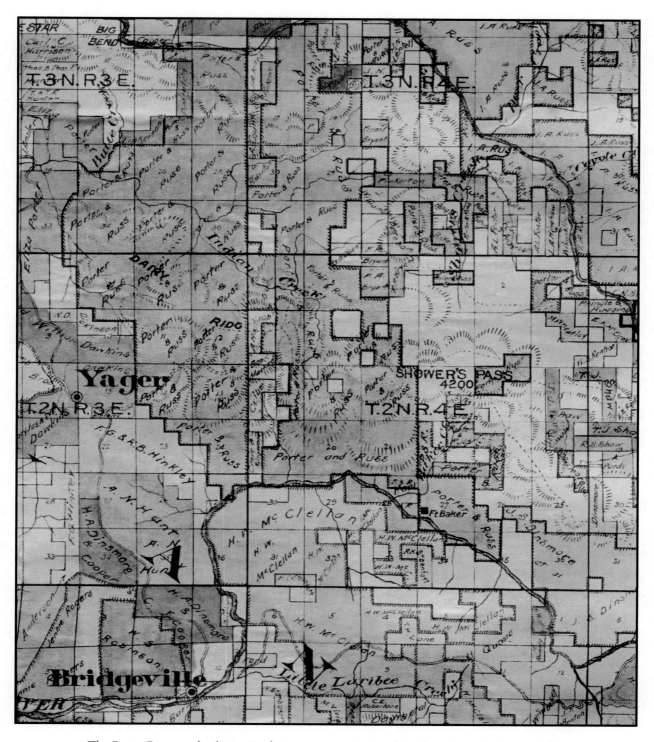

The Porter-Russ ranch, shown in olive green, as it appeared on the 1911 official Humboldt County map. Near its center is the broken line of small homesteads that approximately divide the Russ portion of the ranch (on the left) with the Porter portion (on the right) (EDC).

their neighbor on the north, Tom Sibley, which increased the size of his ranch to about 1,200 acres. The Porters and Sibleys were friends and, according to one of the Porters, they made the transaction because "they knew Tom needed more land to support his family."[1496]

Other families also ranched on the periphery of the Porters' property. In June 1919 Oscar and

The Sonoma Trailblazers relive the Russ-Porter early days as they come up from Dairy Ridge.
When asked what they were carrying in the wagon, the driver answered, "Beer!" (GR).

Dee Stapp and their four children left Eureka by buckboard and headed east. Quite far east, in fact, for they were headed to their new home on Wildcat Creek,[1497] on the far side of the Mad River east of Showers Pass. After three days they reached Little Coyote Flat, where the road ended. The two mules that had pulled the buckboard were now fitted out with pack saddles. One mule carried "blankets, utensils, and enough groceries to last for at least a week." The other mule had two kerosene boxes fitted over its saddle. Into one went Marvin, the eldest son, while Kenneth, the second son, was deposited into the other. Muriel the only daughter, rode on the packsaddle, while "Dee Stapp carried the baby, Ellis, in her arms."[1498]

The Stapps worked hard to improve their homestead. After three years, having met the government's requirements, they received the deed to the property. By then they had accumulated 200 head of hogs, 10 head of cattle, 2 horses and 3 mules. Each year Oscar and the oldest boys would drive a passel[1499] of their hogs to market, taking them south to Dinsmore and then down the Van Duzen to the Pacific Lumber Company's slaughterhouse at Scotia.

When the Stapps' homestead proved up, their eldest son Marvin was nine years old, and it was clear that he and his siblings were not receiving a proper education. The nearest school was 12 miles to the west in Hart's Valley, a short distance from the Showers Pass Post Office, which was run by Ralph Frost. The Hart's Valley business district also included a "quaint store" where "just about anything you wanted could be ordered." Sam Zeron ran a Model T Ford pickup "stage" that would deliver supplies to the store. Lured by these attractions, the Stapps twice moved closer to the school, finally buying a 160-acre property just west of Showers Creek that had previously belonged to William Hagans.[1500] In 1910 Hagans had made the news in spectacular fashion but no doubt wished he hadn't. (See Sidebar 1.)

The first Showers Pass School opened in 1899.[1501] It was located about a mile north of Showers Rock on Coyote Flat,[1502] which was a central location for the families living in the area at that time. By 1910[1503] the supply of students shifted to the northwest, so the school board members took the school apart and moved it to Hart's Valley.[1504]

From the Stapps' new ranch on Showers Creek it was only about five miles to Hart's Valley and the reassembled Showers Pass School.

The Stapp children normally walked there and back, but in stormy weather Oscar Stapp "drove a team of horses or mules with the wagon, often through deep snow, to get the Stapps and neighboring children to school."[1505]

About a mile south of the school at Hart's Valley was a brownish-orange bump on the hillside called, with only approximate accuracy, Red Knoll. This was the site of the Fort Baker Mine, which during World War I produced manganese ore.[1506] In June, 1918, there were about 200 tons of ore on hand, ready to be shipped 28 miles to the railroad at Carlotta.[1507] That year, a total of 24 railcars of Fort Baker manganese were shipped from Carlotta. In 1920, only 6 carloads were shipped.[1508] The mine did well only in wartime.

---

1. William Hagans's Reverse Honeymoon

William Hagans made his appearance in print when Happy Neeley and Bert Foster were arrested for rustling cattle at Fort Baker. The men confessed to the crime but claimed that Hagans was the ringleader. By then Hagans had done two things to make the story more interesting. First, he had fled to Mexico. Second, while doing so he had eloped with Foster's sister and taken her with him. Meanwhile, Hagans's father died in Kansas, which Hagans learned about only after he had crossed into Mexico from San Diego. Hagans thereupon did an about-face and headed to Kansas "to claim the estate." By then, however, the Humboldt County Sheriff's Office was following his movements, and soon Deputy Sheriff Jack McCahan headed east, extradition papers in hand. McCahan "had no difficulty in securing his man" and the pair returned to Eureka. They were accompanied by Hagans's bride, which made the trip a sort of second, perhaps unique, honeymoon. Hagans went on trial in April. He claimed that he did not know that the cattle, which he was seen herding with Neeley and Foster, had been stolen. The jury believed him, and Hagans was acquitted. Meanwhile, Neeley and Foster were receiving three years free room and board at San Quentin.

The Fort Baker Mine on Red Knoll, looking south (JR).

In 1906, the year Robert Porter died, Albert N. Hunt began acquiring land north of Bridgeville. He first purchased ranches that had originally belonged to Dr. Moses Constantine Farrar and Salmon Brown, which gave him a base of about 5,000 acres and brought him to within a half-mile of the southwestern edge of the Russ-Porter ranch near Chimney Rock. Hunt subsequently bought six small homesteads near Showers Pass. They had belonged to Isaac B. Hagans, Francis Oliver, Joseph A. Wagner, Everett Ellingwood, Oliver Liscomb, and Jack Hagans. By 1931 Hunt had added about 2,000 acres to his holdings, including Showers Rock and a band of land around it.[1509] These parcels were at high elevation on or near the ridge north of the Van Duzen. The Hunts acquired additional property nearby, so that what became the Showers Rock Hunt Ranch totaled about 4,000

acres and provided summer range for the Hunts' cattle.[1510] In the 1960s the Hunts purchased the Ackley Ranch, which contained the site of Fort Baker.[1511] Eldredge Ackley had earlier acquired the 1,500-acre ranch from the Porter family at an unknown date.[1512]

The Showers Pass Post Office closed in 1937[1513] but not before it had gained attention for a dramatic rescue attempt. (See sidebar 2.)

The Showers Pass School closed in 1956, after a year in which it only had 6 students.[1514] Just a decade or so earlier it had gained statewide attention. (See sidebar 3.)

About 3 or 4 years after the Russ-Porter Ranch was split up in 1918, the Z. Russ Company, which then owned the Russ half of the old ranch, began renting the Porter's portion of the property. When the Annie Russ Harville Trust took over the Russ holding in 1944, the

2. Rescuing "High Rock"

The snow was deeper than it had been in anyone's memory. At the Showers Pass Post Office, Dave "Barbed Wire" Cassidy, having made his way through the drifting snow, delivered a load of mail. About a hundred yards to the north, Ralph "High Rock" Gordon was skiing in from his ranch. He stumbled and fell in the deep snow.

Back at the post office, Cassidy and others heard a gunshot. Must be High Rock bringing in a letter, they thought, the shot signally Cassidy to wait.

So they waited, but no one showed up. After a time Cassidy left the post office to look for High Rock.

He wasn't far away. Gordon was lying in the snow, a crimson line of blood trailing behind him. His fall had discharged his .45 caliber army automatic, sending a bullet deep into his leg.

Cassidy got help at the post office and the men brought High Rock into the building. They knew immediately that he needed expert medical aid. Cassidy saddled a horse and set out for the nearest phone; it was 15 snow-covered miles away at the Russell Hunt Ranch above Bridgeville. Cassidy, who wasn't called Barbed Wire for nothing, rode through the entire night, breaking trail as he went, and arrived at the Hunts' early the next morning.

Cassidy called the sheriff's office in Eureka, asking that they find a doctor to come to High Rock's aid.

Asking was one thing, but getting the right answer was another. It was said that several doctors refused to go out. Only when a call reached Sam Burre, a recently-minted physician, was there a positive reply. Burre was ready and willing to help, but they needed to know one thing—he'd never ridden a horse.

Deputy Sheriff Roy Nellist drove Burre out. Nellist took Burre to the lower Hunt Ranch, where Cassidy and Walter Sibley got him on board a horse and gave him his first riding lesson: a 17-mile trip, much of it at night, through deeply drifted snow.

They reached Gordon at one o'clock the next afternoon. High Rock was feverish, with a badly infected leg, and Burre realized that Gordon needed to get to a hospital in order to survive.

Burre looked around. There were only three able-bodied men to take Gordon out. They could never do it.

Now Oscar Stapp's 12-year old son went to work. He hiked five miles through the snow to bring additional help, while Burre fashioned a splint and reduced High Rock's fever. Burre then improvised a stretcher.

"High Rock" Gordon on his horse-drawn ambulance sled (HCHS, colorized by JR).

Young Stapp's search soon paid off. Walter and Ray Sibley, each 235 pounds, showed up, took hold of the stretcher, and carried High Rock a mile and a half to the old Porter Ranch headquarters.

The trip was downhill, but it still took five hours. The exhausted rescue party stayed overnight at the ranch house. Strong as the Sibleys were, everyone understood that it would be impossible to carry Gordon by stretcher all the way to Bridgeville.

Now it was "Badger" Kelly who went to work, making a sled that he placed on galvanized metal runners. Sacks of hay were set down to form a mattress, and High Rock, on his stretcher, was placed on top.

Two saddle horses pulled the ambulance sled, with eight men taking turns to help. Even so, the party had to stop every 15 to 25 yards to let the horses rest.

After a full day struggling through the snow, they reached Palace Rock. The horses were nearly done in and had huge blisters on their backs from being rubbed by the ropes that ran from the saddle horns to the sled. The party camped at Palace Rock for the night, quickly eating their entire supply of food—three onions and a loaf of bread. That night two of the men set off for the Hunt ranch. They returned early in the morning with fresh horses and more men.

The rescue party reached the upper Hunt Ranch at about 11 A.M. Here the men had lunch and then went on to the lower Hunt ranch, four miles distant, where they arrived about 6 P.M. An ambulance was waiting there and it sped High Rock to a Eureka hospital. X-rays revealed that the bullet had broken Gordon's femur in three places and remained lodged in the leg.

Gordon stayed in the hospital until the end of May, when Burre took him home to Showers Pass. High Rock had made a full recovery.[1515] By then Gordon and Burre had discovered that they were once schoolmates many years earlier at Freshwater. They hadn't realized this during the rescue because Burre was too busy trying to stay on his horse.[1516]

arrangement continued. In about 1950 the Harville Trust bought out the Porters.[1517]

Then, in 1951, Leland and Esther Rice bought the entire Fort Baker Ranch from the Harville Trust. There followed a period of litigious turbulence. In September 1953 the Rices sued E. Badenhamer and the Coast Pacific Lumber Company, claiming that the defendants were "unlawfully maintaining a mill on the Fort Baker Ranch." The Rices asked for "restitution of the property . . . and $60,000 in damages.[1518] In 1959 the Rices were again in court, suing the Harville Trust, alleging that a 1954 agreement between the Rices and the Trust had been violated for three years, resulting in property damage of $342,000.[1519] Come 1961 and Leland Rice sued the County of Humboldt to compel the county to close Gordon and Stapp

roads, two spurs off of Showers Pass Road that provided access to the ranching families for which they were named. Rice claimed they were not deeded as roads, while the county believed that they qualified as public roads because they had been used as such for over five years.[1520] Further reports about the suits have not been located, but both Gordon and Stapp roads remained opened.[1521]

When the *Humboldt Beacon* ran a report on the Showers Pass area in 1962, the article mentioned the Hart's Valley school, noting that one of the buildings

. . . is headquarters for the Hart Valley Gun Club, and with the use of Coleman lights hung from the ceiling and Coleman stoves to cook on, tables, camp

3. Flowers and Husbands

One year in the 1940s, when Merlynn Stapp was a 12-year-old student at the Showers Pass School in Hart's Valley, she had a chance to enter a contest. The state was offering prizes for the best wildflower collections, which would be exhibited at the state fair.

It was a contest that gave Merlynn a distinct advantage. The Showers Pass area was one of the best places in the county for spring wildflower displays, offering the yellow-golds of California poppies, the blue-purples of lupines, and a rainbow of colors from other flowering plants. Merlynn went to work collecting samples of all the flowers she could find. She mounted them in a display, sent them off to Sacramento, and waited.

After a time Merlyn received word that she'd won one of the top prizes. She went to the fair in Sacramento to see her award-winning display and was told it would be returned to her after the fair ended.

She never got her flowers back.

After Merlynn graduated, she became engaged to Bill Fales, a young man

The first Showers Pass School, relocated at Hart's Valley
among Merlynn Stapp's award-winning flowers (JR).

who lived with the Stapps. One February day in 1949, Fales left the ranch in a jeep, heading west. A heavy snowstorm hit while he was on his way, and his jeep broke down. Fales was six or seven miles from the ranch, but he decided to walk back. It was rough going. He apparently hoped to reach the Showers Pass School in Hart's Valley, where he could make a fire and get something to eat.

Fales never made it. Part way there "he took off his .22 pistol, carefully wrapped the belt around the holster, folded his jacket around it and laid the bundle on the roadway. Ellis Stapp and his wife, heading towards their ranch on skis, saw a piece of Fales's coat showing above the snow and found his body beneath it.

Sixty-seven years later, Merlyn told the stories of her prize-winning flower display and Bill Fales's death. By then she had been married five times. She concluded her account with a short summary of her life: "I stopped collecting flowers, then collected husbands."[1522]

chair and a fine old wood heater to warm the room, it is a comfortable place to cook, eat and relax after a long day in the field by the hunters.[1523]

It was also the place where, if he could have walked but a few hundred yards farther, Bill Fales would have found succor from the blizzard that froze him in the snow. And it was the place where his fiancé-to-be, Merlynn Stapp, had gathered the wildflowers of Showers Pass for her exhibit at the state fair. It was, finally, a place where life and death had crowded together in the great open spaces of the Showers Pass countryside; where the sunlight and storms of existence came and went; and where, if one were patient enough, all the showers, no matter how lengthy, were sure to pass.

Appendix A: The Wrong Place, the Wrong Time

One day in August 1912 Logan Wagner, age 9, and his sister Carmen, age 4, were playing in a hayfield on their family's homestead near Coyote Flat. According to the subsequent newspaper report, "a monster gray eagle swooped down upon them, evidently intending to make the little girl the target of its attack." Logan, however, was armed with a .22 caliber rifle, and he shot the bird, which brought it to the ground. The eagle was down but not out; it spread its wings, extended its talons, and charged Carmen. Logan quickly got between the bird and his sister, and fending off the eagle's attacks, chambered another cartridge, shot the bird in the mouth, and finally killed it with the butt of his rifle.[1524]

Thirteen years passed.

At 11 P.M. on Wednesday, October 7, 1925, a Dyerville truck driver named Henry Sweet picked up hairdresser Carmen Wagner at her parents' home in Eureka. The couple left for a hunting trip in the Showers Pass area. On Sunday the 11th, rancher Walter Craig rode by the Bryant homestead on Coyote Flat. He found Henry Sweet beside his car, dead, with a bullet hole in his back. For ten days searchers

The Wagner homestead, just west of Showers Rock (JR).

looked for any sign of Carmen Wagner. On Friday, October 23, her body was discovered in shallow grave about five miles from the Bryant homestead. Her dog, Pronto, was found nearby, dead from a bullet wound.[1525]

This time Logan Wagner had not been there to protect his sister.

Soon two men were arrested, based on the suspicion that they were involved in the murders. They were part white and part Hupa and were half-brothers. One, Walter David, lived about a mile from Coyote Flat. The other, Jack Ryan, had been seen about the time of the killings riding to his half-brother's cabin. David, it turned out, "had an air-tight alibi and was released." But Humboldt County District Attorney Arthur Hill, who was preparing to run for judge, wanted the case settled. Three months after the murders, Jack Ryan went on trial.[1526]

The trial was long, the deliberations short. Testimony was tainted, and "one of the lawmen who worked for Hill testified that evidence was planted." The jury, which consisted of twelve white males, reached a verdict within 24 hours. They found Jack Ryan not guilty.[1527]

Freed from jail, "Ryan returned to being a cowboy." A fund was established to help repay Ryan and his father the $2,500 they had paid in attorney's fees. Several petitions were circulated that asked for donations, and the Humboldt Times ran an article about the petition from the Iaqua area. The donations there totaled $259, given in amounts from $1 to $25. Most of the local ranch families contributed: the names Fredrickson, Slater, Gift, Shaw, Mullen, Sibley, Fulton, Paddock, Barry, Bjorkstrand, and Hunter were all on the list.[1528]

By then the county had held its election.

Stephen Metzler, a local attorney, had run for district attorney on the pledge that he would find Sweet and Wagner's killer within two years or resign. He won by a landslide, perhaps mostly because he was a "wet" and made it known that he would not enforce the edicts of Prohibition. His stand on the issue was not unexpected, because he owned a still himself.[1529]

Nearly two years passed.

Metzler was worried, for he had not found the murderer. He pressured David and Ryan to confess—either one would do. The district attorney told two deputies that he wanted to put a wire around David's neck "and choke the truth from him."[1530] In October 1927—two years after the murders—Walter David's body was found at edge of a prairie near the Van Duzen.[1531] Metzler's wish was fulfilled, for David's "teeth were kicked in and he was strangled through the mouth with barbed wire."[1532] The district attorney failed to investigate David's death.[1533]

A few months passed.

Metzler still hadn't gained a conviction for the double murders. What he wanted was the conviction, not the murderer. With time growing short to meet his self-imposed deadline to solve the killings, Metzler "hired several men to shadow and terrorize Ryan." They booby-trapped a trail that Ryan regularly rode so that a rifle would fire at him when he came by. No luck. Then two gunmen surprised him as he was being driven across a bridge; Ryan escaped by leaping from the car into the river.[1534] Then Metzler tried a new tactic.

In July 1928 the district attorney "paid a woman $100 to swear a complaint that Ryan had raped her 13-year old daughter. Ryan was immediately arrested. Soon afterward, two

The Bryant homestead, where Henry Sweet's body was found (PD, colorized by JR).

The posse that searched for Carmen Wagner. Showers Rock is in the background (PD, colorized by JR).

other women stepped forward with similar accusations."[1535] Metzler had finally found a plan that worked; he had gotten Ryan back in jail with new charges that could, with perjured testimony, convict him. On September 10, Jack Ryan pled guilty to attacking Rose Sibley, 13, and Hazel Chandler, 16. A third alleged victim, 13-year-old June Zeron, testified against Ryan in court, but Metzler had her case dismissed.[1536] Now everything had finely fallen into place. In an unpublished manuscript, Metzler wrote, "I knew that if [Ryan] were so incarcerated I would wring a [murder] confession from him."[1537]

And wring it, Metzler did. The previous district attorney, Arthur Hill, offered his version of what happened in a subsequent issue of *True Detective Mysteries*:

> The grilling began at seven o'clock on the evening of Wednesday and continued without let-up throughout the night, the officers working in relays and firing a broadside of questions at the suspect.[1538]

Hill failed to provide any details about what actually occurred. After Ryan had pled guilty to the statutory rape charges, Metzler "handcuffed Ryan to a steam radiator and interrogated him for 13 hours."[1539] If the radiator was running on high, Metzler gave new meaning to "giving the third degree" by steaming Ryan at well over a hundred degrees.

An entire night of torturing and intimidation proved to be enough. At 8 A.M. on September 12, Ryan signed a confession admitting that he had killed Walter Sweet and Carmen Wagner. At 3:15 that afternoon he was taken to court, pled guilty to the murders, and was sentenced to life imprisonment by Judge Thomas H. Selvage.[1540] At 7 P.M. Ryan was on his way to San Quentin State Prison.[1541] Justice may sometimes move quickly, but for Jack Ryan, injustice was even quicker.

Not so quickly, justice was meted out to Metzler. Three years after he'd forced Ryan's false confession he was convicted "for selling bootleg liquor out of his office."[1542] Metzler served his term at McNeil Island Federal Penitentiary in Washington state and was released in August 1934. In 1939 he received a full pardon from President Franklin D. Roosevelt.[1543]

Even after Ryan's "confession" many locals insisted that he was innocent. Walter Craig, the man who had discovered Henry Sweet's body, issued a flyer in 1945 that claimed "Jack Ryan Is Not Guilty of Murder," charging Metzler and others of falsely imprisoning Ryan to protect "**three white men**." Instead, Craig claimed, "W. R. Shields and his two sons murdered Henry Sweet and Carmen Wagner, and that Jack Ryan and Walter David met the murderers accidentally and were **forced** by **fear** of **death** to keep silent."[1544]

Others also believed that Shields was the murderer.[1545] One of the posse members who searched for Carmen Wagner's body, William Wonderly, came home from the search and told his wife, "That goddam Bill Shields did it."[1546] In 2001 Sterling Paddock, who had lived in the Kneeland-Iaqua area since the 1910s, said that "Shields killed Carmen Wagner" and that

Sheriff A. A. Ross, Jack Ryan, and District Attorney Arthur W. Hill on the day of Ryan's initial arrest (PD, colorized by JR).

In death Carmen Wagner achieved a level of fame sought by aspiring Hollywood starlets (PD, colorized by (JR).

"Shields had a still at Blocksburg and worked for Metzler."[1547]

Some people were not certain who the murderer was, but they knew it wasn't Ryan. In 1932, not long after Metzler was convicted of selling bootleg whiskey, the State Department of Criminal Identification responded to a request by a Humboldt County rancher to review the Jack Ryan case. Ryan was interviewed by the state agency, but he "gave . . . no new evidence." The case was not reopened.[1548]

Ryan recanted his confession and in 1939 applied for parole. Metzler, who that year received his pardon from Roosevelt, helped assure that Ryan's appeal was denied.[1549]

In 1947 Ryan again applied for parole. The application was denied.[1550] His attempt may

been sidetracked by "psychiatric reports that basically said that Ryan seemed to have a chip on his shoulder and had a bad attitude."[1551] However, other officials at San Quentin who observed his everyday behavior reached a different conclusion, calling Ryan a "model prisoner."[1552]

The following year, federal Indian agents investigated the case. Metzler, who had been reinstated to the State Bar of California after his pardon, was interviewed. He finally told the truth, admitting "that he set Ryan up and that Bill Shields . . . was probably the killer."[1553]

Metzler's confession should have freed Ryan, but instead the federal government's report sat in the state attorney general's office as Ryan waited for days, months, and then years, to receive his release. Finally in 1953, Ryan was paroled,[1554] but even then the terms of his release were punitive: he was ordered to never set foot in Humboldt County.[1555]

Ryan, by now 50 years old, moved to Redding and obtained work as a day laborer on highway projects.[1556] He petitioned three governors for clemency but each time was denied. Finally, in 1969, Governor Roland Reagan commuted Ryan's life sentence to time served.[1557]

In 1956, Metzler, the man who had robbed Ryan of 26 years of his life, died in Los Angeles. He was 70.[1558] Bill Shields died in 1964.[1559] Jack Ryan died in 1978.[1560]

With Ryan's passing, it seemed that the Coyote Flat murder saga had ended. And it no doubt would have, had not a young rancher woman stopped Humboldt County Deputy Sheriff Richard Walton for a chat in October 1983. She told Walton, "You should look into the Jack Ryan case. An innocent man spent his life in prison for crimes he didn't commit."[1561]

The already twisted Coyote Flat murders were about to be twisted even more. But then, finally, they would be unwound.

In seeking out Walton, the ranch woman made an inspired choice. Then in his forties, Walton was fascinated by the history of the West. The Coyote Flat murders were straight out of a Louis L'Amour novel. That alone assured Walton's interest. But more importantly, Walton had a strong sense of justice. As soon as he familiarized himself with the case, he realized that the legal system had been shockingly abused. Walton was hooked.[1562]

Soon Walton was spending almost all of his spare time rewarming what had become a 60-year-old cold case. He spent the next 13 years "reading old newspaper accounts, tracking down surviving participants or their descendants, and reconstructing a case that was never meant to be reopened."[1563] Walton interviewed "almost 400 people, including ranchers, posse members, and bootleggers," half of whom were between 60 and 94 years old. They included state Supreme Court Justice Stanley Mosk, who had worked for the governor in 1939 and knew about Ryan's pardon request. To finance his work, Walton sold his prize collection of over 30 Winchester rifles.[1564]

Near the start of his research, Walton met with newspaper columnist and local historian Andy Genzoli. He told Walton, "Jack Ryan was railroaded," and retrieved "a frail, yellowed manuscript." Genzoli gave it to Walton, indicating that it was what Metzler had written about his handling of the Coyote Flats murders.[1565]

Walton later stated that although the account was biased, the "document became the cornerstone of my investigation."[1566] As Walton continued his inquiry, it became

clear to him that Ryan was innocent. Walton approached Municipal Court Judge John Morrison with the information he'd accumulated. Morrison cast an expert's eye over the evidence and concluded that at least part of the legal process was "a sham," and that Ryan was probably innocent. In 1990 Morrison wrote that his study of the case "results in my opinion that a grave injustice was done to Jack Ryan and that a thorough review by the government will result in a full pardon." Armed with Morrison's statement and the support of other Humboldt County officials, Walton then attempted to obtain something that had never been given before: a posthumous pardon for a convicted murderer.[1567]

Walton wrote then-governor George Deukmejian requesting a review of the case. Soon

At the family's homestead, Carmen Wagner decorated the wall of her upstairs bedroom with this set of cutout images (GR).

Deukmejian's term ended, but in 1991 the State Board of Prison Terms sent a recommendation to the new governor, Pete Wilson, that "a pardon for Jack Ryan be granted on the grounds of innocence."[1568]

But what seemed like a step in the right direction was followed by a stumble. Wilson's office failed to respond to the request. Walton waited, but prospects did not look good. In 1991 and 1992 Wilson granted no pardons, posthumous or otherwise. Walton continued to wait, his hopes sinking, as two more years passed without any action on his request. Finally, in 1995, he went to local assemblyman Dan Hauser for help. On June 13 Hauser wrote Wilson that "At this point, Mr. Walton and I would simply appreciate the courtesy of a response as to the status of the pardon for Jack Ryan. Thank you."[1569]

Ten months passed.

Then, on April 15, 1996, word came from Sacramento: Governor Wilson had "granted a posthumous pardon to a man who was wrongly convicted for a double murder in Humboldt County almost 70 years ago."[1570] The tortuous journey towards justice for Jack Ryan was finally completed.

During the last 20 years of his life Ryan became "very close to a family in Burney," a small town in Shasta County. He befriended the grandmother in the family, and upon "her daughter's death, he helped raise the woman's grandchildren." Ryan was buried in the family's cemetery.[1571]

On the first weekend in June, 1996, Walton and Morrison went to Burney and placed a tombstone on Jack Ryan's grave.[1572] And then Walton spoke the words that Ryan had had waited in vain to hear:[1573]

> Jack Ryan was a young man in the wrong place at the wrong time. He was unjustly railroaded into pleading guilty for crimes he did not commit.[1574]

And then, in the summer sunlight, there was only silence.

Chapter 28

Iaqua

The Iaqua Buttes are a swirl of steep-sided ridges that nearly enclose the headwaters of Lawrence Creek. They drop away to the south across a picturesque tapestry of woodlands and prairies to reach the canyon of North Yager Creek. These sun-facing slopes are incised with several small streams, and it is no wonder that the Tcil-lun-din kai-ya, a Nongatl tribal group, had at least five villages in the vicinity.[1575]

It's unclear how the name "Iaqua" came to be applied to the area. Apparently the word was a term of greeting used by the Athabascan-speaking "mountain" Indians that meant "how do you do?"[1576] In 1850 tiny Humboldt City, the fourth and frailest new town on Humboldt Bay, had an Iaqua Public House,[1577] the same year that the town's "proprietors" built a supply trail to the Trinity River along a route that went by—need it be said?—the mountainside locale soon known as Iaqua.[1578]

The trail that was a boon for the whites soon became a tribulation for the Tcil-lun-din kai-yas. Ranchers were drawn to Iaqua's sunny prairies and abundance of water, and they appropriated much of the land and its resources for their exclusive use, giving no thought for the needs of the Indians who had dwelt there for millennia. The result was the same as it was for most of Humboldt: by the end of the decade, the Iaqua area was enveloped in armed conflict.

John Owen Dinsmore began ranching there in 1859, but soon, as he saw it, "the depredations of the Indians forced him to move his cattle nearer the coast on the Mattole River." In the fall of 1860 Dinsmore sold his stock and

returned to his former residence in Illinois. He came back to Humboldt County in 1861 and ranched in the Eel River valley.[1579] Forty years later, with the Indians dead or displaced, Dinsmore bought land at Eaton Roughs,[1580] near where members of his family in 1906 established the community of Dinsmore.[1581]

In October 1861, at his Iaqua Ranch, Hiram Cooksey found ten of his cattle killed by Indians and three others badly wounded, with arrows sticking in them as if they were oversized pin cushions.[1582] Worried about further attacks, Cooksey removed his family from the ranch that December.[1583] When he returned with a friend the following day he "found the buildings in ashes." His melancholic contemplation of the scene was interrupted by the perpetrators, who fired on the men from ambush. The pair escaped unharmed, but Cooksey's three horses were shot and crippled. Captain George Werk of the Mounted Volunteers reported that "there has not been a day for the last month on which the Indians have not killed stock in that neighborhood." By then Werk's volunteers had disbanded, and it appeared that, lacking protection, the remaining ranchers in the area would have to leave.[1584]

The next report from the Iaqua Ranch came in January 1863, when Wesley Sumption and a man named Hitchcock were looking after the ranch's cattle and "heard the report of an Indian gun,[1585] down in a gulch." Sumption and Hitchcock, hidden by an opportune fog, went down to the gulch, where they found that a party of four Indians had killed a work ox and

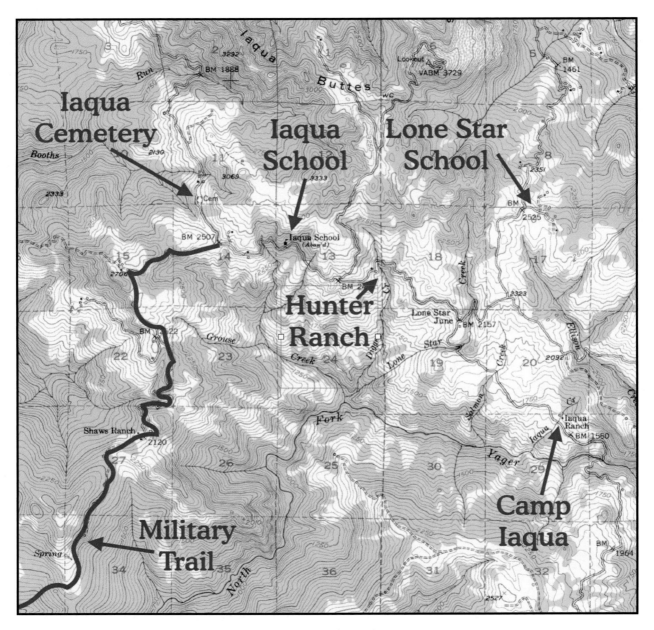

Iaqua area (USGS)

were cutting it up. The two whites shot and killed two of the Indians while the other two escaped.[1586]

That August, Lieutenant Knyphausen Geer and 40 soldiers built Camp Iaqua on part of the Iaqua Ranch.[1587] Various units from the California Mountaineers and the California Volunteers garrisoned the camp for the next three years.[1588] In June 1864 Geer' troops built a trail that connected the 1850 Humboldt City pack train route with the military trail that ran from Fort Humboldt through Blanton and Myrick prairies to Fork Baker. The connecting trail followed the route of today's Tom Shaw Road, running down the ridge between Lawrence Creek and North Yager Creek and then cutting through the Sam Shaw ranch to ford Lawrence Creek about a mile north its confluence with North Yager Creek. The new route shortened the distance between Camp Iaqua and Fort Humboldt by about four miles.[1589] The following month a soldier stationed at Camp Iaqua wrote to the *Humboldt Times* about the camp and ranch upon which it was located. Signing himself "W," he noted that there were about 130 soldiers present,

> . . . made up mostly of hardworking miners whose experience in the mountains of California render them peculiarly fitted for the long and fatiguing marches they at any moment are liable to be called upon to perform.[1590]

But W was more interested in observing the scenery than his fellow soldiers. He looked out from the camp and saw that

> . . . to the south the vision rests upon high promontories and table lands, here and there cluttered with groves of the stately redwood, with the bright greens of the yew tree, and the graceful laurel with their diminutive forms fill up the intervals between their gigantic neighbors.[1591]

One feature on the ranch was especially impressive; "an inexhaustible spring" that filled a basin below it, forming a lake about 220 feet long and 120 feet wide. By then the Iaqua Ranch was owned by George H. Gray and Gus Dinsmore. They butchered some of their stock to provide meat for the troops.[1592]

Gray had recently been a soldier himself. In 1860 he was the third sergeant in the Humboldt Cavalry Company,[1593] a volunteer unit formed in Hydesville that expected to be mustered into service by the governor. When the muster was not forthcoming, some members of the company joined in the multiple massacres of February

The Hunter Ranch sits astride the pack train route through Iaqua (now Kneeland Road) (JR)

1860 that included the well-publicized attack on Indian Island.[1594] According to Dinsmore's niece, Frances Dinsmore Hopkins, "Uncle Gus was one of the raiders" who perpetrated the massacres.[1595]

In September 1865, with the Indian-white conflict winding down, Camp Iaqua was abandoned.[1596] That same year Gray and Dinsmore patented 640 acres directly south of the camp.[1597] In 1875 a traveler found that "old Fort Iaqua is a dry deserted place now."[1598] No mention was made of the Gray and Dinsmore property.

By then a new generation of ranchers had moved into the area. Amos Frame and his wife, Luvanda, who had recently ranched at Yager, purchased property at Iaqua that they used as pasture for their cattle. Eventually they acquired land just north of the Iaqua cemetery astride the county wagon road. Their home became a stopping place for travelers on the Bridgeville-Kneeland stage. The Frame's oldest daughter, Ada, became the Iaqua postmaster. She married Sam Shaw, part of another early-day ranch family whose place was about three miles southwest of the Iaqua cemetery.[1599] In 1907 Luther Sibley purchased the Frame Ranch. The Iaqua Post Office, established first as "Jacqua" in 1880, was changed later that year to Iaqua once the spelling error was corrected. The office closed in 1903, but was reestablished by Sibley in 1909. This time the office lasted until 1920, when it was subsumed by the Kneeland office.[1600]

Isaac Gift, "a large, strong man," his wife Evelyn, and their family arrived in 1868. They had come across the plains in 1864, and when one of their mules died en route Gift took its place in the yoke, helping pull their wagon for the next 48 hours. The Gifts located their ranch at the head of Grouse Creek, about a mile south of the future site of the Iaqua cemetery. Three of their sons continued the Gift ranching operations after Isaac's death in 1881.[1601] James P. and Amelia Fredrickson started a ranch northwest of the Gifts' place in 1870. Their sons, Thorwald and William H., ranched in partnership after their father's death in 1901.[1602]

Being neighbors, the Gifts and the Fredricksons didn't have far to go to see each other. On one occasion the families may have wished they lived farther apart. John H. Gift and his brothers thought to relive a bit of the area's history by dressing up as Indians and going over to the Fredrickson place, where Irene Fredrickson was home alone with her two children. The Gift boys climbed onto the roof and blocked the chimney, hoping that the smoke would drive Irene out of the house. Imagine their surprise when Irene did nothing of the sort but instead got the family's shotgun and fired it through the roof.[1603]

Jeremiah and Elizabeth Mullen homesteaded on Lawrence Creek in 1870. Their sons, William and John, took over "Highland Acres," as the ranch was called, after their father's death. The brothers also purchased their uncle David Mullen's adjacent ranch. After four years William bought out his brother's interest in the ranches and ran them alone. John then moved to a ranch at Kneeland. A third brother, Timothy, had a ranch on the far side of Lawrence Creek.[1604]

In April 1879 a newly minted school teacher, 18-year-old Etta Palmer, arrived at Iaqua for her first job. (See sidebar 1.)

The Iaqua school district had been established in 1876. When Etta Palmer taught there in 1879, it had 11 books in its library. Nine years later the library had grown to 166 books. Classes at the Iaqua School were last held in 1922. For years

1. "I do hate to say good bye to these dear children."

Henrietta "Etta" Palmer received her introduction to Humboldt County when crossing the bar at the entrance to the bay: "All the glass in the pilot house was smashed and the ship heaved to and fro," she wrote to her Aunt Mary, "up and down until my feet and head almost changed places."[1605]

She was coming to teach at Iaqua.

Etta had learned of the teaching position because a friend, Henry Steere, had moved from the Fruitvale district in Oakland, where they both lived, to manage a ranch at Iaqua. He had written his father, the Fruitvale postmaster, that the community needed a teacher and his father had contacted Etta, who accepted the job.[1606]

Once on solid ground in Eureka, Etta contacted a Mr. Scott, who was a friend of postmaster Steere's. Scott, she wrote, was "horrified at my going to Iaqua to teach." He called it "God's forsaken hole," but Etta, once she arrived there, "thought that God was wonderfully merciful in lavishing so much beauty on it."[1607]

Having taken the measure of the place, she added, with her understated eloquence, that

> The people are not so richly endowed as their natural surroundings, for they live in the rudest of houses, but they possess the kindest of hearts and I am becoming attached to them more and more.[1608]

Etta visited the Miller family (she appears to have changed most of the families' names in her letters). Mr. Miller was the local blacksmith. The house, Etta quickly learned, was

> . . . anything but cozy or comfortable. The floor of the living room was tracked with mud, for which she [Mrs. Miller] apologized, saying the men were continually passing in and out with dirty boots. The air was filled with tobacco smoke and things were strewn about helter skelter. The only furniture consisted of chairs of rough, clumsy design made of redwood.[1609]

Nonetheless, Etta needed to stay with the Millers, because the wife of the family she had intended to board with was very sick. But Mrs. Miller said she could not keep Etta as she had nothing with which to make her comfortable.

Then little Denny Miller, who had just had his first day of school with Etta, whispered something in his mother's ear, after which Mrs. Miller agreed to board his teacher. Later Etta learned that Denny had said he would eat less if Etta was allowed to stay—Mrs. Miller had told him earlier that if the teacher lived with them there would not be enough to eat.[1610]

Etta soon determined the cause of the Millers' poverty. It was Mr. Miller, the blacksmith, who

> . . . is worthless. He makes quite a bit of money. If only he would use it on his family. Instead he goes off to Eureka on what they call here, "A bust" and then comes home penniless without even a stick of candy for his two children.[1611]

There was one Indian-white family in Iaqua. The wife, "a squaw," rode her mustang over to meet Etta, who noted, with prim prejudice, that

> I didn't mind her calling, for she had the same curiousity [sic] as her white sisters and her marriage [to a white man] brought her up to their

The Iaqua School struggles to stay upright (JR)

level socially. But when she joined us for dinner I couldn't but help deplore her table manners.[1612]

Later, at school, Etta found that "the half-breed boy was present, but was more neatly dressed than some of the others and was quiet and well behaved." She took more interest in

> . . . little Paul and Dorcas Orfner . . . [who] are pretty kiddies in spite of being pitifully dirty and forlorn in appearance. Little Paul has big brown dreamy eyes and soft brown ringlets all over his head. It was hard to tell whether his skin was fair or dusky owning to the dirt on his face and hands. Dorcas, the little girl, has the sweetest but saddest face, such a yearning look that my heart went out to her. They were both barefoot and scantily clothed otherwise. They live only a few steps from the school in a house that is as shabby as are the children.[1613]

Part way through the school year, Etta was obliged to move when Mrs. Miller took sick. Her new lodging was the Beans' house, which had a combination living room-dining room-kitchen that was perilous to walk across:

> Mr. Bean is so shiftless that he has never nailed down the floor boards. One has to be careful, therefore, where one steps else the far end of the board will fly up and hit one in the face.[1614]

Mrs. Bean desperately wanted a rocking chair, so that she could rock her baby. Mr. Bean promised to get her one the next time he went to town.[1615] He eventually made the trip but came back without the rocker, saying "it cost $1.75 and $1.50 was all it was worth." Etta, who was paying $20 a month board, was enraged and scolded Mr. Bean for his parsimoniousness. Dinner was silent that night. Afterwards Mr. Bean went out saying he had to ask Mr. Simpson, a neighbor, to run an errand for him. Two days later Mr. Simpson came by—with the rocking chair.[1616]

As the school year went by, Etta formed more opinions about Iaqua and its residents, noting that "these people seem utterly unconscious of the beauties of nature by which they are surrounded," but she then reminded herself that "they have to work so hard to get the necessities of life that they do not have time to look upward or about them to see . . . [these] beauties. . . ."[1617]

Once the Iaqua School closed, Iaqua students attended the Lone
Star School, three miles to the east (HCHS, colorized by JR.)

One day Etta rode four miles to have dinner with Mr. and Mrs. Hermit.
They lived in a

> "regulation shack" built like the rest, of rough boards, no paint, no
> decoration of any kind either inside or outside. . . .
>   She [Mrs. Hermit] is a woman of some culture, [who] was educated
> in a boarding school in N Y state. It is the old story of marrying beneath
> her and against her parents [sic] wishes and this is the result—a poverty
> stricken home in the wilderness away from any one who might be com-
> panionable, and with a husband whose environment has not elevated
> him or improved him in any way. He for whom she sacrificed all, is not
> a companion who makes up for the other deficiencies in her life.[1618]

Although the male population of Iaqua, at least in Etta's eyes, were a
pretty useless group, they did make one collective attempt to better their
condition. In 1878 Iaqua, along with Rohnerville, were the only two com-

munities in Humboldt County to form Greenback clubs.[1619] The Greenback Party had gained notice because it advocated the issuing of more paper money (greenbacks), a shorter work day, and restrictions on Chinese immigration: all proposals designed to help white workers and farmers.[1620] In the summer of 1879, the Greenbackers were running a candidate for county supervisor whom Etta found to be "a real roughneck and almost illiterate." Etta, who of course could not even vote, backed the Republican incumbent and persuaded all of the Iaquans to forsake their party's candidate. After the Republican was reelected, he sent Etta a note thanking her for the "wonderful majority" he had received from Iaqua, which was due, he was certain, to the Iaqua teacher's efforts.[1621]

The school year drew to a close. Little Dorcas Orfner, the girl with the "sweetest but saddest face," told Etta that her mother was making her a new dress for the occasion. Dorcas had been clothed in rags when she first came to school, and Etta was "delighted that Mrs. Orfner's pride is sufficiently awakened for her to want a new dress for that dear little girl."[1622]

Etta's work with the children was appreciated. Despite the poverty in the Iaqua school district, she was offered more pay if she returned the next year. When she sent her last letter to Aunt Mary, she hadn't decided if she would come back. Etta closed her letter by saying,

I am looking forward to going home and seeing you all again, yet I dread leaving for I do hate to say goodbye to these dear children.[1623]

Etta did not return to Iaqua. Instead she took a teaching position back home in Fruitvale. Henry Steere, who had often spent time with her in Iaqua, left the ranch there and took a job with the Southern Pacific Railroad. Apparently he kept in touch with Etta because, as he later told his daughter Julia, "I wrote your mother and asked her to marry me." Henry and Etta were wed in Aunt Mary's parlor in January 1883. According to Julia, Etta always regretted not returning to Iaqua and "never spoke of her failure to do so without reproach."[1624]

afterward, it served as a venue for dances and other community events.[1625] Sterling Peterson, who grew up on Bug Creek, over the ridge and across the Mad River, rode horseback to the dances, at which he played the banjo.[1626]

About 1885 Charles Fiebig, by then "a very old man," collected an interesting bird specimen "near Iaqua." It was an immature California condor (*Gymnogyps californianus*). Fiebig was reputedly "a taxidermist of far more than ordinary ability," but someone who "practices the art only as a pastime."[1627] For years the taxidermied condor was on display at Eureka High School.

Although the military installation at the Iaqua Ranch had been closed for 30 years, in 1895 "Fort Iaqua" made the news. The ranch was apparently using that name to attract vacationers. It reportedly was "fast becoming one of the leading summer and health resorts of Humboldt county." In July "a jolly crowd from Rohnerville" arrived, and by evening they had caught "a large string of fish" and shot two bucks, both four-pointers, in a triumph of jollity. Forming part of the party were such well-known Rohnerville families as the Camptons, Lambs, and Feigenbaums. Eureka sent a contingent of visitors that included both the William Carson and John Dolbeer families. A hall was under

construction at the "fort" and when finished would be the scene of a "grand ball."[1628]

By the early 1900s Porter's Hall at Fort Iaqua was regularly making the news. Each year between 1902 and 1904 the Blue Lake Advocate reported on its front page either a dance or a "social time" there. One year "16 jolly young folks" from Maple Creek and nearby Belmont attended, probably crossing the Mad River near Big Bend.[1629]

Improbable as it may seem, for a time the Iaqua area played an important role in ship building. The "extremely long, shallow roots" of Douglas-firs were used for what was called "ship knees." John Gift, his son George, and John Bjorkstrand would dig out the roots and cut them into "about ten-foot lengths in roughly an 'L' shape." These "knees" would be used in the construction of wooden ships to "support deck

Slater Road and part of the Iaqua Buttes (JR)

The Iaqua Ranch in 1995, or is it a century earlier? (JR)

beams and keels." When enough knees had been cut, John Gift "would hitch the six-horse team to a high-seated wagon and haul them to Eureka," where they would be used by shipbuilder Hans Bendixsen.[1630]

The Slater Ranch was located within the confines of the Iaqua Buttes.[1631] There weren't a lot of neighbors. In December 1911 Hugh Slater was absent, so his wife Frances went out to check his trap lines. At the edge of the forest, she found that one of traps had caught "a large black bear" that had almost gotten free. Not a problem for Slater, who took aim with her rifle and shot him dead. She then skinned the bear, threw the skin over her shoulder and started home. The skin proved so heavy that Slater could only carry it a short distance before having to stop and rest. But get it home she did, and then, according to the newspaper article, she "will cure the pelt and make it into a rug to remind her of her experience alone in the woods."[1632]

Ten years later, the Slaters and another animal made the news. This time it was their dog, Sam. Although only ten months old, Sam's job was to guard the Slaters' large flock of sheep. He was charged with staying with the sheep at all times and driving off any coyotes that might be sizing up the flock. When Sam then showed up at the Slater's house one afternoon in the fall of 1921, it was the first time he had failed in his duty. Hugh Slater tried to drive Sam back to the sheep but the dog refused to go. Hugh even tried leading him part way back, but that didn't work either. Finally Slater noticed that "there was something about the look in his eyes and the wag in his tail that [indicated] he was trying to tell something." Hugh then decided to walk back with his dog to the flock, whereupon "Sam seemed joyful and began to jump up and down, barking incessantly. . . ." Finally Sam jumped over a fence near some dense underbrush. Slater followed and soon found Sam in the thicket, next to "a very young lamb that had become separated from the flock and caught in the underbrush."[1633]

In the summer of 1928 a fire lookout was established on the highest of the Iaqua Buttes, with ranger A. A. Wilkie on duty. For 20 years Hugh and Frances Slater staffed the lookout,[1634] which surely had one of the loveliest views imaginable.

Another Frances gained a name for herself in the area. For over 20 years, from the 1940s to 1966, Frances Paddock drove the star route mail stage that went to Iaqua, Yager, Fort Baker, and Mountain View. The ranchers would leave Frances a shopping list at their mailbox and on her next trip she would pick up their groceries in Myrtletown and deliver them with the mail. She "carried a chain saw, ran the route all year long, and sometimes got stuck."[1635]

After World War II, during the Douglas-fir boom, Cornell Paddock built a mill on Lawrence Creek. Years earlier his father, Garf, had peeled tanbark on the same creek.[1636] Residents of the Iaqua area could usually make a living, but they had to work at it.

Several of the families that had come in the 1860s and 1870s stayed on, generation after generation living their lives within a landscape that changed little, if at all, and then, when their time came, joining their parents and grandparents in the Iaqua cemetery. For decades they would pass the long-abandoned Iaqua School, which sat on a grassy knoll among the oaks and lupine, its aging wooden siding growing grayer with the years. And then, at last, it was gone, for the property owner, fearful that it might be burned by hooligans, had taken it down.

After that there was little to distract motorists passing through Iaqua on the Bridgeville-Kneeland Road. Only at the old Sibley Ranch might they slow down, for a herd of goats often stood there upon the pavement, a bleating, obstructing reminder that the area owed its development to the presence of livestock.

Sources

A. J. J. [pseud.]
  1878a A Visit to Petrolia and Upper Mattole.
    Ferndale Enterprise, June 8, 1878:3.
almanac.com
  2022a What does one call a group of hogs?
    Web page. Electronic document, https://
    www.almanac.com/fact/what-does-one-call-
    a-group-of accessed on June 2, 2022.
America's Story
  2020 Andrew Carnegie Grows Up
    Working. Web page. Electronic doc-
    ument, http://library.humboldt.
    edu/humco/holdings/photodetail.
    php?S=spott&CS=All%20Collec-
    tions&RS=ALL%20Regions&PS=A-
    ny%20Photographer&ST=ALL%20
    words&SW=&C=52&R=15 accessed on
    July 19, 2020
American Lumberman
  1912a Among the Northern Redwoods.
    American Lumberman, March 30, 1912.
  1912b Among the Northern Redwoods.
    American Lumberman, April 27, 1912:55.
American Philosophical Society
  2020 American Council of Learned Societies
    Committee on Native American Languag-
    es, American Philosophical Society [ACLS
    Collection]: Detailed Inventory. Web page.
    Electronic document, https://search.am-
    philsoc.org/collections/view?docId=ead/
    Mss.497.3.B63c-ead.xml accessed on
    January 4, 2020.
Anderson, David
  2000 Russ Family Roots Run Deep.
    Times-Standard, May 29, 2000.
  2001a. The story of a Bridge, a boat, and a
    budget. Times-Standard, February 5,
    2001:A1, A8.
Anderson, Kat
  2005 Tending the Wild: Native American
    Knowledge and the Management of
    California's Natural Resources. Berkeley:
    University of California Press.
Anderson, Mary
  1984a Nona James at 80 Descended from
    Genuine Pioneer Stock. Redwood Record,
    September 20, 1984.
  1985a Chinese in Southern Humboldt.
    Redwood Record, April 11, 1985:A-6.
  1987a A lifetime of hunting, trapping.
    Humboldt Historian, March-April 1987:4-6.
  2006 Backwoods Chronicle: A History of
    Southern Humboldt 1849 – 1920. N. p.
Anonymous
  1987 Mount Pierce. Humboldt Historian,
    November-December 1987:12.
  N.d.a. Fragment of map of ranches in Bear
    River valley. Photocopy in author's posses-
    sion.
  N.d.b. Interview by Jerry Rohde with unnamed
    resident of Eel Rock, ca. 2000.
Anonymous [pseud.]
  1876a Notes from Anonymous. Humboldt
    Times, July 19, 1876:1.

Anster, John
  2019 Poems: With Some
  Translations from the German. Web page.
    Electronic document, https://books.
    google.com/books?id=DVhMAAAA-
    cAAJ&pg=PA216&dq=%22the+black+-
    jager%27s+song%22&hl=en&sa=X-
    &ved=0ahUKEwi5r6bWo-fjAhVKD-
    q0KHZeHDHsQ6AEIMjAB#v=onep-
    age&q=%22the%20black%20jager's%20
    song%22&f=false accessed on August 3,
    2019.
anthromuseum.ucdavis.edu
  2021a Clinton Hart Merriam 1855-1942
    American Naturalist and Ethnographer.
    Web page. Electronic document, http://
    anthromuseum.ucdavis.edu/c-hart-merri-
    am-biography.html accessed on June 12,
    2021.
Arcata Leader
  1879a Overland. Arcata Leader, December 6,
    1879:3.
Arcata Union
  1901a Good Old Indian. Arcata Union,
    November 9, 1901:5.
  1913a Interesting Account of Trip by Delegates
    to Redding. Arcata Union, July 10, 1913.
  1919a Bowden Brothers Take Over Shelter
    Cove Wharf Property. Increased Shipping
    Activity Looked For. Arcata Union, Octo-
    ber 23, 1919.
  1925a Redwood Highway article. Arcata Union,
    March 12, 1925:4.
  1926a Redwood Highway article. Arcata Union,
    July 29, 1926:6.
  1927a Another Oil Well for Upper Mattole.
    Arcata Union, September 29, 1927.
  1933a McKee Saw Mill Burns at Weott. Arcata
    Union, July 7, 1933.
Arceneaux, Marc
  2013 Best Western Plus Humboldt House Inn
    Presents Stories of the Inn's Founders &
    Early Garberville. Garberville: Best West-
    ern Plus Humboldt House Inn, 2013.
Arms, L. R.
  N.d. A Short History of the US Army
    Noncommissioned Officer. Webpage.
    Electronic document, http://www.army-
    studyguide.com/imagesvr_ce/1203/a-
    short-history-of-the-us.pdf accessed on
    August 21, 2016.
Asbill, Frank
  1953 The Last of the West. Manuscript
    photocopy: Humboldt State University
    Library, Arcata.
Asbill, Frank, and Argle Shawley
  1975 The Last of the West. New York: Carlton
    Pres, Inc.
askArt
  2019a Margaret Smith Cobb. Web page.
    Electronic document, http://www.
    askart.com/artist/Margaret_Smith_
    Cobb/11181975/Margaret_Smith_Cobb.
    aspx accessed on July 30, 2019.

Aspen Daily Times
    1888a Facts about Wool. Aspen Daily Times,
        October 16, 1888:3.
Atherton, Gertrude
    1945 Golden Gate Country. New York: Duell,
        Sloan & Pearce.
Atkinson, Theodora Kaspar
    2019 Recollections of Stafford. Photocopy in
        possession of author.
Aubrey-Herzog, Jay
    2022 Battle for Boomer Jack. Web page.
        Electronic document, https://www.
        northcoastjournal.com/humboldt/battle-
        for-boomer-jack/Content?oid=2125846
        accessed on April 23, 2022.
avalon.law.yale.edu
    2016 General Orders No. 100: The Lieber
        Code. Web page. Electronic document,
        http://avalon.law.yale.edu/19th_century/
        lieber.asp#sec3 accessed on August 28,
        2016.
aveofthegiants.com
    2016a Redcrest. Webpage. Electronic
        document, http://www.aveofthegiants.
        com/on-the-avenue/redcrest/ accessed on
        July 10, 2016.
Ayer, N. W., and Son
    1921 N. W. Ayer and Son's American
        Newspaper Annual and Directory. Philadel-
        phia: N. W. Ayer & Son.
B [pseud.]
    1878 Letter from a Traveler. Ferndale Enterprise,
        June 28, 1878.
Bailey, Cora
    1900 Cora Bailey Diary: June 1, 1898 through
        September 19, 1900. Copy on file at the
        Humboldt County Historical Society,
        Eureka.
Bair, Marie Melanson
    1989a Summer fun at Boehne's river camp.
        Humboldt Historian, September-October
        1989:11.
Baker, Ray Jerome
    1934a Letter to "Wife." Original in the Bishop
        Museum Archives, Honolulu, Hawaii; filed
        as MS GRP 16, Box 9.5.
    2006 Ray Jerome Baker information from
        Bishop Museum: photographs with identi-
        fying information and selection of mem-
        oirs, diaries, and correspondence. Copy on
        file in the Humboldt County Collection,
        Humboldt State University Library, Arcata,
        CA
Baldo, Chris, and Theron Brown
    2005 Fred C. Holmes – Redwood in His Blood.
        Roots of Motive Power, Inc. Newsletter 23
        no. 3.
Bancroft, Hubert Howe
    1888a History of California, Vol. VI. San
        Francisco: The History Publishers
    2015 Humbert Howe Bancroft's History of
        Utah 1540-1886. Web page. Electronic
        document, http://www.utlm.org/online-
        books/bancroftshistoryofutah_chapter22.
        htm accessed July 31, 2015.
Bancroft Library
    1997 A. L. Kroeber Papers, 1869-1972. Bancroft
        Library, University of California, Berkeley.

    2020 Guide to A. L. Kroeber Papers. Web
        page. Electronic document, https://oac.
        cdlib.org/findaid/ark:/13030/tf3d5n99tn/
        entire_text/ accessed on January 2, 2020.
Baratti, John L.
    N.d. History of Rio Dell 1850 – 1959.
        Photocopy available at the Humboldt State
        University Library, Arcata.
Barber, Mrs. Enos (sic)
    1937 Aged Indian Woman Passes at Blue Lake.
        Humboldt Times, April 1, 1937:4.
Barmazel, Steven
    1996 Murder on Coyote Flat. California Lawyer,
        May 1996:42-44, 86-87.
Barnum, Robert
    2017 Interview with Jerry Rohde on May 24,
        2017.
Bassett, Vicki
    2015 Causes and Effects of the Rapid Sinking
        of the Titanic. Undergraduate Engineering
        Review. Web page. Electronic document,
        http://writing.engr.psu.edu/uer/bassett.
        html accessed on November 24, 2015.
Bauer, JoAnn
    2020a Personal communication with the
        author, November 2, 2020.
    2020b Personal communication with the
        author, November 3, 2020.
Baumgardner, Frank H.
    2006 Killing for Land in Early California. New
        York: Algora Publishing.
Baumhoff, Martin
    1958 California Athabascan Groups.
        Anthropological Records 16, no. 5.
    1963 Ecological Determinants of Aboriginal
        California Populations. Berkeley: Universi-
        ty of California Press.
Baxter, Grace Johnson
    1987a "A Railroad Track and a Hobble Skirt."
        In Humboldt County the Way It Was, volume
        IV, edited by Gayle Karshner. Arcata: The
        Union.
    1987b "Tosaldo Johnson, a Pioneer and his
        Family. In Humboldt County the Way It
        Was, volume IV, edited by Gayle Karshner.
        Arcata: The Union.
Beal, Scoop
    1941a Men Tell Of Attack. Humboldt Standard,
        December 22, 1941:1, 15.
Bean, Walton
    1973 California: An Interpretive History, 2nd
        ed. New York: McGraw-Hill.
Bear River Band
    2021 Wiyot/Mattole History. Web page.
        Electronic document, http://www.brb-nsn.
        gov/our-story/wiyot-mattole-history/ ac-
        cessed on June 28, 2021.
Belcher, Jerry
    1970 U. S. Ousts Youthful Colony from
        Humboldt County Haven. Photocopy con-
        tained in the Petrolia file at the Humboldt
        County Historical Society, Eureka, CA.
Belcher Abstract & Title Co.
    1921-1922 Atlas of Humboldt County,
        California. Eureka: Belcher Abstract &
        Title Co.
Belyk, Robert C.
    2001 Great Shipwrecks of the Pacific Coast.
        New York: John Wiley & Sons, Inc.

Benbow, Michael J.
    2005 A Family's Quest for a Piece of Paradise: The Benbow Hotel as a Symbol of the First Modern Era. M. A. thesis, Humboldt State University.
Bencie, Robin
    1997 Genetic Variation and Inbreeding Depression in the Rare California Endemic, *Astragalus agnicidus* (Leguminosae). M. A. Thesis, Humboldt State University.
    2021a Personal communication with Jerry Rohde, February 8, 2021.
Berg, Ken, and Roxanne Bittman
    1988 Rediscovery of the Humboldt Milk-Vetch. Fremontia, April 1988.
Bess, Carol Robertson
    2020 Alexander Robertson. Web page. Electronic Document, https://web.archive.org/web/20041110213233/http://www.blocksburg.com/robertson_comments.php?id=P31_0_15_0_C accessed via Wayback Machine on August 15, 2020.
Bevington, Douglas
    2009 The Rebirth of Environmentalism: Grassroots Activism from the Spotted owl to the Polar Bear. Washington: Island Press.
Big Trees
    1952 The Big Trees. Web page. Electronic document, https://www.youtube.com/watch?v=UWcMg-yohJs accessed on May 19 2019.
Bishop, Verda
    1991 Interview with Jerry Rohde, May 18, 1991.
Bittermann, Rusty
    2010 The Remarkable Saga of the Coopers of Coopers Mills, Hydesville. Humboldt Historian, Summer 2010:8-16.
Black, Patricia
    2007 Personal interview with Jerry Rohde.
Blackie, W. G.
    MDCCCXCIX (1899) Literary Pastimes of Early Life. Glasgow: Blackie and Son Limited.
BlackPast.org
    2016 Fort Pillow Massacre (1864). Web page. Electronic document, http://www.blackpast.org/aah/fort-pillow-massacre-1864 accessed on September 3, 2016.
Bledsoe, A. J.
    1885 Indian Wars of the Northwest. San Francisco: Bacon & Co.
Blue Lake Advocate
    1900a Article on Judge Hunter's land purchase in Salmon Creek. Blue Lake Advocate, April 17, 1900:3.
    1902a Dance at Porter's hall article, Blue Lake Advocate, May 24, 1902:1.
    1903a Social time at Porter's hall article, Blue Lake Advocate, April 18, 1903:1.
    1904a Social dance at Porter's hall article, Blue Lake Advocate, July 23, 1904:1.
    1918a To Operate Manganese Mine. Blue Lake Advocate, February 9, 1918:8.
    1933a Ralph Gordon Wounded near Showers Pass. Blue Lake Advocate, February 11, 1933.
    1933b Cream of Country News. Blue Lake Advocate, June 3, 1933:3.
    1949a Robert H. Fales, 23, Loses Life During Recent Snowstorm. Blue Lake Advocate, February 19, 1949:2.
BLM
    2017a Patent records for T1S, R2E, Humboldt Meridian. Web page. Electronic document, https://glorecords.blm.gov/results/default.aspx?searchCriteria=type=patent|st=CA|cty=023|twp_nr=1|twp_dir=S|rng_nr=2|rng_dir=E|sec=10|sp=true|sw=true|sadv=false accessed on April 10, 2017.
    2017b Patent records for "Stump" in T3S, R3E, Humboldt Meridian. Web page. Electronic document, https://glorecords.blm.gov/results/default.aspx?searchCriteria=type=patent|st=CA|cty=023|ln=stump|twp_nr=3|twp_dir=S|rng_nr=3|rng_dir=E|m=15|sp=true|sw=true|sadv=false accessed on December 2, 2017.
    2017c Patent records for "McKee" in T4S, R2E, Humboldt Meridian. Web page. Electronic document, https://glorecords.blm.gov/results/default.aspx?searchCriteria=type=patent|st=CA|cty=023|ln=McKee|twp_nr=4|twp_dir=S|rng_nr=2|rng_dir=E|m=15|sp=true|sw=true|sadv=false accessed on December 4, 2017.
    2017d Patent records for "Cruickshank" in T5S, R2E, Humboldt Meridian. Web page. Electronic document, https://glorecords.blm.gov/results/default.aspx?searchCriteria=type=patent|st=CA|cty=023|ln=cruickshank|twp_nr=5|twp_dir=S|rng_nr=2|rng_dir=E|m=15|sp=true|sw=true|sadv=false accessed on December 8, 2017.
    2017e Patent records for "Filkins" in T2S, R4E, Humboldt Meridian. Web Page. Electronic document, https://glorecords.blm.gov/results/default.aspx?searchCriteria=type=patent|st=CA|cty=023|ln=filkins|twp_nr=2|twp_dir=S|rng_nr=4|rng_dir=E|m=15|sp=true|sw=true|sadv=false accessed on December 13, 2017.
    2018a Patent records for Township 3 South, Range 2 East, Humboldt Meridian. Web page. Electronic document, https://glorecords.blm.gov/results/default.aspx?searchCriteria=type=patent|st=CA|cty=023|twp_nr=3|twp_dir=S|rng_nr=2|rng_dir=E|m=15|sp=true|sw=true|sadv=false#resultsTabIndex=0&page=4&sortField=11&sortDir=0 accessed on March 19, 2018.
    2018b Patent records for Township 2 South, Range 2 West, Humboldt Meridian. Web page. Electronic document, https://glorecords.blm.gov/results/default.aspx?searchCriteria=type=patent|st=CA|cty=023|twp_nr=2|twp_dir=S|rng_nr=2|rng_dir=W|m=15|sp=true|sw=true|sadv=false#resultsTabIndex=0&page=6&sortField=11&sortDir=0 accessed on August 13, 2018.

2018c Patent records for "Carothers" in Township 2 South, Range 2 East, Humboldt Meridian. Web page. Electronic document, https://glorecords.blm.gov/results/default.aspx?searchCriteria=type=patent|st=CA|cty=|ln=carothers|twp_nr=2|twp_dir=S|rng_nr=2|rng_dir=E|m=15|sp=true|sw=true|sadv=false accessed on November 11, 2018.

2018d Patent records for "Mowry" and "Robinson" in Township 2 South, Range 2 East, Humboldt Meridian. Web page. Electronic document, https://glorecords.blm.gov/results/default.aspx?searchCriteria=type=patent|st=CA|cty=023|twp_nr=2|twp_dir=S|rng_nr=2|rng_dir=E|sec=12|m=15|sp=true|sw=true|sadv=false accessed on November 12, 2018.

2018e Patent records for Section 29, Township 2 South, Range 3 East, Humboldt Meridian. Web page. Electronic document, https://glorecords.blm.gov/results/default.aspx?searchCriteria=type=patent|st=CA|cty=023|twp_nr=2|twp_dir=S|rng_nr=3|rng_dir=E|sec=29|m=15|sp=true|sw=true|sadv=false accessed on November 28, 2018.

2019a Patent records for Section 12, Township 3 South, Range 3 East, Humboldt Meridian. Web page. Electronic document, https://glorecords.blm.gov/results/default.aspx?searchCriteria=type=patent%7Cst=CA%7Ccty=023%7Ctwp_nr=3%7Ctwp_dir=S%7Crng_nr=3%7Crng_dir=E%7Csec=12%7Cm=15%7Csp=true%7Csw=true%7Csadv=false accessed on August 9, 2019.

2019b Patent for Melissa J. Wilds, formerly Melissa J. Sanford, for property in Section 3, Township 3 South, Range 3 East, Humboldt Meridian. Web page. Electronic document, https://glorecords.blm.gov/details/patent/default.aspx?accession=CA0990   .202&docClass=STA&sid=mm3cmhby.c4w#patentDetailsTabIndex=1 accessed on August 11, 2019.

2019c Patent records for Section 3, Township 3 South, Range 3 East, Humboldt Meridian. Web page. Electronic document, https://glorecords.blm.gov/results/default.aspx?searchCriteria=type=patent|st=CA|cty=023|twp_nr=3|twp_dir=S|rng_nr=3|rng_ir=E|sec=3|m=15|sp=true|sw=true|sadv=false accessed on August 11, 2019.

2019d Patent records for Section 1, Township 4 South, Range 1 East, Humboldt Meridian. Web page. Electronic document, https://glorecords.blm.gov/results/default.aspx?searchCriteria=type=patent|st=CA|cty=023|twp_nr=4|twp_dir=S|rng_nr=1|dr=E|sec=1|m=15|sp=true|sw=true|sadv=false accessed on August 28, 2019.

2019e Patent records for Section 6, Township 4 South, Range 2 East, Humboldt Meridian. Web page. Electronic document, https://glorecords.blm.gov/results/default.aspx?searchCriteria=type=patent|st=CA|cty=|twp_nr=4|twp_dir=S|rng_nr=2|rng_dir=E|sec=6|sp=true|sw=true|sadv=false accessed on August 28, 2019.

2019f Patent records for Section 7, Township 4 South, Range 2 East, Humboldt Meridian. Web page. Electronic document, https://glorecords.blm.gov/results/default.aspx?searchCriteria=type=patent|st=CA|cty=|twp_nr=4|twp_dir=S|rng_nr=2|rng_dir=E|sec=7|sp=true|sw=true|sadv=false accessed on August 28, 2019.

2020a Patent for south half of Section 29 and north half of Section 32, Township Three North Range Three East. Web page. Electronic document, http://www.glorecords.blm.gov/details/patent/default.aspx?accession=CA0910   .076&docClass=STA&sid=kcs4oubq.wgn#patentDetailsTabIndex=1 accessed on July 8, 2020.

2020b Patent for George Bert, for property in Section 27, Township 1 South, Range 1 East, Humboldt Meridian. Web page. Electronic document, https://glorecords.blm.gov/details/patent/default.aspx?accession=0658-425&docClass=MV&sid=pv5d21n5.f13#patentDetailsTabIndex=1 accessed on August 17, 2020.

2020c Patent records for Section 6, T3S, R3E, Humboldt Meridian. Web page. Electronic document, https://glorecords.blm.gov/results/default.aspx?searchCriteria=type=patent|st=CA|cty=023|twp_nr=3|twp_dir=S|rng_nr=3|rndir=E|sec=6|m=15|sp=true|sw=true|sadv=false accessed on August 30, 2020.

2020d Patent records for Section 18, T2S, R2E, Humboldt Meridian. Web page. Electronic document, https://glorecords.blm.gov/results/default.aspx?searchCriteria=type=patent|st=CA|cty=023|twp_nr=2|twp_dir=S|rng_nr=2|rng_dir=E|sec=18|m=15|sp=true|sw=true|sadv=false accessed on September 20, 2020.

2021a Patent record for Charlie Briceland, for property in Section 33, T2S, R2E, Humboldt Meridian. Web page. Electronic document, https://glorecords.blm.gov/details/patent/default.aspx?accession=0658-424&docClass=MV&sid=mss-0dzab.rk5 accessed on March 4, 2021.

Blue Lake Advocate

1893a Harris-Dyerville road story. Blue Lake Advocate, November 4, 1893:2.

1898a Pedrotti wounding story. Blue Lake Advocate, August 8, 1898:2.

1898b Mail routes story. Blue Lake Advocate, October 22, 1898:1.

1900a The Cream of Country News. Blue Lake Advocate, July 14, 1900:2.

1904a Mrs. Grant Johnston bear story. Blue Lake Advocate, April 30, 1904:2.

1914a To Build Yager Creek Bridge. Blue Lake Advocate, February 28, 1914:1.

1920a From Hydesville and Vicinity, Blue Lake Advocate, February 7, 1920:4.

1930a Dinsmore cattle article. Blue Lake Advocate, December 13, 1930:3.

1931a Fred Bair Sells Maple Creek Ranch. Blue Lake Advocate, August 1, 1931:2.

1937a Mollie Brock Died Sunday. Blue Lake
       Advocate, April 3, 1937:1.
1953a Cream of County News. Blue Lake
       Advocate, September 17, 1953:7.
BoatSafe.com
    2015 Ceremony for Renaming Your Boat. Web
          page. Electronic document, http://www.
          boatsafe.com/nauticalknowhow/rename.
          htm accessed on November 27, 2015.
Book Review Digest
    1910a Review of Blaxine. Book Review Digest,
           vol. 6:79.
Boots, Jim
    1964 The Life of an Old Stage Driver and Mule
          Skinner. Humboldt Historian, January-Feb-
          ruary 1964:7.
Borden, Stanley T.
    1949a The Pacific Lumber Co. Western
           Railroader 12, no. 8 (1949):7-11.
    1958a NWP's Carlotta Branch . . . the
           California Midland RR. Western Railroad-
           er, February 1958.
    1963a San Francisco & Northwestern. Western
           Railroader, January 1963.
    1968a Traffic Stopped When Logs Crossed
           Highway at Brown's Mill. Humboldt Histo-
           rian, May-June 1968:2.
Bowcutt, Frederica
    2015 The Tanoak Tree. Seattle: University of
          Washington Press.
Branscomb, Ernie
    2009a "Enoch Percival French and Newton
           Bishop Drury," Ernie's Place (blog), http://
           ernielb.blogspot.com/2009/07/enoch-
           percival-french-and-newton-bishop.html
           accessed on August 5, 2020.
Brekke, Joann Smith
    1990 Interview with Jerry Rohde.
Bridgemeister
    2022a 1917 Alderpoint. Website. Electronic
           document, https://www.bridgemeister.
           com/bridge.php?bid=2232 accessed on
           April 19, 2022.
Britannica
    2021a Sioux Web page. Electronic document,
           https://www.britannica.com/topic/Sioux
           accessed on February 15, 2021.
Brown, Jim
    2008 Folsom Prison. Charleston, SC: Arcadia
          Publishing Co.
Brown, Salmon
    1879a Letter from Bridgeville. Daily Humboldt
           Times, March 7, 1879:3.
Bruff, J. Goldsborough
    1949 Gold Rush. New York: Columbia
          University Press.
Buxton, Katie
    1989 Capetown traced from 1854. Humboldt
          Historian, May-June 1989:22-23.
California Board of Bank Commissioners
    1900 Report of the Board of Bank
          Commissioners. Sacramento: State Printing.
California Bricks
    2018a John B. Hill. Web page. Electronic
           document, http://calbricks.netfirms.com/
           brick.hill.html accessed on September
           22, 2018.

California Department of Engineering, State
Highway Commission
    1914a Plan and Profile of Proposed State
           Highway in Humboldt County, from Shive-
           ly to Jordan Creek.
California Department of Natural Resources,
Division of Forestry
    1949a [Map of] South Half of Humboldt
           County.
California Department of Public Works, Division of
Highways
    1933a Plan and Profile of State Highway in
           Humboldt County between Jordan Creek
           and South Scotia Bridge.
California Highway Bulletin
    N. d. Eliminating the Terrors of the Bell
           Springs Grade. Excerpt without full cita-
           tion, found in the "Transportation-High-
           way 101" file at the Humboldt County
           Historical Society, Eureka, California.
California Military History
    2020a Fort Iaqua. Web page. Electronic
           document, http://www.militarymuseum.
           org/FtIaqua.html accessed on July 4,
           2020.
California State Agricultural Society
    1891 Transactions of the California State
          Agricultural Society During the Year 1890.
          Sacramento.
California State Library
    1923 News Notes of California Libraries. Web
          page. Electronic Document, https://
          www.google.com/books/edition/
          News_Notes_of_California_Libraries/
          Ee4PRNdV0dYC?hl=en&gbpv=1&d-
          q=%22Dobbyn+School%22+humboldt+-
          county&pg=PA466&printsec=frontcover
          accessed on May 10, 2022.
California State Mining Bureau
    1886 Sixth Annual Report of the State
          Mineralogist, Part I. Sacramento.
    1896 Thirteenth report of the State
          Mineralogist. Sacramento.
California State Railroad Museum
    2018. Master Railroad Equipment Roster. Web
           page. Electronic document, https://www.
           californiarailroad.museum/assets/carou-
           sels/CSRM-Public-Roster-7-19-2016.pdf
           accessed on August 9, 2017.
Californian
    1910 Ad for Fort Seward. The Californian,
          December 24, 1910.
    1914 Eel Rock Springs. The Californian,
          August 22, 1914.
Calisphere
    2018a Front view of Tom and Sally Bell. Web
           page. Electronic document, https://cali-
           sphere.org/item/ark:/13030/kt35800395/
           accessed on January 6, 2019.
Canfield, John H.
    2015 The Enduring Lesson Of A Little Log
          Bridge. Web page. Electronic docu-
          ment, https://mattolehistory.wordpress.
          com/2011/04/23/bear-river-bridge-build-
          ing-lesson/ accessed on August 9, 2015.
Caro, Robert
    1975 The Power Broker: Robert Moses and the
          Fall of New York. New York: Vintage Books.

Carr, Ezra S.
1875 The Patrons of Husbandry of the Pacific Coast. San Francisco: A. L. Bancroft and Company.

Carr, John
1891 Pioneer Days in California. Eureka: Times Publishing Company.

Carranco, Lynwood
1982 Redwood Lumber Industry. San Marino, CA: Golden West Books.
1984a No. 1—the born-again engine. Humboldt Historian, May-June 1984:3-5.

Carranco, Lynwood, and Estel Beard
1981 Genocide and Vendetta: The Round Valley Wars of Northern California. Norman, OK: University of Oklahoma Press.

Carranco, Lynwood, and Henry L. Sorensen
1988 Steam in the Redwoods. Caldwell, ID: The Caxton Printers, Ltd.

Carranco, Ruth, and Links Carranco
1977 Briceland Once Center of Thriving Tanbark Industry. Humboldt Historian, November-December 1977:1-2.

Carter, Ernest
1983a "American Tank" was once a place in Humboldt life. Humboldt Historian, May-June 1983:7, 16.

CCH2 Portal
2021 Specimen Records Table for Astragalus agnicidus. Web page. Electronic document, https://www.cch2.org/portal/collections/listtabledisplay.php?db=all&taxa=Astragalus+agnicidus&usethes=1&taxontype=2 accessed on February 8, 2021.

Census Online
2018a 1860 Federal census – Pacific T[o]w[nshi[p]. Web page. Electronic document, http://files.usgwarchives.net/ca/humboldt/census/1860/pg00001.txt accessed on December 17, 2018.

Chadbourne, Addie
N. d. Letter to the Editor. Humboldt Historian. Photocopy of a single page which shows no date.

Chadbourne, David
1991 Interview with Jerry Rohde, May 21, 1991.

Chase, Alice Davis
1986 Recollections of a journey to a 'strange land.' Humboldt Historian, July-August 1986:21-22.

Chernow, Ron
2017 Grant. New York: Penguin Press.

Childs, Richard, et al.
1991a Richard Childs, Robert Childs, and Velma Childs, interview with Jerry Rohde.

Childs, Velma
1986 100-year-old log school restored in Redcrest area. Humboldt Historian, May-June 1986:3-4.

Chivers, Mrs. M. A.
1875 A Lady's Defence of Petrolia. West Coast Signal, April 28, 1875:3.

Christensen, Carl
1989 Surfman describes rescue. Humboldt Historian, March-April 1989:5.

Clark, Julia Steere
N.d.a. A Bit of Background. Copy on file at the Humboldt County Historical Society, Eureka.

N.d.b. A Bit of Conclusion. Copy on file at the Humboldt County Historical Society, Eureka.

Clark, T. K.
1983a Regional History of Petrolia and the Mattole Valley. Eureka: Miller Press.
1983b Wreck of the St. Paul—1908 [sic]. Humboldt Historian, September-October 1983:10-11.

Clever, Fran
1982 Southern Humboldt town names outlive communities. Humboldt Beacon, March 11, 1982:3.
1998 Before the Floods: Early memories of Dyerville, South Fork, Weott, and Burlington. N. p.

Coast and Geodetic Survey
1909 United States Coast Pilot: Pacific Coast, 2nd ed. Washington DC: Government Printing Office.

Cobb, Margaret Smith
1910a Blaxine: Halfbreed Girl. New York: The Neal Publishing Company.

Cockman, George
N.d.a. Personal communication with Jerry Rohde.

Coe, Frederick
2019 The Madrones. Web page. Electronic document, https://www.pacifichorticulture.org/articles/the-madrones/ accessed on September 12, 2019.

Colbruno, Michael
2020 Walter Van Dyke. Blog. Electronic document, http://mountainviewpeople.blogspot.com/2011/05/walter-van-dyke-1823-1905-california.html accessed on August 24, 2020.

Conklin, J. M.
1882 Judge J. M. Conklin Tells About Neighbors of the Mattole Valley. Ferndale Enterprise, April 28, 1882.

Cook, Margarite Drucella
1974a Schumacher story. In The Trail Back:B-19.
1997 The Southern Humboldt Papers. 16 volumes. Photocopy: Humboldt County Library, Eureka.

Cook, Margarite, and Diane Hawk
2001 A Glance Back: Northern Mendocino County History. Piercy, CA: Hawk Mountaintop Publishing.
2006 In the Early Days: Southern Humboldt History 1853-1920. Piercy, CA: Hawk Mountaintop Publishing.

Cooskey, Laura Walker
2004a Honeydew this and Honeydew that . . . . Now . . . and Then: The Journal of the Mattole Valley Historical Society 5(3);1-2.
2004b Honeydew Milltown Swept Away like Sawdust. Now . . . and Then: The Journal of the Mattole Valley Historical Society 5(4);1-4.
2004c Oil Dream creates Petrolia in Lower Mattole. Now . . . and Then: The Journal of the Mattole Valley Historical Society 6(1):1-3.
2011a. A Guide to the Petrolia Cemetery Burials. Now . . . and Then 9(2):5-14.

2017a Mattole Lumber Company: A Man, A Plan, and Tanbark. Now . . . and Then: The Journal of the Mattole Valley Historical Society 10(4):1-6.

2017b Mattole Lumber Co., Pt.2: The Wharf 1908-18: Opening the Valley. Now . . . and Then: The Journal of the Mattole Valley Historical Society 10(4):1-3.

2018a Personal communication from Laura Cooskey to Jerry Rohde, May 23, 2018, 1:08 A. M.

2018b Personal communication from Laura Cooskey to Jerry Rohde, May 23, 2018, 9:28 A. M.

2018c Personal communication from Laura Cooskey to Jerry Rohde, May 22, 2018, 10:12 P. M.

2020a So . . . what happened to the Natives here? Web page. Electronic document, https://web.archive.org/web/20110719234842/http://www.mattolehistory.org/Mattole_Natives.pdf accessed on July 24, 2020.

Cornford, Daniel A.
1987 workers and Dissent in the Redwood Empire. Philadelphia: Temple University Press.

Coy, Owen C.
1923 California County Boundaries. Berkeley: California Historical Survey Commission.
1982[1929] The Humboldt Bay Region 1850 – 1875. Eureka: Humboldt County Historical Society.

Cozzens, Peter
2016a The Earth Is Weeping: The Epic Story of the Indian Wars for the American West. New York: Alfred A. Knopf.
2016b Ulysses S. Grant Launched an Illegal War Against the Plains Indians, Then Lied About It. Web page. Electronic Document, http://www.smithsonianmag.com/history/ulysses-grant-launched-illegal-war-plains-indians-180960787/ accessed on November 12, 2016.

Crain, Jim
1977 Historic Country Inns of California. San Francisco: Chronicle Books.

Crane, William B.
2012 Franz and Bear River Horse, 4th ed. Ferndale: Ferndale Museum.

Crichton, R. Chalmers
1988a Arthur Way: civic leader and racer. Humboldt Historian, July-August 1988.

Crismon, Max
1991a Interview with Jerry Rohde, May 29, 1991.
N.d.a Interview with Jerry Rohde.

Crocker, Clarence E.
2016 Post Offices and Postal Officials: Bivingsville and Glendale, South Carolina 1837-2010. Web Page. Electronic document, http://glendalesc.com/postoffice.html accessed on December 4, 2016.

Crow , Leslie
2017 Pacific Tannery, Wagner Leather Company and Pacific Storage Company: Finding Success in Business for 138 Years. Web page. Electronic document, http://www.leathersmithe.com/california-historical-tanne/the-pacific-tannery-wagner.html accessed on August 12, 2017.

CRTANCS (California Retired Teachers Association North Coast Section), eds.
1989 History of Humboldt County Schools: Volume II – Eureka Area. Eureka: Humboldt County Office of Education.
1993 History of Humboldt County Schools By High School Districts: Volume III – Ferndale Area. Eureka: Humboldt County Office of Education.
1999 History of Humboldt County Schools: Volume IV – Fortuna Area. Eureka: Humboldt County Office of Education.
2001 History of Humboldt County Schools By High School Districts: Volume V – Southern Humboldt Area. Eureka: Humboldt County Office of Education.

Cuddeback Union School District
2019 Area History. Web page. Electronic document, http://www.humboldt.k12.ca.us/cuddeback_sd/area_history.php accessed on March 19, 2019.

Cunningham, Mary Louise
2000a One man's Dream: George Young Builds a Store and a Family in Pepperwood. Humboldt Historian, Winter 2000:15-21.

Curtin, Jeremiah
1940 Memoirs of Jeremiah Curtin. Madison: State Historical Society of Wisconsin.

Curtis, Edward S.
1970[1924]a The North American Indian, Vol. 13. New York: Johnson Reprint Corporation.
1970[1924]b The North American Indian, Vol. 14. New York: Johnson Reprint Corporation.

Daigh, Michael
2015 John Brown in Memory and Myth. Jefferson, NC: McFarland & Company, Inc.

Daily Alta California
1850a Humboldt Correspondence. Daily Alta California, September 20, 1850.
1850b Trinidad—A Journey Overland. Daily Alta California, April 9, 1850.
1850c The Indian Outrages in Napa Valley. Daily Alta California, March 19, 1850:2.
1851a The Eel River Valley. Daily Alta California, August 26, 1851:3.
1864a The Klamath Indian War: Capture and Execution of Two Indian Chiefs. Daily Alta California, April 19, 1864:1.

Daily Evening Bulletin
1871a Schools—Halfbreeds. [San Francisco] Daily Evening Bulletin, November 11, 1871.

Daily Humboldt Standard
1890a Steamer Ajax Wrecked. Daily Humboldt Standard, September 20, 1890.
1907a Promotion Work In Humboldt County. Daily Humboldt Standard, February 5, 1907:3.
1907b Promotion Work in Humboldt County. Daily Humboldt Standard, February 6, 1907:3.
1907c. Promotion Work in Humboldt County. Daily Humboldt Standard, February 11, 1907:3.

1907d Promotion Work in Humboldt County. Daily Humboldt Standard, January 23, 1907:6.

1907e Promotion Work in Humboldt County, Daily Humboldt Standard, February 26, 1907:2.

1907f Fatal Landslide at Upper Mattole. Daily Humboldt Standard, March 29, 1907:2.

1907g Promotion Work in Humboldt County. Daily Humboldt Standard, February 17, 1907:3.

1907e Garberville. Daily Humboldt Standard, April 6, 1907:7.

1910a Steamer Del Norte Rams Lightship. Daily Humboldt Standard, January 5, 1910:1.

1911a Flat Boat Upset in Eel River. Daily Humboldt Standard, March 31, 1911:1.

Daily Humboldt Times
1888a In Memoriam. Daily Humboldt Times, September 20, 1888.

1908a Railroad Work Monday. Daily Humboldt Times, March 29, 1908.

Daily Standard
1895a At Fort Iaqua. Daily Standard, July 19, 1895.

1899a Humboldt Vineyard. Daily Standard, September 26, 1899:3.

1899b Returned Klondiker. Daily Standard, October 2, 1899:3.

1899c Blocksburg Scorching. Daily Humboldt Standard, September 25, 1899:3.

1903a. Carlotta New Railroad Town. Daily Humboldt Standard, August 29, 1903:4.

1911a Flat Boat Upset in Eel River. Daily Standard, March 31, 1911:1.

Daily Star
2020a Twenty Lives Lost. Web page. Electronic document, https://news.google.com/newspapers?nid=1297&dat=19020104&id=0H8TAAAA-IBAJ&sjid=kooDAAAAIBAJ&pg=6762,66972&hl=en accessed on May 30, 2020.

Daily Times-Telephone
1883a Rohnerville Programs. Daily Times-Telephone, April 1, 1883:3.

Dana, Charles A.
1902 Recollections of the Civil War. New York: D. Appleton and Company.

David Rumsey Map Collection
2019 [Map of] San Francisco and North Pacific Railway. Web page. Electronic document, https://www.davidrumsey.com/luna/servlet/detail/RUMSEY~8~1~26792~1100604:San-Francisco-and-North-Pacific-Rai accessed on July 27, 2019.

Davidson, George
1889 Coast Pilot of California, Oregon, and Washington. United States Coast and Geodetic Survey. Washington, DC: Government Printing Office.

Davis, Samuel
2019 Miscellaneous poems, chiefly on divine subjects. Published for the religious entertainment of Christians in general. Web page. Electronic document, https://quod.lib.umich.edu/cgi/t/text/text-idx?c=evans;c-c=evans;view=text;idno=N05397.0001.001;rgn=div2;node=N05397.0001.001:4.1 accessed on August 4, 2019.

Davy, Marguerite Ross
1950a First White Girl Tells Garberville Story. Humboldt Times, September 3, 1950.

1950b Humboldt County's Redwood Parks. Humboldt Times, July 23, 1950.

Dawson, William Leon
1923 The Birds of California, vol. 3. San Diego: South Moulton Company.

Deering, E. R.
1966 The Maple Creek Willie Indian Scholarship Fund. California Education, April 1966:3.

DeLong, Harriet
1971 Book Agent of the 1870's. Humboldt Historian, November-December 1971:1, 9.

Democratic Standard
1880a Garberville has not a Chinaman . . . . Democratic Standard, March 27, 1880:3.

Dengler, Lori
2006. The 1906 Earthquake on California's North Coast. Humboldt Historian, Winter 2006:27-34.

Denny, Edward
1911 Denny's Official Map of the County of Humboldt California. San Francisco: Edward Denny & Co.

Deseret News
1975a Scholar fund running dry. Deseret News, December 26, 1975:4.

Dictionary.com
2019a Firkin. Web page. Electronic document, https://www.dictionary.com/browse/firkin accessed on July 21, 2019.

Dinsmore, Muriel
1975a City "dudes" restore rural lodge. Times-Standard, January 12, 1975:15, 18.

Dinsmore, Trustom R.
1961 John Dinsmore. Humboldt County Historical Society Newsletter, May 1961.2

Director of the Census
1907 Official Register: Persons in the Civil, Military and Naval Service of the United States and List of Vessels. Washington: Government Printing Office.

Dixon, Roland B.
1930 Pliny Earle Goddard (1869-1928). Proceedings of the American Academy of Arts and Sciences 34(12):526-528.

Dolfini, Sally
2004 Good Times at the Stafford Inn. Humboldt Historian, Summer 2004:22-26.

Doolittle, A. J.
1865 Official Township Map of Humboldt Co., Cal. San Francisco: A. J. Doolittle.

Driver, Harold E.
1939 Culture Element Distributions: X: Northwestern California. Anthropological Records 1(6).

Durst, John H.
1883 Afoot up Eel River. Overland Monthly (1)3:250-255.

Easthouse, Keith
2017a School Board Opts to Drill A Well at Whitethorn School. Humboldt Independent, December 12, 2017:1, 5.

EcoTopia
2106a Julia Butterfly Hill. Web page. Electronic document, http://ecotopia.org/ecology-hall-of-fame/julia-butterfly-hill/ accessed on January 3, 2016.

Eddy, J. M.
1893 In the Redwood's Realm. San Francisco: D. S. Stanley & Co.

Edeline, Denis P.
1978 At the Banks of the Eel. N.p.
N. d. The Edeline Family. Excerpt photocopy in possession of author.

Eel Valley Advance
1970a Bark camp article. Eel Valley Advance, April 27, 1980:8.
1970b Route 36: Redwood Empire's Conversation Piece. Eel Valley Advance, November 23, 1970.

Eich, Glenyth L.
1978 "Punkin Center" Researched by Present Resident. Humboldt Historian, January-February 1978:1, 4.
1984 Robinsons' link to Shively goes back four generations. Humboldt Historian, July-August 1984.

Egan, Timothy
2012 Short Nights of the Shadow Catcher. Boston: Houghton Mifflin Harcourt.

Eggenberger, David
1985 An Encyclopedia of Battles. New York: Dover Publications, Inc.

Elliott, Helen, and Fred Elliott
N. d. The Story of Bull Creek. Photocopy in author's possession.

Elliott, Wallace W.
1881 History of Humboldt County, California. San Francisco: Wallace W. Elliott & Co.

Elsasser, Albert B.
1978 Mattole, Nongatl, Sinkyone, Lassik, and Wailaki. In Handbook of North American Indians, vol. 8: California. Robert F. Heizer, ed. Pp. 190-204. Washington: Smithsonian Institution.

Elvidge, Lois
1974 Dobbyn School History Tells of Past Educational Era. Humboldt Historian, November-December, 1974:10.
N. d. Memories of Fort Seward. In The Trail Back 1974:A-21.

Empty Road
2015 Ledger of the Deep: The Mythology of Renaming a Boat. Web page. Electronic document, http://www.theemptyroad.com/ledger-of-the-deep-the-mythology-of-renaming-a-boat/ accessed on November 27, 2015.

Encyclopædia Britannica
2016a Nathan Bedford Forrest. Web page. Electronic document, https://www.britannica.com/biography/Nathan-Bedford-Forrest accessed on October 10, 2016.
2018a John C. Breckenridge. Web page. Electronic document, https://www.britannica.com/biography/John-C-Breckinridge accessed on August 19, 2018.

Encyclopedia.com
2015a Kroeber, Alfred L. Web page. Electronic document, http://www.encyclopedia.com/doc/1G2-3045000665.html accessed on June 8, 2015.

Engbeck, Joseph H. Jr.
2018 Saving the Redwoods. San Francisco: Save the Redwoods League.

Essene, Frank
1942 Cultural Elements Distributions: XXI: Round Valley. Anthropological Records 8:1.

Ethnological Documents
2002 Ethnological Documents Collection of the Department and Museum of Anthropology, University of California, Berkeley, 1875-1958. Berkeley: Bancroft Library. Microfilm: Humboldt State University Library, Arcata.

Eureka Heritage Society
1987 Eureka: An Architectural View. Eureka: Eureka Heritage Society.

Eureka-Humboldt Library
N.d. Index to 1860 Humboldt County census. Photocopy in author's possession.

Eureka Independent
1952a First Truck Freight in Humboldt in 1912. Eureka Independent, March 19, 1952:6.

Eureka Newspapers, Inc.
1949a 1949 Classified Business Directory. Eureka: Eureka Newspapers, Inc.
1965a The One Thousand Year Flood. Eureka Newspapers, Inc., February 15-16, 1965.

Evans, George S.
2007 [1904?] Wylackie Jake of Covelo. Nevada City, CA: Mountain House Books.

Evans, J. Ray
1978 Old Humboldt Paper Company Born of A Shipwreck. Humboldt Historian, January-February 1978:3.

Evans, Raymond
1999 When Fast Food Was A Rabbit. N.p.

Evening Star
1877a Communication. Evening Star, February 21, 1877:3.
1877b Ad for Larabee Hotel. Evening Star, July 25, 1877:1.
1877c Ad for Overland stages. Evening Star, July 25, 1877:1.
1877d From the South. Evening Star, May 10, 1877:1.

Falk, Peggy
2018 Interview with Jerry Rohde, December 5, 2018.

Farager, John Mack, ed.
1998 The American Heritage Encyclopedia of American History. New York: Henry Holt and Company.

Faulkner, Jessie
2002a One Foggy Night . . . The Final Tale of the Alaska. Humboldt Historian, Fall 2002:20-23.
2003a Turbulent times in Shively: Residents recall commute by boat. Times-Standard, November 24, 2003.
2004a Harvest Home. Humboldt Historian, Fall 2004:32-35.

Felt, T. D.
1869 Another Indian Depredation—Heroic Conduct of Mrs. Bowman. Humboldt Times, April 3, 1869.

Ferndale Enterprise
1878a Hansell article. Ferndale Enterprise, August 30, 1878:3.

1878b The Beaumont Bro's. Ferndale Enterprise, July 10, 1878:3.

1880a Article about Blocksburg's Overland Hotel. Ferndale Enterprise, September 10, 1880:3.

1881a A Four Day's Journey Southward. Ferndale Enterprise, August 11, 1881:3.

1882a Editorial Notes. Ferndale Enterprise, July 21, 1882:2.

1884a Mazeppa. Ferndale Enterprise, March 29, 1884:5.

1885a Letter from Garberville. Ferndale Enterprise, December 5, 1885:5.

1885b A Sad Fate. Ferndale Enterprise, November 29, 1885:1.

1886a Death of Joseph Russ. Ferndale Enterprise, October 15, 1886:3.

1886b Local News. Ferndale Enterprise, December 17, 1886:5.

1887b Local News. Ferndale Enterprise, February 11, 1887:5.

1889a An Act of Bravery. Ferndale Enterprise, May 1889.

1890a South Fork Notes. Ferndale Enterprise, June 27, 1890:5.

1891a Upper Eel River and Garberville Notes. Ferndale Enterprise, August 21, 1891:5.

1892a The Town of Petrolia. Ferndale Enterprise, May 13, 1892:1.

1892b Communicated. Ferndale Enterprise, April 1, 1892:4.

1892c From the Alton Journal of Oct 15th. Ferndale Enterprise, October 10, 1892:1.

1893a Over the Grade. Ferndale Enterprise, December 22, 1893:5.

1894a Notice of foreclosure. Ferndale Enterprise, March 30, 1894.

1899a Indian George and family article. Ferndale Enterprise, October 6, 1899.

1899b Bull Creek forest fire article. Ferndale Enterprise, September 1, 1899.

1901a Here and There. Ferndale Enterprise, April 26, 1901:1.

1909a Death of Judge C. G. Stafford. Ferndale Enterprise, July 9, 1909:1.

1912a Crawled Ten Hours With Broken Leg. Ferndale Enterprise, March 29, 1912.

1913a Another Wizard Works Miracles with Plants. Ferndale Enterprise, April 25, 1913.

1913b Writes of Overland Auto Trip. Ferndale Enterprise, July 22, 1913.

1914a Article on Roscoe wedding anniversary. Ferndale Enterprise, June 30, 1914.

1918a Briceland Now Isolated Town. Ferndale Enterprise, August 20, 1918.

1919a Shelter Cove A Lively Town. Ferndale Enterprise, August 15, 1919:7.

1919b Frank Johnson Meets Death in Train Accident. Ferndale Enterprise, September 6, 1919:1.

1924a Grandma Roscoe is Called to Rest. Ferndale Enterprise, June 6, 1924.

1940a Mr. and Mrs. J. Mahan's Part in "Save-the-Redwoods" History is Reviewed. Ferndale Enterprise, January 19, 1940.

1941a June 14 Marks 25th Anniversary of S. S. Bear Wreck. Ferndale Enterprise, June 13, 1941.

1941b Jap Submarine Attacks Tanker Near Cape Mendocino. Ferndale Enterprise, December 26, 1941:1.

1955a Worst Flood! Ferndale Enterprise, December 23, 1955:1.

1955b Eel Valley Swimming Through the Deluge. Ferndale Enterprise, December 23, 1955:1.

Ferndale Semi-Weekly Enterprise

1897a Local Items. Ferndale Semi-Weekly Enterprise, September 24, 1897:4.

1901a Here and There. Ferndale Semi-Weekly Enterprise, April 26, 1901:8.

1901b Under the head of "Good Old Indian. . . ." Ferndale Semi-Weekly Enterprise, November 12, 1901:5.

1903a Killed It With a Hammer. Ferndale Semi-Weekly Enterprise, November 26, 1903:4.

1903b Despite the Superior Court injunction . . . . Ferndale Semi-Weekly Enterprise, April 10, 1903:5.

1904a Triple Drowning in the Mattole River. Ferndale Semi-Weekly Enterprise, March 15, 1904:4.

1907a Banner Presented. Ferndale Semi-Weekly Enterprise, August 20, 1907:4.

1914a Local Notes. Ferndale Semi-Weekly Enterprise, September ***, 1914:5.

Find A Grave

2017 Anna "Annie" Duckett Hunter. Web page. Electronic document, https://www.findagrave.com/cgi-bin/fg.cgi?page=gr&GSln=Hunter&GSiman=1&GScnty=194&GRid=138328341& accessed on April 30, 2017.

2019a Augusta Phillipina Schumacher Jones. Web page. Electronic document, https://www.findagrave.com/memorial/155396461/augusta-phillipina-jones accessed on December 18, 2019.

Finn, J. D. John

2018 Cockiness, incompetence and a labor strike led to a shipwreck. Offbeat Oregon. Web page. Electronic document, https://offbeatoregon.com/1512a.alaska-ship-wreck-368.html accessed on December 4, 2018.

Fisher, Harold

1989 Weott had its own heyday. Humboldt Historian, March-April 1989:20.

Fisher, Harold, and Jane Bryant Fisher

1991 Interview with Jerry Rohde, May 22, 1991.

Fishman, Ram

2006a Albert Etter: The Legacy of a Fruit Explorer. Now . . . and Then: The Journal of the Mattole Valley Historical Society (7)2.

2019 The Ettersburg Apple Legacies. Web page. Electronic document, http://www.greenmantlenursery.com/fruit/etter-apples.htm accessed on September 10, 2019.

Flaherty, F. F.

1934 Etter Brothers Create Earthly Paradise. Humboldt Standard, June 24, 1934.

Fletcher, Randol B.

2011 Hidden History of Civil War Oregon. Charleston, SC: History Press.

Foner, Eric, and John A. Garraty eds.
   1991 The Reader's Companion to American
        History. Boston: Houghton Mifflin Com-
        pany.
Forbes, Stanly
   1886 Official Map of Humboldt County,
        California. San Francisco: Stanly Forbes.
   1896 Official Map of Humboldt County,
        California. San Francisco: Stanly Forbes
Forest Lookouts
   2020a Iaqua Buttes. Web page. Electronic
        document, https://californialookouts.
        weebly.com/iaqua-buttes.html accessed on
        July 8, 2020.
Forrest (pseud.)
   1887 From Forrest. Ferndale Enterprise,
        October 21, 1887:4.
fortwiki.com
   2022a Fort Iaqua. Web page. Electronic
        document, http://www.fortwiki.com/
        Fort_Iaqua accessed on May 30, 2022.
Fountain, Susie Baker
   1960a Strong's Station. Humboldt County
        Historical Society Newsletter, March
        1960:5-6.
   1964a The Settlement of the Humboldt Bay
        Region in 1850. Blue Lake Advocate,
        December 24, 1964:3.
   1965a The Settlement of the Humboldt Bay
        Region in 1850. Blue Lake Advocate, Feb-
        ruary 18, 1965.
   2001 Susie Baker Fountain Papers. 128
        volumes. Microfilm: Humboldt State Uni-
        versity Library, Arcata.
freepages.rootsweb.com
   2018 Frank Kanning Mott. Web page.
        Electronic document, http://freepages.
        rootsweb.com/~npmelton/genealogy/lam-
        ott.htm accessed on November 22, 2018.
French, George
   1997 Any Weott Pastimers Left? Humboldt
        Historian, Summer 1997:39.
Frickstad, Walter N.
   1955 A Century of California Post Offices.
        Oakland: Philatelic Research Society.
Friend, George
   1939 Hardships and Dangers of Early Humboldt
        Life Told by Pioneer of Section. Humboldt
        Times, December 17, 1939:13-14.
Fritz, Emanuel
   1922a A pile of railroad ties . . . . Webpage.
        Electronic document, https://digicoll.
        lib.berkeley.edu/record/15277?l-
        n=en#?c=0&m=0&s=0&cv=0&r=0&xy-
        wh=0%2C-100%2C1500%2C1407
        accessed on October 22, 2020.
   1922b Thousands of split redwood
        grape stakes . . . . Webpage. Elec-
        tronic document, https://digicoll.
        lib.berkeley.edu/record/15280?l-
        n=en#?c=0&m=0&s=0&cv=0&r=0&xy-
        wh=0%2C-95%2C1500%2C1407
        accessed on October 22, 2020.
   1922c A small sawmill on Bull
        Creek . . . . Webpage. Electron-
        ic document, https://digicoll.
        lib.berkeley.edu/record/16076?l-
        n=en#?c=0&m=0&s=0&cv=0&r=0&xy-
        wh=-328%2C0%2C2155%2C1155
        accessed on October 22, 2020.
   1939a Sawmill of Wrigley and
        Russell . . . . Webpage. Electron-
        ic document, https://digicoll.
        lib.berkeley.edu/record/16066?l-
        n=en#?c=0&m=0&s=0&cv=0&r=0&xy-
        wh=-725%2C-12%2C2875%2C1542
        accessed on October 22, 2020.
Fritz-Metcalf Photograph Collection
   2016a Large stump . . . on Holmes Flat.
        Accession # 4879. Webpage. Electronic
        document, http://dpg.lib.berkeley.edu/
        webdb/metcalf/search?keyword=reback&-
        dates=&location=&photographer=&pho-
        tono accessed on May 18, 2016.
   2016b Truck hauling. Jordan Creek. Accession
        # 3091a. Webpage. Electronic document,
        http://dpg.lib.berkeley.edu/webdb/
        metcalf/search?keyword=&dates=&loca-
        tion=&photographer=&photono=3091a
        accessed on May 17, 2016.
   2016c Selective logging by Pacific Lumber
        Company on north slope of Jordan Creek.
        Accession # 3964. Webpage. Electronic
        document, http://dpg.lib.berkeley.edu/
        webdb/metcalf/search?keyword=&-
        dates=&location=&photographer=&pho-
        tono=3964 accessed on May 17, 2016.
   2016d Fire in logging slash on Bridge Creek.
        Accession # 1146. Webpage. Electronic
        document, http://dpg.lib.berkeley.edu/
        webdb/metcalf/search?keyword=&-
        dates=&location=&photographer=&pho-
        tono=1145 accessed on May 18, 2016.
   2016e Camp Coolen . . . at top of Bridge
        Creek incline. Accession # 1421. Webpage.
        Electronic document, http://dpg.lib.berke-
        ley.edu/webdb/metcalf/search?keyword=&-
        dates=&location=&photographer=&pho-
        tono=1421 accessed on May 18, 2016.
   2016f Fire prevention signs used by the Pacific
        Lumber Company . . . . Webpage. Elec-
        tronic document, http://dpg.lib.berkeley.
        edu/webdb/metcalf/search?keyword=&-
        dates=&location=&photographer=&pho-
        tono=2483 accessed on May 19, 2016.
Frost, Ralph C.
   1966 How Showers Pass Was Named. \
        Humboldt County Historical Society
        Newsletter, January-February 1966:2.
Fuller, A. A.
   1873a Upper Eel River. West Coast Signal,
        September 17, 1873:2.
Fugit, Tempus III (pseud.)
   1935. Early History of the Beautiful Mattole
        Valley in Southern Humboldt. Humboldt
        Times, December 29, 1935.
Gaffney-Gorman, Bertha
   1976 Willie Was His Name, And He Had A
        Vision. Sacramento Bee, January 5,
        1976:B4.
Gardner, Susan
   2001 Family member reflects bask on history of
        grand hotel; What happened to the dude
        ranch? Redwood Times, August 17, 2011.
Garner, Bryan A.
   2016 Garner's Modern English Usage. Oxford:
        Oxford University Press.

Garner, James G.
  1965 General Order 100 Revisited. Military
      Law Review 27:1-48.
Gates, Leroy J.
  1883 A Frightful Accident and One of the Most
      Miraculous Escapes from Death on Re-
      cord. Unattributed clipping in the J. W.
      Henderson biography file at the Humboldt
      County Historical Society, Eureka. Grizzly
      Creek Lower Blackburn Carlos Arturo
Gates, Paul W.
  2002 Land and Law in California. West
      Lafayette, IN: Purdue University Press.
Gates, Thomas M.
  N.d. [Map of] Yurok Aboriginal Territory.
      Photocopy in author's possession.
Geer, Knyphausen
  1948 Captain Knyphausen Geer: His Life and
      Memoirs. Humboldt County Historical
      Society Journal.
Genealogy.com
  2018a The Christopher Erin Lindstrom of
      Roseville, CA: Information about Mary
      Anne Roche Singley. Web page. Electronic
      document, https://www.genealogy.com/
      ftm/l/i/n/Christopher-Erin-Lindstrom/
      WEBSITE-0001/UHP-0454.html accessed
      on August 20, 2018.
  2019a Register Report of John Putnam. Web
      page. Electronic document, https://www.
      genealogy.com/ftm/p/u/t/Ed-Putnam/
      BOOK-0001/0043-0275.html accessed on
      August 12, 2019.
Geni
  2018a Willis Wayne Myers. Web page.
      Electronic document, https://
      www.geni.com/people/Willis-My-
      ers/6000000014826422079 accessed on
      November 29, 2018.
  2019a Jane Susanna Logan. Webpage.
      Electronic document, https://www.geni.
      com/people/Jane/6000000041891851055
      accessed on August 11, 2019.
Geniella, Mike
  2001 Benbow turns 75. Press Democrat, July
      18, 2001.
Genzoli, Andrew
  1949a Shelter Cove—Humboldt's Land of
      Paradise. Humboldt Times, September 11,
      1949:17, 23.
  1952a There Was More Than Weather in Sgt.
      McLean's Log Pages! Humboldt Times,
      April 6, 1952:6.
  1952b Story of the Walla Walla. Humboldt
      Times, January 6, 1952.
  1971a Automation Ends Era of Lightship.
      Times-Standard, June 12, 1971:3.
  1972a Eel River Country. Fresno, CA: Mid-Cal
      Publishers.
  1977a Redwood County: With the passing of
      time. Times-Standard, April 15, 1977:28.
  1979a Bridgeville was a lively trip.
      Times-Standard, March 5, 1979.
  1982a Wreck of the S.S. Bear. Humboldt
      Historian, May-June 1982:3-7.
  1982b 'The Poison Oak'—Disappointment on
      the Eel River–. Humboldt Historian,
      March-April 1982:8-9.

  1982c Apples and the 'Great Maria.'
      Humboldt Beacon, January 7, 1982:5.
  1982d Redwood Country. Humboldt Beacon,
      May 12, 1982:5.
  1983a Remembering a daring transition from
      Sail to Steam . . . . Humboldt Historian,
      January-February 1983:18-19.
Genzoli, Andrew M., and Wallace E. Martin
  1972 Redwood Pioneer—a frontier remembered.
      Eureka: Schooner Features.
Gibbs, Anita
  N.d. Term paper on the Oscar Stapp family.
      Photocopy in author's possession.
Gibbs, George
  2016 George Gibbs' Journal of Redick McKee's
      Expedition Through Northwestern
      California in 1851. Web page. Electronic
      document, http://klamathbucketbrigade.
      org/Gibbs_1851JournalMcKeeExpedi-
      tion040406.htm accessed on August 12,
      2016.
Gibbs, James S., Jr.
  1957 Shipwrecks of the Pacific Coast. Portland,
      OR: Binfords & Mort.
Gifford, E. W.
  1939 The Coast Yuki. Anthropos (34)1:292-375.
Gift, Harry E.
  1987 Ship knees harvested in Iaqua area.
      Humboldt Historian, March-April
      1987:17.
Gipson, Naida Olsen
  2005. Babes In Benbow. Humboldt Historian,
      Summer 2005:28-31.
Goddard, Pliny E.
  1903a #1 Sinkyone Notebook. In Selected
      Notebooks of Pliny Earle Goddard Relating
      to Humboldt County Tribes. Jerry Rohde,
      ed. PDF file archived at the Cultural Re-
      sources Facility, Humboldt State Universi-
      ty, Arcata, CA.
  1906a Redwood Creek & Mad River Notebook.
      In Selected Notebooks of Pliny Earle God-
      dard Relating to Humboldt County Tribes.
      Jerry Rohde, ed. PDF file archived at the
      Cultural Resources Facility, Humboldt
      State University, Arcata, CA.
  1906b Lassik 1906 Names of Places Names of
      Plants. [Lassik notebook #2]. Original at
      Special Collections Division, University of
      Washington Libraries.
  1907a Mattole Notebook #1, P. E. Goddard,
      October 1907. In Selected Notebooks of
      Pliny Earle Goddard Relating to Hum-
      boldt County Tribes. Jerry Rohde, ed.
      PDF file archived at the Cultural Resourc-
      es Facility, Humboldt State University,
      Arcata, CA.
  1907b Places V[an] Duzen to Mad River Pete
      [Notebook] #21. In Selected Notebooks of
      Pliny Earle Goddard Relating to Humboldt
      County Tribes. Jerry Rohde, ed. PDF file
      archived at the Cultural Resources Facility,
      Humboldt State University, Arcata, CA.
  1907c [Untitled] Sinkyone Notebook II Albert
      Smith and George Burt [sic]. In Selected
      Notebooks of Pliny Earle Goddard Relating
      to Humboldt County Tribes. Jerry Rohde,
      ed. PDF file archived at the Cultural Re-

sources Facility, Humboldt State University, Arcata, CA.

1907d Untitled Sinkyone Notebook 1 Albert Smith and Sallie [Sally] Bell Interviews. *In* Selected Notebooks of Pliny Earle Goddard Relating to Humboldt County Tribes. Jerry Rohde, ed. PDF file archived at the Cultural Resources Facility, Humboldt State University, Arcata, CA.

1907e 1 Nongatl Peter Van Duzen 1907 [Notebook]. *In* Selected Notebooks of Pliny Earle Goddard Relating to Humboldt County Tribes. Jerry Rohde, ed. PDF file archived at the Cultural Resources Facility, Humboldt State University, Arcata, CA.

1907f Mattole [Notebook] #2. *In* Selected Notebooks of Pliny Earle Goddard Relating to Humboldt County Tribes. Jerry Rohde, ed. PDF file archived at the Cultural Resources Facility, Humboldt State University, Arcata, CA.

1908a Yager 1908 Village Sites copied on cards [Notebook]. *In* Selected Notebooks of Pliny Earle Goddard Relating to Humboldt County Tribes. Jerry Rohde, ed. PDF file archived at the Cultural Resources Facility, Humboldt State University, Arcata, CA.

1908b Sinkyone Notebook IV, July 1908. *In* Selected Notebooks of Pliny Earle Goddard Relating to Humboldt County Tribes. Jerry Rohde, ed. PDF file archived at the Cultural Resources Facility, Humboldt State University, Arcata, CA.

1908c Duzen Mrs. Pete (~ and Mad River) June 15, 1908. PDF file archived at the Cultural Resources Facility, Humboldt State University, Arcata, CA.

1908d Nongatl Van Duzen Pete [Notebook] 18[.] June 17, 1908. *In* Selected Notebooks of Pliny Earle Goddard Relating to Humboldt County Tribes. Jerry Rohde, ed. PDF file archived at the Cultural Resources Facility, Humboldt State University, Arcata, CA.

1908e Peter V. D. June 20 1908 Nongatl [Notebook] 19. *In* Selected Notebooks of Pliny Earle Goddard Relating to Humboldt County Tribes. Jerry Rohde, ed. PDF file archived at the Cultural Resources Facility, Humboldt State University, Arcata, CA.

1908f [Untitled Sinkyone Notebook Charlie Interview July 1908] *In* Selected Notebooks of Pliny Earle Goddard Relating to Humboldt County Tribes. Jerry Rohde, ed. PDF file archived at the Cultural Resources Facility, Humboldt State University, Arcata, CA.

1913a Wayside Shrines in Northwestern California. American Anthropologist (15)4:702-703.

1914a Notes on the Chilula Indians of Northwestern California. University of California Publications in American Archaeology and Ethnology (10)6:265-288.

1914b Chilula Texts. University of California Publications in American Archaeology and Ethnology (10)7:289-379.

1919a Letter from P. E. Goddard to Dr. C. Hart Merriam dated February 25, 1919. Copy in author's possession.

1922a [Untitled Notebook Bear River and some Wailaki, August to September 1922.] *In* Selected Notebooks of Pliny Earle Goddard Relating to Humboldt County Tribes. Jerry Rohde, ed. PDF file archived at the Cultural Resources Facility, Humboldt State University, Arcata, CA.

1923 The Habitat of the Wailaki. American Archaeology and Ethnology, vol. 20. University of California Press.

1929 The Bear River Dialect of Athapascan. University of California Publications in American Archaeology and Ethnology (24)5.

N.d.a Van Duzen [Notebook] #20. *In* Selected Notebooks of Pliny Earle Goddard Relating to Humboldt County Tribes. Jerry Rohde, ed. PDF file archived at the Cultural Resources Facility, Humboldt State University, Arcata, CA.

N.d.b V[an] D[uzen] Songs [Notebook] #23. *In* Selected Notebooks of Pliny Earle Goddard Relating to Humboldt County Tribes. Jerry Rohde, ed. PDF file archived at the Cultural Resources Facility, Humboldt State University, Arcata, CA.

N.d.d #2 Sinkyone [Notebook]. *In* Selected Notebooks of Pliny Earle Goddard Relating to Humboldt County Tribes. Jerry Rohde, ed. PDF file archived at the Cultural Resources Facility, Humboldt State University, Arcata, CA.

N.d.e. Lassik Misc. [Lassik notebook #1]. Original at Special Collections Division, University of Washington Libraries.

N.d.f. Bald Hills [Notebook]. *In* Selected Notebooks of Pliny Earle Goddard Relating to Humboldt County Tribes. Jerry Rohde, ed. PDF file archived at the Cultural Resources Facility, Humboldt State University, Arcata, CA.

Goetzmann, William H., and Kay Sloan
  1982 Looking Far North: The Harriman Expedition to Alaska, 1899. Princeton, NJ: Princeton University Press.

Goldberg, Ami
  1985 Fascinating years at the Ettersburg Ranch. Humboldt Historian, September-October 1985:6-9.

Golla, Victor
  2011 California Indian Languages. Berkeley: University of California Press.
  2015a Personal communication with author regarding Goddard notebook #22, April 30, 2015.
  2015b Personal communication with author regarding certain Athabascan language terms, July 10, 2015.

Golla, Victor, and Sean O'Neill, eds.
  2001 The Collected Works of Edward Sapir. Vol. 14: Northwest California Linguistics. Berlin: Mouton de Gruyter.

Gomez, Melissa
  2021 UC Berkeley removes Kroeber Hall name, citing namesake's 'immoral' work with Native Americans. Web page. Electronic document, https://www.latimes.com/california/story/2021-01-27/uc-berkeley-kroeber-hall accessed on February 2, 2021.

Google Patents
  2019a Gradometer. Web page. Electronic document, https://patents.google.com/patent/US1219341 accessed on April 10, 2019.

Gordon, David E.
  1899a Old Camp Grant. Daily Standard, October 13, 1899:3.
  1899b Over the River. Daily Standard, October 16, 1899:3.
  1899c Along the Road. Daily Standard, October 17, 1899:3.
  1899d Along the River. Daily Standard, October 18, 1899:3.

Grant, Bonnie
  2005 Bonnie Henderson Grant in Children from our One-Room Schools. Blocksburg, CA: Blocksburg Town Hall Association.

Grant, Madison
  1919 Saving the Redwoods. Zoological Society Bulletin, September 1919:92-118.

Gravelmap
  2019 Gravel Routes in California: Whitethorn. Web page. Electronic document, https://gravelmap.com/browse/california accessed on June 23, 2019.

Greenmantle Nursery
  2020a The Ettersburg Apple Legacies. Web page. Electronic document, http://www.greenmantlenursery.com/fruit/etter-apples.htm accessed on September 2, 2020.

Greenson, Thaddeus
  2006a 'Simpler ways of life.' Times-Standard, October 19, 2006.

Gregory, Tom
  1911 History of Sonoma County California with Biographical Sketches of The leading men and women of that county, who have been identified with its growth and development from the early days to the present time. Los Angeles: Historic Record Company.

Greig, Rusty
  1964a Brice's Ferndale – Petrolia Stage Line. Humboldt County Historical Society Newsletter, July-August 1964:1.

Griggs, Gary, and Deepika Shrestha Ross
  2014 California Coast from the Air. Missoula, MT: Mountain Press Publishing Company.

Gudde, Erwin Gustave
  1969 California Place Names. Berkeley: University of California Press.

Guinn, J. M.
  1904 History of the State of California and Biographical Record of Coast Counties, California. Chicago: The Chapman Publishing Co.

Gurnon, Emily
  2004a Buyer Beware. North Coast Journal, April 22, 2004.

  2004b Gem on Ocean Quickly Loses Its Brilliance. Web page. Electronic document, https://www.latimes.com/archives/la-xpm-2004-jun-21-me-sheltercove21-story.html accessed on July 3, 2020.

Hackett, Bob, and Sander Kingsepp
  2019 INJ Submarine I-17. Tabular Record of Movement. Web page. Electronic document, http://www.combinedfleet.com/I-17.htm accessed on June 24, 2019.

Hagemann, David
  N.d. Sam Stockton 1905-1983. Photocopy on file under "Biographies" at the Humboldt County Historical Society, Eureka, California.

Hale, J. J.
  1879a. Card of Thanks. Daily Humboldt times, March 12, 1879:3.

Hamm, Lillie E.
  1890 History and Business Directory of Humboldt County. Eureka: Daily Humboldt Standard.

Hanson, Buck
  1962 The Called Me A "Mule-Skinner." Humboldt County Historical Society Newsletter, March 1962:8.

Hanson, Buck, and Jim Boots
  1963 Memories of the Pacific Oaks Extract Works. Humboldt County Historical Society Newsletter, January-February 1963:13.

Harrington, James Peabody
  1983 The Papers of John P. Harrington in the Smithsonian Institution 1907 – 1957. Microfilm: Humboldt State University Library, Arcata.

Harville, Richard
  1985a Joseph Russ: A noted pioneer of Humboldt. Humboldt Historian, March-April 1985:4-7, 26.

Harville, Ronald P.
  1982 Letter to editor. Humboldt Historian, July-August 1982:17.
  1988 The Story of the Fort Baker Ranch. Santa Barbara: Ronald Patrick Harville.

Hawk, Diane
  2004 Touring the Redwood Highway: Humboldt County. Piercy, CA: Hawk Mountaintop Publishing.

Healdsburg Tribune
  1924a Large Crowd At Grove Dedication. Healdsburg Tribune, August 26, 1924:1.
  1936a Mrs. Georgeson, Ill Few Weeks, Dies in Eureka. Healdsburg Tribune, Enterprise and Scimitar, May 14, 1936:7.

Heartwood
  2018. Heartwood Mountain Sanctuary. Web page. Electronic document, https://www.heartwoodhub.com/emerald-springs-spa-wellness-center/ accessed September 26, 2018.

Heinbach, Orpha
  1986 A child's view of the Shively tunnel project. Humboldt Historian, July-August 1986:12-13.

Heizer, Robert F.
  1993 The Destruction of California Indians. Lincoln NB: University of Nebraska Press.

Heizer, Robert F., ed.
 1972 George Gibbs' Journal of Redick McKee's
    Expedition Through Northwestern Cal-
    ifornia in 1851. University of California
    Berkeley, Archaeological Research Facility,
    Department of Anthropology.
 1978 Handbook of North American Indians,
    vol. 8: California. Washington: Smithso-
    nian Institution.
Heizer, Robert F. and Alan J. Almquist
 1971 The Other Californians. Berkeley:
    University of California Press.
Heizer, Robert F. and Albert B. Elsasser, eds.
 1963 Aboriginal California: Three Studies in
    Culture History. Berkeley: University of
    California Press.
Heller, David
 2020a Personal communication with the
    author, October 30, 2020.
 2020b Personal communication with the author,
    October 31, 2020.
Hendricks, Karen Campbell
 2015. Redway. Humboldt Historian, winter
    2015:20-23.
Hewes, Gordon W.
 1940 Notes, Book III. Photocopy of hand-written
    notebook in author's possession.
Hill, Arthur W.
 1930 Who Killed Beautiful Carmen Wagner?
    True Detective Mysteries, July 1930:20-29;
    84-94.
Hill, Hazel
 1954a Briceland Is Filled With Treasured
    Memories. Humboldt Times, May 16,
    1954: 10.
 1955a Blocksburg Life Was Rough, Ready,
    Happy. Humboldt Times, December
    18,1955:9.
Hill, Jesse Kaufhold
 2020a John Kaufold: "A Hipster before They
    Existed." Web page. Electron-
    ic document, https://kymkemp.
    com/2020/02/21/john-kaufhold-a-hip-
    ster-before-they-existed/ accessed on
    November 12, 2020.
Hillman, Raymond W.
 2007 Fog-bound tragedy remembered.
    Times-Standard, July 20, 2007: A1, A8.
History and Happenings
 2017a Eel Rock. Web page. Electronic
    document, http://historyandhappen-
    ings.squarespace.com/humboldt-coun-
    ty/2016/12/12/eel-rock.html accessed on
    December 23, 2017.
 2019a Island> Irma> Island Mountain. Web
    page. Electronic document, http://his-
    toryandhappenings.squarespace.com/
    trinity-county/2016/2/3/island-irma-is-
    land-mountain.html accessed on February
    16, 2019.
History Vault
 2016 Nathan Bedford Forrest. Web page.
    Electronic document, http://www.history.
    com/topics/american-civil-war/nathan-bed-
    ford-forrest accessed on October 10, 2016.

HNSA
 2018a Lightship Swiftsure. Webpage. Electronic
    document, https://archive.hnsa.org/ships/
    swiftsure.htm accessed on December 19,
    2018.
Hodge, Frederick W., ed.
 1910a Handbook of American Indians North of
    Mexico, part 2. Washington: Government
    Printing Office.
Holland, Herb
 1948a Garberville—The Heart of the Redwoods.
    Humboldt Times, September 19, 1948:9.
Home Herald
 1893a Lamb Bro's ad. Home Herald, March 3,
    1893.
Hosmer, Frances Dinsmore
 N.d. Humboldt Days: Recollections of Frances
    Dinsmore Hosmer, as set down by her
    daughter Anne Hosmer Wrightson.
    Photocopy located in the biography files of
    the Humboldt County Historical Society,
    Eureka.
Hotchkiss, George W.
 1898 History of the Lumber and Forest Industry
    of the Northwest. Chicago: George W.
    Hotchkiss & Co.
House, Freeman
 1999 Totem Salmon. Boston: Beacon Press
House Designers
 2022 How Many Trees Does It Take to Build a
    House? Web page. Electronic document,
    https://www.thehousedesigners.com/arti-
    cles/how-many-trees-does-it-take-to-build-a-
    house.asp accessed on May 3, 2022.
HSU Special Collections
 2018. Swanlund-Baker Photograph Collection
    - Biography. Web page. Electronic doc-
    ument, https://en.wikipedia.org/wiki/
    Ray_Jerome_Baker accessed on August 22,
    2018.
Humboldt & Trinity Toll Road Company
 N. .d Prospectus letter. Copy in possession of
    the author.
Humboldt Beacon
 1910a The Passing of Wm. B. Dobbyn of
    Rohnerville. Humboldt Beacon, May 27,
    1910:7.
 1910b Capitalists Invest in So. Humboldt.
    Humboldt Beacon, May 27, 1910:4.
 1916a The Pacific Lumber Company To Have
    Four Stores In Woods. Humboldt Beacon,
    March 17, 1916.
 1916b "Budds", the Well Known Indian Dies at
    Shively. Humboldt Beacon, March 24,
    1916.
 1922a Redwood Park Is Now Open To The
    Public. Humboldt Beacon, June 16,
    1922:4.
 1922b Dyerville and Bull Creek. Humboldt
    Beacon, May 20, 1922:2.
 1922c Bull Creek Dyerville Items. Humboldt
    Beacon, June 30, 1922:6.
 1922d Dyerville and Bull Creek. Humboldt
    Beacon July 7, 1922:1.
 1922e David Chadbourne leg injury article.
    Humboldt Beacon, August 11, 1922.

1922f What might have resulted in a very serious accident . . . . Humboldt Beacon, September 8, 1922:7.

1922g Dyerville Items of Interest. Humboldt Beacon, October 20, 1922:2.

1923a Dyerville and Bull Creek Items. Humboldt Beacon, February 23, 1923.

1923b Bull Creek Items. Humboldt Beacon, May 11, 1923:1.

1923c Chadbourne has fully recovered . . . . Humboldt Beacon, May 18, 1923:7.

1923d Word was received by friends . . . . Humboldt Beacon, September 14, 1923:3.

1967a Old Pepperwood Mill. Humboldt Beacon, January 5, 1967.

1967b Shively's "Indian Buds." Humboldt Beacon, January 26, 1967:15.

1997a Carlotta's Plans for Fire Hall Are Temporarily in Limbo. Humboldt Beacon, March 20, 1997.

N.d. The Killer Eel. Fortuna, CA: Humboldt Beacon, n.d.

Humboldt County Clerk
1896 Precinct Registers of Humboldt County, State of California. Eureka.

Humboldt County Deeds
N.d. Humboldt County Recorder's Office, Eureka, CA.

Humboldt County Department of Community Development Services
2003 Humboldt 2025 General Plan Update: Agricultural Resources and Policies.

Humboldt County Historical Society Newsletter
1960a The Old-Timer's Corner. Humboldt County Historical Society Newsletter, May 1960:11.

Humboldt County Schools
1944 Directory of Public Schools Humboldt County 1944-1945. Eureka: County Superintendent of Schools.

Humboldt Historian
1965a In Memoriam. Humboldt Historian, July-August 1965.

1968a Article containing information about Redwood House. Humboldt Historian, July-August 1968:1.

1981a Photo of Young's Store, Pepperwood. Humboldt Historian, July-August 1981:11.

1987a U. S. Grant—the West Coast Years. Humboldt Historian, November-December 1987:11-13.

1987b In Memory. Humboldt Historian, March-April 1987:24.

1989a Heroic trek through the deep snow of an earlier year. Humboldt Historian, January-February 1989:14-16.

1995a On The Right Track: Raleigh Christopher. Humboldt Historian, Winter 1995:22.

1996a In Memory: Margaret (Peggy) Satterlee. Humboldt Historian, Fall 1996:46.

1999a Obit for Louise Read Paine. Humboldt Historian, Spring 1999:45.

2002a Southern Humboldt Schools. Humboldt Historian, Spring 2002:6-14.

Humboldt Standard
1883a A. J. Huestis. Humboldt Standard, March 24, 1883.

1907a First Wreck News. Humboldt Standard, July 22, 1907:1.

1907b Promotion Work in Humboldt County. Humboldt Standard, January 14, 1907:6.

1907c Petrol Wagons for Petrolia. Humboldt Standard, August 15, 1907:1.

1907d Banner Presentation and Rally at Petrolia. Humboldt Standard, August 16, 1907:1.

1907e A Gala Day at Petrolia. Humboldt Standard, August 17, 1907:1.

1907f Automobiling in the Mountains. Humboldt Standard, August 18, 1907:1.

1907g A Welcome to Governor Gillett. Humboldt Standard, August 18, 1907:2.

1907h Fatal Landslide at Upper Mattole. Humboldt Standard, March 29, 1907:2.

1908a Indian's Death Creates A Stir. Humboldt Standard, January 17, 1908.

1908b Humboldt and Trinity County Toll Road. Humboldt Standard, February 1, 1908.

1910a Daylight Through Bryan Bluff Tunnel. Humboldt Standard, July 19, 1910:1.

1912a Geo. Tooby Buys A Locomobile. Humboldt Standard, September 19, 1912.

1912b Children Attacked by Huge Gray Eagle. Humboldt Standard, August 10, 1912.

1914a $5,000 Fire Rages at Briceland. Humboldt Standard, July 14, 1914.

1915a Canoe from Fort Seward. Humboldt Standard, August 2, 1915.

1916a S. S. Bear Lost—Survivors Here. Humboldt Standard, June 15, 1916:1-2.

1916b Show 1200 Ft. Depth. Humboldt Standard, June 15, 1916:1.

1916c Tell of Night at Sea. Humboldt Standard, June 15, 1916:1-2.

1916d Alder Point Is Charming Village And Summer Camp. Humboldt Standard, December 13, 1916:1.

1918a Hermanson Signs Up Three Autos. Humboldt Standard, July 6, 1918:4.

1919a School of Sharks Attracted To Shelter Cove Alarm Fishermen. Humboldt Standard, September 20, 1919.

1919b Chester Denmark article. Humboldt Standard, July 26, 1919.

1919c Salmon Brown Is Dead; Kills Self. Humboldt Standard, May 13, 1919.

1919d Gasoline Gave Fury to Fire at Bridgeville. Humboldt Standard, December 16, 1919.

1920a Well Known Indian Woman, 90 Years of Age, Died Mon. Humboldt Standard, January 29, 1920.

1920b Death of Emerson recalls Story Of Early Murder Here. Humboldt Standard December 10, 1920.

1921a Death of Mrs. Martha Cuddeback Recalls Stories of Pioneering. Humboldt Standard, January 22, 1921.

1921b Woodshed Being Repaired for School Use; Fire. Humboldt Standard, August 30, 1921.

1921c Iaqua Dog Guard Sheep Night and Day, Saves Tiny Lamb in Underbrush. Humboldt Standard, September 27, 1921.

1921d Article about Hazeltons. Humboldt Standard, November 2, 1921.

1922a Incendiarism Causes Loss of Over $10,00 On Two Ranches at Fruitland. J. Lower Jailed. Humboldt Standard, September 1, 1922.

1923a Lawyer and Lumberman. Humboldt Standard, November 1, 1923.

1923b Queer Pranks of Wind Work Destruction at Brown's Mill. Humboldt Standard, August 22, 1923.

1923c Dr. J. C. Merriam Fights Fire at Redwood Grove Near Garberville. Humboldt Standard, August 6, 1923.

1924a Franklin K. Lane Memorial Redwood Grove To Be Dedicated In Humboldt On August 24. Humboldt Standard, August 5, 1924.

1924b Over 350 Men Are Employed in Mill and Woods of the Holmes-Eureka [sic] Company. Humboldt Standard, December 24, 1924.

1924c. Dyerville Flat Redwoods Being Cut By Loggers. Humboldt Standard, November 24, 1925

1925a Crew of 50 [sic] Men at Work on Fred Hartsook Resort. Humboldt Standard, June 16, 1925.

1925b Founder of Fruitland Succumbs. Humboldt Standard, March 10, 1925.

1926a Man Who Lived Ten Years in Hollow Tree Is Burned to Death in South Fork Cabin. Humboldt Standard, February 13, 1926.

1926b "Hoop Skirt" Saves Pioneer; Miss Cuddeback Tells Story. Humboldt Standard, July 30, 1926.

1927a George Tooby, Pioneer Resident Of County, Dies In This City. Humboldt Standard, August 3, 1927

1927b New Oil Company Will Drill in Mattole Area. Humboldt Standard, October 27, 1927.

1927c Employment of Chinese at Hartsook's Draws Protest. Humboldt Standard, May 27, 1927.

1927d Sheriff Will Probe Mysterious $200,000 Highway Hotel Blaze, Humboldt Standard, August 8, 1927.

1927e Hartsook's Inn Soon to Reopen. Humboldt Standard, November 21, 1927.

1927f Weott Shingle Mill Destroyed by Fire. Humboldt Standard, July 29, 1927.

1927f Weott Hotel Destroyed by Blaze. Humboldt Standard, August 3, 1927.

1927g Indian Charged with Beating up an Indian Woman. Humboldt Standard, July 20, 1927.

1928a Jennie Sands, Aged Indian Woman, Dies. Humboldt Standard, July 28, 1928:9.

1928b Third Well to Be Sunk at Mattole. Humboldt Standard, January 13, 1928.

1928c One Dead from Fighting Conflagration; Woman is Burned in Oil Explosion. Humboldt Standard, September 29, 1928.

1930a N. W. P. Closes Shively Station. Humboldt Standard, March 13, 1930.

1930b 20,000 Arce Timber Area To Be Opened. Humboldt Standard, December 4, 1930.

1931a Pioneer Doctor of County Dies in Auto Crash. Humboldt Standard, August 21, 1931.

1931b Summer Home Area Sold on Bids. Humboldt Standard, August 26, 1931.

1931c 10,000 Acres of Giant Tres Added to State Parks; Dream Realized. Humboldt Standard, September 14, 1931.

1931d Bull Creek and Dyerville Redwood Forests Purchased for State's Park System. Humboldt Standard, June 22, 1931.

1932a Receiver Named for Hartsook Inn. Humboldt Standard, January 29, 1932.

1932b Move to Open Coyote Flat Murder Fails. Humboldt Standard, December 30, 1932.

1934a Mrs. Minnie Peet Succumbs in Arcata. Humboldt Standard, June 4, 1934:9.

1935a New Mattole Grange Hall Is Dedicated. Humboldt Times, August 12, 1935.

1935b New Logging Operations at Carlotta. Humboldt Standard, August7, 1935.

1937a Rites Held for Indian Woman. Humboldt Standard, April 1, 1937:7.

1937b Conductor and Two Itinerants Escape Death Near Shively. Humboldt Standard, August 6, 1937:1.

1937c Former Humboldt Resident Succumbs. Humboldt Standard, August 28, 1937.

1938a Victim Falls Off Narrow Span. Humboldt Standard, May 30, 1938.

1938b Find Body of River Victim. Humboldt Standard, May 31, 1938.

1938c M'Cann Truck Driver Shot in Skin Chain Row. Humboldt Standard, January 21, 1938.

1938d Hartsook Inn Is Auctioned. Humboldt Standard, October 10, 1938.

1938e Flames Sweep Hostelry to Resist Efforts of Garberville Firemen.

1939a Death Closes Long, Active Career. Humboldt Standard, October 5, 1939.

1939b New Shively Span Opened For Traffic. Humboldt Standard, January 25, 1939.

1939c Helmke Store Name Restored To Alderpoint. Humboldt Standard, June 6, 1939.

1940a Humboldt's Vacation Center Boasts Interesting History. Humboldt Standard, March 30, 1940.

1940b George Burtt, 94, Taken By Death. Humboldt Standard, March 18, 1940.

1940c Death Claims Mrs. Susie Burt, 92. Humboldt Standard, December 13, 1940.

1941a Pioneer, Age 90, Remains Active. Humboldt Standard, April 9, 1941.

1941b Daniel J. East of Iaqua Dies. Humboldt Standard, October 21, 1941.

1947a. Prompt Action By Humboldt Ranch Owner Credited With Saving 11 Lives In Blimp Crash. Humboldt Standard, July 15, 1947.

1947b Jack Ryan Denied Parole. Humboldt Standard, November 8, 1947:1.

1955a Old Eel Rock School Must Serve Again. Humboldt Standard, August 15, 1955:26.

1964a Eye-Witness Story from Stafford Told Standard. Humboldt Standard, December 26, 1964.

1964b Pepperwood Wiped Out, Other Towns Crushed!! Humboldt Standard, December 23, 1964:1.

N.d.a Bull Creek Redwood Park to be Dedicated Sunday. Undated clipping in author's possession.

Humboldt State University Library

2020a [Photo of] Three States Good Roads Rally, Dinsmore enroute to Eureka. Special collections photo #1999.07.3157. Web page. Electronic document, http://library.humboldt. edu/humco/holdings/photodetail. php?S=dinsmore&CS=All%20Collections&RS=ALL%20Regions&PS=Any%20Photographer&ST=ALL%20 words&SW=&C=14&R=1 accessed on August 2, 2020.

Humboldt Times

1854a Mattole River and Valley. Humboldt Times, September 23, 1854:2.

1854b Indians. Humboldt Times, October 28, 1854:2.

1855a Immigration. Humboldt Times, July 21, 1855:2.

1855b Humboldt County Lands. Humboldt Times, June 9, 1855:2.

1855c Indian Hostilities—Three Men Killed. Humboldt Times, January 20, 1855:2.

1856a Eel River Correspondence. Humboldt Times, November 1, 1856:2.

1856b For Shelter Cove. Humboldt Times, July 19, 1856:2.

1856c Murder of J. P. Albee by Indians. Humboldt Times, November 15, 1863:2.

1857a A Digger Shot by Diggers. Humboldt Times, September 26, 1857:2.

1857b. Mendocino reservation Again. Humboldt Times, September 5, 1857:2.

1858a Serious Indian Troubles—Removal or Extermination. Humboldt Times, September 18, 1858:2.

1858b Indian Excitement.—Two White Men Wounded.—Two Indians Killed. Humboldt Times, June 12, 1858:2.

1858c More Indian Outrages.—Man Shot Down in the Trail. Humboldt Times, June 26, 1858:2.

1858d Mad River Indians. Humboldt Times, June 26, 1856:2.

1858e Our Indians. Humboldt Times, July 17, 1858:2.

1858f Fight with the Indians.—One White Man Killed.—Ten Mules Scattered and Missing. Humboldt Times, July 17, 1858:2.

1858g Fight with Indians.—One Man Killed and One Wounded. Humboldt Times, August 7, 1858:2.

1858h What's to be Done? Humboldt Times, August 7, 1858:2.

1858i Horrible Murder by Indians. Humboldt Times, September 18, 1858:2.

1858j Serious Indian Trouble.—Removal or Extermination. Humboldt Times, September 18, 1858:2.

1858k Indian Troubles. Humboldt Times, September 18, 1858:2.

1858l Action of the Citizens of Union. Humboldt Times, September 18, 1858:2.

1858m Gone to Work Right. Humboldt Times, September 18, 1858:2.

1858n No Authority. Humboldt Times, September 25, 1858:2.

1858p Movement of Troops. Humboldt Times, October 23, 1858.

1858q Fight with the Indians. Humboldt Times, October 30, 1858:2.

1858r Ranch Burned by Indians. Humboldt Times, October 30, 1858:2.

1858s Indian Matters. Humboldt Times, November 20, 1858:2.

1858t The Volunteer Expedition in this County. Humboldt Times, November 27, 1858:2.

1858u Volunteers. Humboldt Times, December 4, 1858:2.

1858v Mass Meeting in Mattole Valley. Humboldt Times, September 18, 1858:2.

1858w Trouble with the Indians in Mattole. Humboldt Times, June 19, 1858:2.

1858x Letter from Yager Creek. Humboldt Times, October 9, 1858:2.

1859a The Murdered Men. Humboldt Times, December 24, 1859:2.

1859b From the Volunteers. Humboldt Times, January 1, 1859:2.

1859c Another Volunteer Wounded. Humboldt Times, January 29, 1859:2.

1859d Fight with Indians.—Three Men Severely Wounded. Humboldt Times, January 29, 1859:2.

1859e Our Indian War. Humboldt Times, January 29, 1859:2.

1859f Indian War. Humboldt Times, March 12, 1859:2.

1859g Send Them Out. Humboldt Times, April 23, 1859:2.

1859h More Trouble with Indians. Humboldt Times, May 14, 1859:2.

1859i Another Volunteer Company. Humboldt Times, May 28, 1859:2.

1859j One of the Redwood Indians . . . . Humboldt Times, June 4, 1859:2.

1859k Mattole Valley. Humboldt Times, November 19, 1859:2.

1860a House Burned by Indians. Humboldt Times, October 13, 1860:2.

1860b Re Built. Humboldt Times, September 16, 1860.

1861a Cleaned out Again. Humboldt Times, June 15, 1861:3.

1861b Another White Man Murdered by Indians in the County. Humboldt Times, June 29, 1861:2.

1861c A Large Haul. Humboldt Times, February 9, 1861:3.

1861d Apprenticing Indians. Humboldt Times, March 9, 1861:2.

1861e Kidnapping. Humboldt Times, November 2, 1861:2.

1861f Lieutenant Collins' Command. Humboldt Times, June 22, 1861:2.

1861g Attack by Indians. Humboldt Times, January 19, 1861:2.

1861h Massacre and Plunder by Indians on Upper Eel River and Van Duzen's Fork. Humboldt Times, February 3, 1861:2.

1861i Article about Indians killing cattle on Cooksey Ranch. Humboldt Times, October 12, 1861:3.

1861j Indian Difficulties. Humboldt Times, December 14, 1861:2.

1862a Rain at Hoopa. Humboldt Times, July 12, 1862:3.

1862b Fort Seward. Humboldt Times, February 15, 1862.

1862c Court-Martial. Humboldt Times, July 26, 1862:3.

1862d Murder of J. P. Albee by Indians. Humboldt Times, November 15, 1862:2.

1862f Indian Outrages. Humboldt Times, July 12, 1862:3.

1862g Two Citizens Murdered by Savages. Humboldt Times, July 12, 1862:3.

1862h The Attack at Upper Mad River Ford. Humboldt times, July19, 1962:2.

1863a All Right. Humboldt Times, January 3, 1863:3.

1863b Revenge. Humboldt Times, January 24, 1863:2.

1863c Took in Twenty. Humboldt Times, March 7, 1863:2.

1863d Two Indians Killed. Humboldt Times, January 11, 1863:2

1863e The Mountaineers. Humboldt Times, September 12, 1863:2.

1864d Good Haul of Diggers. Humboldt Times, January 11, 1863:2.

1864a Our Indian War. Humboldt Times, April 2, 1864:3.

1864b Our Mails Again. Humboldt Times, December 3, 1864:2.

1864c Hard on the Indians. Humboldt Times, February 20, 1864:3.

1864d Murdered by Indians. Humboldt Times, March 5, 1864:2.

1864e Indian Matters at Mattole. Humboldt Times, September 17, 1864:2.

1864f Iaqua Correspondence. Humboldt Times, August 27, 1864:2.

1866a Letter from Mattole. Humboldt Times, April 14, 1866:2.

1866b Letter from Mattole. Humboldt Times, May 28, 1866.

1866c Abandoned. Humboldt Times, September 15, 1866:3.

1867a Hog Ranch For Sale [ad]. Humboldt Times, May 18, 1867:2.

1867b Road Improvements. Humboldt Times, July 6, 1867:3.

1869a After the Redskins. Humboldt Times, April 3, 1869.

1869b Mattole Items. Humboldt Times, August 28, 1869:3.

1869c Another Indian Depredation. Humboldt Times, January 23, 1869:3.

1874a Hydesville and Van Duzen Road. Humboldt Times, March 4, 1874:3.

1874b A New Enterprise. Humboldt Times, February 7, 1874:3.

1875a The Kneeland Prairie and Round Valley Road. Humboldt Times, May 18, 1875.

1876a Letter to editor. Humboldt Times, July 7, 1876.

1877a Notes from Hydesville. Humboldt Times, December 1, 1877:1.

1878a Exports from Shelter Cove. Humboldt Times, September 14, 1878:3.

1878b Petrolia Is Swept By Flame. Humboldt Times, April 27, 1878.

1879a Supervisors. Humboldt Times, May 14, 1879:3.

1880a Camp Grant. Humboldt Times, February 25, 1880.

1880b Iron Railing for Mackey graves article. Humboldt Times, December 18, 1880.

1880c Pleasure Resort. Humboldt Times, July 14, 1880.

1881a Strong's Summer Resort. Humboldt Times, June 25, 1881.

1891a Fruitland article. Humboldt Times, September 2, 1891:3.

1891b Bank of Eureka foreclosure article. Humboldt Times, June 23, 1891:3.

1892a The Fruitland Company, Incorporated. Humboldt Times, February 27, 1892:2.

1892b Real Estate Transfers. Humboldt Times, March 27, 1892:2.

1892c Humboldt's Orchards. Humboldt Times, August 21, 1892:4

1894a Article about the Fruitland Company. Humboldt Times, February 11, 1894:4.

1894b Allard ad for Fruitland property. Humboldt Times, October 10, 1894:2.

1895a Lawsuit article. Humboldt Times, February 16, 1895:4.

1896a Enterprise Etchings. Humboldt Times, February 2, 1896:1.

1903a Asbill-Ellery. Humboldt Times, June 7, 1903:9.

1907a Columbia's Dead Number 90. Humboldt Times, July 23, 1907:1, 3.

1907b Shelter Cove Survivors. Humboldt Times, July 23, 1907:3.

1907c Blames Officers of Both Boats. Humboldt Times, September 7, 1907:1.

1909a Old Pioneer Is Dead. Humboldt Times, October 31, 1909.

1911a Victim of Three Painful Accidents in One Hour. Humboldt Times, July 11, 1911.

1911b Leaves Bequest To Mrs. Tooby. Humboldt Times, January 8, 1911.

1911c Entire Town of Carlotta Is Sold. Humboldt Times, March 29, 1911:1.

1911d Cherries Are Now Ripe . . . . Humboldt Times, June 11, 1912:3.

1911e Poison Oak Aground. Humboldt Times, February 22, 1911:8.

1911f Craft Will Float Again. Humboldt Times, February 23, 1911:8.

1911g River Plays False. Humboldt Times, February 26, 1911:3.

1911h Will Attempt Salvage. Humboldt Times, March 11, 1911:8.

1911i Derrick Ready to Operate. Humboldt Times, March 17, 1911:4.

1911j Poison Oak to Float. Humboldt Times, March 22, 1911:5.

1911k Freight and Horse Are Lost in Deep Hole. Humboldt Times, March 31, 1911:6.

1911l Boat Stranded up River. Humboldt Times, October 5, 1911:3.

1912a Modern Hotel at Fort Seward Will Be Opened Within Ninety Days. Humboldt Times, August 7, 1912.

1912b Famous Poison Oak May Run on Humboldt Bay. Humboldt Times, October 5, 1912:1.

1913a Chico Construction Co. Is Awarded Contract to Build Dyerville Bridge. Humboldt Times, March 12, 1913.

1913b Humboldt Strawberries to go by Parcels Post. Humboldt Times, January 5, 1913.

1913c Hindley Will Build Bull Creek-Mattole Road. Humboldt Times, August 29, 1913.

1913d Boys Testify for Father in $5000 Suit. Humboldt Times, November 5, 1913.

1913e Dinsmores Deny Story of Plaintiff. Humboldt Times, November 6, 1913.

1913f Young Homesteader Is Awarded $2,500 Damages by Jurors. Humboldt Times, November 7, 1913.

1913g Earl burns' Young Son Commences Suit against Dinsmores for $10,000. Humboldt Times, November 8, 1913.

1913h Albert Schmidt Postmaster for Eighteen Years. Humboldt Times, March 15, 1913.

1914a Old Timer! Do You Remember When~. Humboldt Times, May 31, 1931.

1915a Albert F. Etter Gets Gold Medal. Humboldt Times, December 21, 1915.

1916a Vessel is Looted of Articles of Value by Crew. Humboldt Times, June 18, 1916:1.

1918a "Hobo Jack" Trainman's Mascot Pays Visit to Eel Rock People. Humboldt Times, July 22, 1918:6.

1918b Showers Pass Manganese Mine Ready to Ship. Humboldt Times, June 9, 1918.

1919a Shelter Cove Is Now Tent City of 1000. Humboldt Times, August 8, 1919.

1919b Brief Outline of the Life of W. H. Roscoe, Pioneer of Mattole. Humboldt Times, January 18, 1919.

1919c Indians Stole Durham Bull and Held Potlach; Bull Creek Named. Humboldt Times, March 23, 1919.

1920a Blaze Destroys Blocksburg Store. Humboldt Times, July 18, 1920.

1921a Shively Burns As Firemen Work. Humboldt Times, September 22, 1921.

1922a Boys Thrown into Creek by Old Bridge. Humboldt Times, March 12, 1922.

1923a Garberville News Briefly Told. Humboldt Times, May 23, 1923:8.

1924a Humboldt County in fight with Lumber Co. for Trees. Humboldt Times, November 25, 1924.

1925a Highlights on Contest over Redwoods Seen in Court Room. Humboldt Times, February 12, 1925:2.

1925b People Win Redwoods in Days Fight. Humboldt Times, February 12, 1925:1-2.

1925c Day by Day Synopsis of Coyote Flat Murder Mystery. Humboldt Times, October 24, 1925:3.

1926a Friends Raise Funds to Reimburse Jack Ryan and His Father. Humboldt Times, April 22, 1926.

1928a Jack Ryan Pleads Guilty to Charges in Two Girl Cases. Humboldt Times, September 11, 1928:1-2.

1928b Jack Confesses Murders at Coyote Flat; Is Given Life. Humboldt Times, September 13, 1928:1, 11.

1929a Burris Bros. Announce Big Project. Humboldt Times, April 23, 1929.

1930a Anthropologist Conducts Indian Research Work. Humboldt Times, August 16, 1930:7.

1930b Shively Ferry Cable Snaps. Humboldt Times, March 2, 1930.

1930c Inquest Held for Clarence Burt. Humboldt Times, April 14, 1930:3.

1931a Humboldt Tomatoes Shipped. Humboldt Times, September 12, 1931.

1931b Eureka Firm To Build New Dyerville Bridge. Humboldt Times, April 30, 1931.

1931c Naming of World's Tallest Tree to Feature Dedication of Dyerville Redwood Park. Humboldt Times, September 10, 1931.

1932a When Shively Ferry Sank. Humboldt Times, February 16, 1932.

1932b Old Timer Do You Remember When. Humboldt Times, September 1, 1932.

1932c Famous Author Visits Benbow. Humboldt Times, August 3, 1932.

1935a Will Visit Old Home in Walls, Shetland Islands. Humboldt Times, May 10, 1935.

1935b Grange Hall Burns in Upper Mattole. Humboldt Times, January 1, 1935.

1935c Young and Ambitious at 76. Humboldt Times, September 12, 1935.

1935d Young and Ambitious at 76. Humboldt Times, September 12, 1935.

1937a Survivor of Massacre Dies. Humboldt Times, January 24, 1937.

1937b Well Known Members of N.W.P. Meet Terrible Fate; Locomotive Turns Over. Humboldt Times, August 7, 1937:1.

1937c Showers Pass Post Office Closes Doors. Humboldt Times, March 7, 1937.

1938a "A Poet of the Redwoods." Humboldt Times, June 10, 1938.

1939a Death of Thomas Bell Brings To Light Strange Early Day Story. Humboldt Times, May 14, 1939:12.

1939b Unconditional Decree for Former Official Signed by President Roosevelt. Humboldt Times, March 11, 1939:1.

1940a Last Survivor of Pioneer Days Massacre Succumbs. Humboldt Times, January 20, 1940.

1940b Yager and Jordan Creeks to be Future Log Source. Humboldt Times, October 4, 1940.

1948a Shively Maps Bridge Drive. Humboldt Times, January 25, 1948:1.

1949a Workman Washed Off Shively Span. Humboldt Times, February 23, 1949.

1952a Directory of Humboldt County Lumber Mills. Humboldt Times, January 13, 1952:8, 10.

1955a Blocksburg article. Humboldt Times, August 18, 1955.

1956a Blaze Destroys Historic Hotel in Fort Seward! Humboldt Times, April 29, 1956:1.

1957a Mattole Bridge Collapses. Humboldt Times, May 12, 1957.

1960a Ft. Seward Lumberman Bids High. Humboldt Times, August 5, 1960.

1960b Five Injured When Train Hits Truck Near Fort Seward. Humboldt Times, October 8, 1960:1.

1962a Maple Creek Willie's Generosity Provides Indian Scholarships. Humboldt Times, October 11, 1962:17.

1964a Warehouse, Gasoline Station, 3 Homes Burn; One Man Hurt. Humboldt Times, February 22, 1964.

Humboldt Weekly Standard
1891a Assessment Notice. Humboldt Weekly Standard, August 13, 1891:2.

1891b Notice of Assessment. Humboldt Weekly Standard, July 9, 1891:3.

Humboldt Weekly Times
1874a Wagon Road Bill. Humboldt Weekly Times, March 7, 1874:2.

1874b Wagon Road Bill. Humboldt Weekly Times, March 7, 1874:2.

1875a Van Duzen bridge article. Humboldt Weekly Times, January 2, 1875:3.

1881a Tan bark article. Humboldt Weekly Times, July 30, 1881.

Hunt, Albert R.
2004 Field interview with Jerry Rohde, April 4, 2004.

Hunt, Aurora
1962 The Army of The Pacific And the Unsung Valor of its Men. Montana: The Magazine of Western History, Spring 1962:49-61.

Hunt, Chris
1998. Ettersburg: Nothing Left Today. Times-Standard, August 28, 1998.

Hunt, James A., and Arthur E. Johnson
2001 Family Stories. Humboldt Historian, Fall 2001:6-15.

Hunt, L. C.
1982 Report on six-month's old Fort Humboldt. Humboldt Historian, May-June 1982:12.

Inforuptcy.com
2021a Case number: 1:19-bk-10071 – Fruitland Vineyards LLC Northern California Bankruptcy Court. Web page. Electronic document, https://www.inforuptcy.com/browse-filings/california-northern-bankruptcy-court/1:19-bk-10071/bankruptcy-case-fruitland-ridge-vineyards-llc accessed on May 26, 2021.

Impr. [pseud.)
1858 Indian Women.—Their Treatment. Trinity Weekly Journal, January 9, 1858:2.

Indian Historian
1965 Maple Creek Willie . . . . The Indian Historian, February 1965:8.

Indian War Papers
1860a Affidavit of James McAtee . . . March 8, 1860. Inventory of the Military Department. Adjutant General. Indian War Papers, folder F3753.555.

1860b Petition by citizens of Yager Creek and Van Dousnes [sic] Fork to Governor Downey to call to active service the Humboldt Cavalry Company of volunteers to protect citizens from Indians. Written in Hydesville, Humboldt County, February 23, 1860. Inventory of the Military Department. Adjutant General. Indian War Papers, folder F3753.439.

International News Service
1915 Press Reference Library. New York: International News Service.

Irvine, Leigh H.
1915 History of Humboldt County, California. Los Angeles: Historic Record Co.

"J"
1880 Letter from Petrolia. Ferndale Enterprise, December 9, 1880:3.

Jackson, Dorothy
1984 Letter to the Editor. Humboldt Historian, November-December 1984:27.

James, Jerry
1921[?]a Statement regarding L. K. Wood and Gregg Party. Photocopy available, as part of the "Wiyot History Papers," in the Special Collections, Humboldt State University Library, Arcata.

James, Nona
1984 Interview with Mary Anderson, September 12, 1984. Photocopy in possession of author.

Jameson, B. T., T. D. Felt, and Kennerly Dobyns
1852 Letter to "Fellow Citizens," January 15, 1852. Original at the Humboldt County Historical Society, archived as object # 2014.054.07.

Jeans, Ivan
1984 Pete McCloud: Mad River Recluse. Trinity [Yearbook] 1984.

Jepson, Willis Linn, et al.
1911 California Tanbark Oak. U. S. Department of Agriculture, Forest Service, Bulletin 75.

Johnson, Lauren M.
2021 UC Berkeley removes the name on a school building over an anthropologist's controversial past. Web Page. Electronic document, https://www.cnn.com/2021/01/27/us/uc-berkeley-removes-kroeber-from-anthropology-building-trnd/index.html accessed on June 28, 2021.

Johnson, Warren B.
1887 From the Pacific to the Atlantic: Being and Account of a Journey Overland from Eureka, Humboldt County, California, to Webster, Worcester Co., Mass., with a Horse, Carriage, Cow and Dog. Webster, MA: John Cort.

Johnston, Richard
1882 Narrative. Transcription, produced by Richard Roberts, available at the Ferndale Museum, Ferndale, CA.

Join California
2018a November 6, 1906 General Election. Web Page. Electronic document, http://www.joincalifornia.com/election/1906-11-06 accessed August 2, 2018

Jones, Alice Goen, ed.
1981a Trinity County Historic Sites. Weaverville, CA: Trinity County Historical Society.

Jordan, Mike
    1947a Rolling, Pitching Lightship Marks 'Sign
        Post' To Protect Shipping. Humboldt
        Times, February 9, 1947.
Jorgensen, Skip, and Mary Ellen Boynton
    2019 When butter was gold. Our Story, March-
        April 2019.
Kanahele, Charlene
    1990 Renfroe's mountain hospitality. Humboldt
        Historian, January-February 1990:12-13.
Karshner, Gayle, ed.
    1987a The Way It Was, Humboldt County
        Volume IV. Arcata: The Union.
Kaufman, George S., and Edna Ferber
    N. d. Dinner at Eight. New York: Samuel
        French, Inc.
Keesey, Beatrice
    1982 Letter to the Editor. Humboldt Historian,
        November-December 1982:21.
Kelsey, C. E.
    1971 Census of Non-reservation California
        Indians, 1905 - 1906. Berkeley: Archaeo-
        logical Research Facility, Department of
        Anthropology.
Kelsey, Arthur
    1982. Emergency—Mountain-country style . . . .
        Humboldt Historian, September-October
        1982:9.
Kemp, Bruce
    1983 Native American History: The Lolangkok
        Sinkyone in: Humboldt Redwoods State
        Park General Plan Cultural Resources
        Element.
Kilkenny, Matina
    N.d. Note regarding the name "Redway."
        Photocopy in author's possession.
Kinman, Seth
    2010 Seth Kinman's Manuscript and Scrapbook.
        Ferndale, CA: Ferndale Museum.
Kircher, John C. and Gordon Morrison
    1993 Ecology of Western Forests. Boston:
        Houghton Mifflin Company.
Kneiss, Gilbert
    1956 Redwood Railways. Berkeley: Howell
        North.
Knight, Mrs. John [Topsy]
    [1921?]a Statement regarding reservations and
        attacks by whites on Indians. Photocopy
        available, as part of the "Wiyot History
        Papers," in the Special Collections, Hum-
        boldt State University Library, Arcata.
    [1921]b Statement regarding reservations and
        attacks by whites of Indians living on Eel
        River. Photocopy available, as part of the
        "Wiyot History Papers," in the Special
        Collections, Humboldt State University
        Library, Arcata.
Knuth, Margaret
    1989 Shipwreck survivor tells her story.
        Humboldt Historian, March-April 1989:3-5.
Krei, Melvin A.
    N.d.a Sinking of the Emidio. Copy of typescript
        in author's possession.
Kroeber, A. L.
    1908a Notes on California Folk-Lore. Journal of
        American Folk-Lore xxi:37-38.
    1919 Notes and Queries: Sinkyone Tales.
        Journal of American Folk-Lore, April-June
        1919.

    1925 Handbook of the Indians of California.
        Washington: Government Printing Office.
    1929a Pliny Earle Goddard. American
        Anthropologist, New Series, (31)1:1-8.
    2021a The Nature of Land-Holding Groups in
        Aboriginal California. Web page. Electronic
        document, https://digitalassets.lib.berkeley.
        edu/anthpubs/ucb/proof/pdfs/ucas056-
        003.pdf accessed on February 2, 2021.
    1976b Yurok Myths. University of California
        Press, Berkeley and Los Angeles, California.
    1997 Papers, 1869-1972. Microfilm available at
        the Humboldt State University Library,
        Arcata.
Kühl, Stefan
    2000 Nazi Connection: Eugenics, American
        Racism, and German National Socialism.
        Oxford: Oxford University Press.
L. [pseud.]
    1877a Communication. Evening Star, July 24,
        1877:1.
Lacey, James, and Williamson Murray
    2013 Moment of Battle: The Twenty Clashes
        That Changed the World. New York:
        Bantam Books.
La Motte, H. D.
    N.d. Statement of H. D. La Motte. Original at
        the Bancroft Library, University of Califor-
        nia Berkeley.
Larribie [pseud.]
    1877a From the South. Evening Star, May 10,
        1877:1.
Larson, William E. et al.
    2011 Archaeology of the Smith Creek
        Watershed, Humboldt County, California.
        Archaeological Research Center, Depart-
        ment of Anthropology, California State
        University, Sacramento.
LeBaron, Gaye
    2019a Glory days of North Coast railroads are
        history. Web page. Electronic docu-
        ment, https://www.pressdemocrat.com/
        news/2962068-181/glory-days-of-north-
        coast accessed on April1, 2019.
Leeper, David Rohrer
    1950 The Argonauts of 'Forty-Nine. Columbus,
        OH: Long's College Book Company.
Legier, Jules
    1958. Mattole Indians: 1854 to the Present.
        Photocopy of paper for History 198 class,
        on file under "History—Settlement Period
        1850-75 Indian Wars" in the Humboldt
        County Collection, Humboldt State Uni-
        versity Library, Arcata, CA.
Lentell, J. N.
    1898 Official Map of Humboldt County
        California. N. p.
    1901 Map of Humboldt County 1901. San
        Francisco.
    1905 Map of Mendocino County. San Francisco.
Lesher, David
    1996 Dead Man's Name Finally to Be Cleared.
        Los Angeles Times, April 15, 1996:A1,
        A18-A19.
Lewis, Al, et. al.
    1991 Interview by Jerry Rohde with Al Lewis,
        Ed Lewis, and Blanche Lewis Tompkins,
        July 29, 1991.

Lewis, Ed
2001 Bull Creek, as I saw it in 1931. Photocopy in possession of author.
Lewis, Oscar, ed.
1966 The Quest for Qual-A-Wa-Loo. Oakland, CA: Holmes Book Company.
Library of Congress
2019a Washington as Land Speculator. Web site. Electronic document, https://www.loc.gov/collections/george-washington-papers/articles-and-essays/george-washington-survey-and-mapmaker/washington-as-land-speculator/ accessed on July 20, 2019.
library.humboldt.edu
2016 Tooby and Prior Photo Album – Finding Aid. Web page. Electronic document, https://library.humboldt.edu/humco/holdings/ToobyAid.htm accessed on October 31, 2016.
lighthousefriends.com
2018 Punta Gorda Lighthouse. Web page. Electronic document, http://lighthousefriends.com/light.asp?ID=63 accessed on August 10, 2018.
2019 Cape Mendocino Lighthouse. Web page. Electronic document, http://www.lighthousefriends.com/light.asp?ID=25 accessed on June 24, 2019.
Literary Digest
1918 A Million from Novels. Literary Digest, March 2, 1918:32-33.
Logan, Jane
1964a Memories of Jane Logan. Humboldt County Historical Society Newsletter, May-June 1964.
London, Jack
2019 Navigating Four Horses North of the Bay. Sunset Magazine Web page. Electronic document, https://www.sunset.com/travel/california/jack-london-archival-essay accessed on February 7, 2019.
Long, Clarence D.
1960 Wages and Earnings in the United States 1860-1890. Princeton, NJ: Princeton University Press.
Look Robert C.
N. d. Diary. Notes made from original by author on February 1, 1992.
Lost Coast Outpost
2015a Karuk Leader Amos Tripp Passes; Services at Redwood Acres Monday. Web page. Electronic document, http://lostcoastoutpost.com/2014/apr/12/karuk-leader-amos-tripp-passes-services-redwood-ac/ accessed on April 26, 2015.
Loud, Llewellyn L.
1918 Ethnogeography and Archaeology of the Wiyot Territory. University of California Publications in American Archaeology and Ethnology 14:3.
Lowry, Mabel
1982 The History of the Telephone in Bear River Valley. Photocopy in author's possession.
1986 Early Ranch Days in Bear river Valley. Humboldt Historian, November-December 1986:12-13, 16-17.

N.d. The Big Bear River Fire of 1945. Photocopy in author's possession.
1995 Bear River School. Humboldt Historian, Fall 1995:17-18.
lyricsplayground.com
2018 Lyrics to Dardanella. Web Page. Electronic document, https://lyricsplayground.com/alpha/songs/d/dardanella.html accessed on December 5, 2018.
M. H. [pseud.]
1877 From "The Island" to Eagle Prairie. West Coast Signal, August 15, 1877:1.
Machi, Mario
1984 Gem of the Lost Coast: A Narrative History of Shelter Cove. Eureka: Eureka Printing Co., Inc.
Machi, Mary Ann
2012a The Sinking of the Yacht Flamingo. Humboldt Historian, Fall 2012:36-38.
2015a Email communication with Jerry Rohde dated October 19, 2015.
2015b Shelter Cove Chronology. Copy in possession of author.
2015c Robarts Family Info. Copy in possession of author.
2015d Email communication with Jerry Rohde dated November 10, 2015.
2015e Email communication with Jerry Rohde dated November 26, 2015.
Machi, Mike
2012a Ray family tree. Copy in possession of author.
Madera Tribune
1924a Memorial to Franklin Lane. Madera Tribune, August 25, 1924:3.
1947a Bessie Blimp Bangs Hilltop. Madera Tribune, July 15, 1947:1.
Madley, Benjamin
2016a An American Genocide: The United States and the California Indian Catastrophe, 1846-1873. New Haven: Yale University Press.
Makepeace, Anne
2002 Edward S. Curtis: Coming to Light. Washington DC: National Geographic Society.
Malte-Brun, Conrad
2015[1824] Universal Geography: or A Description of All Parts of the World, on a New Plan, According to the Great Natural Divisions of the globe; Accompanied with Analytical, Synoptical, and Elementary Tables. Web page. Electronic document, https://archive.org/details/universalgeograp07malt accessed on August 5, 2015.
Margolin, Malcolm
1981 The Way We Lived. Berkeley: Heyday Books.
Marine Insight
2020 Dry Docking of Ships – Understanding Stability and Docking Plan. Web page. Electronic Document, http://ernielb.blogspot.com/2009/07/enoch-percival-french-and-newton-bishop.html accessed on August 5, 2020.

Mark West Area Chamber of Commerce
    2020   Mark West Area History. Web page. Electronic document, http://www.mark-west.org/history/markwesthistory.cfm accessed on August 24, 2020.

Martin, Mel
    N.d.   Interview with Jerry Rohde

Martin, Wallace
    1983   Sail and Steam on the Northern California Coast 1850 – 1900. San Francisco: National Maritime Museum Association.

Mathison, Ray
    1998   The History of Alderpoint. Eureka: Eureka Printing Co.

Mattole Restoration Council
    2018.   Mission and History. Web page. Electronic document, http://www.mattole.org/about/mission-history/ accessed on August 12, 2018.

Mays, Tom
    2018   "The California Mutiny." Unpublished manuscript, January 11, 2018. Microsoft Word file.

McBride, Viola Russ
    1995a   How Ranches Got Their Names. N. p.: Viola Russ McBride.
    1998a   Settlers and Indians on Bear River: Tales Remembered. Humboldt Historian, Summer 1998:20-25.

McLean, Louise
    1917   Discovery of Humboldt Bay. Overland Monthly (LXX) 2.

McCloskey, Bruce
    1982   Letter to editor. Humboldt Historian, September-October 1982:16.

McClure, William, and Ruth McClure
    2013   The Japanese Ambassador's Visit. Humboldt Historian, Winter 2013:34-37.

McCormick, Evelyn
    1963a   Dwight Felt Sr. article. Humboldt Times, June 2, 1963:7.
    1986a   Locomotive proved fatal to nine men. Humboldt Historian, March-April 1986:7-8.
    N.d.a   Living With The Giants. Rio Dell: Evelyn McCormick.
    N.d.b.   Dobbyn School: A History Traced. Humboldt Beacon, n.d.

McGuire, Michael
    1979   Petrolia cemetery is being brought back to life. Times-Standard, June 5, 1979.

McKinney, John
    2018   Wildest Coastline in California. Web page. Electronic document, http://articles.latimes.com/1992-08-09/travel/tr-6108_1_king-range-coast accessed on June 1, 2018.

McNamara, Robert
    2015   Doughface. Web page. Electronic document, http://history1800s.about.com/od/1800sglossary/g/Doughface.htm accessed on August 9, 2015.

McTavish [pseud.?]
    1885a   Down the Coast. Daily Humboldt Standard, September 30, 1885:3.
    1885b   Englewood to Rio Dell. Daily Humboldt Standard, July 21, 1885:3.
    1885c   Camp Grant. Daily Humboldt Standard, July 16, 1885:3.
    1885d   On the Road. Daily Humboldt Standard, June 3, 1885:3.
    1885e   Phillipsville. Daily Humboldt Standard, June 30, 1885:3.
    1885f   By Rail. Daily Humboldt Standard, May 27, 1885:3.
    1885g   Blocksburg. Daily Humboldt Standard, June 2, 1885:3.
    1885h   Bridgeville. Daily Humboldt Standard, May 29, 1885:3.
    1885i   Down the South Fork. Daily Humboldt Standard, June 19, 1985:3.

measuringworth.com
    2016a   Web page. Electronic document, https://www.measuringworth.com/uscompare/relativevalue.php accessed on July 28, 2016.
    2016b   Web page. Electronic document, https://www.measuringworth.com/uscompare/relativevalue.php accessed on August 21. 2016.
    2016c   Web page. Electronic document, https://www.measuringworth.com/us-compare/relativevalue.php accessed on October 31, 2016.
    2017a   Web page. Electronic document, https://www.measuringworth.com/uscompare/relativevalue.php accessed on August 7, 2017.
    2018a   Web page. Electronic document, https://www.measuringworth.com/calculators/uscompare/result.php?year source=1864&amount=270000.00&year result=2017 accessed on March 27, 2018.
    2020a   Web page. Electronic document, https://www.measuringworth.com/calculators/uscompare/relativevalue.php accessed on November 16, 2020.

Melendy, Howard B.
    1962a   The Overland Automobile Stage: 1908-1914. Blue Lake Advocate, November 1, 1962:2.
    1962b   The Overland Automobile Stage: 1908-1914. Blue Lake Advocate, October 25, 1962:2.
    1962c   The Overland Automobile Stage: 1908-1914. Blue Lake Advocate, November 22, 1962:2.
    1962d   The Overland Automobile Stage: 1908-1914. Blue Lake Advocate, November 29, 1962:2.
    1962e   The Overland Automobile Stage: 1908-1914. Blue Lake Advocate, November 8, 1962:2.

Merriam, C. Hart
    1918a   The Acorn, a Possibly Neglected Source of Food. National Geographic Magazine (34)2 (August 1918):129-137.
    1921a   California Journal 1921, vol. 1. Photocopy at the Cultural Resources Facility, Humboldt State University, Arcata.
    1922a   California Journal 1922, vol. 1. Photocopy at the Cultural Resources Facility, Humboldt State University, Arcata.
    1923a   California Journal 1923, vol. 1. Photocopy at the Cultural Resources Facility, Humboldt State University, Arcata.

1923b Application of the Athapaskan Term Nung-kahhl. American Anthropologist, vol. 25:276-277.

1966 Ethnographic Notes on California Indian Tribes. Berkeley: University of California Archaeological Research Center 68, part 1.

1976 Ethnogeographic and Ethnosynonymic Date from Northern California Tribes. Contributions to Native California Ethnology from the C. Hart Merriam Collection 1.

1993 C. Hart Merriam Papers Relating to Work with California Indians, 1850-1974. Berkeley: University of California Library Photographic Service, 1993.

Merriam, C. Hart, and Zenaida Merriam Talbot
1974 Boundary Descriptions of California Indian Stocks and Tribes. Berkeley: Archaeological Research Facility, Department of Anthropology.

Merriam, John C.
1938 "Forest Windows" in Published Papers and Addresses of John Campbell Merriam, vol. 3. Washington: The Carnegie Institution of Washington, 1897-1903.

Merriam-Webster
2019a Jehu. Web page. Electronic document, https://www.merriam-webster.com/dictionary/jehu accessed on June 24, 2015.

Metsker, Charles F.
1949 Metsker's Atlas of Humboldt County, California. Tacoma, WA: Charles F. Metsker.

militarymuseum.org
2019a The Attack on the SS Emidio. Web page. Electronic document, http://www.militarymuseum.org/Emedio.html accessed on June 24, 2019.

2016a Humboldt Volunteers. Web page. Electronic document, http://www.militarymuseum.org/ accessed on October 9, 2016.

2022a Fort Baker. Web page. Electronic document, http://www.militarymuseum.org/FtBakerI.html accessed on May 30, 2022.

2022b Fort Iaqua. Web page. Electronic document, http://www.fortwiki.com/Fort_Iaqua accessed on May 30, 2022.

Miller, Rowetta Faye Stapp
2013 The Stapp Family Journey to Humboldt County. Humboldt Historian, Winter 2013:24-28.

Mills, Ellen L., ed.
1985 The Papers of John Peabody Harrington in the Smithsonian Institution: 1907 – 1957, Volume 2. White Plains, New York: Kraus International Publications.

Milota, Marilyn Keach
1993a Humboldt County California Abstracts of Death Records 1873-1925, vol. I. Photocopy available at the Humboldt Room, Humboldt County Library, Eureka.

1993b Humboldt County California Abstracts of Death Records 1873-1925, vol. II. Photocopy available at the Humboldt Room, Humboldt County Library, Eureka.

2001a Humboldt County California Abstracts of Death Records 1926-1935. Photocopy available at the Humboldt Room, Humboldt County Library, Eureka.

2003a Humboldt County California Abstracts of Death Records 1936-1947. Photocopy available at the Humboldt Room, Humboldt County Library, Eureka.

Miner, George "Buck"
1996. The Origin of the Mattole: Through the Eyes of a Salmon. Petrolia, CA: George "Buck" Miner.

Monroe, George
1981 Letter to the Editor. Humboldt Historian, November-December 1981:19.

Monroe, Thomas H.
1962 Notes on the Albee Family. Transcription of a speech given to the Humboldt County Historical Society, on file in the Biography collection at the Humboldt County Historical Society, Eureka, CA.

Morgan, Ruth E.
1982a Thorn had the 'worst' school building in California . . . . Humboldt Historian, January-February 1982:16.

1982b Kids tried to terrify their teacher. Humboldt Historian, July-August 1982:15.

1982c Fire came close but it just wouldn't take Whitethorn School. Humboldt Historian, May-June 1982:16.

Morley, S. Griswold
1938 The Covered Bridges of California. Berkeley: University of California Press.

Morrison Carol "Mori"
1991. Interview with Jerry Rohde, March 7, 1991.

Morrison, Clyde
1960 Discrepancies and Corrections: Captain Knyphausen Geer's Memoirs. Humboldt County Historical Society News Letter, May 1960.

1962a Silas W. Morrison: Part III. Humboldt County Historical Society Newsletter, January 1962:9-10.

1962b Silas W. Morrison: Part IV. Humboldt County Historical Society Newsletter, March 1962:13-14.

Morrison, Sid
1979 Ranches in Bear River. Photocopy in possession of author.

Mortenson, Alice
1990 Interview with Jerry Rohde on December 14, 1990.

Moungovan, Mrs. T. O.
1964a Shelter Cove Scalping. Mendocino County Historical Society Newsletter (3)1:7-8.

Mountaineer (pseud.)
1864 Camp Grant Correspondence. Humboldt Times, December 3, 1864:2.

Mulcahy, J. A.
1970 Letter to the Editor. Humboldt Historian, January-February 1970:2.

Mulley, Alice Y.
1999 Wild River. Humboldt Historian, Fall 1999.

Murphey, Edith V. A.
1941 Out of the Past: A True Indian Story. California Historical Society Quarterly 20(4):349-364.

Murray, Ellen
    1987a The hazards and joys of ranch life.
        Humboldt Historian, July-August 1987:10-
        13.
    1987b Adventure started in Redway. Humboldt
        Historian, July-August 1987:14-17.
Myers, Geraldine
    1992 Phone interview with Jerry Rohde.
Nace, Ted
    2003 Gangs of America: The Rise of Corporate
        Power and the Disabling of Democracy. San
        Francisco: Berrett-Koehler Publishers, Inc.
Nash, Glen
    1985a Blue Slide bridges and their builders.
        Humboldt Historian, March-April
        1985:21-22.
    1988a Benbow: the place and family. Humboldt
        Historian, January-February 1988:3-8.
    1988b The triumphs and trials of Benbow.
        Humboldt Historian, March-April
        1988:14-19.
    1989a Blake's colorful roll in phone history.
        Humboldt Historian January-February
        1989:3-5
    1996a Making a Living, Making a Life in
        Humboldt County. Eureka: Globe Prop-
        erties.
Neibur, H.
    1867. Another Route for the Proposed Wagon
        Road. Humboldt Times, December 7,
        1867:2.
Neiss, Gilbert H.
    1956. Redwood Railways. Berkeley:
        Howell-North.
Nelson, Byron Jr.
    1988 Our Home Forever: The Hupa
        Indians of Northern California. Salt Lake
        City: Howe Brothers.
New York Botanical Garden
    2020 Astragalus agnicidus Barneby. Web page.
        Electronic document, http://sweetgum.
        nybg.org/science/world-flora/mono-
        graphs-details/?irn=16879 accessed on
        May 9, 2020.
New York Historical Society
    2016 What does the 'S' in Ulysses S. Grant
        stand for? Web page. Electronic document,
        http://blog.nyhistory.org/ulysses-grant/
        accessed on October 4, 2016.
New York Lumber Trade Journal
    1917 Obituary of John Sedgwick Noyes. New
        York Lumber Trade Journal, September 15,
        1917:28B
New York Times
    1864a The Fort Pillow Massacre. New York
        Times, May 3, 1864.
    2020a Pacific Steamship Walla Walla Wrecked.
        Web page. Electronic document, https://
        timesmachine.nytimes.com/timesma-
        chine/1902/01/04/issue.html accessed
        on May 30, 2020.
Nixon, Stuart
    1966 Redwood Empire. New York: E. P.
        Dutton.
Noble, Nancy Burnell
    1980. Letter Box. Humboldt Historian,
        September-October 1980:15.

Nomad (pseud.)
    1881 Notes from South Fork. Humboldt
        Times, April 22[?], 1881:3.
Nomland, Gladys Ayer
    1931a A Bear River Shaman's Curative Dance.
        American Anthropologist, New Series,
        January-March, 1931:38-41
    1935 Sinkyone Notes. University of California
        Publications in American Archaeology and
        Ethnology (36)2.
    1938 Bear River Ethnography. Anthropological
        Records (2)2.
Nomland, Gladys Ayer, and A. L. Kroeber
    1936 Wiyot Towns. University of California
        Publications in American Archaeology and
        Ethnology (35)5.
North Coast Journal
    2021a Notice of Impending Power to Sell
        Tax-Defaulted Property. North Coast Jour-
        nal, May 27, 2021:32-33.
Northern Californian
    1858a Indian Affairs. Northern Californian,
        December 15, 1858:2.
    1860a Hydesville Volunteers. Northern
        Californian, February 8, 1860:3.
Northrup, Cynthia Clark, and Elaine C. Prange
Turney
    2003 Encyclopedia of Tariff and Trade in U. S.
        History. Westport CT: Greenwood Publish-
        ing Group.
Norton, Jack
    1979 Genocide in Northwestern California:
        When Our Wolds Cried. San Francisco:
        Indian Historian Press.
nps.gov
    2016a About the Homestead Act. Webpage.
        Electronic document, https://www.nps.
        gov/home/learn/historyculture/abouth-
        omesteadactlaw.htm accessed on July 13,
        2016.
OAC
    2018a Guide to C. Hart Merriam Papers, Vol.
        2. Web page. Electronic document, http://
        www.oac.cdlib.org/findaid/ark:/13030/
        tf1z09n5qh/entire_text/ accessed on
        April 2, 2018.
Obarr, O. W.
    1999 Little Histories of the Road: Carlotta. The
        Northwesterner, Spring-Summer 1999:26.
Ober, James
    1973 Humboldt History. Photocopy of student
        paper in Rio Dell file at the Humboldt
        County Historical Society, Eureka.
O'Hara, Susan Pritchard
    N. d. History of Humboldt Redwoods State
        Park. Photocopy available at Special Collec-
        tions, Humboldt State University Library,
        Arcata.
O'Hara, Susan J. P., and Alex Service
    2013 Northwestern Pacific Railroad: Eureka to
        Willits. Charleston, SC: Arcadia Publish-
        ing.
O'Hara, Susan J. P., and Dave Stockton
    2012 Humboldt Redwoods State Park.
        Charleston, SC: Acadia Publishing.
Olsen, Michele
    2020a The First Netherland Fruit & Land
        Culture Association. Copy of manuscript
        in author's possession.

Ommen, Terry L.
  2012 Wild Tulare County: Outlaws, Rogues &
        Rebels. Charleston, SC: The History Press.
Open Jurist
  2015 223 U. S. 365 –Metropolitan Redwood
        Lumber Company v. Charles P. Doe. Web
        page. Electronic document, http://open-
        jurist.org/223/us/365/metropolitan-red-
        wood-lumber-company-v-charles-p-doe- ac-
        cessed on November 11, 2015.
Oregon Daily Journal
  1920 Sad Story of Man Who Saved Bulb
        Industry is Told. Oregon Daily Journal,
        November 28, 1920:4.
Oregon Encyclopedia
  2020a Chemawa Indian School. Web page.
        Electronic document, https://oregonen-
        cyclopedia.org/articles/chemawa_ indi-
        an_boarding_school/#.X1UWsi2z13Q
        accessed on September 6, 2020.
Oregon Historical Quarterly
  2001 Edgar Horner and the Wreck of the *Alaska*.
        Oregon Historical Quarterly 102(1):72-85.
Orton, Richard H.
  1890 Records of California Men in the War
        of Rebellion, 1861 To 1867. Sacramento:
        State Printing Office.
Osgood, Wilfred H.
  1944 Biographical Memoir of Clinton Hart
        Merriam 1855-1942. Web page. Electronic
        document, http://nau.edu/uploadedFiles/
        Centers-Institutes/Merriam-Powell/
        Forms/cmerriam_Osgood_bio_NAS.pdf
        accessed on July 6, 2015.
OSU
  2017 Tanoak. Oregon State University, Oregon
        Wood Innovation Center. Web Page.
        Electronic document, http://owic.oregon-
        state.edu/tanoak-lithocarpus-densiflorus
        accessed on September 13, 2017.
Ott, Melissa
  2017 The Tanoak (Notholithocarpus
        densiflorus), A Significant Santa Cruz Na-
        tive Plant. Web page. Electronic document,
        https://ventana2.sierraclub.org/santacruz/
        node/216 accessed on August 4, 2017.
Pacific Reporter
  1901 Pacific Reporter, volume 62. St. Paul: West
        Publishing Company.
  1918 Nelson v. Thomas et al. Web page.
        Electronic document, https://www.
        google.com/books/edition/The_Pacif-
        ic_Reporter/rvQ7AAAAIAAJ?hl=en&gb-
        pv=1&dq=%22C.+S.+Thomas%22+El-
        la+Thomas%22%22John+Nelson%22&p-
        g=PA398&printsec=frontcover accessed
        on October 31, 2020.
Paddock, Sterling, and Bill Paddock
  2001 Interview with Jerry Rohde, September
        29, 2001.
Palmer, Henrietta
  1879a Letter to Aunt Mary, April 2, 1879.
        Copy on file at the Humboldt County
        Historical Society, Eureka.
  1879b Letter to Aunt Mary, April 30, 1879.
        Copy on file at the Humboldt County
        Historical Society, Eureka.

  1879c Letter to Aunt Mary, May 5, 1879. Copy
        on file at the Humboldt County Historical
        Society, Eureka.
  1879d Letter to Aunt Mary, June 6, 1879. Copy
        on file at the Humboldt County Historical
        Society, Eureka.
  1879e Letter to Aunt Mary, June 25, 1879. Copy
        on file at the Humboldt County Historical
        Society, Eureka.
  1879f Letter to Aunt Mary, August 3, 1879. Copy
        on file at the Humboldt County Historical
        Society, Eureka.
Palmer, T. S.
  1954 In Memoriam: Clinton Hart Merriam. The
        Auk 71:2.
Palmrose, Robert
  2013 Where Is Sherwood? A History of the
        Overland Auto Stage Company. Humboldt
        Historian, Winter 2013:10-19.
Pardee, Mike
  1951 Garberville—Center of Eel river Industry.
        Press-Democrat, December 2, 1951:1,3.
Parker, Stanley
  1984 Brown's Camp and its gentleman boss.
        Humboldt Historian, July-August
        1984:18-20.
  1988a Reflections of Holmes Lumber Company.
        Humboldt Historian, May-June 1988:3-7,
        14.
  N.d. Palco Past: A Social History of Scotia
        and the Pacific Lumber Company: Neigh-
        bors—Brown's Camp. Photocopy on file at
        the Humboldt County Historical Society,
        Eureka, CA.
parks.ca.gov
  2020a Richardson Grove State Park. Web page.
        Electronic document, https://www.parks.
        ca.gov/?page_id=422 accessed on August
        20, 2020.
Parrish, Justine
  1965 Harrowing Rescues Along Southern
        Humboldt Flooded Areas Brought Out
        Best. Humboldt Standard, January 7, 1965.
Parsnips, Louella [pseud.]
  2013a Captain Marble's Matrimonial Mania.
        Humboldt Historian, Spring 2013:26-28.
Pavlik, Bruce, et al.
  1992 Oaks of California. Los Olivos, CA:
        Cachuma Press.
PBS
  2015a Harriman Expedition Retraced: The
        1899 Expedition. Web page. Electronic
        document, http://www.pbs.org/harri-
        man/1899/1899.html accessed on July 6,
        2015.
  2015b Harriman Expedition Retraced: C. Hart
        Merriam 1855-1942. Web page. Electronic
        document, http://www.pbs.org/harri-
        man/1899/1899_part/participantmerri-
        am.html accessed on July 6, 2015.
Peattie, Donald Culross
  1954 Avenue of the Giants. Holiday, March
        1954.
  1991 A Natural History of Western Trees.
        Boston: Houghton Mifflin Company.
Peterson, Stirling
  1984. Personal communication with the author.

Pfremmer, Esterfay
  1976 Letter to the Editor. Humboldt Historian, May-June 1976:33.

Phegley, Milton
  1991 Rain or shine, the Harris Post Office delivered. Humboldt Historian, September-October 1991:18-20.

Pierce, Helen Thomas
  1976 The Thomas-Wimer Family. Photocopy in the biography files, Humboldt County Historical Society, Eureka.

Pinches, Bill
  2006 In-person interview with Jerry Rohde, November 3, 2006.

Platt, Tony
  2019a. Saving the Redwoods: The Eugenic Connection. Web page. Electronic document: https://www.homeworkmarket.com/sites/default/files/qx/16/02/16/03/platt_saving_the_redwoods_the_eugenic_connection.doc accessed on December 5, 2019.

Polk
  1950 Polk's Eureka (California) City Directory 1949-1950 Including Arcata and Humboldt County. San Francisco: R. L. Polk & Co.

Polk-Husted
  1914 Eureka City and Humboldt County Directory 1914-15. Web page. Electronic document, https://www.google.com/books/edition/Polk_Husted_Directory_Co_s_Eureka_City_a/pMZLAQAAIAAJ?hl=en&gbpv=1 accessed on November 1, 2020.

postalhistory.com
  2016a Post Offices California Redcrest. Webpage. Electronic document, http://www.postalhistory.com/postoffices.asp?task=display&searchtext=redcrest&state=CA&county=&searchtype=word accessed on July 10, 2016.

Powers, Alfred
  1949 Redwood Country. New York: Duell, Sloan & Pierce.

Powers, Stephen
  1872a The Northern California Indians, No.1. Overland Monthly (8)4.
  1872b Afoot and Alone; A Walk from Sea to Sea by the Southern Route. Hartford, CT: Columbian Book Company.
  1976[1877] Tribes of California. Berkeley: University of California Press.

Pritchard, Margaret
  1987a Dyerville gone but its history lives. Humboldt Historian, March-April 1987:9-13, 16.
  1987b Business end of Dyerville experience. Humboldt Historian, May-June 1987:18-21.
  1987c Dyerville crossing had its perils. Humboldt Historian, July-August 1987:18-21.
  1987d Dyerville: stage roads to highway. Humboldt Historian, September-October 1987:22-24.

Pritchard, Margaret, and Susan Pritchard O'Hara
  1991 Interview with Jerry Rohde, April 30, 1991.

Pro-Football-Reference-Com
  2015a Dave Lewis. Web page. Electronic document, http://www.pro-football-reference.com/players/L/LewiDa22.htm accessed on April 26, 2015.

Rambler [pseud.]
  1887a Notes from Southern Humboldt. Daily Humboldt Times, July 19, 1887:3.

Randles, Anthony
  1966 Punta Gorda Lighthouse article. Humboldt Times, April 17, 1966:17.

Raphael, Ray, and Freeman House
  2011 Two Peoples, One Place. Revised edition. Eureka: Humboldt County Historical Society.

Rathjen, Mark
  1989 New life for aging hotel. Times-Standard, September 10, 1989.

Rayle, D. E.
  2014. The Golden Spike Story. The Northwesterner, Fall-Winter 2014:7-15.

readtheplaque.com
  2019 Cape Mendocino Lighthouse. Web page. Electronic document, https://readtheplaque.com/plaque/cape-mendocino-lighthouse accessed on June 26, 2019.

Redwood Coast
  2012 Redwood Coast City Street Map. Burnaby, BC: GM Johnson & Associates Ltd.

Redwood Monastery
  2017 A Short History. Web page. Electronic document, http://www.redwoodsabbey.org/Life/History/ accessed on December 10, 2017.

Reed, Anna
  1986a Anna Reed describes 1872 horseback trip to Humboldt. Humboldt Historian, March-April 1986:18-20.
  1904a A Heroine of Humboldt. Northern Crown, May, 1904:7-10.

Reger, June
  2005 The Murphy Family. In. Children from our One-Room Schools. Blocksburg, CA: Blocksburg Town Hall Association.

Reichard, Gladys
  1922 Wiyot, Yurok Texts. In. Gladys Reichard filed notebooks on Wiyot Indians, [ca. 1920-23]. Bancroft Library microfilm, collection number: BANC MSS 2004/111c.

Reis, Peggy
  2005 Margaret "Peggy" Woodman Reis. In. Children from our One-Room Schools. Blocksburg, CA: Blocksburg Town Hall Association.

Richardson, Claude
  2002 Interview with Jerry Rohde on November 2, 2002.

Rigby, Ken
  2016. Phone interview with Jerry Rohde on December 2, 2016.

Ringwald, George
  2003a The Shelter Cove Saga: From land scam to popular resort. North Coast Journal, August 28, 2003. Web page. Electronic document, http://www.northcoastjournal.com/082803/cover0828.html accessed on December 2, 2015.

2003b Boom Time: Its troubled past largely forgotten, Shelter Cove is going gangbusters. North Coast Journal, September 4, 2003. Web page. Electronic document, http://www.northcoastjournal.com/090403/news0904.html#anchor272215 accessed on December 2, 2015.

Roberts, Ann
2009 Kiwelattah Through the Eyes of Seven Settlers. Humboldt Historian, Spring 2009:24-27.

Robinson, John
1964a The Redwood Highway: Part II—Building the Road. California Highways and Public Works, July-August 1964:24-33.
1964b The Redwood Highway: Part I—Early history of Transportation in the Northern Coastal Counties. California Highways and Public Works, May-June 1964:2-11.

Robinson, W. W.
1948 Land in California. Berkeley: University of California Press.

Rochester Democrat and Chronicle
1903 Obituary of Col. Henry T. Noyes. Rochester Democrat and Chronicle, December 1, 1903:12.

Rohde, Jerry
1991a Taking a long ride through local history. Redwood Record, October 29, 1991:3.
1992a Elinor Elegy: Part I. Redwood Record, May 12, 1992:3.
1992b Two families endure a S. Humboldt flood. Redwood Record, May 19, 1992:3.
1992c Elinor elegy: The Conclusion: The waters recede. Redwood Record, May 26, 1992:3.
2000a Alice, Elinor, and the Great Flood. Humboldt Historian, Winter 2000:4, 36-37.
2001a Benbow SRA Campground Cultural Resources Investigation: Historical Review. Copy in author's possession.
2002a Bull Creek Beginnings. Humboldt Historian, Summer 2002:36-37.
2004a Hunt Ranch Ethnographic and Historical Review. Copy in author's possession.
2005a Field notes of interview by author with Henry and Billye Tsarnas at the Tsarnas mill site, July 22, 2005.
2005b Phone interview by author with Billye Tsarnas, July 19, 1905.
2008a The Sonoma Gang. Web page. Electronic document http://www.northcoastjournal.com/humboldt/the-sonoma-gang/Content?oid=2127928 accessed on October 22, 2013. Also available in: North Coast Journal, September 11, 2008:14-15, 17-19.
2010a Genocide & Extortion. Web page. Electronic document http://www.northcoastjournal.com/news/2010/02/25/genocide-and-extortion-indian-island/ accessed on October 29, 2011. Also available, without endnotes, in: North Coast Journal, February 25, 2010:10-17.
2014a Both Sides of the Bluff. Eureka: MountianHome Books.
2016a An American Genocide. Web page. Electronic document, https://www.northcoastjournal.com/humboldt/an-american-genocide/Content?oid=4116592 accessed on February 28, 2021.
N.d.a. Notes copied from ornithological display at Eureka High School, Eureka.

Rohde, Jerry, and Gisela Rohde
1992 Humboldt Redwoods State Park: The Complete Guide. Eureka, CA: Miles & Miles.
1994 Redwood National & State Parks: Tales, Trails, & Auto Tours. McKinleyville, CA: MountainHome Books.
2022 Southern Humboldt Indians. Arcata, CA: The Press at Cal Poly Humboldt.

Rohde, Jerry, and Donald Verwayne
2005 Tsarnas Mill Site. State of California—The Resources Agency, Department of Parks and Recreation Primary Record.

Rohnerville Herald
1887a The Standard of Monday says: . . . Rohnerville Herald, November 2, 1887:2.
1887b Stage Line ad. Rohnerville Herald, November 2, 1887:2.
1888a Samples . . . . Rohnerville Herald, January 18, 1888:3.
1888b Ed. B. Barnum . . . . Rohnerville Herald, February 22, 1888:3.
1888c A Summer Resort. Rohnerville Herald, February 29, 1888:3.
1888d Drowning of G. W. Charles. Rohnerville Herald, February 29, 1888:3.

Romo, Cheryl
1998 The Mystery of Hans Weisel and the Bar-W. American West, September-October:66-71.

Roscoe, Ken
1991. Heydays in Humboldt. N. p.: ILLIANA Limited.

Roscoe, Neb
1996. Heydays in Mattole. McKinleyville, CA: ILLIANA Limited.

Roscoe, James
1985a The days of Chief Lassik and his people were sadly numbered. Humboldt Historian, March-April 1985.
1985b An Ethnohistory of the Mattole. Photocopy of a Humboldt State University paper in possession of author.

rosieradiator.com
2018 The Guinness Book of World Records. Web page. Electronic document, http://rosieradiator.com/id3.html accessed on September 26, 2018.

Rowley, Max
2004a tracing the Sonoma trail. Humboldt Historian, Spring 2004:29-33.

Rubalcava, Leann
1999 A Walkway to the Giants: Phillipsville in focus. Humboldt Historian, Winter 1999:26-30.

Ruggles, June
1990 Interview with Jerry Rohde, April 30, 1990.

Russell, Angus
1991 Interview with Jerry Rohde, May 25, 1991.

Sacramento Daily Union
1863a Alleged Kidnapping in Mendocino. Sacramento Daily Union, March 26, 1863:2.

Sacramento Union
  1921 Forty-Eight Are Lost In Shipwreck. Sacramento Union, August 8, 1921:1-2.

Sam, Mrs. Jane
  1921a Revised statement regarding Indian Island Massacre, date March 27/21. Photocopy available, as part of the "Wiyot History Papers," in the Special Collections, Humboldt State University Library, Arcata.
  [1921?]a Statement regarding L. K. Wood and Gregg Party. Photocopy available, as part of the "Wiyot History Papers," in the Special Collections, Humboldt State University Library, Arcata.
  [1921?]b Statement regarding Indian Island Massacre. Photocopy available, as part of the "Wiyot History Papers," in the Special Collections, Humboldt State University Library, Arcata.
  [1921?]c Taken to Reservation. Photocopy available, as part of the "Wiyot History Papers," in the Special Collections, Humboldt State University Library, Arcata.
  [1921?]d Revised statement regarding L. K. Wood and Gregg Party. Photocopy available, as part of the "Wiyot History Papers," in the Special Collections, Humboldt State University Library, Arcata.
  [1921?]e Taken to Reservation [revised version]. Photocopy available, as part of the "Wiyot History Papers," in the Special Collections, Humboldt State University Library, Arcata.

San Francisco Call
  1895a The Horrible History of Round Valley. San Francisco Call, October 21, 1895:8-9.
  1902a George White, Round Valley King, Is Dead. San Francisco Call, June 10, 1902:4.
  1911a Change at Post office, Irma, Trinity County. San Francisco Call, October 26, 1911:9.

San Francisco Chronicle
  1983a California's Oil History. San Francisco Chronicle, March 21, 1983.

San Francisco Daily Alta
  1867a The Late Terrible Slaughter in Mendocino County. San Francisco Daily Alta, October 26, 1867.

San Jose Woman's Club
  2019 San Jose Woman's Club. Web page. Electronic document, https://sjwomansclub.org/all-about-sjwc/ accessed on December 7, 2019.

Saul, Barbara Canepa
  1992a Alfred Augustus (A.A.) Hadley. Humboldt Historian, July-August 1992:8-13.

Save-the-Redwoods League
  1931 Annual Report. Copy on file at Special Collections, Humboldt State University Library, Arcata.
  1939a Annual Report. Copy on file at Special Collections, Humboldt State University Library, Arcata.

Schroeder, Merlynn
  2016 Pone interview with Jerry Rohde, January 27, 2016.

Schwarzkopf, Chet
  1948a Weott—Town with Olympic Setting. Humboldt Times, December 5, 1948:5.
  1948b Miranda—Town With A Unique School. Humboldt Times, November 21, 1948:15,17.
  1949a Bridgeville—Heart Of The Upland Empire. Humboldt Times, May 1, 1949:32.
  1949b Pepperwood—Resorts and Gardens Join. Humboldt Times, March 6, 1949:13, 17.
  1949c Holmes And Larabee—Live And Let Live. Humboldt Times, June 12, 1949:17, 28.
  1949d Redcrest-Englewood—People Return. Humboldt Times, April 3, 1949:13, 17.
  1949e Shively—A Man Said It Was Paradise. Humboldt Times, February 6, 1949.
  1949f South Fork – McCann – Dyerville—Big Land. Humboldt Times, July 24, 1949:13, 15.
  1949g Ettersburg and Briceland—Smiling Land. Humboldt Times, June 26, 1949:17, 31.
  1949h Phillipsville—Climate and Setting Lure. Humboldt times, August 14, 1949:13, 15.
  1949i Petrolia—The Heart of a Hidden Valley. Humboldt Times, April 17, 1949:13, 17.
  1949j Myers Flat—Business And Living Are Good. Humboldt Times, May 15, 1949: 17, 21.
  1949k Carlotta—A Pioneer Family named It. Humboldt Times, March 20, 1949:11, 15.
  1949l Bridgeville—Heart of the Upland Empire. Humboldt Times, May 1, 1949:32, 16.

Scott, Jeremiah, Jr.
  1997a Curless Family Leaves a Legacy. Humboldt Historian, Fall 1997:22-26.
  2018a The Ray Brothers, the Kinsey Family, and Boy Scout Troop 54. Humboldt Historian, Summer 2018:28-33.

Scott, Lynford
  1985a The Great Maria used sail and push on the Eel. Humboldt Historian, May-June 1985:9.
  1986a A summer outing and climb up Bear Buttes. Humboldt Historian, March-April 1986:12-13.
  1989 Family album of early railroad images. Humboldt Historian, July-August, 1989:3-7.
  1999 Looking Back at 90 Years.... Eureka: Lynford Scott.

Searson, Mrs. [Jane Duncan]
  [1921?]a Statement regard early Indian-white relations, murders by whites, massacre at Rio dell. Photocopy available, as part of the "Wiyot History Papers," in the Special Collections, Humboldt State University Library, Arcata.
  [1921?]b Revised statement regard early Indian-white relations, murders by whites, massacre at Rio dell. Photocopy available, as part of the "Wiyot History Papers," in the Special Collections, Humboldt State University Library, Arcata.

seasky.org
  2019a Miranda. Web page. Electronic document, http://www.seasky.org/solar-system/uranus-miranda.html accessed on August 9, 2019.

Secrest, William B.
  2004 California Feuds. Sanger, CA: Quill Driver Books/Word Dancer Press.
SFGATE
  1996a Posthumous Pardon for Unjust Conviction/Man imprisoned 25 years for 2 murders. Web page. Electronic document, https://www.sfgate.com/news/article/Posthumous-Pardon-For-Unjust-Conviction-Man-2986296.php accessed on June 5, 2022.
Seidner, Carrie
  1939a Letter to "Friend" [Lucy Allard], dated July 24, 1939. Photocopy available, as part of the "Wiyot History Papers," in the Special Collections, Humboldt State University Library, Arcata.
  N.d.a. Portion of letter [page 1 is missing] to Mrs. Allard. Photocopy available, as part of the "Wiyot History Papers," in the Special Collections, Humboldt State University Library, Arcata.
Shelton, Heather
  2001a The Benbow tradition. Times-Standard, July 22, 2001.
Shepherd, Marvin
  2011 The Sea Captain's Odyssey: A Biography of Captain H. H. Buhne 1822-1895. Walnut Creek, CA: Georgie Press.
Shields, David S.
  2013 Still: American Silent Motion Picture Photography. Chicago: University of Chicago Press.
Shipyard Log
  2020 Knees from Trees. Web page. Electronic document, http://boothbayharborshipyard.blogspot.com/2008/09/knees-from-trees.html accessed on July 8, 2020.
Silvey, Jack
  1985a Living Legends: Dr. Niles dedicated to students, science. Humboldt Historian, July-August 1985:3-5.
  1995a A Tribute to Dr. Doris Kildale Niles. Humboldt Historian, Fall 1995:37-38.
  1998a Bridges Span Time in Mountain Community. Humboldt Historian, Winter 1998:32-39.
Slocum, Bowen & Co.
  1881 History of Napa and Lake Counties, California. San Francisco: Slocum, Bowen & Co.
Smith, Clara
  N.d. Elinor. Section of photocopy of Smith family history in possession of Jerry Rohde.
Smith, Eric Krabbe
  1990 Lucy Young or T'tcetsa: Indian-White Relations in Northwest California, 1846-1944. M. A. thesis, University of California, Santa Cruz.
Smith, Gladys
  1995 Albert Felix Etter, Hybridizer. Pacific Horticulture, Summer 1995:16-22.
Smith, Jean Edward
  2001 Grant. New York: Simon and Schuster.
snac
  2018. Baker, Ray Jerome, 1880-1972. Web page. Electronic document, http://snacco-operative.org/view/9988283 accessed on August 22, 2018.
Snyder, John w.
  1984 The Bridges of John B. Leonard 1905 to 1925. Concrete International, June 1984:58-67.
Sonoma Democrat
  1867a The Little Lake Vendetta. Sonoma Democrat, November 2, 1867:1.
Southern Humboldt Life and Times
  1997a Eel Rock/Fruitland Ridge. Southern Humboldt Life and Times, July 29, 1997:12.
Sparks, Virginia
  1986 Memo on Larabee, Weott, and Fruitland. Photocopy on file at the Humboldt County Historical Society, Eureka.
Spartacus Educational
  2016 Fort Pillow Massacre. Web page. Electronic document, http://spartacus-educational.com/USACWpillow.htm accessed on September 3, 2016.
Speece, Darren Frederick
  2017 Defending Giants. Seattle: University of Washington Press.
Speegle, Will N.
  1931a Benbow Dam article. Humboldt Times, October 4, 1931.
  1945a Hospitality De Luxe. Humboldt Times, April 7, 1945.
  1947a Early Days in Blocksburg. Humboldt Times, July 6, 1947.
Spencer, Ed B.
  1895 Business Directory of Humboldt Count: 1895-6. Eureka: E. B. Spencer.
St. John, Fern
  1959 Some Like It Englewood, Some Like It Redcrest—It's the Name That Matters. Humboldt Times, November 7, 1959.
  1968a Shively Ferry Stirs Memories. Humboldt Historian, November-December 1968:3, 6.
  1968b Wagon Freighters Helped Create N. W. P. Humboldt Historian, July-August 1968:3.
  1968c Showers Pass School on Fort Baker Ranch Headquarters for Hart Valley Gun Club. Humboldt Beacon, July 4, 1968:12.
  1969 Historic Old Bridges Part of Humboldt's Past. Humboldt Beacon, May 1, 1969.
  N.d.a Saga of Henry Millsap's 75 Years In Pepperwood; He's Still Alive, Stayed to the Last, Ready to Fight, in The Killer Eel. Fortuna, CA: Humboldt Beacon, n.d.
  N.d.b [Article on Englewood School]. Photocopy with date and title missing, located in the Eureka clipping file in the Humboldt Room, Eureka Main Library.
Standard Publishing Co.
  1893 Eureka Business Directory 1893-4. Eureka: Standard Publishing Co.
Stansberry, Linda
  2016 Bridgeville. Web page. Electronic document, https://www.northcoastjournal.com/humboldt/bridgeville/Content?oid=3552638 accessed on April 8, 2019.

Startare, Lillie
  2015 Personal communication with Jerry
        Rohde, October 16, 2015.
State of California, California Highway Commission
  1914a Plan and Profile of Proposed State
         Highway In Humboldt County from Dyer-
         ville to Shively. As Built Plans.
  1914b [Plan and Profile of Proposed State
         Highway In Humboldt County from Mi-
         randa to Dyerville.] As Built Plans.
  1922a First Biennial Report of the Division of
         Highways. Sacramento.
  1928a Sixth Biennial Report of the Division of
         Highways. Sacramento.
  1931a Plan and Profile of Proposed State
         Highway In Humboldt County from
         Dyerville to
Shively. As Built Plans.
State of California, Department of Engineering
  1912 Third Biennial Report. Sacramento.
State of California, Department of Natural
Resources, Division of Forestry
  1949a [Map of] South Half Humboldt County.
State of California, Department of Public Works,
Division of Highways
  1937 Plan and Profile of State Highway in
        Humboldt County, between Stegemeyer
        Bluffs and Myers. As Built Plans.
State of California, Division of Mines
  1927 California Journal of Mines and Geology,
        October 1941.
State of California, Resources Agency, Department
of Water Resources, Northern District
  1975. Van Duzen River Basin Environmental
        Atlas. Sacramento, Calif.
Stindt, Fred A.
  1987 The Northwestern Pacific Railroad.
        Kelseyville, CA: Fred A. Stindt.
  1988 The Northwestern Pacific Railroad 1964-
        1985 vol. 2. Kelseyville, CA, Fred A.
        Stindt.
Stindt, Fred A., and Guy L. Dunscomb
  1964 The Northwestern Pacific Railroad:
        Redwood Empire Route. Redwood City,
        CA: Fred A. Stindt and Guy L. Dunscomb.
Strobridge, William F.
  1994 Regulars in the Redwoods: the U. S. Army
        in Northern California, 1852-1861. Spo-
        kane, WA: Arthur H. Clark Co.
Stockton, Dave
  2004 The Man from Whiskey Flat. Humboldt
        Redwoods Interpretive Association News-
        letter, Summer 2004.
Stone, A. K.
  1913. Fort Seward—The Embyro Metropolis.
        Eureka Herald, December 7, 1913:33.
Stuart, John D., and John O. Sawyer
  2001 Trees and Shrubs of California. Berkeley:
        University of California Press.
Subcommittee of the Committee on Indian Affairs:
House of Representatives
  1926 Hearing . . . on H. R. 8036 and H. R.
        9497. Washington DC: Government
        Printing Office.
Sunset
  1951 Article on Eel River. Sunset, March 1951.

  2021a Wine Tasting in Humboldt County. Web
         page. Electronic document, https://www.
         sunset.com/travel/california/humboldt-coun-
         ty-wine accessed on May 24, 2021.
Surveyor General's Office
  1858a [Map of] Township № 1 North Range
         № 3 West, Humboldt Meridian. San Fran-
         cisco: Surveyor General's Office.
  1858b [Map of] Township № IV North Range
         № II East, Humboldt Meridian. San Fran-
         cisco: Surveyor General's Office.
  1871a [Map of] Township № 1 North Range
         № 1 East, Humboldt Meridian. San Fran-
         cisco: Surveyor General's Office.
  1871b [Map of] Township № 1 North Range
         № 2 East, Humboldt Meridian. San Fran-
         cisco: Surveyor General's Office.
  1871c [Map of] Township № 1 South, Range
         № 2 East, Humboldt Meridian. San Fran-
         cisco: Surveyor General's Office.
  1872a [Map of] Township № 1 South, Range
         № 3 East, Humboldt Meridian. San Fran-
         cisco: Surveyor General's Office.
  1872b [Map of] Township № 1 North, Range
         № 5 East, Humboldt Meridian. San Fran-
         cisco: Surveyor General's Office.
  1872c [Map of] Township № 1 North, Range
         № 3 East, Humboldt Meridian. San Fran-
         cisco: Surveyor General's Office.
  1872d [Map of] Township № 2 North, Range
         № 5 East, Humboldt Meridian. San Fran-
         cisco: Surveyor General's Office.
  1872e [Map of] Township № 1 North, Range
         № 5 East, Humboldt Meridian. San Fran-
         cisco: Surveyor General's Office.
  1873a [Map of] Township № 2 South, Range
         № 4 East, Humboldt Meridian. San Fran-
         cisco: Surveyor General's Office.
  1873b [Map of] Township № 3 South, Range
         № 5 East, Humboldt Meridian. San Fran-
         cisco: Surveyor General's Office.
  1873c [Map of] Township № 2 South, Range
         № 5 East, Humboldt Meridian. San Fran-
         cisco: Surveyor General's Office.
  1873d [Map of] Township № 1 South, Range
         № 4 East, Humboldt Meridian. San Fran-
         cisco: Surveyor General's Office.
  1873d Map of] Township № 2 South, Range
         № 4 East, Humboldt Meridian. San Fran-
         cisco: Surveyor General's Office.
  1874a [Map of] Township № 3 South, Range
         № 2 East, Humboldt Meridian. San Fran-
         cisco: Surveyor General's Office.
  1875a [Map of] Township № 4 South, Range
         № 3 East, Humboldt Meridian. San Fran-
         cisco: Surveyor General's Office.
  1875b [Map of] Township № 3 South, Range
         № 3 East, Humboldt Meridian. San Fran-
         cisco: Surveyor General's Office.
  1875c [Map of] Township № 4 South, Range
         № 1 East, Humboldt Meridian. San Fran-
         cisco: Surveyor General's Office.
  1876a [Map of] Township No. 2 South, Range
         No. 3 East, Humboldt Meridian. San Fran-
         cisco: Surveyor General's Office.
  1876b [Map of] Township № 4 South, Range
         № 4 East, Humboldt Meridian. San Fran-
         cisco: Surveyor General's Office.

1876c [Map of] Township № 3 South, Range
       № 4 East, Humboldt Meridian. San Fran-
       cisco: Surveyor General's Office.
1876d [Map of] Township № 2 North, Range
       № 2 East, Humboldt Meridian. San Fran-
       cisco: Surveyor General's Office.
1879a [Map of] Township № 2 South, Range
       № 2 East, Humboldt Meridian. San Fran-
       cisco: Surveyor General's Office.
1885a [Map of] Township № 1 South, Range
       № 2 East, Humboldt Meridian. San Fran-
       cisco: Surveyor General's Office.

Swales, Thomas
       1863 Last Will and Testament. Photocopy in
             "Probate Papers," accession number
             83:39.4, Ferndale Museum archives.

Swanlund-Baker
       2018a Photo of Albert and Sallie Smith at
              Briceland Store. Web page. Electronic
              document, http://library.humboldt.
              edu/humco/holdings/photodetail.
              php?S=Albert%20smith&CS=All%20
              Collections&RS=ALL%20Regions&PS=A-
              ny%20Photographer&ST=ALL%20
              words&SW=&C=6&R=1 accessed on
              January 8, 2019.
       2018b Photo of Albert and Sallie Smith at
              Briceland. Web page. Electronic document,
              http://library.humboldt.edu/humco/
              holdings/photodetail.php?R=0&S=Al-
              bert%20smith&CS=All%20Collec-
              tions&RS=ALL%20Regions&PS=A-
              ny%20Photographer&ST=ALL%20
              words&SW=&C=6 accessed on January
              8, 2019.

Sweasey, Earla Reynolds
       1975 School Story Brings Memories. Humboldt
             Historian, January-February, 1975:5.

Tam, J. H.
       1885 Humboldt County, California Directory,
             1885-1886. N.p.

tapdanceroom.com
       2019 Meet the Tap Dance Director. Web page.
             Electronic document, http://www.
             tapdanceroom.com/Tap-Dance-Instructor-
             About-Us-San-Francisco-CA.html accessed
             on March 31, 2019.

Taussig, F. W.
       1893 The Duties on Wool and Woolens.
             Oxford: Oxford University Press.

Taylor, Addie Louise
       1917 Little Mountain Girl Is Unable To Get
             Schooling But Writes Interestingly. Hum-
             boldt Time, February 4, 1917.

Taylor, Maralee
       1980 Where Is Weott? Humboldt Historian,
             July-August 1980:3-5.

Teague, Vera Snider
       1975. From Buckskin to Team Bells. Ukiah,
             CA: The Letter Shop.

The Writer
       1914a. Writers of the Day. The Writer, vol. XXVI.

Thomas, John L.
       1968 Kunz, [sic] Ben Arthur Trials In Ericson
             Case Recalled. Trinity 1968 Yearbook.

Thornbury, Delmar L.
       1923 California's Redwood Wonderland:
             Humboldt County. San Francisco: Sunset
             Press.

Timberman
       1920a Stockton. The Timberman, September
              1920:48.

Times-Standard
       1968a New Phillipsville P. O. Is in Service.
              Times-Standard March 5, 1968.
       1973a There's something for every citizen at
              Honeydew store. Times-Standard, May 16,
              1973:2.
       1973b Fire ravages Hartsook Inn. Times-
              Standard, June 13, 1973.
       1990a. Its 1906 Again. Times-Standard, July 6,
              1990:A-1.
       1993a Richard Redwood Childs obit.
              Times-Standard, September 23, 1993:B-11.
       1995 Historical Hotel Burns. Times-Standard,
             June 29, 1995:1.
       2009a Jay Martin Dinsmore obit. Times-
              Standard, May 24, 2009:C-6.
       N.d.a. Article on Dinsmore Lodge. Undated
              clipping located in the "Dinsmore" file in
              the Special Collections at the Humboldt
              State University Library.

Tooby, Arthur N.
       1983 Memories of old Harris hotel. Humboldt
             Historian, July-August 1983:12.

Townes, John E.
       1850. Letter to editor. Daily Alta California,
             June 26, 1850:2.

Townsend, Charles H.
       1886 Four Rare Birds in Northern California:
             Yellow Rail, Emperor Goose, European
             Widgeon, and Sabine's Ruffed Grouse. The
             Auk, vol. 3. New York: L. S. Foster.

Tracy, Eleanor Ethel
       1992a Schoolma'am: The Letters of Eleanor
              Ethel Tracy: Alder Point, California March-
              June 1903. Compiled by Harriet Tracy
              DeLong. Eureka: Eureka Printing Co.
       1993a Schoolma'am: The Letters of Eleanor
              Ethel Tracy: Harris, California 1905-1906.
              Compiled by Harriet Tracy DeLong. Eure-
              ka: Eureka Printing Co.

Tracy, M. D.
       2018 17 Dead; 43 Missing; when Steamer
             Alaska Sank Saturday Night. Web page.
             Electronic Document, https://www.
             wrecksite.eu/docBrowser.aspx?1361?5?1
             accessed December 11, 2018.

Trail Back
       1974 The Trail Back 100 Years. Garberville,
             CA: Redwood Record.

Trinity Journal
       1860a The dwelling of old Seth Kinman . . . .
              Trinity Journal, July 14, 1860:2.

Trinity Weekly Journal
       1858a Organization of Indian Fighters. Trinity
              Weekly Journal, October 16, 1858:2.
       1859a More Humboldt Indian Troubles.
              Trinity Weekly Journal, May 21, 1859:2.

tuccycle.org
       2015a Tour of the Unknown Coast. Web page.
              Electronic document, http://www.tuccycle.
              org/ accessed on December 15, 2015.
       2015b Ride Information. Web page. Electronic
              document, http://tuccycle.org//
              rides/100_mile_route accessed on Decem-
              ber 15, 2015.

Turk, E. E.
    1861a Lieut. Collins' Command. Humboldt
          Times, June 15, 1861:3.
Turner, Dennis W. and Gloria H. Turner
    2010 Place Names of Humboldt County, 2nd
          Ed. California. Orangevale, CA: Dennis
          W. & Gloria H. Turner.
Tuttle, Don
    1982 Investigation of Coastline Retreat at
          Shelter Cove, California. Copy on file at
          Humboldt County Natural Resources,
          Public Works.
    2016a Personal communication with Jerry
          Rohde regarding Shively Road, August 2,
          2016.
Tyrrell, A. J.
    1932 The Pioneers Reach Humboldt. Ferndale
          Enterprise, March 18, 1932.
Udseth, Dan
    1996a Detective Finds Justice in Bridgeville
          Case. Times-Standard, June 6, 1996:A6, A8.
Urban Dictionary
    2019a mirada. Web page. Electronic document,
          https://www.urbandictionary.com/define.
          php?term=mirada accessed on August 13,
          2019.
U. S. Coast Survey
    1854 Preliminary Survey of Harbors of the
          Western Coast of the United States: Cres-
          cent City Harbor, Harbor of Mendocino
          City, Shelter Cove, Port Orford on Ewing
          Harbor. Web page. Electronic document,
          http://historicalcharts.noaa.gov/histori-
          cals/preview/image/CP367C accessed on
          November 30, 2015.
    1870a Part of Humboldt Bay, California.
          Register № 1176.
    1870b Part of Humboldt Bay, California.
          Register № 1174.
Underwood, Emily
    2020 An Unlikely Resurrection. Flora (3)2.
United States Bureau of the Census
    1860a Federal Census, Humboldt County,
          California, Mattole Township.
    1900a Federal Census, Indian Population,
          Humboldt County, California, South Fork
          Township.
    1900b Federal Census, Indian Population,
          Humboldt County, California, Mattole
          Township.
    1910a Federal Census, Indian Population,
          Humboldt County, California, Van Duzen
          Township.
United States Bureau of Land Management
    2016a General Land Office record for
          Township 3 South, Range 4 East, Section
          17, Humboldt Meridian. Web page. Elec-
          tronic document, http://www.glorecords.
          blm.gov/results/default.aspx?searchCri-
          teria=type=patent|st=CA|cty=023|twp_
          nr=3|twp_dir=S|rng_nr=4|rng_dir=E|se
          c=17|m=15|sp=true|sw=true|sadv=false
          accessed on December 15, 2016.
    2016b General Land Office record for
          Township 3 South, Range 4 East, Section
          8, Humboldt Meridian. Web page. Elec-
          tronic document, http://www.glorecords.
          blm.gov/results/default.aspx?searchCri-
          teria=type=patent|st=CA|cty=023|twp_

          nr=3|twp_dir=S|rng_nr=4|rng_
          ir=E|sec=8|m=15|sp=true|sw=true|sad-
          v=false accessed on December 15, 2016.
    2016c General Land Office record for
          Township 2 South, Range 5 East, Section
          20, Humboldt Meridian. Web page. Elec-
          tronic document, http://www.glorecords.
          blm.gov/results/default.aspx?searchCri-
          teria=type=patent|st=CA|cty=023|twp_
          nr=2|twp_dir=S|rng_nr=5|rng_
          dir=E|sec=20|sp=true|sw=true|sadv=false
          accessed on December 16, 2016.
    2016d Record of Land Patents for "Kneeland"
          in Township 2 South, Range 5 East.
          Web page. Electronic document, http://
          www.glorecords.blm.gov/results/
          default.aspx?searchCriteria=type=pat-
          ent|st=CA|cty=023|ln=kneeland|twp_
          nr=2|twp_dir=S|rng_nr=5|rng_
          dir=E|m=15|sp=true|sw=true|sadv=false
          accessed on December 18, 2016.
    2016e Record of Land Patents for "Hoglen" in
          Township 2 South, Range 5 East. Web
          page. Electronic document, http://
          www.glorecords.blm.gov/results/
          default.aspx?searchCriteria=type=pat-
          ent|st=CA|cty=023|ln=hoglen|twp_
          nr=2|twp_dir=S|rng_nr=5|rng_
          dir=E|m=15|sp=true|sw=true|sadv=false
          accessed on December 18, 2016.
    2018a Record of Land Patents for Section 18,
          Township 2 South, Range 2 East, Humboldt
          Meridian. Web page. Electronic document,
          https://glorecords.blm.gov/details/patent/
          default.aspx?accession=CA1090   .232&d-
          ocClass=STA&sid=dbz2g1e3.v55 accessed
          on September 21, 2018.
    2018b Record of Land Patent for Joseph D.
          Smith in Section 1, Township 5 south,
          Range 3 East, Humboldt Meridian. Web
          page. Electronic document, https://glo-
          records.blm.gov/details/patent/default.
          aspx?accession=CA1090   .201&doc-
          Class=STA&sid=qnscm2jw.fsw#patentDe-
          tailsTabIndex=1 accessed on September
          24, 2018.
United States Circuit Courts of Appeals
Reports, vol. 11
    1895 Noyes et al. v. Barnard. Web page.
          Electronic document, https://books.
          google.com/books?id=f-JNAQAAIAA-
          J&pg=PA425&lpg=PA425&dq=alger+-
          noyes+van+duzen&source=bl&ots=RM
          ag_V6UU&sig=ACfU3U3PhqthBlyo-
          jY0VcYliF2HzaSOA8g&hl=en&sa=X-
          &ved=2ahUKEwi61vWlkLjiAhULWK-
          0KHXTACFcQ6AEwC3oECAcQAQ#v=o-
          nepage&q=alger%20noyes%20van%20
          duzen&f=false accessed on May 26, 2019.
United States Coast & Geodetic Survey
    1940 Cape Mendocino and Vicinity.
          Washington, DC.
United States Congress, House of Representatives
    1897 Tariff Hearings before the Committee on
          Ways and Means. Congressional serial
          set issue 3543. Washington: Government
          Printing Office.
    2015 Ex. Doc. 282. Congressional Edition,
          vol. 2561:1-21. Web page. Electron-

ic document, https://books.google.
com/books?id=LT9HAQAAIAA-
J&q=282#v=snippet&q=282&f=false
accessed on August 3, 2015.

United States Department of Agriculture
1920a Trinity National Forest, California: 1920
[map]. Washington DC: United States
Department of Agriculture, Forest Service.
[A version of this map, catalogued at the
Bancroft Library as G4362.T7E1 1920;
.U5; Case XD, contains annotations and
hand colorings done by C. Hart Merriam
to show the names of Indian tribes and
their boundaries in the Humboldt-Men-
docino-Trinity area.]
1937a Yearbook of Agriculture 1937. United
States Department of Agriculture.
2015a Clinton Hart Merriam. Web page.
Electronic document, http://www.aphis.
usda.gov/wps/portal/aphis/ourfocus/
wildlifedamage/sa_programs/sa_nwrc/sa_
history/ct_clinton_hart_merriam/!ut/p/
a0/04_Sj9CPykssy0xPLMnMz0vMAfG-
jzOK9_D2MDJ0MjDzd3V2dDDz93HwC-
zL29jAwMTfQLsh0VAXWczqE!/ accessed
on June 2, 2015.
2015b Tanoak. Web page. Electronic document,
http://plants.usda.gov/plantguide/pdf/
cs_lide3.pdf accessed on June 4, 2015.

United States Department of the Interior
1978a National Register of Historic Places
Inventory—Nomination Form: Carlotta
Hotel. Web page. Electronic document,
https://npgallery.nps.gov/NRHP/
GetAsset/34762081-f74c-4bea-88d0-
f54eb89a48c3 accessed on May 19, 2019.
1981a National Register of Historic Places
Inventory—Nomination Form: Lower
Blackburn Grade Bridge. Web page. Electronic document, https://npgallery.nps.
gov/NRHP/GetAsset/NRHP/81000148_
text accessed on May 19, 2019.

United States Department of the Interior,
Geological Survey
1949a Garberville, California. Quadrangle.
1949b Alderpoint, California. Quadrangle.
1940a Iaqua Buttes, California. Quadrangle.
1951a Scotia, California. Quadrangle.
1969a Redcrest, California. Quadrangle.
1969b Weott, California. Quadrangle.

United States House of Representatives
1858 Executive Documents . . . During the First
Session of the Thirty-Fifth Congress 1857-
'58. Washington: James B. Stedman.

United States Office of Education
1910 Annual Report of the Commissioner of
Education, vol. 1. Washington DC: Government Printing Office.

United States Senate
1890. Executive Documents of the Senate of the
United States for the First Session of the
Fifty-First Congress 1889-'90. Washington
DC: Government Printing Office.

United States War Department
1897a The War of the Rebellion: A
Compilation of the Official Records of the
Union and Confederate Armies; Series 1 -
Volume 50 (Part I). Washington DC: Gov-
ernment Printing Office.

1897b The War of the Rebellion: A
Compilation of the Official Records of the
Union and Confederate Armies; Series 1 -
Volume 50 (Part II). Washington DC: Gov-
ernment Printing Office.

uscglightshipsailors.org
2018 Blunt's Reef Lightship. Web page.
Electronic document, http://www.
uscglightshipsailors.org/blunts_reef_light-
ship_lv83_wal508.htm accessed on
December 19, 2018.

Van Deliner, Bernice
1984 James Ervin Wood—Garberville/Ranch
Founder. Humboldt Historian, January-February 1984:3-7.

Van Dyke, Walter
1891 Early Days in Klamath. Overland Monthly,
vol. XVII, No. 104 Second Series, August
1891.

Van Kirk, Susie
2019a National Register of Historic Places
Inventory—Nomination Form for Carlotta Hotel. Web page. Electronic document, https://npgallery.nps.gov/NRHP/
GetAsset/34762081-f74c-4bea-88d0-
f54eb89a48c3 accessed on April 1, 2019.
N.d.a. Merrifield Family. Copy in author's
possession.

Vatnsdal, Russell L.
1957 Ettersburg: A History of Humboldt
County, California. Unpublished paper
located in the "Ettersburg" file in the Humboldt County Collection, Humboldt State
University Library, Arcata.

Verdi, Anne F.
1974 William F. Notley: Early Californian.
Noticias del Puerto de Monterey
(18)10:17-21.

Vincent, Paul
1983 A Tale of Tanbarkiing: What Happened
at Briceland and Shelter Cove. Humboldt
Historian, January-February 1983:3-8.

Vinyard, Lucille
1990. Interview with Jerry Rohde, December
20, 1990.

Volunteer [pseud.]
1862 From Fort Seward. Humboldt Times,
March 22, 1862:3.

"W"
1859a Letter from Cape Mendocino. Humboldt
Times, November 12, 1859:2.
1859b Mattole Valley. Humboldt Times,
November 19, 1859:2.

"W" (2)
1864a Iaqua Correspondence. Humboldt Times,
July 26, 1864:2.

Walker, Laura
1996 The Early Days of Mattole Road. Mattole
Restoration Newsletter, Winter 1996.

Waltmann, Henry G.
1971 Circumstantial Reformer: President Grant
& the Indian Problem. Arizona and the
West 13(4):323-342.

Walton, Rachel [Richard H.]
2022a Personal communication with Jerry
Rohde, May 30, 2022.

Walton, Richard H. [Rachel]
2006 Cold Case Homicides. Boca Raton,
Florida: Taylor & Francis.

Ward, Charles Willis
    1915a Humboldt County California. Eureka: Ward-Perkins-Gill Co.

Wasserman, Laura, and James Wasserman
    2019 Who Saved the Redwoods? New York: Algora Publishing.

Water Resources Control Board
    2017 Executive Director's Report, September 19, 2017.

waterboards.ca.gov
    2016a In the Matter of Water Quality Certification for Shively Community Bridge – Low-Flow Railcar Crossing, Eel River Project. Web page. Electronic document, http://www.waterboards.ca.gov/northcoast/board_decisions/water_quality_certification/pdf/2014/140407_ShivelyCommBridge_401.pdf accessed on July 28, 2016.

Waterman, T. T.
    1992[1920] Yurok Geography. Trinidad, CA: Trinidad Museum Society.

Way, Dave
    1947a J. Fairhurst Says Industry is Permanent. Humboldt Standard, November 17, 1947.

waymaking.com
    2019 SS Emidio Memorial. Web page. Electronic document, http://www.waymarking.com/waymarks/WMF8RW_SS_Emidio_Memorial_Crescent_City_CA accessed on June 24, 2019.

WeatherDB
    2016 Alderpoint, California Average Rainfall. Web page. Electronic document, https://rainfall.weatherdb.com/l/562/Alderpoint-California accessed on November 14, 2016.

Weekly Humboldt Times
    1858a Indian Matters—Movement of the Volunteers. Weekly Humboldt Times, November 20, 1858:2.
    1860a Indian Hostilities—Volunteer Company. Weekly Humboldt Times, February 4, 1860:2.
    1860b Volunteer Company—Immediate Action Necessary. Weekly Humboldt Times, February 11, 1860:2
    1863a Good Haul of Diggers. Weekly Humboldt Times, January 17, 1863:2.
    1879a Our Wool Interest. Weekly Humboldt Times, November 8, 1879.

Weigel, Lawrence E.
    1976 Pre-Contact Cultural Ecology of the Nongatl Indians of Northwestern California. Humboldt Journal of Social Relations 4:1.

Werelate.org
    2017 John Henry Hunter. Web Page. Electronic document, http://www.werelate.org/wiki/Person:John_Hunter_(55) accessed on April 30, 2017.

West Coast Signal
    1871a Stage line ad. West Coast Signal, September 20, 1871:3.
    1874a Stage Line Extended. West Coast Signal, September 30, 1874:3.
    1875a Completed. West Coast Signal, August 4, 1875:3.
    1875b From the Bay to Yagerville. West Coast Signal, September 29, 1875.
    1876a Ad for B. Blockburger. West Coast Signal, January 12, 1876:4.
    1876b Mattole Valley. West Coast Signal, July 26, 1876:3.
    1876c From the Wagon Road. West Coast Signal, December 16, 1876.
    1876d Good Road. West Coast Signal, November 1, 1876:3.
    1876e Bullard & Sweasey stage line ad. West Coast Signal, August 16, 1876:1.
    1877a Ad for Eel River House. West Coast Signal, September 5, 1877:4.
    1877b Splendid Road. West Coast Signal, August 15, 1877:1.
    1878a Completion of the Garberville and Shelter Cove Road to the Coast Route Road. West Coast Signal, November 6, 1878:3.
    1878b Overland from San Francisco. West Coast Signal, September 4, 1878:1.

Western Directory Co.
    1920 Eureka City Directory. Long Beach: Western Directory Co.

Wheeler, Jessie
    1997a Bridge Speech. Photocopy on file at the Humboldt County Historical Society, Eureka, CA.
    2014a Interview with Jessie Wheeler, October 31, 2014.
    2015a Phone interview with Jerry Rohde, May 31, 2015.
    2017a The Heyday of Bridgeville. Sr. News, June 2017:1, 4.

Whistle Punk
    2005 Metropolitan Redwood Lumber Company. Whistle Punk, July 2005:6.

White, Ralso
    N.d. Ralso White Collection, College of the Redwoods Library, Eureka, CA.

White, Ronald C.
    2016 American Ulysses: A Life of Ulysses S. Grant. New York: Random House.

Whiteshot, Charles A.
    1905. The Oil Well Driller. Mannington, WV: Charles A. Whiteshot.

Wichels, Ernest D.
    2017 How it all began. Web page. Electronic document, http://www.solanoarticles.com/history/pdf/pdf_files/how_it_all_began.pdf accessed on August 6, 2017.

Wikimedia Commons
    2018a Category: Fred Hartsook. Web page. Electronic document, https://commons.wikimedia.org/wiki/Category:Hartsook_Photo accessed on September 25, 2018.

Wikipedia
    2015a Dave Lewis (punter). Web page. Electronic document, http://en.wikipedia.org/wiki/Dave_Lewis_(punter) accessed on April 26, 2015.
    2015b Pliny Earle Goddard. Web page. Electronic document, http://en.wikipedia.org/wiki/Pliny_Earle_Goddard accessed on June 1, 2015.
    2105c Clinton Hart Merriam. Web page. Electronic document, https://en.wikipedia.org/wiki/Clinton_Hart_Merriam accessed on July 4, 2015.

2015d Ticino. Web page. Electronic document, https://en.wikipedia.org/wiki/Ticino accessed on August 5, 2015.

2015e Sylvanus Morley. Web page. Electronic document, https://en.wikipedia.org/wiki/Sylvanus_Morley accessed on August 7, 2015.

2015f Cadastre. Web page. Electronic document, https://en.wikipedia.org/wiki/Cadastre#Cadastral_surveys accessed on August 9, 2015.

2015g Public Land Survey System. Web Page. Electronic document, https://en.wikipedia.org/wiki/Public_Land_Survey_System accessed on August 9, 2015.

2015h Historical ranking of Presidents of the United States. Web page. Electronic document, https://en.wikipedia.org/wiki/Historical_rankings_of_Presidents_of_the_United_States#2013_Gallup_poll accessed on August 9, 2015.

2015i Cordelia Botkin. Web page. Electronic document, https://en.wikipedia.org/wiki/Cordelia_Botkin accessed on November 9, 2015.

2015j Notleys Landing, California. Web page. Electronic document, https://en.wikipedia.org/wiki/Notleys_Landing,_California accessed on November 10, 2015.

2015k Hail, Columbia. Web page. Electronic document, https://en.wikipedia.org/wiki/Hail,_Columbia accessed on November 25, 2015.

2016a Julia Butterfly Hill. Web page. Electronic document, https://en.wikipedia.org/wiki/Julia_Butterfly_Hill accessed on January 3, 2016.

2016b Luna (tree). Web page. Electronic document https://en.wikipedia.org/wiki/Luna_(tree) accessed on January 3, 2016.

2016c Fort Humboldt State Historic Park. Web page. Electronic document, https://en.wikipedia.org/wiki/Fort_Humboldt_State_Historic_Park accessed on August 25, 2016.

2016d Albert Sidney Johnson. Web page. Electronic document, https://en.wikipedia.org/wiki/Albert_Sidney_Johnston accessed on August 25, 2016.

2016e Lieber Code. Web page. Electronic document, https://en.wikipedia.org/wiki/Lieber_Code accessed on August 28, 2016.

2016f Department of the Pacific. Web page. Electronic document, https://en.wikipedia.org/wiki/Department_of_the_Pacific accessed on August 30, 2016.

2016g Battle of Fort Pillow. Web page. Electronic document, https://en.wikipedia.org/wiki/Battle_of_Fort_Pillow accessed on September 3, 2016.

2017a Northwestern Pacific Railroad. Web page. Electronic Document, https://en.wikipedia.org/wiki/Northwestern_Pacific_Railroad#cite_note-6 accessed on November 25, 2017.

2017b List of English terms of venery, by animal. Web page. Electronic document, https://en.wikipedia.org/wiki/List_of_English_terms_of_venery,_by_animal accessed on November 27, 2017.

2017c Black Friday (1869). Web page. Electronic document, https://en.wikipedia.org/wiki/Black_Friday_(1869) accessed on December 6, 2017.

2018a White Motor Company. Web page. Electronic document, https://en.wikipedia.org/wiki/White_Motor_Company accessed on January 6, 2018.

2018b Great Flood of 1862. Web page. Electronic document, https://en.wikipedia.org/wiki/Great_Flood_of_1862#Northern_California accessed on January 14, 2018.

2018c Franklin Knight Lane. Web page. Electronic document, https://en.wikipedia.org/wiki/Franklin_Knight_Lane#Later_life_and_legacy accessed on April 1, 2018.

2018d Thomas A. Scott. Web page. Electronic document, https://en.wikipedia.org/wiki/Thomas_A._Scott accessed on May 27, 2018.

2018e Asphalt. Web page. Electronic document, https://en.wikipedia.org/wiki/Asphalt accessed on July 29, 2018.

2018f James Gillett. Web page. Electric document, https://en.wikipedia.org/wiki/James_Gillett accessed August 2, 2018.

2018g. Independence Party (United States). Web page. Electronic document, https://en.wikipedia.org/wiki/Independence_Party_(United_States) accessed on August 2, 2018.

2018h Tank Locomotive. Web page. Electronic document, https://en.wikipedia.org/wiki/Tank_locomotive#Saddle_tank accessed on August 9, 2018.

2018i. Dawes Act. Web page. Electronic document, https://en.wikipedia.org/wiki/Dawes_Act accessed on August 13, 2018.

2018j Mercalli intensity scale. Web page. Electronic document, https://en.wikipedia.org/wiki/Mercalli_intensity_scale accessed on August 19, 2018.

2018k Ray Jerome Baker. Web page. Electronic document, https://en.wikipedia.org/wiki/Ray_Jerome_Baker accessed on September 23, 2018.

2018l Fred Hartsook. Web page. Electronic document, https://en.wikipedia.org/wiki/Fred_Hartsook accessed on September 24, 2018.

2018m Frank K. Mott. Web page. Electronic document, https://en.wikipedia.org/wiki/Frank_K._Mott accessed on November 22, 2018.

2018n Tudor Revival architecture. Web page. Electronic document, https://en.wikipedia.org/wiki/Tudor_Revival_architecture accessed on November 24, 2018.

2018o White Pass. Web page. Electronic document, https://en.wikipedia.org/wiki/White_Pass accessed on November 28, 2018.

2018p Shootout on Juneau Wharf. Web page. Electronic document, https://en.wikipedia.org/wiki/Shootout_on_Juneau_Wharf accessed on November 28, 2018.

2018q Wang Wang Blues. Web page. Electronic document, https://en.wikipedia.org/wiki/Wang_Wang_Blues accessed on December 10, 2018.

2019a History of California's state highway system. Web page. Electronic document, https://en.wikipedia.org/wiki/History_of_California%27s_state_highway_system#cite_note-1907-117-39 accessed on April 6, 2019.

2019b Russell A. Alger. Web Page. Electronic document, https://en.wikipedia.org/wiki/Russell_A._Alger accessed on May 26, 2019.

2019c Aaron T. Bliss. Web page. Electronic document, https://en.wikipedia.org/wiki/Aaron_T._Bliss accessed on May 26, 2019.

2019d Pottawatomie massacre. Web page. Electronic document, https://en.wikipedia.org/wiki/Pottawatomie_massacre accessed on June 21, 2019.

2019e Common Carrier. Web page. Electronic document, https://en.wikipedia.org/wiki/Common_carrier accessed on October 17, 2019.

2019f List of Governors of California. Web Page. Electronic document, https://en.wikipedia.org/wiki/List_of_governors_of_California accessed on November 5, 2019.

2019g Nineteenth Amendment to the United States Constitution. Web page. Electronic document, https://en.wikipedia.org/wiki/Nineteenth_Amendment_to_the_United_States_Constitution accessed on December 7, 2019.

2020a Pink Pearl. Web page. Electronic document, https://en.wikipedia.org/wiki/Pink_Pearl_(apple) accessed on Sedan Day, September 2, 2020.

2021a Lakota people. Web page. Electronic document, https://en.wikipedia.org/wiki/Lakota_people accessed on February 14, 2021.

2021b George Hearst. Web page. Electronic document, https://en.wikipedia.org/wiki/George_Hearst accessed on June 12, 2021.

2022a Iaqua. Web page. Electronic document, https://en.wikipedia.org/wiki/Iaqua,_California accessed on May 30, 2022.

WikiTree
2017a Frederick Alexander Duckett. Web page. Electronic document, https://www.wikitree.com/wiki/Duckett-858 accessed April 30, 2017.

Wildwood, Nellie
1876a The Bear River Region. West Coast Signal, October 11, 1876:3.

Wilson, Melinda, and Jerry Lesandro
2004 Milking Cows at Bear River. Humboldt Historian, Summer 2004:28-33.

Winkler, Charles
1995a A Case Unravels. Times-Standard, July 9, 1995:A1, A6.

Womack, Della
1985 Interview with unnamed interviewer. Copy in author's possession.

Wood, Lewis K.
1856 Northern Coast of California—Its Early Settlement. Humboldt Times, April 26, 1856.

1863 Northern Coast of California—Its Early Settlement. Humboldt Times, February 7, 1863.

1872a Discovery of Humboldt Bay: L. K. Wood's Narrative. West Coast Signal, March 20, 1872:1.

1872b The Discovery of Humboldt Bay—Letter from Lewis K. Wood, Esq. West Coast Signal, March 20, 1872:2.

Work Projects Administration
1940a The National Guard of California 1849-1880, Part 1. Sacramento.

1940b The National Guard of California 1849-1880, Part 2. Sacramento.

WorthPoint
2018 RPPC Phillipsville Garberville CA Resort Lodge Humboldt Redwood Hwy Eureka Photo. Web page. Electronic document, https://www.worthpoint.com/worthopedia/rppc-phillipsville-garberville-ca-22056928 accessed on April 2, 2018.

Worthen, Evelyn Shuster
1996 The Unfolding Drama of Bridgeville, a Former Stagecoach Town: As Told By a Country School Teacher. Eureka: E. S Worthen.

Wrecksite
2018a. S S Alaska (+1921). Website. Electronic document, https://www.wrecksite.eu/wreck.aspx?23643 accessed on December 13, 2018.

Wright, Harold Bell
1942 The Man Who Went Away. New York: Harper & Brothers.

Wrigley, Irving
1991 Interview with Jerry Rohde, May 31, 1991.
N.d. Interview with Jerry Rohde

www.flickr.com
2016a 1913 Locomobile. Web page. Electronic document, https://www.flickr.com/photos/carlylehold/29364889913/ accessed on October 31, 2016.

Wright, Warren B.
1975 Sheep shearing time at the Drewry Ranch.

Yarborough, Bridget M.
1976 "S.S. Emidio" Ends Voyage In CC Port. Del Norte Triplicate Bi-Centennial Edition:193.

Y. Z. (pseud.)
1859 Letter to the Editor. Northern Californian, December 28, 1859:2.

Zachary, Jean
1986 Some glimpses of history from Moody Road areas. Humboldt Historian, January-February 1986:16-21.

Endnotes

1. Merriam 1998:reel 9, frame 285.
2. Goddard 1907c:35-46, 1907d:10.
3. Goddard 1907c:43.
4. Goddard 1907c:44-45.
5. Goddard 1923:107.
6. Merriam 1976:90; Goddard:1965:107.
7. Goddard 1923:107.
8. Humboldt Standard 1883a; Turner and Turner 2010:130; Gibbs 2016:21.
9. Irvine 1915:952-953.
10. Doolittle 1865.
11. Rowley 2004a:33.
12. Surveyor General's Office 1876b.
13. Doolittle 1865; Surveyor General's Office 1871c, 1872a, 1873a, 1876a, 1876b, 1876c.
14. Doolittle 1864; Surveyor General's Office 1876b.
15. Fountain 2001:(39)163.
16. Fountain 2001:(39)163.
17. Cook 1997:(5)55.
18. Irvine 1915:916.
19. Cook and Hawk 2006:103. Other accounts claim that Enoch Jewett acquired 10,000 acres from Redd (Irvine 1915:916; Cook 1997:(5)55), but if so, Jewett did not hold on to the entirety. A review of later property maps makes the 2,400-acre figure more likely.
20. Cook and Hawk 2006:103.
21. Anonymous 1876:1.
22. Fountain 2001:(89)311; Cook and Hawk 2006:101.
23. Evening Star 1877b:1, 1877d:1; Cook and Hawk 1997:(12)1; Cook and Hawk 2006:54. Cook and Hawk give the year as 1878, but the Evening Star, reporting in real time, has it completed by April 1877.
24. Cook and Hawk 2006:54, 102.
25. Cook and Hawk 2006:101.
26. As of 2019, the barn was still standing.
27. Cook and Hawk 2006:105.
28. Cook and Hawk 2006:102.
29. Frickstad 1955:42.
30. Forbes 1886.
31. Monroe 1981:19.
32. Cook and Hawk 2006:102.
33. CRTANCS 2001:139.
34. McTavish 1885d:3.
35. Asbill and Shawley 1975:189-191.
36. Rambler 1887a:3.
37. Fountain 2001:(89)152, 169, 170.
38. Cook and Hawk 2006:106, 108;
39. Speegle 1945a.
40. Humboldt Standard 1927a.
41. Tooby 1983:12.
42. Fountain 2001:(62)200, (106)137.
43. Asbill and Shawley 1975:186.
44. DeLong 1971:1.
45. Ferndale Enterprise 1878b:3.
46. Cook and Hawk 2006:27-28.
47. Fountain 2001:(33)350.
48. Fountain 2001:(33)350.
49. Fountain 2001:(33)350.
50. Asbill and Shawley 1975:188.
51. Asbill and Shawley 1975:186.
52. Blue Lake Advocate 1898a:2.
53. Blue Lake Advocate 1898b:1.
54. Tracy 1993a:9, 11-12.
55. Tracy 1993a:11-12.
56. Tracy 1993a:11.
57. Tracy 1993a:11, 14.
58. Which still bloomed avidly above nearby Spruce Grove a century later.
59. Tracy 1993a:17.
60. Tracy 1993a:18.
61. Tracy 1993a:40, 42-43, 45.
62. Tracy 1993a:49.
63. Tracy 1993a:49.
64. Tracy 1993a:53-55.
65. Tracy 1993a:14, 44.
66. Tracy 1993a:55.
67. Tracy 1993a:56.
68. Tracy 1993a:57.
69. Tracy 1993a:58.
70. Tracy 1993a:68.
71. Tracy 1993a:74.
72. Tracy 1993a:78-79.
73. Tracy 1993a:78.
74. Tracy 1993a:80.
75. Tracy 1993a:81-82.
76. Tracy 1993a:84.
77. Denny 1911; Lentell 1898.
78. Tracy 1993a:95, 97.
79. Cook and Hawk 2006:109.
80. Cook 1997:(3)78, (7)137; Cook and Hawk 2006:98.
81. Cook and Hawk 2006:98. On October 16, 1914, sergeant John Drewry and guard Joe Kerr were making their rounds at Folsom State Prison when they were attacked by Frank Cheeks (prisoner #9336) and Gordon Phelps (prisoner #8149), who had unlocked their cell door with a makeshift key fashioned from a piece of wire. The convicts were armed with a dumbbell and knife. In the ensuing struggle, both guards dropped their pistols. Kerr managed to break free and alert the other prison guards, but Drewry was stabbed to death by Cheeks. The prisoners, now armed with the guards' pistols, ran into the prison yard, where Kerr killed Phelps with a shot through the head. Cheeks exchanged shots with guard Frank Maher, who was in the yard tower. Maher was wounded in the leg and died 12 days later after the wound became infected. Cheeks managed to get outside of the prison and hid along the nearby American River. He was serving a life sentence for murdering a Tulare County rancher and had already made a spectacular escape attempt, when he launched himself out the window of the train that was taking him to his trial. Cheeks was soon caught after that episode and this time he was also quickly captured, being found in a Loomis rooming house. He was tried for Drewry's murder, found guilty, and sentenced to be hanged. He subsequently made another escape attempt, which was foiled, and was executed on August 27, 1915 (Ommen 2012; Brown 2008:45).
82. Cook and Hawk 2006:97.
83. Cook 1997:(5)35
84. Metsker 1949:92.
85. Cook 1997:(3)78.
86. library.humboldt.edu 2016; Fountain 2001:(27)319; Cook 1997:(11)150.

87. Denny 1911.
88. Denny 1911; Belcher Abstract & Title Co. 1921:3.
89. Denny 1911:15.
90. Metsker 1949:92.
91. Fountain 2001:(27)319.
92. Humboldt Standard 1912a.
93. www.flickr.com 2016a. Converted to 2015 dollars, Tooby's Locomobile would cost $135,000—more than enough for even a Tesla (MeasuringWorth 2016c).
94. Humboldt Times 1911b.
95. Cook 1997:(12)32.
96. Blue Lake Advocate 1893a:2.
97. Cook and Hawk 2001:76.
98. Humboldt Times 1911e.
99. San Francisco Call 1911a:9; Denny 1911; History and Happenings 2019a.
100. The store and post office were observed by the author in 2005.
101. Cook 1997:(6)125.
102. History and Happenings 2020a.
103. Polk-Husted 1914:234.
104. Carranco and Beard 1981:194. There is further complexity: Kate Robertson Asbill had a friend named Carrie Morrison, who owned the Palace Hotel in Ukiah (Carranco and Beard 1981:206). It is not known if she was related to Carrie Morrison Robertson, a much younger woman, nor is it known if George Robertson, Carrie Robertson's husband, was related to Kate Robertson Asbill.
105. Lentell 1898.
106. Humboldt Times 1903a:9.
107. Carranco and Beard 1981:194.
108. Although in this last case, it should be mentioned that an early name for Douglas-fir was Douglas spruce (Peattie 1991:171).
109. Phegley 1991:20.
110. Phegley 1991:20.
111. Turner and Turner 2010:175.
112. Phegley 1991:20.
113. Or 500, depending on which paragraph of the article is being read.
114. Eddy 1893:65.
115. Wright 1975.
116. It is unclear from the available accounts whether the party set forth from the town of Sonoma or simply from some unnamed location in Sonoma County.
117. Coy 1982:66-67; Turner and Turner 2010:130; Gibbs 2016:120.
118. Coy 1982:67; Turner and Turner 2010:130.
119. Townes 1850:2.
120. U. S. War Department 1897a:79.
121. Doolittle 1865.
122. Gordon 1899a:3.
123. Surveyor General 1871c, 1876a.
124. Lentell 1905.
125. Rowley 2004a:33.
126. Blue Lake Advocate 1893a:2.
127. California Highway Bulletin 1916:5.
128. Doolittle 1865; Surveyor General 1876b.
129. Forbes 1886.
130. Goddard 1907d:10.
131. Trail Back 1974:17.
132. Reed 1986a:18.
133. Trail back 1974:2.
134. Forbes 1886.
135. Irvine 1915:698

136. Goddard 1908a:89-90.
137. U. S. Bureau of Land Management 2016a.
138. Forbes 1886.
139. Ferndale Enterprise 1890a:5.
140. State of California, Department of Natural Resources, Division of Forestry 1949a. The "hotel" was actually on the south side of the road, not the north side as mapped.
141. Pritchard 1987d:22.
142. U. S. Bureau of Land Management 2016b.
143. Lentell 1898; Denny 1911; Turner and Turner 2010:180.
144. McCormick n.d.a:12.
145. Turner and Turner 2010:104-105.
146. Turner and Turner 2010:162.
147. Speegle 1945b.
148. Robinson 1964b:10.
149. Turner and Turner 2010:70.
150. Rohde 2014:48-50.
151. Nixon 1966:156.
152. Melendy 1962b:2; Palmrose 2013:12.
153. Melendy 1962a:2.
154. Palmrose 2013:12.
155. Palmrose 2013:2.
156. Wickipedia 2018a.
157. Melendy 1962b:2.
158. Ober 1973.
159. Irvine 1915:1080; Palmrose 2003:11.
160. Fountain 2001:(79)100.
161. Melendy 1962c:2.
162. Irvine 1915:1080-1081.
163. Melendy 1962a:2.
164. Palmrose 2013:14.
165. Irvine 1915:1080-1081.
166. Irvine 1915:1081; Palmrose 2013:15.
167. Ferndale Enterprise 1913b.
168. Irvine 1915:1081.
169. Melendy 1962c:2.
170. Palmrose 2013:17.
171. Melendy 1962c:2.
172. Melendy 1962d:2.
173. Belcher Abstract & title Co. 1921:3.
174. St. John 1968b:3.
175. St. John 1968b:3.
176. St. John 1968b:3.
177. St. John 1968b:3.
178. St. John 1968b:3.
179. St. John 1968b:3.
180. Goddard 1903a:19; Goddard 1908b:53-54; Ethnological Documents 2002:reel 12(4):35-45, 186.
181. Ethnological Documents 2002:reel 12(4):70.
182. Merriam 1993:(30)419.
183. United States War Department 1897a:303-304.
184. Reed 1896a:18.
185. This later became East's Ferry, which was, appropriately, just east of Grizzly Bluff (Turner and Turner 2010:16).
186. Humboldt Times 1874b:3.
187. Humboldt Times 1879a:3.
188. CRTANCS 2001:117.
189. CRTANCS 2001:117.
190. Cook 1997:(10)14.
191. Cook 1997:(10)14; CRTANCS 2001:118.
192. CRTANCS 2001:160.
193. Durst 1883:253.
194. This is how the name appears in the Humboldt County deed records (Humboldt County Deeds

n.d.:Book B2:179). Elsewhere the spelling is given as Giesmann (McTavish 1885c:3), Gisseman (Seco 1880a), and as Giesman (Humboldt Times 1885d:3).

195. Humboldt Times 1885d:3.
196. McTavish 1885c:3.
197. McTavish 1885c:3.
198. Fountain 2001:(71)133.
199. Olsen 2020a.
200. Olsen 2020a.
201. Olsen 2020a; Van Hinte 1985:653-654.
202. Koch was a professional promoter who subsequently became involved in other land schemes. By 1897 he was secretary and treasurer of the Texas Colonization Company, owners of 51,000 acres of south Texas land, on which it was "proposed to settle a colony of Hollanders, with the expectation of making them good American citizens" (Chicago Directory Company 1897:231).
203. Humboldt Weekly Standard 1891a:2; Olson 2020a.
204. Humboldt Times 1891b:3.
205. Humboldt Weekly Standard 1891b:3; Olson 2020a.
206. Humboldt Times 1891a:3.
207. Olson 2020a.
208. Humboldt Times 1892b:2.
209. Humboldt Times 1892c:4.
210. Humboldt Times 1892c:4
211. Humboldt Times 1896a:1.
212. Humboldt Times, 1894a:4.
213. Humboldt Times 1895a:4.
214. Humboldt Times 1894b:2.
215. Irvine 1915:643.
216. Humboldt Times 1879a:3.
217. Cook 1997:(10)14.
218. Belcher 1921:2.
219. Blue Lake Advocate 1900a:2.
220. Humboldt Standard 1922a.
221. Humboldt Standard 1925b.
222. Cook 1997:(4)14.
223. Humboldt Standard 1925h.
224. American Lumberman 1912b:55.
225. Blue Lake Advocate 1893a:2.
226. Melendy 1962d:2.
227. Metsker 1949:62.
228. Belcher 1921:2; Carranco 1982:175.
229. Metsker 1949:62; Rohde and Verwayne 2005:5-6.
230. Rohde and Verwayne 2005:6.
231. Rohde and Verwayne 2005:6.
232. Rohde and Verwayne 2005:6.
233. Rohde and Verwayne 2005.
234. Rohde and Verwayne 2005:6.
235. Rohde 2005a.
236. Rohde 2005a, 2005b.
237. Palmrose 2013:17.
238. Melendy 1962d:2; 1962e:2.
239. Palmrose 2013:17.
240. Sunset 2021a.
241. The enjoyment was endangered. By 2019 the winery was in bankruptcy court (Inforuptcy.com 2021a) and in 2021 the property was listed as being tax delinquent for five years and soon would be subject to sale (North Coast Journal 2021a:33). It began to look like Fruitland would witness a second agricultural debacle more than a century after the first. But then new owners took over the winery, and as of 2022, the Fruitland vineyard was again fruitful.
242. Merriam 1998:reel 31:frames 93, 97.
243. Essene 1942:89.
244. Cook and Hawk 2006:112. Gurshorn C. Armstrong had property on the South Fork Eel at the same time Thomas Armstrong had his ranch on the main Eel (Fountain 2001:[31]143). The two are sometimes conflated (Fountain 2001:[61]20).
245. Cook and Hawk 2006:112. The 1865 county map locates "T. Armstrong" about two miles north of Spruce Grove (Doolittle 1865).
246. McTavish 1885d:3.
247. Surveyor General's Office 1873b.
248. Irvine 1915:606; Mathison 1998:4.
249. library.humboldt.edu 2016.
250. Cook 1997:(12)1; Fountain 2001:(72)225-226. Cook's information indicates that the road reached Alder Point in the spring; Fountain's account claims it happened in the fall.
251. Cook and Hawk 2006:112.
252. Fountain 2001:(72)225-226.
253. Evening Star 1877a:3.
254. Forbes 1886.
255. Fountain 2001:(61)22.
256. Two sources give the year as 1878 (Cook and Hawk 2006:54; Cook 1997:[12]1) but the Eureka Evening Star carries a report from April 25, 1877, that "the road is finished through Cahto" a community in Mendocino County (Eureka Evening Star 1877d:1).
257. West Coast Signal 1878b:1.
258. Friend 1937:14. A later source states that the bridge was completed in 1890 (Mathison 1998:4).
259. Mathison 1998:3. Mathison refers to horses being at the "stage stop," but the horses were probably also used by individual postal riders carrying the mail.
260. Elliott 1881:185.
261. Irvine 1915:622.
262. McTavish 1885d:3; Forbes 1886.
263. Carranco and Beard 1981:218. More is told about White in the chapter on Eel Rock.
264. Lentell 1898; Carranco and Beard 1981:228.
265. Fountain 2001:(24)18-19.
266. Blue Lake Advocate 1893a:2. George W. Charles drowned in February 1888 (Rohnerville Herald 1888
267. Humboldt Standard 1916d:1.
268. Forbes 1886.
269. Lentell 1898.
270. Spencer 1895:147.
271. Tracy 1992a.
272. Frickstad 1955:41-42.
273. Irvine 1915:600.
274. Irvine 1915:738.
275. Lentell 1898.
276. Pacific Reporter 1901:34-36; Carranco and Beard 1981:239-257.
277. Irvine 1915:693.
278. Tracy 1992a 40-41. Dyke was apparently unconcerned that mapmakers had incorrectly rendered his last name since 1886, using first "Doyle" (Forbes 1886) and then coming somewhat closer with "Dike" (Lentell 1898).
279. Tracy 1992a:20, 23.
280. Tracy 1992a:69.
281. Mathison 1998:7.
282. Irvine 1915:473.
283. Irvine 1915:804.
284. Irvine 1915:473.

285. Frickstad 1955:41.
286. Mathison 1998:8, 10.
287. In the United States, a fourth-class post office was on the bottom rung of the postal ladder. According to one account, "persons with reasonable cause could make application for a post office in their community. It could be a business man, a company or group of interested residents. If approved, a small fourth class post office would be opened on private property, most often in the applicant's place of business, home or another place of their choice. The exception to this rule was that no post office could be located in, or joining a bar room. The applicant was most often named as Postmaster/Postmistress" (Crocker 2016).
288. Irvine 1915:473.
289. Irvine 1915:473.
290. Irvine 1915:738.
291. Humboldt Historian 1965a.
292. Mathison 1998:8.
293. At some point the industrious McNight also built the Alderpoint water system, but the date is uncertain (Mathison 1998:12).
294. Cook 1997:(5)89.
295. Mathison 1998:10.
296. Gregory 1911:470.
297. Fountain 2001:(61)15.
298. Mathison 1998:13.
299. Mathison 1998:16. The school playground equipment consisted of "a swing in the old oak on the west side of the schoolhouse, a baseball and bat."
300. Mathison 1998:17.
301. Mathison 1998:30.
302. Asbill and Shawley 1975:362.
303. Irvine 1915:139.
304. Mathison 1998:23.
305. Mathison 1998:26.
306. Mathison 1998:23.
307. Mathison 1998:24-25.
308. Humboldt Standard 1916d:1.
309. Cook 1997:(2)28.
310. Humboldt Standard 1916d:1.
311. Mathison 1998:28.
312. Mathison 1998:28, 36.
313. Mathison 1998:38.
314. Mathison 1998:28-29.
315. Mathison 1998:18.
316. Mathison 1998:30.
317. Humboldt Standard 1916d:1.
318. Fountain 2001:(61)15.
319. Humboldt Standard 1916d:1.
320. Belcher Abstract & Title Co. 1922:12.
321. Bridgemeister 2022a.
322. Mathison 1998:35.
323. Mathison 1998:36.
324. Mathison 1998:40-41.
325. Bridgemeister 2022a.
326. Mathison 1998:43.
327. Cook 1997:(2)31.
328. Mathison 1998:18.
329. Mathison 1998:44-45.
330. Mathison 1998:46.
331. Mathison 1998:44.
332. Mathison 1998:55.
333. Mathison 1989:55.
334. Cook 1997:(2)28.
335. Humboldt Standard 1939c.
336. Humboldt Historian 1995a:22.
337. Mathison 1998:68-70.
338. Mathison 1998:70-71.
339. Mathison 1998:71.
340. Mathison 1998:71-72, 74-75.
341. Mathison 1998: 75-77.
342. Mathison 1998:76-77.
343. Fountain 2001:(61)18. This excerpted letter has been edited slightly for clarity.
344. Fountain 2001:(61) 18.
345. "6 Whereby the world that then was, being overflowed with water, perished: 7 But the heavens and the earth, which are now, by the same word are kept in store, reserved unto fire against the day of judgment and perdition of ungodly men." (King James Version.)
346. Humboldt Times 1964a.
347. Cook 1997:(2)30.
348. Mathison 1998:78-79.
349. Mathison 1998.
350. Goddard 1906b:40.
351. Goddard 1906b:24-25; Ethnological Documents 2002:12(4)221.
352. Long Valley is south of Laytonville in Mendocino County.
353. U. S. War Department 1897a:982.
354. U. S. War Department 1897b:37.
355. U. S. War Department 1897b:50.
356. U. S. War Department 1897b:170.
357. Carranco and Beard 1981:145.
358. Humboldt Times 1863a:3
359. The Herald made the common mistake of conflating numerous southern Humboldt tribal groups (Sinkyone, Lassik, etc.) under the misnomer Wailaki in its various spellings.
360. Humboldt Times 1863b:2.
361. Murphey 1941:354.
362. Humboldt Times 1863c:2.
363. Fountain 2002:(24)28.
364. Forbes 1886. Forbes's map actually shows the owner as H. T. Fairbanks, but this author believes that fair or otherwise there was only one bank, not two or more.
365. California Board of Bank Commissioners 1900:177.
366. Fountain 2002:(62)238.
367. Denny 1911.
368. Humboldt Beacon 1910b:4.
369. freepages.rootsweb.com 2018.
370. Wikipedia 2018k.
371. The Californian 1910.
372. Humboldt Beacon 1910b:4.
373. The Californian 1910.
374. Fountain 2002:(89)324.
375. Fountain 2002:(71)30.
376. Fountain 2002:(71) 30.
377. Humboldt Times 1912a.
378. Humboldt Times 1912a.
379. Humboldt Times 1914a.
380. Rayle 2014:12-13.
381. Irvine 1915:121-122.
382. Irvine 1915:125.
383. Irvine 1915:420, 423.
384. Wikipedia 2018n.
385. The vessel may have been the Poison Oak. An account of its often-amusing misadventures will be found in the chapter on Shively.
386. Mathison 1998:52.
387. Humboldt Standard 1915.

388. Thornbury 1923:83.

389. Thornbury 1923:164-165.

390. Press Reference Library 1915:335; Belcher Abstract & Title Co. 1921:3, 1922:12.

391. Stone 1913:33.

392. Elvidge n. d.:A-21.

393. Reis 2005:127

394. CRTANCS 2001:123. This account refers to the "Trinity Lumber Company," leaving "National" out of its name.

395. Humboldt Times 1952a:8-10.

396. Humboldt Times 1956a:1.

397. Humboldt historian 1996a:46.

398. Metsker 1949:93.

399. Cook 1997:(VIII)44.

400. Humboldt Times 1960b:1.

401. Cook 1997:(4)6.

402. Cook 1997:(4)13.

403. Bair 1989a:11.

404. U. S. War Department 1897a:633-634.

405. Hunt 1962:49-50.

406. U. S. Department 1897a:691.

407. U. S. Department 1897a:723

408. Wikpedia 2018b.

409. Humboldt Times 1862a:3.

410. Mays 2018.

411. U. S. War Department 1897a:559.

412. U. S. War Department 1897a:843.

413. U. S. War Department 1897a:843.

414. U. S. War Department 1897a:842.

415. U. S. War Department 1897a:803.

416. Humboldt Times 1862c:3.

417. Mays 2018.

418. Humboldt Times 1862b:3.

419. U. S. Department 1897a:181.

420. U. S. War Department 1897a:908.

421. Volunteer 1862:3.

422. A startling change of gender for a season traditionally associated with the feminine. Viz: "The faith in their happy eyes/Comes surely from our Sister the Spring/When over the sea she flies . . . ." (Belloc, "The South Country.")

423. Volunteer 1862:3.

424. Surveyor General's Office 1873a.

425. Humboldt Standard 1919b.

426. Forbes 1886.

427. Humboldt Standard 1937c; BLM 2017e.

428. Fountain 2001:(127)346.

429. San Francisco Call 1895a:8.

430. Carranco and Beard 1981:217.

431. Carranco and Bear 1981:220.

432. Carranco and Beard 1981:239-240.

433. Carranco and Beard 1981:240-241.

434. Carranco and Beard 1981:242-243.

435. Carranco and Beard 1981:244.

436. Carranco and Beard 1981:229-230.

437. Carranco and Beard 1981:244.

438. Carranco and Beard 1981:245.

439. Carranco and Beard 1981:250.

440. Carranco and Beard 1981:251.

441. Carranco and Beard 1981:252-257.

442. Lentell 1898.

443. Californian 1914:30.

444. Cook 1997:(10)14.

445. Frickstad 1955:42.

446. Aubrey-Herzog 2022.

447. Humboldt Times 1918a:6.

448. CRTANCS 2001:6.

449. Fountain 2001(71)445; History and Happenings 2017a.

450. Sunset 1951a:30.

451. The Metsker atlas from 1949 shows only the older road (Metsker 1949:76), but the Forest Service map from the same year shows the new road in place (State of California, Department of Natural Resources, Division of Forestry 1949a).

452. Humboldt Standard, 1955a:26.

453. Humboldt Historian 2002a:12. The article also claims that an Eel Rock School existed since 1889, but this is not substantiated by other records. The article may have conflated the Eel Rock School with the Eel River School, which operated at least as early as 1890 but was located downriver west of Loleta (Hamm 1890:21).

454. Fountain 2001:(71)445.

455. Humboldt Standard, 1955a:26.

456. Humboldt Times 1952a.

457. Fountain 2001:(71)445.

458. Southern Humboldt Life and Times 1997a:12.

459. Anonymous n.d. The author received this information from an unidentified local in response to the question, "where is Eel Rock?"

460. Hanson 1962:8.

461. Cook 1997:(6)87.

462. Felt 1869. Anna Morrison Reed later wrote a more detailed account in her magazine, the Northern Crown (Reed 1904a).

463. Fountain 2001:(62)379.

464. Reed 1904a.

465. Schwarzkopf 1949f:13.

466. Surveyor General 1872a.

467. Schwarzkopf 1949f:13.

468. McTavish 1885c:3.

469. Humboldt Times 1880a; Schwarzkopf 1949f:13.

470. Schwarzkopf 1949f:13.

471. Blue Lake Advocate 1893a:2.

472. Turner and Turner 2010:70.

473. Robinson 1964b:10.

474. Irvine 1915:98.

475. CRTANCS 2001:154-155.

476. Cunningham 2000a:15-20.

477. Cunningham 2000a:20.

478. Frickstad 1955:47.

479. Frickstad 1955:45.

480. Ferndale Enterprise 1919b:1.

481. Humboldt Standard 1938c.

482. Schwarzkopf 1949f:13.

483. Schwarzkopf 1949f:13.

484. Belcher Abstract & title Co. 1921:2.

485. CRTANCS 2001:154.

486. Anderson 2001a:A1, A8.

487. Dana 1902:61.

488. He was baptized Hiram Ulysses Grant but was always called by his middle name. The congressman who assisted Grant with his application to West Point erroneously put his name down as Ulysses S. Grant. His diploma and commission from the military academy listed him as such, and Grant failed to persuade the army to correct the mistake. He gave up and thereafter signed his name "Ulysses S. Grant" (New York Historical Society 2016).

489. Lacey and Murray 2013:262.

490. U. S. War Department 1897b:643, 655.

491. Smith 2001:84-88; White 2016:118-121; Chernow 2017:82-87.

492. U. S. War Department 1897b:655.

493. Goddard 1903a:19; Goddard 1908b:53-54; Ethnological Documents 2002:reel 12(4):35-45, 186.
494. U. S. War Department 1897b:643.
495. Coy (1982:65-66) makes reference to the original Sonoma Trail coming down the South Fork Eel, indicating that "in later times the trail kept to the ridge between this branch and the main stream . . . ."
496. Humboldt Times 1861c:3.
497. Doolittle 1865.
498. Surveyor General 1871c.
499. Humboldt Beacon 1910a:7.
500. Guinn 1904:1169.
501. Gordon 1899a:3.
502. Guinn 1904:1169.
503. Gordon 1899a:3.
504. Turner and Turner 2010:73.
505. Turner and Turner 2010:73.
506. Humboldt Beacon 1910a:7.
507. Guinn 1904:1169-1170.
508. Irvine 1915:1029-1031.
509. Fuller 1873:2.
510. Ferndale Enterprise 1878a:3.
511. Rohde 2014a:49.
512. Humboldt Times 1932b.
513. Durst 1883:253.
514. Humboldt Weekly Times 1881a.
515. Cook 1997:(VIII)14.
516. The use of white oak for maul heads is noteworthy, ergo this note. Oregon white oak is better known for its use by ranchers for fence posts since its "heartwood . . . lasts so long in contact with the soil." The species used for maul heads was usually the canyon live oak, whose "tough and strong and shock-resistant" wood gave it the nickname maul oak (Peattie 1991:425-426, 446).
517. Daily Times-Telephone 1883a:3.
518. McTavish 1885c:3.
519. Tamm 1890:121, 123.
520. Well might readers (and my editor) ask, "what does 'six stalks" mean?" A diligent search has revealed no answer, so I will offer the assumption that this was the number of corn stalks that each entrant could present for the judges' inspection.
521. California State Agricultural Society 1891:592-593.
522. Belcher Abstract & Title Co. 1921:2.
523. Gordon 1899b:3.
524. Gordon 1899a:3
525. Irvine 1915:1029-1031.
526. Irvine 1915:535.
527. Lentell 1898.
528. Metsker 1949:45.
529. Irvine 1915: 827-828, 1238.
530. Fountain 2001:(70)88.
531. Fountain 2001:(70)87.
532. Humboldt Historian 1999a:45.
533. CRTANCS 2001:65-66.
534. Rohde 2014:50; Fountain 2001:(32)89.
535. Fountain 2001:(32)89.
536. Turner and Turner 2010:220.
537. Scott 1999:26, 28-29.
538. Turner and Turner 2010:220.
539. Irvine 1915:1251.
540. Humboldt Standard 1926a.
541. Pinches 2006.
542. Clever 1998:15, 19.
543. Clever 1998:20-21.
544. Schwarzkopf 1949f:13.
545. Schwarzkopf 1949f:13.
546. Humboldt Beacon n.d. The article states that the southerly section of the bridge washed out, but this is contradicted by the current condition of the bridge, which shows the newer replacement sections to the north.
547. Eureka Newspapers 1965a.
548. The dog is not dead, he's only resting.
549. Wikipedia 2017a.
550. Rohde 1991a:3.
551. "Time consumes all things."
552. Rohde 2014:50.
553. Forbes 1886.
554. Merriam 1993:(30)413.
555. Schwarzkopf 1949d:17.
556. Pritchard 1987a:12.
557. Bureau of Land Management 2017a.
558. Surveyor General's Office 1871b.
559. Schwarzkopf 1949d:13; Childs 1991.
560. Frickstad 1955:42.
561. Bureau of Land Management 2017a.
562. McTavish 1885b:3.
563. Frickstad 1955:42-43.
564. Ferndale Enterprise 1890a:5.
565. Ferndale Enterprise 1891a:5.
566. Fountain 2001:(62)338.
567. St. John n.d.b.
568. Schwarzkopf 1949d:13.
569. Childs 1991a:5.
570. Times-Standard 1993a:B-11.
571. Childs 1991a:5.
572. As per an "Englewood Inn" postcard.
573. Falk 2018. This building is shown in a postcard from Young's Studio from about 1911. Schwarzkopf (1949d:13) confusingly refers to it as the Englewood Inn.
574. Schwarzkopf 1949d:13; Fountain 2001:(62)338. Schwarzkopf reports the purchase occurred in 1920, but Fountian's source is a contemporary newspaper account, and its date is thus used here.
575. Schwarzkopf 1949d:13.
576. Childs 1991a:2.
577. Clever 1982:3; Childs 1991a:1-2.
578. Childs 1991a:1, 5
579. St. John 1959; Childs 1991a:1, 5.
580. Childs 1991a:5.
581. St. John 1959.
582. St. John 1959; Turner and Turner 2010:196.
583. Schwarzkopf 1949d:13.
584. postalhistory.com 2016a.
585. Hawk 2004:86-88.
586. Hawk 2004:84.
587. Baldo and Brown 2005:39-42.
588. aveofthegiants.com 2016a.
589. Childs 1986:3-4; Childs et al. 1991.
590. Merriam 1993:(30)420.
591. Goddard 1907b:36.
592. Goddard 1907b:29-40.
593. Goddard 1908b:105-108.
594. Doolittle 1865; Surveyor General's Office 1871b; Coy 1982:65-66.
595. Coy 1982:226.
596. U. S. War Department 1897a:79.
597. Rohde 2014:48-54.
598. Goddard 1907b:39.
599. Goddard 1907b:40
600. U. S. War Department 1897a:79.
601. Turner and Turner 2010:162.

602. U. S. War Department 1897a:79.
603. U. S. War Department 1897a:79.
604. U. S. War Department 1897a:79. The reference to the "mail trail" is ambiguous. One such trail ran just east of the main Eel as it crossed Larabee Creek. Another route, called "Bur's [Burr's] Trail, is mapped as coming south from the Van Duzen area to cross the ridge just west of Chalk Mountain. While not labeled specifically as another mail trail, it is seems likely that it is this route that Ketchum referred to when he went "over the mountain" and then across the "mail trail." The reasons for this belief are three: 1) this route would have departed the Van Duzen about three miles downriver from McAtee's Crossing; this would fit with the camping place of the detachment, which Ketchum indicated was about "three miles below the crossing." 2) The crossing of the other trail was about four miles farther down the Van Duzen, a location that would have taken the detachment a considerable time to reach from their camp of the previous night before they took the trail south. 3) the route from Chalk Mountain would probably have brought the detachment to a meeting with Larabee Creek near the village of No-le-bi, which is the only known site in the area that would have corresponded with Ketchum's description of "a large ranch" of Indians. (Surveyor General's Office 1871b, 1871c, 1872c; Belcher Abstract & Title Co. 1922:13).
605. U. S. War Department 1897a:79.
606. Goddard 1907b:33-35.
607. Sam 1921e.
608. Goddard 1907b:33.
609. Goddard 1907b:36.
610. Fuller 1873:2.
611. Humboldt Standard 1910a:1.
612. Scott 1999:26-27.
613. Scott 1989:6.
614. Irvine 1915:971.
615. Stindt and Dunscomb 1964:37.
616. Irvine 1915:285.
617. CRTANCS 1999:103. More than 30 years earlier, when Georgeson lived in Blocksburg, he married Ella T. Thompson, who had been the teacher at the Larabee School, which at that time was located on upper Larabee Creek, about nine miles north of Blocksburg (Humboldt Standard 1939a; Humboldt Times 1935a; CRTANCS 2001:149).
618. Clever 1998.10.
619. CRTANCS 1999:100, 103.
620. Forbes 1886.
621. Parker 1988a:5; Schwarzkopf 1949c:17.
622. Humboldt Beacon 1916a.
623. Belcher Abstract & Title Co. 1921:2, 1922:13.
624. Fritz-Metcalf Photograph Collection 2016d.
625. Carranco and Sorensen 1988:216-217; Fritz-Metcalf Photograph Collection 2016e, 2016f.
626. Humboldt Beacon 1916a.
627. Carranco and Sorensen 1988:217.
628. Stindt 1987:156.
629. Belcher Abstract & Title Co. 1922:13.
630. CRTANCS 1999:106-107.
631. Crismon 1991a.
632. Humboldt Standard 1938a, 1938b.
633. Rohde and Rohde 1992:123; Ruggles 1990.
634. Crismon 1991a.
635. Humboldt Times 1938a.

636. Humboldt Times 1938a.
637. Crismon 1991a.
638. Schwarzkopf 1949c:28.
639. Schwarzkopf 1949c:28.
640. CRTANCS 1999:100, 106, 108.
641. Frickstad 1955:46.
642. CRTANCS 1999:102.
643. Evans 1999:61-62.
644. Evans 1999:62-63.
645. Evans 1999:63.
646. Evans 1999:63-64.
647. Evans 1999:64.
648. Evans 1999:64-65.
649. Evans 1999:64-66.
650. Evans 1999:66.
651. Evans 1999:66-67.
652. Evans 1999:68-72.
653. Rohde 2022:98.
654. Merriam 1993: reel 9, frames 169-170.
655. Loud 1918:273.
656. Harrington 1983:reel 1:716.
657. Schwarzkopf 1949c:17.
658. Eich 1978:1.
659. Lentell 1898.
660. There is confusion about this date. Parker gives the Shaw purchase as January 6, 1905, but doesn't provide the location. He later claims that Holmes Eureka bought two 80-acre parcels on the flat in 1908 (Parker 1988a:5). Carranco and Sorensen (1988:115) state that "in 1905 Holmes Eureka Lumber Company also acquired timber across the Eel River from Shively." Eich (1978:1) indicates that by 1906 Holmes Eureka was paying taxes on the property on the flat and that the company had taken over the land in 1905. It appears that Parker didn't realize that the Shaw property was at Holmes and confused the purchase date with the date when Holmes Eureka started cutting timber on the flat.
661. Schwarzkopf 1949c:17; Eich 1978:1.
662. Fountain 2001:(79)100.
663. Frickstad 1955:44.
664. Borden 1963a:13.
665. Unlike logging railroads, which usually serve only their parent company, a common carrier railroad serves the general public (Wikipedia 2019).
666. Schwarzkopf 1949c:17; Parker 1988a:5.
667. Irvine 1915:1080-1081; Borden 1963a:13; Fountain 2001:(79)100. Irvine's biography of Smythe indicates that he started his Holmes-to-Sherwood run in 1910, but this is contradicted by the 1908 newspaper article found in Fountain, which gives September 1908 as the date.
668. Eich 1978:1.
669. At least according to one exuberant report.
670. Eich 1978:1.
671. Fountain 2001:(71)234.
672. Irvine 1915:872, 1,000.
673. Eich 1978:4.
674. Belcher Abstract & Title Company 1922:13.
675. Eich 1978:4.
676. Parker 1988a:5.
677. This would be enough wood to build about fourteen 1,500-square-foot houses (House Designers 2022).
678. Schwarzkopf 1949c:17; Fritz-Metcalf Photograph Collection, 2016a. It is impossible to determine if the sources are describing the same tree, but the accounts correspond so closely as to make the match almost certain.

679. Parker 1988a:5.
680. Schwarzkopf 1949c:17.
681. Eich 1978:4.
682. Schwarzkopf 1949c:17.
683. Eich 1978:1
684. Irvine 1915:993-994.
685. Irvine 1915:994.
686. Eich 1978:4; Martin n.d.
687. Belcher Abstract & Title Company 1922:12.
688. Schwarzkopf 1949c:17.
689. Hagemann n.d.
690. Schwarzkopf 1949c:17.
691. Hagemann n.d.
692. Turner and Turner 2010:126.
693. Schwarzkopf 1949e.
694. Baratti, n.d. 5-6.
695. Baratti n.d.:8.
696. Schwarzkopf 1949e.
697. Milota 1993a:88.
698. Under the Homestead Act of 1862, homesteaders had five years in which to build a house and farm a 160-acre land parcel. Two neighbors or friends then had to confirm that these improvements had been made. A total of $18 in fees and commissions had to be paid during the process. The homesteader then received a patent for the land, signed by the current President of the United States (nps.gov 2016a).
699. Schwarzkopf 1949e.
700. Fuller 1873a:2.
701. Merriam 1993(1)322. He states here that the "Lo-lahn-kok . . . [claimed] main Eel from Shively to Scotia." Elsewhere Merriam indicates that the group held the main Eel "from Shively to Dyerville" (Merriam 1993:(9)153). I have taken the two statements together as indicating Lolahnkok control of the main Eel from Scotia to the mouth of the South Fork at Dyerville. No Indian from this stretch of the Eel was ever interviewed by an ethnographer. Merriam's information comes from George Burtt, a Lolahnkok from Bull Creek. However, Pliny Goddard's informant Charlie indicated that Sinkyone territory (which would have included the Lolahnkok group) extended north only to the High Rock area, some seven miles upriver from Shively (Ethnological Documents 2002:reel 12(4):31-33). I have used Merriam's information because I believe that his informant George Burtt was more familiar with the Shively area than was Charlie, who appears to have traveled down the Eel only as far as the High Rock area.
702. Fuller 1873a:2.
703. Surveyor General's Office 1871b.
704. Faulkner 2004a:33.
705. Rohde 2014a:48-50.
706. West Coast Signal 1877b:1.
707. Schwarzkopf 1949e; St. John 1968a:3.
708. Humboldt Beacon 1967b:15.
709. St. John 1968a:3.
710. Personal observation of the author's.
711. St John 1968a:3.The article does not give the daytime fee for the ferry, but presumably it was less. Converted into 2015 dollars, the nighttime charge would be about $11.70 (measuringworth.com2016a).
712. Humboldt Times 1932a.
713. St. John 1968a:3, 6.
714. St. John 1968a:3, 6.

715. Faulkner 2003a. This account states that the motor was added in 1949; it is unclear what relationship this boat had with the "14-foot skiff" that operated in 1948 as a substitute for the partly washed-out summer bridge (Humboldt Times 1948a:1).
716. Eich 1984:4.
717. Faulkner 2003a.
718. Humboldt Standard 1939b; Humboldt Times 1948a:1.
719. Faulkner 2003a.
720. Humboldt Standard 1939b; Humboldt Times 1948a:1.
721. Humboldt Times 1949a.
722. M. H. 1877:1. The author has concluded that the initialed individual was Martha Herrick, whose husband Rufus had filled the same issue of the Signal with his effulgent praise of the same roadwork.
723. McTavish 1885b:3.
724. There are at least three dates given for the arrival of the railroad at the future site of Elinor. Carranco and Sorensen (1988:141) claim the rail line reached the area in 1906. Borden (Borden 1949a:10), writing in 1949, claims the event took place in July 1898 while the same Borden (Borden 1963a:7) writing in 1963 has changed his mind and gives the year as 1892 Borden's 1892 date is supported by Eddy's 1893 map, which shows the railroad line ending at the approximate location of Elinor (Eddy 1893:6).
725. Borden 1963a:7.
726. Orpha Heinbach inspected the partly completed tunnel with her father and two sisters. She reported that "the bluff is high and steep, and the water around the foot of it a dark green." The Heinbachs first went into the south end of the tunnel, finding "petrified shells" in the bluff side and about eight large timbers framing the entrance. Orpha noted that "the tunnel is cut wider at the top than at the bottom." The Heinbachs then went to the north entrance, "finding it much the same as the other . . ." but noting "there were not so many shells" (Heinbach 1986:12-13).
727. Stindt 1988a:119.
728. Schwarzkofp 1949e.
729. Frickstad 1955:46.
730. Genzoli 1982:8. Bump's original record of events on the Eel has not been located. An alternate version of the Poison Oak's exploits was written by Lynford "Bud" Scott, brief portions of which are used here. For his complete account, see: Scott 1999:51-52, 57-61. The Humboldt Times carried several reports about the Poison Oak that describe incidents somewhat similar to—but far from being exactly like—those in the Bump-Genzoli version. For readers who would like to leaven the Bump - Genzoli version with the newspaper accounts, there follows a "headline history" of the events reported by the Times, which includes citations for the articles. Humboldt Times: 1911e Poison Oak Aground; 1911f Craft Will Float Again; 1911g River Plays False; 1911h Will Attempt Salvage; 1911i Derrick Ready to Operate; 1911j Poison Oak to Float; 1911k Freight and Horse Are Lost in Deep Hole; 1911l Boat Stranded up River. 1912b Famous Poison Oak May Run on Humboldt Bay.
731. Genzoli 1982:8-9.
732. Genzoli 1982:9.
733. Genzoli 1982:9.

734. Genzoli 1982:9.
735. Genzoli 1982:9.
736. Genzoli 1982:9.
737. Genzoli 1982:9.
738. Genzoli 1982:9.
739. Genzoli 1982:9.
740. Genzoli 1982:9.
741. Genzoli 1982:9.
742. Genzoli 1982:9. Scott 1999:52, 59.
743. Genzoli 1982:9; Scott 1999:52, 59.
744. Genzoli 1982:9.
745. Genzoli 1982:9.
746. Schwarzkofp 1949e.
747. Irvine 1915:816; Schwarzkofp 1949e.
748. Faulkner 2003a.
749. Schwarzkofp 1949e.
750. Irvine 1915:816; Schwarzkofp 1949e; Faulkner
      2003a.
751. Faulkner 2004a:33.
752. Keesey 1982:21.
753. Irvine 1915:138.
754. Irvine 1915:963.
755. Fountain 2001:(62)348.
756. Irvine 1915:967-968; Eich 1984:3.
757. Jackson 1984:27.
758. Eich 1984:6.
759. Humboldt Beacon 1967b:15.
760. Humboldt Beacon 1916b.
761. Humboldt Times 1921a.
762. Humboldt Times 1930b.
763. Humboldt Standard 1930a.
764. Humboldt Times 1931a.
765. Humboldt Standard 1937b:1; Humboldt Times
      1937b:1. McCormick (1986a) incorrectly report-
      ed the wreck as involving engine 184, which was
      in two other wrecks that each killed three railroad
      workers This error was corrected by O'Hara and
      Service (2013:104) in their book on the North-
      western Pacific Railroad.
766. Tuttle 2016a.
767. St. John 1968a:6.
768. waterboards.ca.gov 2016a
769. Schwarzkofp 1949e.
770. Eich 1984:6.
771. Faulkner 2003a.
772. Merriam 1993:reel 30, frame 413; reel 9, frame 154
      left.
773. Turner and Turner 2010:148.
774. Frickstad 1955:45.
775. Fuller 1873a:2.
776. Fountain 2001:(62)283.
777. Rohde 2014a: 48-54.
778. West Coast Signal 1877a:4.
779. Stuart and Sawyer 2001:402.
780. Durst 1883:252-253.
781. Frickstad 1955:45.
782. Ferndale Enterprise 1887b:5.
783. Lentell 1898.
784. Still known as "Hazeltine" to the newspapers.
785. McTavish 1885b:3.
786. Irvine 1915:1058.
787. Belcher 1922:13.
788. Schwarzkopf 1949b:13.
789. Turner and Turner 2010:15.
790. Ferndale Enterprise 1891a:5.
791. Nash 1989a:4. The Barkdull family figured in
      another interesting naming. John and Nancy
      Barkdull lived in the Mattole Valley in the
      1860s. When a daughter was born there, she

was believed to be the first Humboldt County
white child born south of Cape Mendocino. Her
parents promptly named her Mendocino Barkdull
(Miner 1996:35).
792. Irvine 1915:998.
793. Fountain 2001:(83)362.
794. California, Department of Engineering, State
      Highway Commission 1914a:4; Humboldt Histo-
      rian 1981a:11.
795. California, Department of Engineering, State
      Highway Commission 1914a:3; Denny 1911;
      Belcher 1921:1, 1922:13.
796. Thornbury 1923:85.
797. Cunningham 2000a:15-17. Much of Cunningham's
      information about the Young family is also found
      in Irvine 1915:999-1001.
798. Cunningham 2000a:17.
799. Genzoli 1982:9; Humboldt Times: 1911e.
800. Cunningham 2000a:20-21.
801. Cunningham 2000a:20-21.
802. Cunningham 2000a:21.
803. Cunningham 2000a:21.
804. Lentell 1898; Denny 1911; Polk-Husted 1914;
      Irvine 1915:285; Humboldt Standard 1941a;
      Humboldt Beacon 1967a. The Beacon article
      claims that French "owned and operated" the mill
      but Irvine, a contemporaneous source, indicates
      that Georgeson was the owner. The 1914-1915
      county directory lists French as a "timber cruiser"
      and Georgeson as "pres Laurel Co: (Polk-Husted
      1914:245-246).
805. Davy 1950b.
806. Branscomb 2009a.
807. American Lumberman 1912a:65.
808. Marine Insight 2020.
809. Schwarzkopf 1949b:13.
810. Humboldt Beacon 1967a.
811. Schwarzkopf 1949b:13.
812. Irvine 1915:285.
813. Humboldt Beacon 1967a.
814. Humboldt Times 1931a.
815. Schwarzkopf 1949b:13.
816. Schwarzkopf 1949b:13.
817. Hawk 2004: 89, 91, 93.
818. Schwarzkopf 1949b:13.
819. Hawk 2004:94.
820. Schwarzkopf 1949b:13.
821. Schwarzkopf 1949b:13.
822. Ferndale Enterprise 1955a:1, 1955b:1.
823. Humboldt Standard 1964b:1.
824. Eureka Newspapers, Inc. 1965a.
825. Eureka Newspapers, Inc. 1965a.
826. Russell 1991.
827. Humboldt Beacon. N.d.
828. Russell 1991.
829. St. John. N.d.a.
830. Russell 1991.
831. Turner and Turner 2010:47.
832. Carranco and Sorensen 1988:133.
833. There are at least three dates given for the arrival
      of the railroad at the future site of Elinor. Car-
      ranco and Sorensen (1988:141) claim the rail line
      reached the Elinor area in 1906. Borden writing
      in 1949 (1949a:10), believes the event took place
      in July 1898, while Borden writing in 1963
      (1963a:7) has changed his mind and gives the year
      as 1892. The latter date is supported by Eddy's
      1893 map (1893:6) that shows the railroad line
      ending at the approximate location of Elinor.

834. Lentell 1898; Borden 1949a:10.
835. Ober 1973. Meakin's name is spelled Meekan in another account (Turner and Turner 2010:47.
836. Denny 1911; Turner and Turner 2010:47; Rohde 2014a:48-54.
837. Baxter 1987a:48.
838. Borden 1949a:10.
839. Murray 1987a:11. Murray probably well knew of whom she spoke: she succeeded Elinor (whose name she spells Eleanor) as Tom Fleming's wife. The other versions are summarized in Turner and Turner 2010:83.
840. Irvine 1915: 442.
841. Ober 1973.
842. Ober 1973.
843. State of California, Department of Natural Resources, Division of Forestry 1949a; U. S. Department of the Interior, Geological Survey 1951a; Carranco and Sorensen 1988:216-217; Fritz-Metcalf Photograph Collection 2016b, 2016c.
844. Schwarzkopf 1949b:17; Mortenson 1990; photo of Elinor School.
845. Schwarzkopf, anticipating the errors of a later generation, misapplies the word "nimrod." It is supposed to be a synonym for a skillful hunter, referring to King Nimrod of Shinar, who is so described in Genesis. More recently, 20th-century slang has equated a nimrod with someone who is "a simpleton, dunderhead, [or] blockhead" (Garner 2016:627). In Schwarzkopf's case, nimrod apparently refers to someone who fishes, in this case in the Eel River.
846. Schwarzkopf 1949b:17.
847. Brekke 1990.
848. Brekke 1990.
849. Rohde 1992a; Smith, n.d.
850. Rohde 1992a; Smith, n.d.
851. Rohde 1992a; Smith, n.d.
852. Rohde 1992a; Smith, n.d.
853. Rohde 1992a; Smith, n.d.
854. Mortenson 1990; Rohde 1992a, 1992b; Smith n.d.
855. Rohde 1992b; Smith, n.d.
856. Mortenson 1990; Rohde 1992b; Smith, n.d.
857. Mortenson 1990; Rohde 1992b.
858. Mortenson 1990; Rohde 1992b.
859. Mortenson 1990; Rohde 1992b.
860. Rohde 1992b; Smith n.d.
861. Ober 1973.
862. Mortenson 1990; Rohde 1993c.
863. Ober 1973.
864. Mortenson 1990; Rohde 1993c.
865. Rohde 2000a.
866. Loud 1918:273. See Rohde (2014:10) for a discussion of the Wiyot-Athabascan boundary in the area.
867. Merriam 1993:(9)169.
868. Surveyor General's Office 1871a.
869. Durst 1883:252.
870. McTavish 1885b:3.
871. Elliott 1881:165, 178, 211.
872. Humboldt Standard 1923a.
873. Lentell 1898.
874. Ferndale Enterprise 1909a:1.
875. Parker 1984:19.
876. Parker 1984:19.
877. California, Department of Public Works, Division of Highways 1933a:1.
878. Parker 1984:19.
879. Turner and Turner 2010:38. Even as late as 1949, no name for the locale appeared on the maps (Metsker 1949:29). This was rectified by the 1951 USGS topographic map, but by then Brown's Mill had become Stafford (United States Department of the Interior, Geological Survey 1951a).
880. Parker 1984:19; Parker n.d.:6.
881. Parker 1984:20.
882. Parker 1984:20.
883. Borden 1968:2 Parker 1984:20. The lower figures are Borden's, the higher Parker's.
884. Parker 1984:20; Borden 1968:2.
885. Parker 1984:20.
886. Humboldt Standard 1923b.
887. Humboldt Standard 1923b.
888. Borden 1968a:2; Parker 1984:20.
889. Dolfini 2004:23.
890. Fountain 2001:(83)118; Dolfini 2004:23. Dolfini states that a "former office building" became the inn, but as the inn was two stories tall, it seems much more likely that it was the "cookhouse and bunkhouse" that was converted, as reported in Fountain.
891. California Department of Public Works, Division of Highways 1933a:1, 5-6; Dolfini 2004:23. The reroute was approved by the highway department in 1933; one newspaper article indicates it was completed in 1936 (Fountain 2001:(83)118.
892. Atkinson 2019.
893. U. S. Department of the Interior, Geological Survey 1951a.
894. Atkinson 2019.
895. Fountain 2001:(83)118.
896. Dolfini 2004:23, 26; Atkinson 2019.
897. Dolfini 2004:24. Dolfini refers to "hewed ewes" but in writing a phrase that she initially heard, has almost certainly confused her homophones.
898. Atkinson 2019.
899. Atkinson 2019.
900. Humboldt Standard 1964a.
901. Fountain 2001:(83)118.
902. Wikipedia 2016b.
903. Wikipedia 2016a, 2016b; EcoTopia 2016a
904. Goddard 1906b:39.
905. When recording habitation locations in the Dobbyn Creek area, Goddard refers to them as "winter camps." However, these sites contained house pits, which would qualify them as villages.
906. Goddard 1906b:9-13; Ethnological Documents 2002:12(4)220.
907. Goddard 1906b:39.
908. Goddard 1906b:29-37; Ethnological Documents 2002:12(4)220.
909. Goddard 1906b:20-22, 40; Ethnological Documents 2002:12(4)220.
910. Goddard 1906b:40.
911. Goddard 1906b:24-25; Ethnological Documents 2002:12(4)221.
912. Goddard 1906b:43.
913. Murphey 1941:354; Humboldt Times 1863b:2.
914. Essene 1941:89.
915. Humboldt Times 1867a:2.
916. Humboldt Times 1861d:2.
917. It is unclear where this station was located. The most likely place, given its name, was at the mouth of Larabee Creek, which was where the mail trail crossed.
918. Doolittle 1865.

919. Humboldt Beacon 1910a:7; Surveyor General's Office 1871c. The Beacon obituary claims Dobbyn moved to Rohnerville in 1872; two other sources give the year as 1875 (Fountain 2001:(52)51; Guinn 1904:1169).
920. Two biographies and an obituary fail to mention Dobbyn's connection with the creek, but other sources claimed he owned land in the area (Turner and Turner 2010:73; Fountain 2001:(72)9, (52)51).
921. Murphey 1941:355, 364. Murphey, in interviewing the Lassik woman Lucy Young, learned that Young was related to "Bill Dobbins' mother. At the time of the interview Dobbins was living with Young and her husband at Round Valley.
922. Forbes 1886.
923. Elvidge 1974:10.
924. "Dobbyns" is the rendering given by the CRTANCS authors. Other accounts, however, give it as "Dobbyn" (McCocrmick n.d.; California State Library 1923:466).
925. Elvidge 1974:10.
926. Sweasey 1975:5.
927. CRTANCS 2001:74. The water situation had no doubt been improved by the addition of a Fawcett.
928. Elvidge 1974:10.
929. Belcher Abstract & Title Co. 1922:6.
930. Silvey 1985a:3-5; 1995a:37-38.
931. Elvidge 1974:10.
932. Cook 1997:(10)12.
933. Elvidge 1974:10.
934. Thornbury 1923:83.
935. Mathison 1998:44.
936. Polk 1950:743.
937. Mathison 1998:73; United States Department of the Interior, Geological Survey 1949b. Mathison refers to "Lindorff," first name not given. Polk lists him as Sig Lindroth (Polk 1950:743), and the Humboldt Times has Sid Lindroth (Humboldt Times 1960a).
938. Humboldt Times 1960a.
939. Belcher Abstract & Title Co. 1922:15; CRTANCS 2001:69.
940. Goddard 1906b:40.
941. Ethnological Documents 2001:12(4):176-185.
942. Lentell 1898.
943. Irvine 1915:605-606.
944. Madley 2016:290, 292; Bledsoe 1885:345.
945. Irvine 1915:698. The Curlesses reportedly brought the first sheep into the Blocksburg area (Anderson 1987a:4) although the 1859 date given by Anderson is incorrect.
946. Turner and Turner 2010:191; Fountain 2001:(24)49; Humboldt Times 1955a.
947. Cook 1997:(2b)1.
948. Friend 1939:13.
949. McTavish 1885g:3; Daily Humboldt Standard 1907b:3.
950. Daily Humboldt Standard 1907b:3.
951. McTavish 1885g:3. McTavish renders Coates as "Coots."
952. Asbill and Shawley 1975:194-195.
953. United States Bureau of Land Management 2016d.
954. Surveyor General 1873c.
955. The spelling of the family's name varies. The land office document rendered it "Hoglen," while Friend gives it as Hoagland. The Trinity County Historical Society and the United States Geological Survey use Hoaglin. A grave in the Blocksburg Cemetery is for "Ellen A. Hoaglen," however, and since that was apparently the rendering used by the family, it is that spelling that is used in this account.
956. United States Bureau of Land Management 2016e.
957. Friend 1939:13.
958. Fountain 2001:(74)265; Ferndale Semi-Weekly Enterprise 1897a:3.
959. United States Bureau of Land Management 2016c.
960. San Francisco Daily Alta 1867a: Sonoma Democrat 1867a:1; Secrest 2004:122-127.
961. Fountain 2001:(72)78.
962. Hill 1955a:9.
963. Fountain 2001:(24)16-17.
964. West Coast Signal 1876a:4.
965. Evening Star 1877b:1.
966. McTavish 1885g:3.
967. Fountain 2001:(125)333.
968. Frickstad 1955:41.
969. Cook 1997:(2b)15.
970. Daily Humboldt Standard 1907b:3.
971. Cook 1997:(2b)1.
972. Hill 1955a:9.
973. Evening Star 1877d:1.
974. Evening Star 1877c:1.
975. Larribie 1877a :1.
976. L. 1877a:1.
977. Speegle 1947a.
978. Johnson 1887:7.
979. Speegle 1947a.
980. Elliott 1881:162.
981. Cook 1997:(5)88.
982. Cook 1997:(5)89.
983. Cook 1997:(5)88: Irvine 1915:792-793.
984. Ferndale Enterprise 1880a:3; Daily Humboldt Standard 1907b:3.
985. Curtin 1940:435.
986. Northrup and Turney 2003:374.
987. United States House of Representatives 1897:1426.
988. Taussig 1893:5-7.
989. Weekly Humboldt Times 1879a.
990. United States House of Representatives 1897:1426.
991. Aspen Daily Times 1888a:3.
992. Eddy 1893:65.
993. Cook 1997:(2b)14-15; Cook and Hawk 2006:116
994. Elliott 1881:185.
995. Cook 1997:(2b)4.
996. Elliott 1881:159.
997. Cook and Hawk 2006:116.
998. Cook 1997:(2b)8.
999. Hill 1955a:9.
1000. Cook and Hawk 2006:116.
1001. Cook and Hawk 2006:115.
1002. Friend 1937:13.
1003. Blue Lake Advocate 1893a:2.
1004. Fountain 2001:(24)17.
1005. Daily Standard 1899c:3.
1006. Fountain 2001:(24)17.
1007. Humboldt Times 1920a.
1008. Humboldt Standard 1921b.
1009. Thornbury 1923:82-83.
1010. Cook 1997:(2b)15.
1011. Hill 1955a:9.
1012. Thornbury 1923:82.
1013. Reger 2005. The entire sidebar is based on her charming account.
1014. Reger 2010.

1015. Ethnological Documents 2002:12(4)175-185
1016. Goddard 1908a:70, 91.
1017. Goddard 1908a:61-62, 64-66; Ethnological Documents 2002:12(4)184-185.
1018. Goddard 1908a:63-64.
1019. U. S. War Department 1897a:12.
1020. U. S. War Department 1897a:12.
1021. Turk 1861a:3.
1022. U. S. War Department 1897a:12.
1023. U. S. War Department 1897a:908.
1024. By the author, at least.
1025. Surveyor General 1873d.
1026. Humboldt Times 1864f.
1027. The location referred to is actually Little Burr Creek, a tributary of Larabee Creek. Another stream, Burr Creek, flows into the South Fork of the Van Duzen River.
1028. Bledsoe 1885:197-198; Friend 1939:13; Harrington 1983:(32)758 left.
1029. Friend 1939:14.
1030. Bess 2020. Bess claims that the ranch grew to "nearly 20,000 acres," but the land maps from 1886 and 1898 show only a fraction of that amount (Forbes 1896; Lentell 1898).
1031. Various spellings were used for the last name of notorious Indian killer Hank Larabee.
1032. Surveyor General 1873d.
1033. Humboldt Times 1875a.
1034. Frickstad 1955:44.
1035. Hamm 1890:14.
1036. Surveyor General 1872e; Turner and Turner 2010:43.
1037. Irvine 1915:622, 897; Turner and Turner 2010:103. Burr Creek Station and French appear to have either been very close together or different names for the same location.
1038. Turner and Turner 2010:67.
1039. Friend 1939:14.
1040. Friend 1939:14.
1041. Friend 1939:14.
1042. Friend 1939:14.
1043. CRTANCS 1999:149-151.
1044. Sparks 1986.
1045. "B" 1878:3.
1046. McTavish 1885h:3.
1047. Frickstad 1955:44.
1048. CRTANCS 1999:42-44.
1049. Grant 2005:149.
1050. CRTANCS 1999:42.
1051. "Thus passes the glory of the school."
1052. Surveyor General's Office 1872b.
1053. Goddard n.d.a.:76-77, 82-83.
1054. Goddard n.d.a.:76; Ethnological Documents 2002:12(4)232
1055. Goddard 1908a:48.
1056. Fountain 2001:(89)455.
1057. Turner and Turner 2010:80.
1058. Dinsmore 1961:2.
1059. This may have been Greene Bartlett, an "old hunter," who located Bartlett Springs in Lake County in 1870 (Slocum, Bowen & Co. 1881:206).
1060. Dinsmore 1975a:15; Turner and Turner 2010:80.
1061. Dinsmore 1961:2.
1062. Denny 1911.
1063. Times-Standard n.d. The article claims the lodge was built in 1901, but that was before the Dinsmores bought the property.

1064. Turner and Turner 2010:72.
1065. Humboldt Times 1913d, 1913e, 1913f, 1913g. After the verdict was in, little Lee Burns also sued the Dinsmore brothers—for $10,000 (Humboldt Times 1913g). It is unclear what became of this suit.
1066. Kanahele 1990:12-13.
1067. Humboldt County Historical Society Newsletter 1960a:11; Milota 2001a:82.
1068. Fountain 2001:(71)14.
1069. Denny 1911; Turner and Turner 2010:146. Denny shows "Kunz" just barely in Trinity County. Turner and Turner list "Kuntz" in Humboldt County "almost to the Trinity County line."
1070. Lentell 1898; Turner and Turner 2010:146.
1071. San Francisco Call 1895a:9. Much of the story of Ericson's murder comes from a lengthy article in the October 21, 1895, San Francisco Call upon which Carranco and Beard based their account (1981:235-236). Another version of the murder was written by the great-grandson of Benjamin Arthur, one of the five conspirators allegedly involved in the murder (Thomas 1968:36-42).
1072. Carranco and Beard 1981:217, 235-236.
1073. Carranco and Beard 1981:236.
1074. San Francisco Call 1895a:8.
1075. Carranco and Beard 1981:236.
1076. Carranco and Beard 1981:236.
1077. Belcher Abstract & Title Co. 1922:16. In 1907 Van Duzen Pete and the ethnographer Pliny Goddard came down the Mad River and passed "a large flat with [a] deserted big white house." It was George Ericson's place, still vacant 21 years after he had been murdered (Goddard 1907b:100).
1078. Dinsmore 1975a:15, 18.
1079. Blue Lake Advocate 1930a:3.
1080. Times-Standard 2007a:C-7.
1081. Times-Standard 2009a:C-6.
1082. Dinsmore 1975a:15.
1083. Dinsmore 1975a:15.
1084. Greenson 2006a.
1085. Goddard 1908a:46-54; Ethnological Documents 2002:12(4)174-175.
1086. Goddard 1907b:20.
1087. Humboldt Times 1861f:2; U. S. War Department 1897a:18-19.
1088. "Larrabee" is the spelling used by his family (Russell-Wilson 2006). Various spellings have appeared over time, with "Larabee" being used on the U. S. Geological Survey maps (U. S. Department of the Interior, Geological Survey 1951a, 1969b). Since this last version is in continuing contemporary use, it will be used here.
1089. Irvine 1915:322-323, 452.
1090. "Northern" Burr Creek runs through Burr Valley and meets the South Fork Van Duzen about a mile northeast of Larabee Valley. "Southern" Burr Creek lies several miles to the southwest, heading on the west side of the Larabee Buttes and flowing down to a confluence with Larabee Creek (Turner and Turner 2010:43.
1091. Lentell 1898; Denny 1911; Belcher Abstract & Title Co. 1922:13. Rohde 2010a; Fountain 2001:(107)299. Hagans's last name is misspelled as "Hagins" in the latter document.
1092. Irvine 1915:323.
1093. Russell-Wilson 2020.
1094. Fountain 2001:(107)299. The township where

Larabee's ranch was located was not officially mapped until 1872; only then could the land have been legally acquired for ownership (Surveyor General's Office 1872e).

1095. Rohde 2010a; Fountain 2001:(107)299. Hagans's last name is misspelled as "Hagins" in the latter document.

1096. The exact location of Larabee's ranch house has been debated for decades, but a 1934 letter to the Ferndale Enterprise appears to have solved the mystery. J. A. Adams wrote that his father's Larabee Valley homestead contained "the grave of a white woman killed by the Indians" (Ferndale Enterprise 1934a). Various maps show an F. R. Adams owning land in sections 11 and 14, T1N, R4E, (Belcher Abstract & Title Co. 1922:13; Metsker 1949:80). No other Adams is shown owning property in the Larabee Valley area on any of the other detailed county maps. The woman referred to was almost certainly Ann Quinn, the cook at the Larabee-Hagans ranch.

1097. Daily Evening Bulletin 1860a:2. The author refers to Larabee as "L——."

1098. U. S. War Department 1897a:10-11.

1099. Bledsoe 1885:338; U. S. War Department 1897a:7.

1100. Irvine 1915:323.

1101. Fountain 2001:(62)314, 453.

1102. Ferndale Semi-Weekly Enterprise 1901a:8.

1103. CRTANCS 1999:39.

1104. Silvey 1985b:7.

1105. Belcher Abstract & Title Co. 1922:13, 16.

1106. Silvey 1985b:7.

1107. State of California, Department of Natural Resources, Division of Forestry 1949a; Robinson 1964b:8-9.

1108. Belcher Abstract & Title Co. 1922:13, 16.

1109. Blue Lake Advocate 1929a.

1110. Blue Lake Advocate 1932a.

1111. Blue Lake Advocate 1933a.

1112. Blue Lake Advocate 1937b.

1113. CRTANCS 1999:39.

1114. CRTANCS 1999:39.

1115. Humboldt Times 1952a:8; Metsker n.d.

1116. Schneider n.d.

1117. Irvine 1915:936.

1118. Schneider n.d.

1119. Schneider n.d.

1120. Clayton n.d.

1121. Schneider n.d.

1122. Belcher Abstract & Title Co. 1922:13.

1123. Belcher Abstract & Title Co. 1922:13.

1124. Schneider n.d.

1125. Schneider n.d.

1126. Clayton n.d.

1127. Social Education 2020a. Schneider gives the date as April 10, but what could you expect from an "alien enemy"?

1128. Schneider n.d.

1129. Schneider n.d.

1130. Schneider n.d.

1131. The 1921 county map shows three Rackliff parcels: one directly west of Petrolia, one just northeast of the mouth of the Mattole, and one southeast of Punta Gorda on the coast (Belcher Abstract & Title Co. 1922:4). The "home ranch that was willed to Jenny's siblings was reportedly "south of the Mattole" (Clayton n.d.), which would locate the parcel south of Punta Gorda.

1132. Clayton n.d.

1133. Schneider n.d.; Clayton n.d.

1134. Schneider n.d.

1135. Schneider n.d.

1136. Schneider n.d.; Clayton n.d.

1137. Goddard 1907b: 16,21, 25-27; N.d.a.:83. Goddard does not record any Nongatl name for the area that became Bridgeville. Curtis, however, claims that the Sinkyone word for Bridgeville was "Gitel" (Kroeber 1925:145), while Merriam's Lolahnkok informant George Burtt calls the place "Ahn-sin-tah-che-be" (Merriam 1993:(30)420). These are probably later-day names for the town of Bridgeville rather than references to any Kit-tel ki-ya site on the location.

1138. Goddard 1907b:23-25.

1139. U. S. War Department 1897a:303-306.

1140. Doolittle 1865.

1141. Fountain 2001:(117)124.

1142. Indian War Papers 1860a.

1143. Doolittle 1865.

1144. Bledsoe 1885:196; Bitterman 2010:16. Bitterman and Bledsoe both give the year as 1869, but the year on Drinkwater's grave marker is 1868.

1145. Friend 1939:13. Friend's account differs from Bledsoe's on several points. In those cases Friend's information is used because he was in the area at the time of the incident, whereas Bledsoe's version was secondhand.

1146. Bledsoe 1885:197-198.

1147. Friend 1939:13.

1148. Carr 1891:310.

1149. Harrington 1983:reel 32:758 left. The information comes from an interview with the Chimariko Indian Abe Bush (Miles 1985:76).

1150. Friend 1939:13.

1151. Harrington 1983:reel 32:758 left.

1152. Friend 1939:13.

1153. Friend 1939:13.

1154. Jones, et al. 1981:327

1155. The information in this paragraph is from a later research project display, photos of which are in the author's possession.

1156. Humboldt Times 1869c.

1157. Elliott 1881:180.

1158. The spelling of the family's name varied. The land office document rendered it "Hoglen," while Friend gives it as Hoagland. The Trinity County Historical Society and the U. S. Geological Survey use Hoaglin. However, a grave in the Blocksburg Cemetery is for "Ellen A. Hoaglen," and since that was apparently the rendering used by the family, it is that spelling that is used in this account.

1159. Fountain 2001:(70)66.

1160. Belcher Abstract & Title Co. 1922:13.

1161. Worthen 1996:22.

1162. Friend 1939:13.

1163. Schwarzkopf 1949a:16.

1164. Forbes 1886; Lentell 1898; Denny 1911; Belcher Abstract & Title Co. 1922:13.

1165. Silvey 1998:33.

1166. Romo 1985:66-67.

1167. Irvine 1915:329.

1168. Elliott 1881:179; Irvine 1915:654-655. Robinson's daughters give the date as 1869 (Schwarzkopf 1949a:16).

1169. Schwarzkopf 1949a:16; Turner and Turner 2010:200.

1170. Surveyor General's Office 1872c.
1171. Belcher Abstract & Title Co. 1922:13.
1172. Romo 1985:67.
1173. Romo 1985:66-70.
1174. Elliott 1881:188; Forbes 1886.
1175. Elliott 1881:188.
1176. Humboldt Standard 1919c.
1177. Daigh 2015:228.
1178. Dootlittle 1865. See, for example the Coast Survey's maps of the east side of Humboldt Bay (U. S. Coast Survey 1870a, 1870b).
1179. Coy 1982:75.
1180. Coy 1982:75-77.
1181. Coy 1982:225.
1182. Coy 1982:280-281.
1183. Coy 1982:283.
1184. Neibur 1867a:2.
1185. Humboldt Times 1874a:3
1186. Coy 1982:284; Humboldt Times 1874a, 1874b.
1187. Rohde 2014:200-201.
1188. Redwood Coast 2012; Gravelmap 2019.
1189. Humboldt Times 1875a; West Coast Signal 1875a:3.
1190. West Coast Signal 1874a:3.
1191. Nash 1985:21.
1192. Fountain 2001:(70)71.
1193. Fountain 2001:(79)25.
1194. Fountain 2001:(79)25-26.
1195. Fountain 2001:(79)26.
1196. Humboldt Weekly Times 1875a.
1197. Turner and Turner 2010:37.
1198. West Coast Signal 1875a:3.
1199. Humboldt Times 1875a.
1200. West Coast Signal 1876d:3.
1201. Friend 1937:13.
1202. Wheeler 2015a.
1203. West Coast Signal 1876e:1.
1204. Evening Star 1877b:1, 1877d:1; Cook and Hawk 1997:(12)1; Cook and Hawk 2006:54. Cook and Hawk give the year as 1878, but the Evening Star, reporting in real time, has it completed by April 1877.
1205. Elliott 1881:209.
1206. Blue Lake Advocate 1893a:2.
1207. Frickstad 1955:42
1208. Fountain 2001:(70)61.
1209. Fountain 2001:(70) 61.
1210. Humboldt Standard 1920b.
1211. Brown 1879a:3.
1212. Brown 1879a:3; Hale 1879a:3.
1213. Arcata Leader 1879a:3.
1214. Wheeler 1997a:2.
1215. Arcata Leader 1879a:3.
1216. Johnson 1887.
1217. McTavish gives Barnum's middle initial as "S" but other sources have it as "B."
1218. McTavish 1885h.
1219. Rohnerville Herald 1888 c3.
1220. Fountain 2001:(70)80.
1221. Fountain 2001:(70)70.
1222. Where Henry then became a Coxswain.
1223. Cook 1997:(3)42-43.
1224. Silvey 1998a:34.
1225. Silvey 1998a:34.
1226. Schwarzkopf 1949l:16.
1227. Worthen 1996:38.
1228. Schwarzkopf 1949l:16.
1229. Fountain 2001:(70)63.
1230. Humboldt Standard 1919d.
1231. Schwarzkopf 1949l:16.
1232. Worthen 1996:39.
1233. Wheeler 2017a:4.
1234. Wheeler 2014a.
1235. Worthen 1996:39.
1236. Silvey 1998a:35-36.
1237. Worthen 1996:48.
1238. Schwarzkopf 1949:32.
1239. Humboldt Times 1952a:8.
1240. Way 1947a.
1241. Schwarzkofp 1949:16.
1242. Silvey 1998:36-38.
1243. Little known because the author has just recently created it.
1244. Fountain 2001:(89)406.
1245. West Coast Signal 1876c; Humboldt Weekly Times 1874a.
1246. Humboldt Times 1861c:3; the portion of this trail that passed through the future site of Strong's Station is shown on the 1871 Surveyor General's map (Surveyor General 1871b).
1247. Humboldt Times 1909a.
1248. Humboldt Times 1871e:2.
1249. West Coast Signal 1871c:2.
1250. B 1878:3.
1251. Humboldt Times 1880c.
1252. Humboldt Times 1881a.
1253. Humboldt Times 1909a.
1254. McTavish 1885f:3.
1255. Humboldt Times 1909a.
1256. Humboldt Times 1911:3
1257. Thornbury 1923:81.
1258. Fountain 1960a:6.
1259. Fountain mentions Alger as the sole purchaser in 1887. The 1898 county map shows Bliss as co-owner (Lentell 1898).
1260. Rohde 2014:32-33.
1261. Fountain 1960:6.
1262. Wikipedia 2019b.
1263. Fountain 1960a:6.
1264. Wikipedia 2019b.
1265. Wikipedia 2019b.
1266. Wikipedia 2019b, 2019c.
1267. Hotchkiss 1898:122, 125-126.
1268. Hotchkiss 1898:76-77.
1269. Lentell 1898.
1270. U. S. Circuit Courts of Appeals Reports 1895:424-425.
1271. New York Lumber Trade Journal 1917:28B.
1272. U. S. Circuit Courts of Appeals Reports 1895:424-425.
1273. U. S. Circuit Courts of Appeals Reports 1895:424-425. This amount reflect the subtraction of Barnard's 7.5% commission from the sale price.
1274. Measuringworth.com 2020a.
1275. Borden 1958:3.
1276. Lentell 1898.
1277. Apparently Noyes-Alger had acquired 455.22 additional acres after their original purchase.
1278. Humboldt Times 1903a:8.
1279. Fountain 1960:6.
1280. Fountain 2001:(89)406.
1281. Fountain 2001:(89)406.
1282. U. S. Department of the Interior, Geological Survey 1969a.
1283. Goddard n.d.a.:74; Goddard 1929:323.
1284. Norton 1979:155.

1285. Rohde 2014:109.

1286. Norton 1979:62; Rohde 2014:88-89.

1287. Cuddeback Union School District 2019. The sources for this report are not given.

1288. Fountain 2001:(32)442, (119)116; State of California, Resources Agency, Department of Water Resources, Northern District 1975: Plate 6, Sheet D.

1289. Humboldt Times 1862g:3; Humboldt Standard 1926b.

1290. Humboldt Standard 1926b.

1291. Doolittle 1865; Humboldt Standard 1921a.

1292. Humboldt Standard 1926b.

1293. Humboldt Standard 1921a.

1294. Humboldt Standard 1926b.

1295. Fountain 2001:(32)442.

1296. Humboldt Standard 1926b.

1297. Humboldt Standard 1862g:3; Doolittle 1865. The crossing was probably where the "Indian Valley and Yager Creek Trail" went across the Mad River, in Section 20, Township 2, North, Range 5 East, Humboldt Meridian (Surveyor General's Office 1872d).

1298. Irvine 1915:1167.

1299. Irvine 1915:183.

1300. Lentell 1898; Schwarzkopf 1949k:11; Van Kirk 2019a.

1301. Van Kirk 2019a.

1302. Irvine 1915:183.

1303. Borden 1958a:3.

1304. Borden 1958a:3.

1305. Borden 1958a:5.

1306. Daily Standard 1903a:4.

1307. Daily Standard 1903a:4.

1308. Turner and Turner 2010:54. Various sources claim that the name was given by either John M. Vance (Schwarzkopf 1949K:11; Turner and Turner 2010:54;) or B. F. Porter, a railroad employee who may have been courting favor with his boss, John M. Vance (Obarr 1999:26).

1309. Borden 1958a:5.

1310. LeBaron 2019a.

1311. Root Creek is about two miles downriver from Grizzly Creek.

1312. Fountain 2001:(50)109.

1313. A scan of this unique map is in the author's possession.

1314. Van Kirk 2019a.

1315. Irvine 1915:181-182.

1316. Fountain 2001:(70)71.

1317. Humboldt Times 1911

1318. Nash 1996a:37-38.

1319. Ward 1915a:62-63.

1320. Nash 1996a:41-41.

1321. Oregon Daily Journal 1920:4.

1322. Fountain 2001:(70)100.

1323. Irvine 1915:1010-1011. One wonders if the cows would have especially enjoyed Ruby's rendering of the Moo-nlight Sonata.

1324. Knab 1981:4; State of California, Department of Natural Resources, Division of Forestry 1949a; Turner and Turner 2010:9.

1325. Knab 1981:4.

1326. Carter 1983a:7; Turner and Turner 2010:9.

1327. Fountain 2001:(70)114.

1328. Fountain 2001:(70)99.

1329. Dawson 1923a:1488.

1330. Denny 1911; Belcher Abstract & Title Co. 1921:14; Carranco and Sorensen 1988:116.

1331. Humboldt Standard 1924

1332. Borden 1958a:5.

1333. Belcher 1921:1.

1334. Borden 1958a:5.

1335. Borden 1958a:5; Carranco and Sorensen 1988:214-215.

1336. Belcher Abstract & title Co. 1922:13; Humboldt Standard 1930b.

1337. Borden 1958a:9; Turner and Turner 2010:195.

1338. Carranco and Sorensen 1988:214-215.

1339. Rigby 2016. Carranco and Sorensen (1988:215) map the rail line as ending near Flanigan Creek. The 1950 USGS quad for the area shows the tracks terminating about a quarter-mile south of the creek, but also shows that the tracks, which are doubled there, then turn into two roads (U. S. Department of the Interior, Geological Survey 1950a). This suggests that Rigby is correct in claiming that the eastern end of the rail line was converted into a logging road.

1340. Carranco and Sorensen 1988:118, 214-215; Turner and Turner 2010:17.

1341. Humboldt Standard 1935b; Borden 1958a:5; Metsker 1949:46-47, 63-64.

1342. U. S. Department of Interior 1978a.

1343. Borden 1958a:9.

1344. Carranco and Sorensen 1988:149.

1345. Borden 1958a:9.

1346. Carranco and Sorensen 1988:214-215.

1347. Humboldt Times 1940b.

1348. A logging arch is a large piece of arch-shaped steel, with each end attached either to wheels or treads and pulled by a tractor. A spool attached to the apex of the arch held a cable, one end of which was rigged to encircle one end of a log. The cable was wound in enough to elevate the near end of the log, so that only the far end rested on the ground. The tractor would pull the arch forward to yard (haul) the log to a landing. The arch allowed the elevated front end of the log to avoid hanging up on obstacles, such as low stumps or rocks (Labbe and Carranco 2001:4-5).

1349. Humboldt Times 1940b.

1350. Borden 1958a:5.

1351. Borden 1958a:9.

1352. Schwarzkopf 1949K:11.

1353. Schwarzkopf 1949K:11.

1354. Schwarzkopf 1949K:11.

1355. Big Trees 1952.

1356. U. S. Department of Interior 1978a.

1357. Times-Standard 1990a:A-1.

1358. Times-Standard 1995a:1.

1359. Humboldt Beacon 1997a.

1360. Humboldt Times 1874a.

1361. Forbes 1886.

1362. Nash 1985:21.

1363. Fountain 2001:(79)57.

1364. Gates 1883.

1365. Gates 1883.

1366. Hamm 1890.

1367. Rohnerville Herald 1888a:3.

1368. Rohnerville Herald 1888a:3.

1369. Genzoli 1979a. Wiley's account mentions that the "Van Duzen River has to be crossed six times" before arriving at Bridgeville, but it is unclear why this was necessary (or even possible) if the route along the north side of the Van Duzen was in place.

1370. Lentell 1898.
1371. Tracy 1993a.
1372. Belcher Abstract & Title Co. 1922:13.
1373. Denny 1911.
1374. Evening Star 1877c:1; West Coast Signal 1878b:1; Tam 1885:14.
1375. Lentell 1898.
1376. Robinson 1964b:8.
1377. Denny 1991.
1378. Denny 1911; State of California, Department of Engineering 1912:204-207.
1379. Arcata Union 1913a.
1380. Humboldt State University Library 2020a.
1381. Eureka Independent 1952a:6.
1382. State of California, Department of Engineering 1912:204-207; Robinson 1964b:8-9.
1383. Fountain 2001:(62)344.
1384. U. S. Department of the Interior 1981a.
1385. Or perhaps in 1923. In a 1984 magazine article, John W. Snyder gives the year as 1922 (Snyder 1984:64), but in the 1981 National Register form he prepared, the year is given as 1923 (U. S. Department of the Interior 1981a). Local historian Glen Nash, writing about the bridges in 1985, states the contracts for both bridges were let in 1922 but does not provide a date for their construction (Nash 1985a:21).
1386. U. S. Department of the Interior 1981a; Arcata Leader 1979a:3.
1387. Snyder 1984:61, 64; Nash 1985a:21-22; Stansberry 2016.
1388. Nash 1985a:21-22.
1389. The latter device was patented by William Christopher Mobbow in 1917. It was "designed for use in indicating the dip, inclination or grade of a road or other surface, and particularly as an attachment for automobiles and other road vehicles" (Google Patents 2019a).
1390. Fountain 2001:(91)129.
1391. Had no one learned from the destructive 1912 drive of the Mack truck?
1392. Fountain 2001:(91)129.
1393. Fountain 2001:(91)129.
1394. Eel Valley Advance 1970b.
1395. The ethnographer Pliny E. Goddard and the Nongatl Indian Van Duzen Pete examined the Yager Creek drainage, naming and locating village sites and tribal groups on North Yager and Middle Yager creeks. No mention was made of South Yager Creek, except for its name, Se-das-tin-kok, which meant "housed from lots of rocks" (Goddard 1908a:9). Pete did indicate that a Nongatl tribal group called the Kun-te-bi kay-ya lived on Kun-te-bi, which was what they called Yager Creek (Goddard n.d.a.:61), but this appears to be the name for the lower creek, below where the branches joined.
1396. Humboldt Times 1858x:2
1397. One source speaks of the "coastal prairies, oak savannas, prairie patches in coastal redwood forests, all rich in plant species diversity and kept fertile through centuries of Indian burning . . ." (Anderson 2005:76). The same source indicates that "the Yurok, Wiyot, Hupa, Chilula, Nongatl, Mattole, Sinkyone, Cahto, and Yuki" all engaged in "burning for better seed crops" (Anderson 2005:263).
1398. Fountain 2001:(70)101.

1399. Humboldt Times 1875a.
1400. West Coast Signal 1875b.
1401. Frickstad 1955:47.
1402. Forbes 1886.
1403. Anster 2019:216.
1404. Blackie MDCCCXCIX:99.
1405. Humboldt Times 1859g:2.
1406. Humboldt Times 1859h:2.
1407. Humboldt Times 1859h:2.
1408. Trinity Journal 1859a:2.
1409. Trinity Journal 1859a:2.
1410. Bledsoe 1885:293.
1411. Genzoli 1982:5.
1412. Humboldt Times 1859i:2.
1413. Bledsoe 1885:293-295.
1414. The quote is probably from Samuel Davies: "My Cattle graze upon a thousand Hills, And feed unnumber'd in the fertile Vales. So various, so unbounded is my Store, The greediest Wish can comprehend no more" (Davies 2019a:17). The full stanza, as given here, does not suggest the sense of incipient impoverishment that Y. Z. intended to convey.
1415. Y. Z. 1859:2.
1416. Weekly Humboldt Times 1860a:2.
1417. Weekly Humboldt Times 1860b:2.
1418. Bledsoe 1885:300.
1419. Indian War Papers 1860b.
1420. Heizer 1993:156.
1421. A full account of the massacres is given in "Genocide and Extortion" (Rohde 2010a).
1422. Coy 1982:197.
1423. According to the White family papers, they were living "on South Yager (near Bridgeville) in 1859" (White n.d.).
1424. White 1884.
1425. White 1884.
1426. White n.d.
1427. White 1884.
1428. The most comprehensive account of the Indian killings is contained in Madley 2016a. Raphael and House provide a lengthy list of massacres (Raphael and House 2011).
1429. Frickstad 1955:47.
1430. Hamm 1890:153.
1431. Fountain 2001:(39)286.
1432. Fountain 2001:(82)382.
1433. Fountain 2001:(82)382.
1434. Lentell 1898.
1435. Denny 1911.
1436. Thornbury 1923:137.
1437. Thornbury 1923:137.
1438. Irvine 1915:1219.
1439. Humboldt Standard 1941b.
1440. Rohde 2014a:122-124.
1441. Humboldt Times 1935c.
1442. Humboldt Standard 1941b.
1443. Belcher Abstract & Title Co. 1922:13.
1444. Irvine 1915:1218.
1445. Belcher Abstract & Title Co. 1922:13.
1446. CRTANCS 1999:229.
1447. Frickstad 1955:47.
1448. This, at least, is the last year a teacher is shown for the school (CRTANCS 1999:229). The 1944-1945 directory for Humboldt County public schools lists Yager as "suspended" (Humboldt County Schools 1944:33).
1449. Doolittle 1865; Surveyor General's Office 1876d.

1450. Fountain 2001:(52)2.
1451. Tyrrell 1932.
1452. Doolittle 1865.
1453. Fountain 2001:(117)95.
1454. Humboldt Times 1869c.
1455. There were three reported attacks by Humboldt County Indians in 1869, the last such recorded in the county (Coy 1982:195-196).
1456. Humboldt Times 1869c:3.
1457. Hamm 1890:153. Elliott 1881:179.
1458. Humboldt Historian 1968a:1.
1459. Humboldt Times 1877a:1.
1460. Lentell 1898; Denny 1911; Belcher Abstract & Title Co. 1922:13; Metsker 1949:47, 64.
1461. Fountain 2001:(52)102; Irvine 1915:930; Home Herald 1893a.
1462. CRTANCS 1999:169. There are two versions of this document. The one used here, which has more complete information, covers the Redwood House School on pages 169-171. The less complete version has its coverage on pages 171-173.
1463. Ferndale Enterprise 1892c:1.
1464. Carter 1983a:7.
1465. CRTANCS 1999:169-170; Metsker 1949:47.
1466. CRTANCS 1999:171.
1467. Bevington 2009; Speece 2017:194, 220-221.
1468. Turner 2010:196; Frost 1966:2.
1469. Goddard 1907b:16, 21; n.d.a.: 83.
1470. Goddard 1908a:29-30; Ethnological Documents 2002:12(4):147-152.
1471. Goddard 1907b:90-93, 119-122.
1472. Works Progress Administration 1940a:239-240.
1473. Weekly Humboldt Times, November 20, 1858:2.
1474. Goddard n.d.f.:114.
1475. Weekly Humboldt Times, November 20, 1858:2.
1476. militarymuseum.org 2022a.
1477. See the Fort Seward chapter in this book.
1478. Turner and Turner 2010:219.
1479. U. S. War Department 1897a:992.
1480. Humboldt Times 1862; U. S. War Department 1897a:81.
1481. U. S. War Department 1897b:608-609.
1482. U. S. War Department 1897b:609.
1483. Humboldt Times 1863e:2.
1484. militarymuseum.org 2022b.
1485. Harville 1988:10.
1486. Harville 1988:10-13.
1487. Harville 1988:14.
1488. Harville 1988:8-9, 24-25. Harville believed that there had been a military outpost on Indian Creek and that a "barracks" building, which may have been a log cabin, at one time existed there. However, a search of army records finds no mention of any "Fort Baker" after the original one on the Van Duzen was abandoned in 1863.
1489. Harville 1988:16. The story, if false, would have been an attempt at pulling the wool over the readers' eyes.
1490. Harville 1988:17.
1491. Harville 1988:14-15.
1492. Friend 1939.
1493. Lentell 1898.
1494. Harville 1988:17, 19.
1495. Denny 1911.
1496. Harville 1988:75.
1497. Miller 2013:28.
1498. Gibbs n.d.:1-2.
1499. Readers may smile at the use of this quaint term, but it is one of two collective nouns correctly used for a group of hogs (almanac.com 2022a). The other word, "team," might easily conjure up an image of the hogs pulling a wagon.
1500. Gibbs n.d.:3-5.
1501. CRTANCS 1989:47.
1502. Belcher Abstract & Title Co. 1922:13.
1503. In 1910 Maud Frost taught at "the one-room school in Hart's Valley" (Wooden n.d.:2). Her brother was Ralph Frost, the postmaster.
1504. Harville 1988:43.
1505. CRTANCS 1989:50.
1506. Blue Lake Advocate, 1918a:8; State of California, Division of Mines 1927:518.
1507. Humboldt Times 1918b.
1508. State of California, Division of Mines 1927:518-519.
1509. Denny 1911; Belcher Abstract & Title Co. 1922:13; Metsker 1949:81; Hunt and Johnson 2001:7-8.
1510. Hunt and Johnson 2001:12.
1511. Rohde 2004a.
1512. Harville 1988:75.
1513. Humboldt Times 1937c.
1514. CRTANCS 1989:47-48.
1515. Blue Lake Advocate 1933b:3.
1516. This sidebar is based on the following sources: Blue Lake Advocate 1933a:2; Harville 1988:63-65; Humboldt Historian 1989a:14-16.
1517. Harville 1988:75.
1518. Blue Lake Advocate 1953a:7.
1519. Fountain 2001:(89)316.
1520. Fountain 2001:(89)316.
1521. And were driven by this author in the 1990s.
1522. This sidebar is based on the following sources: Blue Lake Advocate 1949a:2; Harville 1988:66; Schroeder 2016. Merlynn Schroeder passed away a few weeks after I interviewed her.
1523. St. John 1968c:12.
1524. Humboldt Standard 1912b.
1525. Humboldt Times 1925c:3.
1526. Walton 2006; Barmazel 1996:86.
1527. Walton 2006; Barmazel 1996:86.
1528. Humboldt Times 1926a.
1529. Barmazel 1996:86.
1530. Barmazel 1996:86.
1531. Hunt 2002.
1532. Lesher 1996:A1.
1533. Lesher 1996:A18.
1534. Lesher 1996:A19.
1535. Lesher 1996:A19.
1536. Humboldt Times 1928a:1.
1537. Barmazel 1996:86.
1538. Hill 1930:94.
1539. Barmazel 1996:86.
1540. Humboldt Times 1928b:1, 11.
1541. Udseth 1996a:A8.
1542. Barmazel 1996:86.
1543. Humboldt Times 1939b:1.
1544. Harville 1988:59.
1545. In 1996 Walton was quoted by writer Steve Barmazel as saying that Metzler "knew all along that Bill Shields was the killer," but, summarized Barmazel, Metzler didn't have the evidence to convict him, "so he substituted Jack Ryan's name." When I contacted Walton (who is now Rachel Walton) in 2022, she told me that "I have

become friends with the real killers families as a result of their cooperation with me, and for their protection, I have not divulged anything further until they pass." Walton added: "William Shields did not kill Carmen Wagner.....he was a prime suspect to be sure, but there is so much more to this story." Walton indicated that she has 20 banker boxes of material on the case, which "will go to the Humboldt Historical Society when I pass..." (Walton 2022).

1546. Barmazel 1996:87.
1547. Paddock and Paddock 2001.
1548. Humboldt Standard 1932b.
1549. Winkler 1995a:A6.
1550. Humboldt Standard 1947b:1.
1551. Barmazel 1996:87.
1552. Lesher 1996:A19.
1553. Barmazel 1996:87.
1554. Barmazel 1996:87.
1555. Lesher 1996:A19.
1556. Lesher 1996:A19.
1557. SFGATE 1996.
1558. Winkler 1995a:A6.
1559. Winkler 1995a:A6.
1560. SFGATE 1996.
1561. Barmazel 1996:43-44.
1562. Barmazel 1996:44.
1563. Walton 2006.
1564. Walton 2006.
1565. Barmazel 1996:44.
1566. Barmazel 1996:44.
1567. Winkler 1995a:A6.
1568. Winkler 1995a:A6.
1569. Winkler 1995a:A6.
1570. SFGATE 1996.
1571. Lesher 1996:A19.
1572. Udseth 1996a:A6.
1573. Lesher 1996:A19.
1574. SFGATE 1996.
1575. Goddard 1907e:3; Ethnological Documents 2002:12(4):166-170.
1576. A visitor to Humboldt County in February 1851 reported this usage (Bruff 1851:479).
1577. Shepherd 2011:75.
1578. Daily Alta California 1850a.
1579. Irvine 1915:677.
1580. Dinsmore 1961:2.
1581. Times-Standard n.d.
1582. Humboldt Times 1861i:2
1583. Fountain 2001:(109)67.
1584. Humboldt Times 1861j:2;Works Project Administration 1940b:343-344; Fountain 2001:(109):67.
1585. How it was that the sound of the gun indicated that it belonged to Indians was not explained.
1586. Humboldt Times 1863
1587. Geer 1948:23: California Military History 2020a.
1588. U. S. War Department 1897b: 711-713, 817, 885, 963, 1007, 1109-1111, 1267, 1271-1274.
1589. U. S. War Department 1897a:277; Lentell 1898; Denny 1911; Belcher Abstract & Title Co. 1922:14.
1590. "W"(2) 1864a:2.
1591. "W"(2) 1864a:2.
1592. "W"(2) 1864a:2:Fountain 2001:(32):65-66; Irvine 1915:391; Hosmer n.d.:1.
1593. Norton 1979:155.
1594. Rohde 2010a.
1595. Hosmer n.d.:4.
1596. Humboldt Times 1866c:3.
1597. BLA 2020a.
1598. West Coast Signal 1875b.
1599. Shaw 1983:14; Lentell 1898; Denny 1911; Belcher Abstract & Title Co. 1922:14.
1600. Irvine 1915:1134-1135; Denny 1911; Belcher Abstract & Title Co. 1922:14; Frickstad 1955:44.
1601. Irvine 1915:1135-1136; Lentell 1898; Denny 1911; Belcher Abstract & Title Co. 1922:14.
1602. Irvine 1915:1189-1190; Lentell 1898; Denny 1911; Belcher Abstract & Title Co. 1922:14.
1603. Startare 2015.
1604. Irvine 1915:1003; Lentell 1898.
1605. Palmer 1879a.
1606. Clarke n.d.a.
1607. Palmer 1879a.
1608. Palmer 1879a.
1609. Palmer 1879b.
1610. Palmer 1879b.
1611. Palmer 1879b.
1612. Palmer 1879c.
1613. Palmer 1879c.
1614. Palmer 1879d.
1615. Palmer 1879d.
1616. Palmer 1879d, 1879e.
1617. Palmer 1879e.
1618. Palmer 1879f.
1619. Cornford 1987:52.
1620. Foner and Garrity 1991:473-474; Faragher 1998:377.
1621. Palmer 1879f.
1622. Palmer 1879f.
1623. Palmer 1879f.
1624. Clarke n.d.b.
1625. CRTANCS 1989:38-39; Peterson 1985.
1626. Peterson 1984.
1627. Rohde n.d.; Townsend 1886:491.
1628. Daily Standard 1895a:4.
1629. Blue Lake Advocate 1902a:1, 1903a:1, 1904a:1.
1630. Gift 1987a:17; Shipyard Log 2020.
1631. State of California, Department of Natural Resources, Division of Forestry 1949a.
1632. Humboldt Standard 1911a; Forest Lookouts 2020.
1633. Humboldt Standard 1921c.
1634. Forest Lookouts 2020.
1635. Fountain 2002:(26)475; Paddock and Paddock 2001.
1636. Paddock and Paddock 2001.

About the Author

Jerry Rohde has researched Humboldt County history and written about it for over 30 years. He has served as the ethnogeographer and historian for Humboldt State University's Cultural Resources Facility for over 20 years and has authored or co-authored seven books and written more than 500 reports for state and local agencies and various Indian tribes. His History of Humboldt County People and Places series is planned to include seven books, of which *Southeast Humboldt Hinterlands* is the fourth. Jerry and his wife Gisela live in South Stumpville, a Eureka suburb.

Made in the USA
Monee, IL
15 June 2023

bf908a5c-4314-444f-afba-7e21d39137d6R01